ENDANGERED EXCELLENCE

SUNY series in Ancient Greek Philosophy

Anthony Preus, editor

ENDANGERED EXCELLENCE
ON THE POLITICAL PHILOSOPHY OF ARISTOTLE

PIERRE PELLEGRIN

Translated by Anthony Preus

Cover art © Virginie Berthemet

Original French edition: L'Excellence menacée: Sur la philosophie politique d'Aristote © Classiques Garnier, 2017

Published by State University of New York Press

© 2020 State University of New York

All rights reserved

No part of this book may be used or reproduced in any manner whatsoever without written permission. No part of this book may be stored in a retrieval system or transmitted in any form or by any means including electronic, electrostatic, magnetic tape, mechanical, photocopying, recording, or otherwise without the prior permission in writing of the publisher.

For information, contact State University of New York Press, Albany, NY
www.sunypress.edu

Library of Congress Cataloging-in-Publication Data

Names: Pellegrin, Pierre, author. | Preus, Anthony, translator.
Title: Endangered excellence : on the political philosophy of Aristotle / Pierre Pellegrin ; translated by Anthony Preus.
Description: Albany : State University of New York, 2020. | Series: SUNY series in Ancient Greek Philosophy | Includes bibliographical references and index.
Identifiers: LCCN 2020000968 (print) | LCCN 2020000969 (ebook) | ISBN 9781438479576 (hardcover : alk. paper) | ISBN 9781438479569 (pbk. : alk. paper) | ISBN 9781438479583 (ebook)
Subjects: LCSH: Aristotle—Political and social views. | Democracy. | Political science.
Classification: LCC JC75.D36 P45 2020 (print) | LCC JC75.D36 (ebook) | DDC 320.01—dc23
LC record available at https://lccn.loc.gov/2020000968
LC ebook record available at https://lccn.loc.gov/2020000969

10 9 8 7 6 5 4 3 2 1

Contents

Translator's Note	vii
Abbreviations	ix
Introduction: "Our Ancestors the Greeks"	1
Chapter 1 The Philosopher in Politics	17
Chapter 2 A Biological Politics?	67
Chapter 3 The Endangered Happiness of the City	95
Chapter 4 Citizen, City, Constitution	171
Chapter 5 On the Positive Use of Deviance	235
Chapter 6 The Legislator	269
Chapter 7 The Theoretical Tools of the Legislator	305
Chapter 8 Political Matter	345
Conclusion	383
Bibliography	401
Index	409

Translator's Note

I have tried to capture the spirit of Pierre Pellegrin's French in my English version; that effort has been considerably assisted by his careful reading of the translation, and his many suggestions for improvement. Translations of Aristotle and of other ancient texts have often been assisted by standard translations but amended to cohere with Pellegrin's excellent translations of these same passages into French. I have tried to find translations of modern authors into English, and to use those where possible. They are noted in the footnotes and bibliography. Otherwise, I have translated the originals into English, again very often with Pellegrin's advice and suggestions.

It should also be noted that Pierre Pellegrin has written a totally new conclusion for the present volume; the conclusion is translated from this new text, not from the original French edition.

Abbreviations

APo	*Posterior Analytics*
APr	*Prior Analytics*
DA	*De Anima*
DC	*De Caelo*
EE	*Eudemian Ethics*
EN	*Nicomachean Ethics*
Eum.	*Eumenides*
GA	*Generation of Animals*
HA	*History of Animals*
IA	*Progression of Animals*
Met.	*Metaphysics*
PA	*Parts of Animals*
Phys.	*Physics*
Rep.	*Republic*

Introduction

"Our Ancestors the Greeks"

Studying ancient Greek political philosophy goes to the very root of our relations with the Greeks, that is to say, to the root of a peculiar and fertile mystification. It is said that the fantasized tie that the West today maintains with ancient Greece, that has taken five centuries, maybe eight, to construct, has become remarkably distorted in the last several decades. The retreat of classical studies should be in fact both the cause and a result of this weakening, but after all the number of people knowing Greek was never that great. This distancing involves so to speak every domain. Our new approach to the history of knowledge probably played an important, perhaps fundamental, role, in the divorce between the Greeks and us. For a long time, in fact, historians of science have accepted the illusion of a direct descent from ancient speculations to modern disciplines. The fact that our sciences use, even for their names, many Greek terms has contributed to that illusion. In fact, it is tempting to think that there, as almost everywhere else, the same words refer to the same realities and that, therefore, modern physics directly follows ancient *physikē*. This is a matter of a historical problem of first importance, opposing a continuist vision of the progress of the human spirit, which thinks that all scientists over the centuries have been dedicated to the same tasks, posing to themselves the same questions, and that science would then be the structure that they have built together, to which each has contributed his or her stones, and the discontinuist conception developed by the French school of the history of science, founded by Gaston Bachelard, which simultaneously refuses to consider the progress of science as a simple addition of discoveries and insists on the new and irreducible character of the sciences in relation to previous intellectual constructions. Thus, it is necessary to recognize that there is hardly more than a relationship of homonymy between ancient physics and that of Galileo and Newton, and in any case these two do not belong to the same history.

Greek, and more generally Greco-Roman, antiquity provides first-class material for thinking about the complex relationships between historical continuity and discontinuity, one of the subjects of the magnificent and somewhat forgotten 1969 work of Michel Foucault, *The Archaeology of Knowledge*.[1] It's exceptional material because the Greeks and Romans have left us an impressive number of texts that have been continuously edited, translated, analyzed, imitated, and invoked. Our relationship to classical antiquity has also long been privileged because the West, like its cultural ancestors before them, the Byzantines and Islamics, has thought of Greek and Roman thinkers as direct participants in their theoretical debates. An exceptional fate, because despite attempts to revive "the spirit of medieval philosophy" by Christians trying to slow the irreversible decline of Christianity, the Medieval Latin world, for example, has not had that sort of survival—it has for a long time been relegated to the category of obsolete intellectual universes.

What would be the basis of a continuity between us and the Greeks, when important elements of their cultural constructions and ours do not belong to the same history? Foucault has been especially sensitive to these discontinuities that are like the material of historical continuity: "In short, the history of thought, of knowledge, of philosophy, of literature seems to be seeking, and discovering, more and more discontinuities, whereas history itself appears to be abandoning the irruption of events in favour of stable structures."[2] We will return to Foucault in our conclusion. Michel Foucault and *The Archaeology of Knowledge* form the frame of this study.

Nevertheless, even staying within the history of the sciences this Bachelardian position needs to be modified on several points; I will mention the three most important. First, the Greeks have left us theoretical constructions that we cannot simply delete from the history of science. Obviously, in mathematics no one would dream of expelling the Hellenic

---

1. In French, Michel Foucault, *L'archéologie du savior* (Paris: Gallimard, 1969), English translation, *The Archaeology of Knowledge*, trans. A. M. Sheridan Smith (New York: Routledge, 2002).

2. Foucault, *L'archéologie du savior*, 13, trans. Sheridan Smith, *Archaeology of Knowledge*, 6.

and Hellenistic contributions from the discipline, but the same goes for speculations based upon mathematics, the hydrostatics of Archimedes as well as astronomy, even though geocentric, based on the hypothesis of orbits composed of circular movements: the hypotheses of Eudoxus and Calippus, as well as those of Ptolemy, based on a system of homocentric spheres, as false as they are, are still part of the same history of science. Next, there are other fields involved that we have sometimes thrown too hastily into the bitter abyss of pre-science. That is true of Aristotle's biology, something that I have studied for a very long time. From the start I was sensitive to its aspect that is radically strange from the point of view of modern science, notably as it takes positions dictated by metaphysical or ideological prejudices. How should we understand, for example that Aristotle has "observed" that women have fewer sutures in their skulls than men? Today I would be much more inclined to consider Aristotle as a "true" biologist. We must recognize that the Bachelardian schema functions much less well in biology than in physics.[3] Finally, if we consider only the most impressive physics of antiquity, that of Aristotle, we must surely recognize that it has posed problems that subsequently required a scientific treatment. Thus the "law" of falling bodies posited by Aristotle that establishes a relationship between the weight of the body and the speed of its fall, or more generally large sections of Aristotelian kinematics fall under a physical theory that happens to be false rather than under an alleged physical theory. That was also the case with the homocentric spheres mentioned above.

Also, the various "human sciences," even if they don't belong to the same history as their Greek equivalents, even when they bear the same name, nevertheless have all or nearly all a Greek, even Aristotelian, prehistory or "archaeology." That's one of the bases of the extraordinary resurgence of interest in Aristotle since the 1960s: when we excavate to ensure the foundations of our disciplines, we hit Aristotelian strata. And there is, "last but not least," the case of philosophy that, at least in its university practice, pretends to continue our relationship with the Greeks.

But the domain in which our relationship to the Greeks seems to us somehow direct, and that which concerns us directly here, is that of politics, in the largest sense of the word. In that domain many of us feel directly illuminated by the Greek sun. The opinion that the Greeks invented

---

3. I have tried to give some reasons for that fact in the introduction to my translation of the *Parts of Animals*, Aristote, *Les Parties des animaux* (Paris: GF-Flammarion, 2011).

politics, and especially democracy, and by the same token the very idea of citizenship, is all the more rooted in our common consciousness that it is far from being completely false. That position became even more legitimate in the middle of the twentieth century with a decisive turning point for our approach to Greek matters.

That turning point was brought about by Jean-Pierre Vernant and his colleagues and students taking up ancient studies in the years 1960–1980. They not only reinforced for us the idea that in political matters the Greeks have spoken to us *directly*, but they have made us see in the political organization of Greek society an ultimate explanation of the special characteristics of the Hellenic cultural era. We must recognize from the start that Vernant and his colleagues are real historians who are, as such, aware of the differences between antiquity and the modern world, open to a relativistic approach to cultural facts and receptive to the irreducible element of exoticism that ancient Greece has for us. Thus, if any charges are to be brought against Vernant, they would not include schematism. To be sure, Vernant uses some unfortunate phrases. Thus, when he begins the last chapter of his famous *Mythe et pensée chez les Grecs*[4] with this statement: "Rational thought has, as it were, its personal credentials in order: its date and place of birth are known. It was in the sixth century BC, in the Greek cities of Asia Minor." That's a remarkable example of an expression that goes beyond the thought of its author, as Vernant himself recognized, since he did not intend in any way to deny rational thought to the non-Greek people of antiquity.

It may be useful, as a foretaste of what will follow, to remember very schematically what Vernant has taught us. His central thesis asserts that what seems to distinguish the Greeks from their neighbors is the birth of an original form of social organization, the city (*polis*). The corollary to this thesis, hardly expressed by Vernant and his colleagues but always present, is that all the ideas and practices that the Greeks have constructed from this *political* break, like those that concern the exercise of power, citizenship, public space, relation to the law, are those that still shape our democratic values. That is why we do not feel ourselves tied as directly to the "others," the apolitical barbarians.

---

4. Jean-Pierre Vernant, *Mythe et pensée chez les Grecs* (Paris: Maspéro, 1962), trans. J. Lloyd and J. Fort, *Myth and Thought Among the Greeks* (New York: Routledge, 1983), 343. This work, justly celebrated, is a collection of articles that appeared in 1962 from François Maspéro, a "progressive" publisher from whom Hellenists hardly ever appear.

This thesis rests on the historical fact that at a certain moment power stopped being founded on a relationship between divine entities handed down through princes and priests in relation to or anointed by them, but started to depend on the ability of some to persuade those who had become their *fellow citizens* by rational arguments. This new organization of power is symbolized above all by the assembly of citizens in the *agora*, where many aspects of collective life had passed through the sieve of contradictory rational discussion. Thus one is witness at the birth of political institution, which, in competition with other institutions (religious, family, professional, etc.), ultimately dominated them.

Vernant writes,

> The human group [that of the Greek cities and even of the proto-cities found in Homer] makes itself in this image: beside individual private homes there is a center where public affairs are debated, and this center represents all that is "common," the collectivity as such. In this center each one feels equal to everyone else; no one is subject to another. In this free debate that is instituted in the center of the *agora*, all citizens are defined as *isoi*, equals, *homoioi*, similar. We see the birth of a society where the relation between man and man is thought under the form of a relation of identity, symmetry, reversibility.[5]

Vernant discerns a "contamination" of every level of Greek society by this new political structure. Thus the crucial idea of *isonomia*, which in the political domain designates the equality of rights of all citizens, is applied in medicine in the famous passage of Alcmaeon of Croton, who says that health, and thus life itself, presupposes an isonomic equilibrium of the powers that compose the body, while illness is the *monarchy* of one of the powers (hot, cold, dry, moist, sweet, bitter, etc.).[6] Isonomia is applied even to the whole universe, since in Anaximander's cosmology, for example, Earth is immobile in the center of the universe because it

---

5. Vernant, *Mythe et pensée chez les Grecs*, 154 (trans. note: A. Preus translation; in the translation published by Zone Books New York in 2006 you find the passage on p. 371).

6. Cf. Pseudo-Plutarch, *Placita Philosophorum (Opinions of the Philosophers)*, ed. G. N. Bernardakis (Leipzig: Teubner, 1893), 911A, and Stobaeus, *The Greek Anthology*, ed. W. R. Paton (Cambridge, MA: Loeb, 1857–1921), 4.36.

"is not dominated by anything" (ὑπὸ μηδενὸς κρατουμένη).[7] In an article both brilliant and dense, Charles Mugler shows that *isonomia* is the basic principle of atomism and that it was posited in a manner more general and in a way more "pure" by Democritus than it would be by Epicurus. This superiority of Democritean atomism over Epicurean atomism has been asserted several times by Mugler.[8] We should note that he expresses the indeterminate and undecidable nature of the universe of the Atomists in terms of justice and law: "justice is thus rendered by this homogeneous distribution to everything that exists" (232); Democritus "grants the same right of existence to everything that is possible" (236).

The political space thus created is that of men, not of women, outside the home, not within, of written laws, not of customs, of civic deities and not of chthonic and/or mystical cults, of reason and not of dank psychic enthusiasms. Science and philosophy would have arisen directly from this process of politicizing Greek space, because they put into operation compelling demonstrations valid for any human mind, and in ethics, for example, imperatives would be based on reason and not on certainties transmitted by what one may call the collective consciousness of a particular population. Vernant meant to show us, among other things, that it was only in a city that Socrates could have sought universal definitions of various virtues.

The forms of knowledge too become both rational and public, with the primary consequence that they can be understood as accessible to everyone and teachable, often for a fee. The example of medicine is remarkable. One can get an idea of the transformation we are talking about by looking at the greatest figure of ancient medicine, Hippocrates. The medical school that he founded on the island of Cos brought together old and new. The old is that medicine, an activity closely tied to religion by way of the cult of Asclepius, rests on a traditional form of teaching, that is, that it is not propounded in a reasoned oral presentation but is *transmitted* from predecessors to their successors, generally carried out within a lineage. Thus, physicians tried to insert themselves into one of the lineages descending from the god Asclepius himself, by one of his

---

7. Hippolytus, *Refutation of All Heresies*, trans. J. M. MacMahon, 1.6.3, available online at NewAdvent.org.

8. Charles Mugler, "L'isonomie des atomistes," *Revue de Philologie* 30 (1956): 231–250, see also his "Sur quelques particularités de l'atomisme ancien," *Revue de Philologie* (1953): 141–174.

two sons, Podalirius or Machaon. The family of Hippocrates, for example, pretended to descend from Podalirius, and Hippocrates was initiated into medicine by his father and grandfather, who is supposed to have written medical works. His sons and his son-in-law were members of his school. The new aspect is that Hippocrates proposed a theory of medicine that everyone could examine and thus also criticize, even if none of the texts that have come down to us under his name can be attributed to him with certainty. He is also the person who, it is said, was the first to teach medicine for a fee.[9]

The *school*, which replaced the lineage brotherhood and was no longer located in a temple, is the new form of association within which knowledge is transmitted. The physicians doubtless preceded the philosophers in the "schoolization" of knowledge in Greece, since the school of Hippocrates was founded about 420 BCE, the Platonic Academy around 387, and the Presocratic schools earlier than Hippocrates were not institutions presupposing a life entirely or mainly common among its members, as were the medical and philosophical schools in classical, Hellenistic, and Roman antiquity.[10] Nevertheless we must note that it is not certain that the school of Hippocrates (and this applies equally to the Academy during the lifetime of Plato) imposed on its students any doctrinal orthodoxy at all, because it was not until the third century BCE that Herophilus of Chalcedon brought from philosophy to medicine a *school* practice that would make its students not only live with their teacher but be held to defend his teachings against those of rival schools. Among the philosophers doubtless the first "school" in the full sense of the word, producing an orthodoxy, was Aristotle's Lyceum. However, the teachings of the master were discussed and developed by his disciples and successors; this was the case in the Lyceum, the Stoa, and, to a lesser degree, the Epicurean school.

Of course the victory of political rationality was never complete. There were perverse usages, like those of the Sophists, at least in the picture of them that the philosophers like Plato and Aristotle have given us, and there

---

9. Several years ago, I tried to give a *political* reading of the difference, long noticed by specialists, between Cnidian medicine, with its empirical reputation, and Coan medicine (that of Hippocrates), with a rational reputation. Cf. Pierre Pellegrin, "Médecine hippocratique et philosophie," in D. Gourevitch, M. Grmek, P. Pellegrin, *Hippocrate. De l'Art medical* (Paris: Livre de Poche, 1994), 14–40.

10. The Pythagoreans formed an association that was closer to a religious sect than to a school.

still existed large areas of social life that continued to follow prepolitical logics, for example within familial cults or initiatory religious associations like that of the Mysteries of Eleusis, that surely often got the upper hand over the political process in certain decisions that citizens were led to take concerning their individual or collective life. It's really only in Plato's *Republic* that the family, the most important prepolitical institution, was dissolved into the city. That is a crucial *political* problem and is treated as such by Aristotle; we will come back to that. Nevertheless it remains, conformably with the position of Vernant, that the texts of the philosophers, orators, historians, even the dramatists, show that the Greeks had a clear awareness of the difference between them and those they called "barbarians"; the fact that they lived in cities was, in their eyes, an important part of that specialness. As for Aristotle, he lived at the end of a historical movement that began with the founding of cities, and no one was more conscious than he of the break that that foundation represented.

But that which interests us above all is the application of this rational approach that would thus be fundamentally a political one, to politics itself. Doubtless the Greeks, according to the written works that have come down to us, mainly agreed in considering city life as founded on relationships between rational beings, even if no one could imagine a city bereft of all religious practices. But the relations between the religious and the rational were not, in ancient Greece, the same as those that have been constructed in the case of "true" religions, revealed religions, and in any case the political sphere did not have to worry about any threats from various religious institutions. This is true to the point that when in mythical thought human unhappiness was often seen as caused by human ignorance of divine commandments or agreements, with the rise of the city, social evil was subsequently understood as coming from a lack of rationality. Thus, political theoreticians, who were immediately presented as reformers in charge of a refoundation of the city according to rational criteria, are as ancient as politics itself.

We will never be grateful enough to Vernant for having liberated us from a false and pernicious approach to Greece. Presenting himself as the one who, following his teacher Louis Gernet and according to the title of Gernet's most famous work (*An Anthropology of Ancient Greece*),[11] contrib-

---

11. Louis Gernet, *Anthropologie de la Grèce antique* (Paris: Maspéro, 1968), a posthumous collection of articles by J.-P. Vernant in 1968 published by François Maspéro. Louis Gernet died in January 1962.

uted to put ancient Greek society under the theoretical yoke of historical anthropology, Vernant took up opposition to the previous approach, that of the "Greek Miracle." In detaching the ancient Greeks from ordinary historical causality and pretending that their genius was something miraculous ("because it was they"), the theory of the "Greek Miracle" served above all to give us made-to-measure ancestors who helped us feel ourselves to be what we pretend to be. Tremendous historical, anthropological, and sociological research has apparently not completely destroyed this idea, since it is periodically reborn from its ashes.[12]

Today, however, it seems to me that the break that Vernant established should be relativized. Not, obviously, that Vernant falls back into the reactionary ethnocentrism of our old teachers, since he has thoroughly applied the methods of critical history and historical anthropology to ancient societies. But to bring everything together to the birth of the city (a kind of Marxist schema, but based on politics more than on economics), isn't that in a way a kind of reintroduction of the Greek Miracle? Because it is a fact that the city appeared in the Greek cultural era and not elsewhere. Why? Vernant has the wisdom to avoid identifying one or several causes of this appearance. In a sense, the analyses of Vernant and his friends recover the *ideological* role of the theory of the Greek Miracle, even if in a subtle and altered manner. Because the image of Greek politics and democracy that they give us would be that which we would expect to make the Greeks the ancestors of modern politics and democracy as we would wish they would be, and unhappily, that they are not.

Doubtless we should soften Vernant's description, in the first place because the Greeks surely were rather strongly aware of the particularity of Hellenic politics according to the regime under which they themselves lived. But Vernant fell into the same Athens-centric illusion as the majority of his colleagues. Because not only were most cities not democratically governed, but the democracies of the Greek world from the sixth to the fourth centuries BCE, other than the mother of all democracies, Athens, were often regimes imposed by force on cities that fell to Athenian impe-

---

12. See, for example, the book by Sylvain Gouguenheim, *Aristote au Mont Saint-Michel* (Paris: Seuil, 2008), which (re)constructs a mythical Western rationality that goes from the Greeks to the Medieval Latins, via the Romans, but carefully avoiding the Arabs. I have said (almost) everything bad that I have to say about this book in Pierre Pellegrin, "Aristote arabe, Aristote latin. Aristote de droite, Aristote de gauche," *Revue philosophique de la France et de l'Étranger* (Janvier–Mars 2009): 79–89.

rialism. Here is an example taken from Thucydides (1.115.2). Samos and Miletus went to war, and Miletus having been worsted, appealed to Athens:

> In this they were joined by certain private persons from Samos itself, who wished to revolutionize the government. Accordingly, the Athenians sailed to Samos with forty ships and set up a democracy; took hostages from the Samians, fifty boys and as many men, lodged them in Lemnos, and after leaving a garrison in the island returned home.

Thus democracy was established at Samos. We will see that for Aristotle cities are in a way more or less political according to the regime under which they live.

Besides, historians have noted that Athenian democracy conformed very little to that which we expect from a democracy. The great majority of the population (women, slaves, foreigners) was excluded from political life. In 317 BCE Demetrius of Phaleron, who had been put in charge of Athens under the control of Macedonia, carried out a census that counted twenty-one thousand citizens, ten thousand metics, and four hundred thousand slaves. Doubtless among the slaves were counted the women, less certainly among the metics, but it is almost certain that that was not the case for citizens, which means that there were over twenty thousand wives and daughters of citizens being excluded from citizenship. Some modern historians have contested these numbers because it seems difficult that Athens at that time had nearly five hundred thousand inhabitants, but at least it gives an order of magnitude. In oligarchical cities it was worse, and the body of citizens was often unbelievably restricted, not to mention tyrannies and other monarchies. Although Plato, both in the *Republic* and in the *Laws*, did not seem to be excessively concerned about this sort of demographic lack of equilibrium, Aristotle sometimes reveals that he is conscious of the danger. We must also recognize on this point that Vernant, more than many others, was conscious of the limits and corrections that we need to bring to our spontaneous image of Greek democracy.[13]

Another historical remark, to notice a point, truly gigantic, that casts a singular shadow over Vernant's account, which we must recognize as somewhat idyllic. This point has in any case been well seen by Aristotle.

---

13. On this matter, there is a book that is still worth reading, Moses Finley, *Démocratie antique et démocratie moderne* (Paris: Payot, 1976), with a long essay by Pierre Vidal-Naquet, "Tradition de la démocracie grecque."

As we have said, the Athenians, who serve as a model for Vernant, were always, to the end, fierce partisans of birthright (*jus sanguinis*). Claude Vatin, as well as Claude Mossé,[14] who is far from giving up her Athens-centrism, have shown clearly that "the maximum enlargement of the political body is not incompatible with the closing of the civic body."[15] That is, Athenian democracy developed in two directions: on the one side, lift as much as possible the census restrictions that prevented many Athenians from participating in political life because they had too small an inheritance, and, on the other, to avoid any contamination of the civic body by the two great dangers that threatened it, slaves and foreigners, two groups largely overlapping, since there was the very strong tendency of all slave systems to look for their slaves among foreign populations. And in that paragon of Athens-centrism, Pericles's famous funeral oration presented in 431 BCE for the Athenian soldiers who had died in combat, according to Thucydides, who reported the speech, he praised the

> Ancestors, for it is both just and proper that they should have the honor of the first mention on an occasion like the present. They dwelt in the country without break in succession from generation to generation, and handed it down free to the present time by their valor.

For the Athenians there was, *prior to the establishment of political relations* (and "prior" here should be understood as much in a logical as chronological sense), a dream of ethnic purity that dazes us. When we read Aristotle's *Politics*, we get the impression that the crucial problem for any city is that of determining by law the *political* criteria for citizenship. Thus, Aristotle thinks that a well-governed city should not give civic rights to artisans. But even before legislating to decide who is legitimately a citizen, Athens formed a human group, established on genetic and not political criteria, of people who could be citizens. This practice is demonstrated by the formation of "civic lists" where potential citizens are inscribed as members of a deme. One of the major events of the political history of Athens was the periodic revision of these civic lists. Thus, according to the *Constitution of Athens* ascribed to Aristotle (26.4), because the number

---

14. Claude Vatin, *Citoyens et non-citoyens dans le monde grec* (Paris: SEDES, 1984); Claude Mossé, *Politique et société en Grèce ancienne. Le 'modèle' athénien* (Paris: GF-Flammarion, 1995).
15. Vatin, *Citoyens et non-citoyens dans le monde grec*, 70.

of citizens had become too great, Pericles decided to limit citizenship to men descended from Athenians on both sides, maternal and paternal. In Athens, citizenship, in the sense of the prerogatives that attached to the status of citizen, was extremely difficult to obtain. Athenians were more than willing to share the *duties* of citizenship with noncitizens: thus, metics paid a special tax and were liable for military service. But even the orator Lysias, who assisted the return of the democracy in 404 BCE, did not acquire citizenship. This obsession with purity of blood was so entrenched among the Athenians that they went so far as to refuse to apply the common idea that people settled in a location are formed by migration. Nicole Loraux has clearly shown that, right to the level of myth, Athenians wanted to remain *purely*, in every sense of that word, with each other; we remember that according to their main origin myth they pretended to be born from their land (autochthonous).[16]

Historically, we see that legislation had a tendency to resist marriages with foreigners, and worse yet, with slaves, on the one hand firmly rejecting from citizenship children born of such unions, and punishing fraud on this point in a pitiless way on the other. It's also because of this obsession with purity of blood that Athens had a very strong prohibition against adultery. Claude Vatin remarks correctly that women, whom all cities excluded from full citizenship, were nevertheless closer than foreign men—they were called πολίτις, the feminine form of πολίτης, or "citizeness." Ethnically pure material, although not a sufficient condition for the existence of a citizen, was a necessary condition. So in Athens citizenship was in the first place a matter of birth, that is, of family. That is a crucial point that causes some difficulty for Vernant's schema.[17]

Before offering a specifically political critique at the beginning of *Politics* 3, in one of the rare passages in his works that is straightforwardly

---

16. Cf. Nicole Loraux, *Né de la terre. Mythe et politique à Athènes* (Paris: Seuil, 1996). In a remarkable little book William K. C. Guthrie finds in many Greek populations this pretention to autochthony but remarks that "above all other Greeks the Athenians boasted of this distinction." William K. C. Guthrie, *In the Beginning: Some Greek Views on the Origin of Life and the Early State of Man* (London: Methuen & Co., 1957), 23.

17. We ought to note here that modern democracies have sometimes shared these characteristics with ancient democracies. In the apartheid era, South Africa was certainly a democracy with great attention to the rights of its citizens, except that the great majority of the population was excluded from this civic contract. Until recently, Germany maintained a citizenship rule, based on a birthright, so strict that Turks who had lived for several generations in Germany, without having any remaining relationship at all with the country of origin of their ancestors, were refused German citizenship,

ironic, Aristotle begins by showing the absurdity of the Athenian position—he does not attribute it specifically to Athens, since he talks about Larissa—on the ground that it leads to an infinite regress. In order to be an Athenian citizen, one had to have parents who were Athenians, whose parents in turn had to have been Athenians, and so on. In fact Aristotle does not challenge the attribution of citizenship in a city transmitted by way of birth, but he is much too aware of the vagaries, twists, and turns of history to be able to believe that this way of acquiring citizenship could be definitive and unchangeable, and he notes that the principle is challenged when there are historical upheavals: we will return several times to the occasional necessity of opening up the body of citizens following a "lack of men" caused by a war. For the most part, the Greeks did not accept, even hypothetically, the idea that people could become fellow citizens simply by sharing the common ethical and political values, as the American and French revolutions affirmed. Doubtless that idea has, unfortunately, lost some force in our societies. Philosophers like Plato and Aristotle are doubtless closer than others when they claim that citizenship in the excellent city is for men who share a certain number of virtues. But for Aristotle the demand for virtue is for fellow citizens and, for him as for all the Greeks, the idea of "foreigner" remains full of implications.

One may say simultaneously that a more careful reading of Aristotle would have enabled Vernant to bring necessary amendments to his sketch, but also that in general Aristotle conforms to the essence of Vernant's position in that, as we will see, politics, although not definitory of human nature, is no less an important property that colors every level of society in which it appears.

The Greeks, That Is to Say, Aristotle

It is all the more regrettable that Vernant did not read Aristotle more carefully, because he is the only really political thinker in antiquity, and perhaps in the entire history of philosophy. There would be many ways

---

while the descendants of seventeenth-century German immigrants to the Caucasus, no longer speaking German, gained German citizenship easily. Germany has recently modified its legislation, yielding to pressure from the EU, but powerful movements in favor of birthright are currently appearing in Europe along with the increase of power of populist movements. In any case, in a country like France, the right of residency is rarely invoked to acquire French nationality; that is mainly conferred by the fact of being the issue of parents themselves already citizens.

of showing that the place of Aristotle in *our* approach to the Greek political reality is more significant than that of other philosophers, historians, and ancient thinkers of the social reality of antiquity. Let us be satisfied, even before any precise analysis, with the following fact. When we read the surviving ancient Greek texts, two characteristics inevitably strike us, we could say two invading *presences*. The one, which is far from being distinctive to the Hellenic world, but is clearly a nearly absolute rule in all societies of the same period, is that of slavery; the other, proper to the Greeks, is the city (*polis*). These two realities are not, properly speaking, part of the unconscious of the Greeks, because none of them were ignorant of their presence, but they were so close and so pervasive that they didn't have the idea of trying to think about them explicitly and precisely.

Thus for slavery. Slaves were *so much there*, everywhere and always, that they became invisible. Pierre Vidal-Naquet has remarked that even utopia did not succeed in erasing the reality of slavery, even of reducing its massiveness. Those who, like Aristophanes, imagined an extreme social subversion, that rule by women would represent, simply did not conceive that such a subversion could abolish slavery, since the city of women continues to have slaves.[18] Zeno of Citium, the founder of Stoicism, wrote a *Republic* in the Cynical vein that was part of his thought. He described a society of sages (composed solely of sages, or mixing sages and non-sages—interpreters are not in agreement about that) in which all social usages would be overturned. All institutions would be suppressed—no courts, no temples, no money; not only is the institution of marriage abolished, but there is a regime of absolute sexual freedom and, last but not least, the very marks of sexual difference are abolished, since men and women wear the same clothing.[19] But apparently not a word about slavery, although that institution is at least as invasive as that of marriage. The same for the revolutionary (pro)positions of the Cynics, who counted among natural practices both incest and cannibalism: in the name of its founding conventions culture seems to go against our sexual impulses in forbidding us certain partners and also against our need of food by forbidding us to eat the bodies of our dead relatives. On the other hand, slavery did not seem to them to

---

18. See Pierre Vidal-Naquet, "Slavery and the Rule of Women in Tradition, Myth and Utopia," in *Myth, Religion and Society*, ed. R. L. Gordon (Cambridge: Cambridge University Press, 1981).

19. See Harold Caparne Baldry, "Zeno's Ideal State," *Journal of Hellenic Studies* (1959): 3–15.

be an unnatural institution. To be sure, Diogenes of Sinope finally did without his slave, but only when his slave had run away, which proves that he had one, and we know his name—Manes. In fact, the actions and words of Diogenes reported by Diogenes Laertius tend to show that the cynical philosopher thought, like most people of his era, that the state of slavery was naturally appropriate for people who had mental and/or ethical qualities inferior to those of "normal" people. Diogenes Laertius tells us twice that Diogenes declared himself winner in athletic competitions "in the category of men," and that the official winners ought to be included "in the category of slaves" (6.33 and 43). When someone asked Diogenes why we call slaves *andropoda* ("man-footed"), he answered, "because they have the feet of men, and a soul like yours, you who ask me that question" (6.67). For the Cynics too, "slave" is an insult.

If we remember the place and functions that Plato grants to women in his *Republic* and blame him for the silent presence of slaves in the Platonic dialogues, it reinforces in us the impression that gender difference was for ancient thinkers a *question*, and slavery was not. Aristotle was the only ancient philosopher who put forward a theoretical analysis of the phenomenon of slavery; we will have to clarify the content and goals of that analysis. But Aristotle was also the only ancient philosopher to try to think through that peculiarly Greek reality, the city, which amounts to saying, as we have already pointed out, that he was the only political thinker. We will, in what follows, take the terms "political," "politician," "politically," in their proper sense as that which relates to the *polis*, or city. Oddly enough, among the orators, poets, and even philosophers, who are constantly referring to the city, none asks himself or herself "what is a city?" We will return to these social objects common to the Greeks and theoretically absolutely proper to Aristotle. The Aristotelian theory of slavery will be examined in the appropriate place when it is a matter of the place to which Aristotle assigns it, within the family. As for the city, it will be absent from none, so to speak, of the pages that follow.

When one writes a work on a subject it is because one believes that the subject has not been satisfactorily treated heretofore. The interpretation of Aristotle's political philosophy has been, for the last several decades, the object of a great deal of attention, many publications, and automatically, one may say, remarkable progress. Some of the theses presented in this book nevertheless propose a reorientation of the reading of whole sections of the political philosophy of the man from Stagira. But, of course, "new" does not always mean "true."

This work was originally imagined as a collection of articles dedicated to Aristotelian political philosophy. In view of how much my own positions have evolved, I had at the beginning the intention of revising these articles before publishing them until I realized that I had to write a book, for at least two reasons. First, because it would be the most economical solution, to the extent that revision is sometimes harder work than writing in the first place. One of the principal results of that decision is that I have often engaged in self-plagiarism in reusing the theses and even many of the expressions used in the articles in question. The second reason is entirely different: in gathering my articles, I realized that, on the one hand, on almost all the important subjects that were discussed in them, Aristotle came to positions that separated him, sometimes to a significant degree, from those of other ancient thinkers, and on the other hand, that these positions gave him a decidedly "modern" appearance. Without wanting to make Aristotle an immediate participant in today's debates—a procedure that I have just condemned in this introduction—I think that it does not lack interest to note the degree to which Aristotle's political philosophy finds an echo in ways of thinking that are radically foreign to him. But it is more striking to consider these original positions together than to study them one by one.

CHAPTER 1

The Philosopher in Politics

Let us begin with a chapter that reviews well-known aspects of Aristotelian ethics that Aristotelian "professionals," who may be looking for more original analyses, may skip, reading only its appendix. Aristotle is the only thinker to present a real conceptual analysis of the *polis*. But that is surely not enough to permit us to say that he was the first and only one, at least among ancient philosophers, to think about politics. He obviously was not the only one to take an interest in what we call political philosophy. One might even ask whether there was any philosopher, at least in the ancient world, who did *not* discuss the organization of human society. In his analysis of the treatises "On Nature" of the Presocratics, Gerard Naddaf finds their common architecture composed of three levels: cosmogony, anthropogony, and politigony.[1] That means that every philosopher worthy of the name had to deal in rational terms with the universe, the human race (often among other living kinds), and human society. Naddaf extends this schema to Hesiod, to the Sophists, and to Plato, and he may be right. In any case it seems incongruous when an ancient philosopher does not offer his opinion on either the origin or nature of human societies. In proposing that philosophy is called to investigate all things, the Presocratic philosophers claimed that they had something to say about politics, and if we are generally ignorant of the content of their claims, it is mainly due to the loss of the relevant texts.

---

1. Gerard Naddaf, *The Greek Concept of Nature* (Albany: State University of New York Press, 2005).

And since in moral and political matters it is not far from analysis to prescription, philosophers have often put on the robe of moral preacher and social reformer. That's a fundamental characteristic of philosophy that has continued to the present day, joining a cognitive approach to a practical and prescriptive approach, both rational. Remember the Kantian "program": What can I know? What ought I do? For what may I hope?

It could happen that certain philosophers have *abandoned* entire areas to which their speculations might be supposed to apply. Aristotle himself notes, in a famous passage in the *Parts of Animals*, that "in the time of Socrates . . . the study of nature left off and philosophers turned toward the useful virtues, that is, politics" (I.1, 642a2). It really is a matter of abandonment, since, according to the *Phaedo*, Socrates had at first tried to philosophize in the manner of the Presocratics, before he decided that he was unable to deal with questions of cosmology, religion, and physics. Plato put an end to the pose—simultaneously abusive and dangerous in his eyes—of the autonomy of ethics, founding it again on the cosmic order that only the philosopher may apprehend. As for politics, it never disappeared completely from the philosophical program. Thus, even when in the Hellenistic schools, ethics won out over politics and became one of the three parts of philosophy, political questions were always thoroughly debated among philosophers, even when some of them advised avoiding public life, as the Epicureans did.

In fact, Aristotle inaugurated a new attitude of philosophy toward politics, and that was as much because of new historical circumstances as because of his own special epistemological stance. It is very difficult to decide if these two factors interacted with each other and, if that is the case, to what degree. Aristotle was de facto outside the *polis*. Foreigner in Athens, Macedonian subject, former teacher of the young Alexander of Macedon, his father the friend of King Philip II, Aristotle found himself, as it happened, in a unique situation, that of a companion of a prince, but who got his intellectual development in the milieu of *citizens*. This was an almost untenable situation, as we will see, for someone who thought that the perfect form of human community was the city. It was also a very uncomfortable position for a philosopher who was a member of Plato's Academy, and thus a resident of Athens, where the anti-Macedonian sentiment was as strong as the Macedonian threat was real. The danger that Philip II represented for Athens in particular and the life of the city in general was in fact perfectly identified by the Greeks. Thus, Aristotle took his last journey, shortly before his death, to avoid the vindictiveness of the

Athenians, heartened by the announcement of the death of Alexander. We are told that he said at the time that he wanted to prevent the Athenians from repeating the injustice that they had committed against Socrates. We will have more to say about the relationships between Aristotle's historical situation and his political philosophy at the end of the present chapter.

As for the epistemological perspective, it's worth remembering the essential, since it is so characteristic of Aristotle's way of thinking. If one looks from a distance at Greek philosophy before Aristotle, that is, up to Plato, one sees that ethical-political speculation appears in it as an element in an organic whole. Thinkers who claim to explicate reality by describing the generation of things from their first component elements articulate cosmogony, zoogony, and politogony by accounting for them by the same principles. Thus Democritus, who was perhaps the major theoretical opponent of Aristotle, even more than Plato, claimed that the atoms, by their shapes and combinations, explained not only how the universe was formed, how life appeared and developed, why the sun is hot and why the sea is blue, but also the reality and functioning of the human soul.

Plato gave this conception that one may call "total" an accomplished form, and as we have most of his writings, which is not the case for the thinkers who preceded him, it is Plato who, in opposition to Aristotle, has best incarnated one of the two great ways of thinking, reductionism and pluralism, whose opposition has given structure to the history of philosophy as to the history of the sciences. In fact, it is not only in morals and politics that, as the poet Coleridge said, everyone is born either a Platonist or an Aristotelian. For Plato, there is only one way to do science, and even only one science, the "dialectic" of the *Republic*, which is therefore the science of everything. This, among many others, is also the position of Descartes, for whom "philosophy is like a tree" of which the various parts have sprouted from a common trunk, and above all, from common roots. Despite the differences that seem to us, and are, enormous, Plato shares this position with Democritus, though Democritus is a "mechanist" and Plato a devoted partisan of natural teleology. Kant, on the other hand, adopts a fundamentally Aristotelian attitude when he distinguishes the domains of nature and freedom without subsuming them under a single entity. This opposition reappears in the sciences, in the modern sense of the word. From time to time particular areas escape, or claim to escape, the conceptual frame of the dominant science. That was the case, for example, for thermodynamics, which seemed to be an exception to the laws of classical mechanics, but it was above all the case for all forms of vitalism that, from Aristotle to Georges Canguilhem and Ernst Mayr, would claim, against all mechanisms from Democritus to molecular biology, to extricate the living from the exclusive dominion of the physical-chemical sciences. This fight between a vitalism that affirms the specificity of the living and a mechanistic reductionism pervades Aristotle's entire zoological works.

Aristotle put forward a coherent and "hard" version of pluralism. It rests on two postulates. First, that of the isolation of genera, according to which one may distinguish various genera of objects in the world and that to each of these genera corresponds its own science. Thus, lengths and numbers being two distinct genera, geometry and arithmetic are two different sciences, which work together only with difficulty. In fact, Aristotle's position is less fixed than it first appears, since the extent of a genus depends on ongoing research—thus living things, animals, birds, and raptors can be taken as genera in different investigations—and since he accepts (how could he do otherwise?) the general theory of proportions, which applies as well to lengths as to numbers, but also to times, speeds, and so on. Nevertheless, it remains that physics, whose object is all beings that have in themselves the source of their changes, does not communicate with mathematics whose objects are unchangeable, whatever their exact ontological status otherwise. We know how much of an obstacle that separation constituted for the birth of modern physics, but there, too, Aristotle violates at the margin the rule that he laid down and does not miss the opportunity to introduce a certain number of calculations into his physical demonstrations.

The second postulate, a kind of extension and radicalization of the first, posits that there are different types of science, and notably that it is necessary to distinguish practical sciences from theoretical sciences. The theoretical sciences *contemplate* (one of the senses of the verb θεωρεῖν in Greek, the root sense being "to see") their objects and present a demonstrative discourse about them. For Aristotle, in a very Platonic vein, there is no theoretical science except of that which is not only universal, but also unchangeable. The three great theoretical sciences are mathematics, whose object is immobile and embedded in matter; physics, which studies material objects in movement; and theology, which thinks about the being that is separate from matter and immobile. The way that Aristotle envisages the theoretical science of physics, which applies, to the extent that it is a theoretical science, to immovable objects at the same time as it is applied to entities by definition in motion, does not interest us here.

At the same time, I will not go into the problem, tempting though it is, of the degree to which Aristotle adhered completely to this contemplative conception of knowledge that supposes that the knowing subject does not intervene in the construction of the object of knowledge.

As a rule, ethics and politics are classified as "practical sciences." For the moment let us accept this distinction, though we will need to make it more precise and amend it. They are certainly *sciences*; that is, they are meant to give the person who has them an acquaintance more universal than a simple empirical approach to the phenomena.[2] There is a passage in the *Eudemian Ethics* that illustrates in a particularly strong manner, both in its substance and form, this claim that politics is scientific:

> In every investigation, arguments stated in philosophical form are different from those that are non-philosophical; hence we must not think that theoretical study of such a sort as to make manifest not only the nature of a thing but also its cause is superfluous even for the political student, since that is the philosophic procedure in every field of inquiry. (1.6, 1216b35, trans. Rackham)

Not only is politics a *philosophical* study, one that offers arguments (λόγοι) put forward in a *philosophical* way (φιλοσόφως), but it also articulates the two great interrogations that characterize scientific research, the "fact" and the "why." And yet, when we look at the texts that propose a program of this kind, the beginning of book 2 of the *Posterior Analytics* (89b29), for example, one gets the impression (but is it well founded?) that Aristotle thinks there uniquely or principally of the theoretical sciences.

But in taking as object human action (*praxis*), the practical sciences are distinguished from the theoretical sciences at several points. In the first place, they do not consider objects distinct from the subject itself as do the theoretical sciences that "contemplate" a reality that they cannot modify, or as what Aristotle sometimes calls the "productive sciences," that is, techniques.[3]

---

2. The expression "practical science" (ἐπιστήμη πρακτική) appears only once in Aristotle, and possibly not at all, since Jacques Brunschwig, in his edition of the *Topics*, suppresses "practical" in the only passage that speaks expressly of science "theoretical, practical, and productive" (6.6, 145a15, 18). But when the *Metaphysics* speaks of "thought" (*dianoia*, E.1, 1025b25) theoretical, practical, and productive, it's clearly the same doctrine.

Next, it is difficult for them to apply deterministic schemas that are normal in mathematics and physics, because the domain of practical sciences is that of human freedom, which entails the possibility of unpredictable decisions, and of the absolute uniqueness of events, which makes it delicate to apply explanatory schemas. Delicate, but not totally impossible, otherwise the practical sciences would not be sciences. Finally, the practical sciences, as their name indicates, are concerned with *practice*, that is, they aim at transforming the reality that they study. In the *Nicomachean Ethics* Aristotle asserts successively, and not far apart, that "since the present inquiry does not aim at theoretical knowledge like the others—for we are inquiring not in order to know what excellence is, but in order to become good, since otherwise our inquiry would have been of no use" (2.2, 1103b26), while he makes fun of those who make ethics a theory, comparing them to sick people who are satisfied to read the prescriptions of their physician, before declaring, "Next we must consider what virtue is" (1105b29). The contradiction is only apparent, since "to those who desire and act in accordance with a rational principle knowledge about such matters will be of great benefit" (1.1, 1095a10). But who these people are, and what the true function of practical understanding is, which depend on the people to whom they are addressed, will all become clear below.

But the difference between theoretical and practical sciences is not only epistemological. In fact, we must not forget that "science" (ἐπιστήμη) is for Aristotle, and indeed for other ancient philosophers, and ultimately to a certain degree for us, a twofold reality. On the one side, it is a body of propositions logically related to each other; but on the other, it is

---

3. In the *Eudemian Ethics* (1.5, 1216b10), Aristotle opposes theoretical sciences that "have no other end except to get to know and to contemplate the nature of things that are the subjects of the sciences" (giving as examples astronomy, physics, and geometry) to the productive sciences, giving as examples medicine and politics. Rather than a sign of immaturity (the *Eudemian Ethics* having not yet developed the doctrine that is found in book E of the *Metaphysics*) it is better to see this as an adaptation to the needs of the moment: Aristotle wants to oppose the sciences that have as their only goal understanding to those that aim at a practical result. As elsewhere, we find this *partial* appeal to certain doctrines. Thus, in the last chapter of *Politics* I Aristotle distinguishes rational and irrational parts of the soul, which would mean that this rather restricted description was conceived before the refinements we find in the *De Anima*. But it is enough to note that the passage in the *Politics* does not need more than the distinction between rational and irrational. Nevertheless, it remains that practical and productive sciences are different from each other, and that politics and ethics are practical sciences.

also a *virtue*, that is to say an excellent state of the person who knows, since it is a matter, in the case of science, of an intellectual virtue, not an ethical virtue.[4] And one may well say, in English, that such and such an individual has mathematical science or knows mathematics because he or she has mastered the system of theorems or, more likely today, a (small) part of that system. When that individual has thoroughly mastered this theoretical material, he or she is an excellent mathematician. But the radical difference between theoretical and practical sciences can be found in these two aspects that every science possesses. On the one hand, the architecture of a science like mathematics, and that of a science like politics, are very different, as what we said above has already suggested: politics does not offer demonstrations, nor theorems of the kind that are typical of mathematics. And, on the other hand, the excellences (virtues) of those who practice theoretical sciences and of those who deal with the practical sciences are also very distant from each other.

To put things in Aristotelian terms, theoretical excellence and practical excellence are not identical and are not embodied in the same people, except by accident. Thus, Aristotle contrasts Anaxagoras and Pericles, each of them excellent in one of these domains. The one who properly bears the name "philosopher" is the one who is excellent in the theoretical domain. But he simply would not have the qualities that would make him the best political man. Speculative intelligence is not, in fact, always a big help, even if it can sometimes be, when one has to resolve problems posed by contingent concrete situations in which one must know how to decide at the right moment. In a justly famous book, published in 1963, *La Prudence chez Aristote* (Prudence in Aristotle), Pierre Aubenque proposes an impressive picture of this man who is excellent in the practical realm, the "prudent" (φρόνιμος). One of Aubenque's main theses is that the prudent person, taking Pericles as an example, cannot count on any norm external to himself to decide which actions ought to be done or avoided, because he is himself the norm.[5] Thus the philosopher loses the mastery of all things assigned to him by Plato and notably, crucially

---

4. Let us say once and for all that the term *aretē* (ἀρετή) can be translated equally well by "virtue" or by "excellence."

5. Cf. *Nicomachean Ethics* 3.6, 1113a29, "The good man judges each class of things rightly, and in each class the truth appears to him." Furthermore, 9.4, 1166a12: "Excellence and the good man seem to be the measure of every class of things." Perhaps we should take that as a hendiadys meaning, "the virtue of the virtuous man."

for us, he is no longer entitled to govern the city. We will thus have to redefine the role of the philosopher vis-à-vis politics.

Before we turn to that, it is useful to make a remark that should give more emphasis to what I said above about the difference between Plato and Aristotle, and in a general way about the difference between theoretical and practical science. In fact, the *Republic* said that the philosopher should rule in the city. But Plato seems to have evolved on this point—we can allow ourselves this claim because Plato's writings can be arranged in a more or less approximate chronological order. That might reduce Aristotle's originality, but we will show that that is not at all the case.

On the second point, doubtless Plato's *Statesman* is the most useful. At the beginning of the dialogue the Stranger posits a distinction: within science (ἐπιστήμη) we must distinguish two kinds, of which the text gives as examples "arithmetic and certain other techniques" and "the technique of the carpenter and every other manual laborer" (258d). "Divide all the sciences in this way, in calling one kind 'practical' and the other 'only cognitive' (μόνον γνωστικήν)" (258d), the Stranger asks Young Socrates. It seems to me that this μόνον deserves a "strong" interpretation, not meaning "pure" ("purely cognitive" sciences, as most of the recent translators have rendered it),[6] but as indicating a kind of superiority of the practical sciences: these are not "only cognitive," meaning that they are also that. For Plato, the carpenter is assuredly a bearer of knowledge, that is, his science is *cognitive*. But, like carpentry, all the practical arts "use (their knowledge) to complete those material objects they cause to come into being from not having been before" (trans. Rowe). In this part of the *Statesman*, "practical" means "productive," but Plato has already seen difficulties with this thesis when, in the *Sophist* (219b–c), he distinguished productive arts from arts of acquisition. That means that Plato, unable to think the *practical* and thus to really distinguish it from the theoretical, is obliged to include politics among the cognitive sciences.[7] We are all

---

6. C. J. Rowe: "purely theoretical"; H. N. Fowler: "pure sciences."

7. At 259c–d a remarkable comparative word—we will see an example just as ambiguous from Aristotle in the next chapter. "Then do you want us to assert that the king is more closely related to the theoretical sort of knowledge than to the manual or generally practical sort?" (trans. Rowe), the Stranger asks. But the double sense of μᾶλλον permits us to understand, "The king has closer affinities with cognitive science rather than with manual arts and in general practical arts." Nevertheless, the two comparatives that follow (μᾶλλον, οἰκειότερον) allow the royal science (politics) to participate somewhat in the practical.

the same rather far from the Aristotelian distinction between action and production.

Concerning the first point, we see that Plato is satisfied if a philosopher counsels a prince if the prince has no political knowledge. The *Statesman*, again, takes account of this novel situation:

> Well then, won't we say that the person who is clever at giving advice to a king of a country, although he is himself a private individual, himself has the expert knowledge that the ruler himself ought to have possessed? (259a, trans. Rowe)

And the *Laws* is perhaps even more clear on this point:

> It looks as if your position is this: the best state will be the product of a dictatorship, thanks to the efforts of a first-rate legislator and a well-behaved dictator, and this will be the quickest and easiest way to bring about the transformation. (4.710d, trans. Saunders)

But the initial Platonic structure is in no way overturned. The true ruler or legislator is the one who possesses political knowledge. But it is still the philosopher who is master of this science. If, by misfortune, the de facto ruler does not have it, the best would be for him or her to associate with someone who does have it. Doubtless behind this proposition, but between the lines, is the idea that the tyrant may have special abilities that bring it about that he or she, in a particular situation, is in power, and not the philosopher: the one might be more determined, more tough than the other. But we are very far from the Aristotelian thesis that the excellence of the ruler and that of the philosopher are different and depend on different sorts of knowledge that coincide only *accidentally* in the same person.

This opposition between theoretical and practical reappears within the practical science that politics itself is. Every practical science must articulate the speculative and the practical, which presupposes that they were previously separated. That's a problem that does not arise at all for the theoretical sciences. But politics, in a way the paradigmatic practical science, pushes this separation farther than do the others. This is shown by a passage at the end of the *Nicomachean Ethics* that not only contrasts theoretical and practical sciences but also the practical sciences with one another:[8] "In the other sciences the same people are found offering to teach the arts and practicing them, e.g. doctors or painters" (10.10, 1180b32); in politics, however, we see that this is not the case. The text in which the quotation occurs merits attention. Aristotle sees a proof of the decoupling of theory and practice in the case of the art of politics in the fact that those who claim to teach it, the Sophists, would be entirely unable to exercise the function of a statesman, and that reciprocally in the case of statesmen, "they are found neither writing nor speaking about such matters, though it were a nobler occupation perhaps than composing speeches for the law-courts and the assembly" (1183a3). That's what makes rulers seem to be purely empirical,[9] something that Aristotle absolutely refuses to attribute to them, and the *Politics* as a whole is the best witness to this refusal. "Still, experience seems to contribute not a little" to the activity of governing (1181a9), and, contrary to what the Sophists claim, legislation is a difficult art, with this interesting remark: it's not enough to consider existing laws and "to choose those that people regard highly" (1181a16); the laws themselves do not teach us how to make them.

There is therefore, in regard to politics, a duality that distinguishes it from all other practical-productive sciences, and that brings it about that the practitioner and the theoretician are not one and the same person. To be sure, medicine, which Aristotle cites in his list of sciences, also knows this kind of difference. In fact, it must take account of the absolute singularity of the situations into which it is led to intervene, always assuming that the physician is master of a range of knowledge, in this case the branch of natural science, in the Aristotelian sense of the word, which deals with what would later be called anatomy and physiology. That's what leads Aristotle to say that "it behooves the natural scientist to obtain a clear view of the first principles of health and disease."[10] And, as in the case of politics where the person who has scientific knowledge of legislation would not make a good statesman, the theoretician, here the "biologist," would not necessarily make a good doctor to the extent

---

8. Without, as I said above, the word "practical" appearing in the text. Aristotle here makes the same blend of practical and productive sciences that he made in the passage in the *Eudemian Ethics* cited in a previous note. Medicine, in fact, cannot be considered as a practical science in the strict sense.

9. "Some think that their action is based on a certain empirical ability more than on thought" (1180a1).

10. *Sense and Sensibilia* 1, 436a17 (trans. J. I. Beare).

that he lacks that "quickness of mind"[11] that enables him to grasp the specific details in the individual case. But ultimately, if not all biologists are good doctors, at least Aristotle makes all good doctors biologists: "Those physicians who are cultivated and learned make some mention of natural science, and claim to derive their principles from it."[12] Politics, on the other hand, separates more clearly the two functions of the statesman (magistrate) and legislator. This separation reflects a distinction within excellence itself, since Aristotle carefully distinguishes the prudence of the legislator from that of the magistrate, as we will see when the time comes.

Obviously, the same person might be both a theoretician of legislation and find himself engaged in the political life of the city; Aristotle cites the cases of Lycurgus and of Solon. Furthermore, the legislator knows full well that the laws that he proposes to the city will ultimately be applied in totally singular circumstances, even if they would then receive, as we will see, the support of *decrees* (ψηφίσματα). That's what Aristotle says in the last chapter of the *Nicomachean Ethics*, where there is perhaps an allusion to the important collection of constitutions and laws of various cities and peoples that Aristotle, doubtless assisted by his associates and students in the Lyceum, put together to serve him as documentation: "Surely, then, collections of laws, and of constitutions also, may be serviceable to those who can study them and judge what is good or bad and what enactments suit what circumstances" (1181b6).

But in the distinction that Aristotle applied at the beginning of the last chapter of *Politics* 2, between theoreticians who have never taken part in political activities and those who have also been statesmen, the latter seem to be a kind of exception. The conjunction of theoretical and practical political abilities in the same individual appears to be a kind of "accident" in the Aristotelian sense of the word. In any case, this relative familiarity of the legislator with particular cases does not give him the ability to be an excellent ruler of the city. But, and this is absolutely crucial, the person who has excellence in the practical science of politics is not the good magistrate who applies good laws well, but the legislator who establishes or rectifies these laws. This is the person, as we will see, who is

---

11. That's how I translate the word ἀγχίνοια, studied in the last chapter of *Posterior Analytics* 1.
12. *On Life and Death* 5, 480b26 (trans. G. R. T. Ross).

the major factor in the goodness of the citizens, that is, this is the person who bests fulfills the criteria of the practical science called "politics." To put it another way, practical excellence is the excellence of the legislator. I will try to provide a more solid basis to what I am asserting here a bit arbitrarily when I examine the difference that Aristotle makes between "legislative prudence" and "political prudence."[13]

If we return to the three Kantian questions that one may apply to the Aristotelian enterprise, it would be the theoretical sciences that would be charged with replying to the question, "What can I know?" It is probably politics, and we will soon see why, which would be the most likely to answer the question, "What ought I do?" But it is indeed the task of ethics to answer the question, "What may I hope for?" Like all ancient philosophers, in fact, Aristotle answers this question by saying that the goal of human life is happiness and that the practical sciences, ethics and politics, do not achieve their calling unless they assist human beings, or rather, and we will see why, *men*, to attain happiness. But, in fact, this question goes beyond the boundaries of ethics and politics, because the idea of happiness crosses the great divide between theoretical and practical knowledge, since, notably at the end of the *Nicomachean Ethics*, Aristotle distinguishes, as we will have occasion to recall, theoretical happiness—it would be better to call it "contemplative"—from practical happiness. But for the moment we are more interested in practical happiness. Indeed, the practical sciences of ethics and politics each teach us something different about happiness.

To put it in very general terms, the Aristotelian analysis of the *polis* establishes that life in the city is a necessary condition for perfect (practical) happiness. That means, among many other things, that this perfect happiness is a happiness for citizens only, not for women, children, or slaves. Furthermore, it is not just any city that can assure the happiness of its citizens, but, as we will see in detail, a city with the right constitution. To designate this political form of happiness Aristotle does not use the normal term for "happiness" (εὐδαιμονία) but the expression "good life" (εὐ ζῆν). I will again refer to the difference between εὐδαιμονία and εὐ ζῆν, but only to admit that I have almost nothing to say about it. Aristotle's ethical analyses establish a very strong tie between happiness, there designated by the term εὐδαιμονία, and virtue (ἀρετή). This is a position common to nearly all ancient ethicists, even though there are obviously important nuances between the Socratic and Aristotelian positions, and

---

13. Below, pp. 199ff.

even more important differences between Aristotle and his Hellenistic successors. Assuredly, Aristotle does not claim, as Socrates did, that vice is purely ignorance, nor does he think, as did the Stoics, that virtue alone assures happiness and that the fact that one is in good health or diseased, free or imprisoned and tortured, rich or poor, is indifferent. For Aristotle, one cannot be happy without a minimum of what he calls, like his predecessors and contemporaries, "external goods," and we will see that there is even a good reason that virtue presupposes a certain amount of wealth.[14] Nevertheless it remains that the basic idea is the same for (nearly) all the philosophers of antiquity: only virtuous people are happy. That's why ethics has the most to say about happiness.

The virtue in question here is ethical virtue, and not intellectual (or dianoetic) virtue. Ethical virtue is an excellence that results from an apprenticeship. In the *Nicomachean Ethics*, Aristotle offers the following list of intellectual virtues: art, science, prudence, wisdom, and intelligence (6.3, 1139b16). It's not possible to examine in depth the intellectual virtues here, not even their relations with the ethical virtues. We can at least note the difficulty posed by the inclusion of prudence (φρόνησις) in the list of intellectual virtues while prudence is, as has been said, the perfected form of the ethically virtuous man and it is the prudent person who serves as the reference point to define ethical virtue.

So, let us make a brief detour through ethical virtue, without which there is no happiness, traversing, once again, well-beaten paths. Doubtless Aristotle had no difficulty persuading his contemporaries to accept that virtue is a *state*. The word ἕξις (*hexis*) is sometimes translated "disposition," but it is better to reserve this word to translate διάθεσις; state or habitual state is probably the least inaccurate translation. Etymologically deriving from the verb ἔχειν, to have, to possess, it indicates a stable and lasting possession of a quality. *Hexis* is translated into Latin by *habitus*. In the passage of the *Nicomachean Ethics* that establishes that virtue is a state, or more precisely, that "state" is the genus of the virtue that he is trying to define, by adding to the genus the specific difference,[15] Aristotle carries

---

14. "Certainly no one will dispute the propriety of that partition of goods which separates them into three classes, viz. external goods, goods of the body, and goods of the soul, or deny that the happy man must have all three" (*Pol.* 7.1, 1323a24, trans. Jowett).

15. Cf. 1106a14: "We must, however, not only describe it as a state, but also say what sort of state it is. Δεῖ δὲ μὴ μόνον οὕτως εἰπεῖν, ὅτι ἕξις, ἀλλὰ καὶ ποία τις." The expression ποία τις is a way of designating the "species."

out the demonstration by a method that he often uses, the exhaustive list. As there are in the soul, he says, just three sorts of realities—affects, capacities, and states—and virtue does not belong to either of the first two classes, it is a state. Fear, for example, is an affect (*pathos*): we feel it without having made any intervening choice and it moves us. The capacity (*dynamis*) of feeling fear is something that we have by nature and it does not have *value*. A state, on the other hand, is something that is not given to us automatically, we acquire it because we have decided for it and, for that reason, it has a value, that is, it can be considered as good or bad. Courage and cowardice are habitual states.

Thus, one cannot say that the ethical virtues are taught in the sense in which the intellectual virtues are taught, but they have these two characteristics, contradictory only in appearance, to be simultaneously acquired and natural. They are acquired because it is by the repetition of virtuous (or vicious) acts that the individual acquires a virtuous (or vicious) state. Aristotle does not feel any need to demonstrate this idea, since it was widely shared in his day. Otherwise said, virtue is fundamentally a matter of education: the person who has been habituated to courage or to generosity from childhood will become courageous or generous. Doubtless he will become both, because Aristotle agrees with the Platonic doctrine that the virtues imply each other. The same goes for the vices. Ethical virtues are also natural because, in a nature naturally good, good people are in agreement with that nature.

More precisely, when Aristotle defines virtue as "a state concerned with choice, lying in a mean relative to us, this being determined by a rule in the way a prudent person would determine it" (*EN* 2.6, 1106b36), one must understand that this state has become a situation almost unchangeable, all the more so because it provides us with satisfaction: the courageous person feels satisfaction in acting courageously. Aristotle goes so far as to make pleasure and displeasure the criterion of the virtuous act in that if someone does a good action or avoids a bad action, if, for example, he does not run away from the enemy or abstains from committing adultery, but it costs him or he does it for fear of shame or punishment, he is not virtuous, but *continent*: "the whole concern both of excellence and of political science is with pleasures and pains," says *Nicomachean Ethics* 2.2, 1105a10.[16] For Aristotle, as for the ancients in

---

16. Cf. *Nicomachean Ethics* 2.2, 1104b8: "Moral excellence is concerned with pleasures and pains." It would be very interesting to try to identify the pleasure that accompanies

general, pleasure is a crucial question for ethics, and it is hardly surprising that the *Nicomachean Ethics* discusses it at length, twice, perhaps because of bad harmonizing by an editor. We will see in the next section that pleasure is also a political question. But we will not deal with the question, although very important, of the type of pleasure that the vicious find in the exercise of their vice, for no one truly doubts that the profligate loves his profligacy and the greedy person gets satisfaction by amassing treasures.

Virtue is thus a state, a stable and pleasant state, that the virtuous person has no reason to abandon. One might even say that he does not find any motive force that pushes him to abandon it, and for that reason the virtuous person is *naturally* the producer of virtuous acts, while people today tend to think that virtuous acts are what make the one who does them virtuous. That's why the prudent person, the paragon of virtue, is the norm for virtuous actions. In given circumstances, therefore, an act will be virtuous because the prudent person does it (or would do it). This will take an extreme form among the Stoics, for whom everything that the Sage does, whether he pillages, rapes, or kills, is good because, definitively anchored in virtue, he cannot do anything but good.

Two problems thus appear to us that we cannot avoid because they will be politically crucial. The first, perhaps the principal difficulty of ancient ethical theories, consists of explaining why virtue, which makes those who possess it happy, is so rare and vice so common. Such modes of conduct take a turn both incomprehensible and scandalous in the case of *intemperance* (ἀκρασία) in which an individual chooses the bad, when he knows where the good is, and knows that it is in his interest to choose the good. Ancient moralists, and following them modern interpreters, especially those writing in English, have put considerable effort into elucidating the way in which philosophers who were not provided with the convenience of supposing human nature vicious because of original sin have attempted to resolve this problem. We notice immediately that this question has a political version. A virtuous city, and thus happy, ought, in fact, to have a remarkable stability if, at least, we leave to the

---

the virtuous act. People today easily conceive that it is, in some circumstances, "the pleasure of being good," and, at the same time, we easily conceive it as narcissistic. We also know, as Christians, the morbid pleasure of suffering while doing virtuous acts. But the ancient Greeks were surely talking of something else.

side adventitious problems coming from the external world. But neither virtue nor stability reigns in the world of cities . . .

The second problem is that of the audience for the ethical treatises. Because ultimately virtuous people have no need of dissertations about virtue, and it would need a good deal of naïveté to think that such dissertations could tear the vicious away from their vice. One of the great theses of Aristotelian psychology, in fact, is that contrary to what the Socratic tradition claimed, knowledge moves nothing. Knowing what is good and bad never pushes anyone toward the first and away from the second, nor the opposite. I will not pursue or avoid anything unless a *desire* impels me. Possibly protreptic or hortatory works could create a desire by appealing to *sentiments* like indignation or shame, but in no case could a treatise defining "virtue" turn a vicious person away from vice. So, ethical treatises are addressed neither to the virtuous nor to the vicious.

Aristotle's answer to the first question is, schematically speaking, that there is a difference between the natural and the spontaneous, and that which is truly natural to us ought to be revealed to us, this revelation being one of the tasks assigned to philosophy. Aristotle shared this approach with the other ancient moralists, even if their explanations of this initial blindness were not the same: ignorance for some, presence of an ineradicable irrational component in human beings for the others. We see it in this remarkable passage from the *Nicomachean Ethics*:

> Now if arguments were in themselves enough to make men good, they would justly, as Theognis says, have won very great rewards, and such rewards should have been provided; but as things are, while they seem to have power to encourage and stimulate the generous-minded among the young, and to make a character that is gently born, and a true lover of what is noble, ready to be possessed by excellence, they are not able to encourage the many to nobility and goodness. For these do not by nature obey the sense of shame, but only fear, and do not abstain from bad acts because of their baseness but through fear of punishment; living by passion they pursue their own pleasures and the means to them, and avoid the opposite pains, and have not even a conception of what is noble and truly pleasant, since they have never tasted it. . . . It is hard, if not impossible, to remove by argument the bad traits that have long since been incorporated in the character. (10.9, 1179b4)

The moralist, and especially as we will soon see, the legislator, find themselves up against people, and notably men, whom they must lead to virtue for the sake of their own happiness, but who are attracted by vice, its works and ways, and that in a manner more or less irresistible, if they do not find, outside themselves, the power to resist it.

In the same passage in the *Nicomachean Ethics*, Aristotle reminds us of his idea of the acquisition of virtue by *habituation* (ἔθος), recalling the tripartition he had presented in book 1, chapter 10: some think that virtue is given by nature, that is, by divine favor, others that it is acquired through teaching, and still others by habituation (1179b20). "By nature" here means "in a spontaneous and effortless manner," alluding to certain individuals who, without incentives or constraints, find their satisfaction in virtuous behavior. Such people exist, but we understand why, given their small number, Aristotle attributes their condition to divine favor. . . . We must also note that in this chapter as elsewhere Aristotle in no way asserts the absolute impotence of arguments to have ethical effects. Ethical arguments, in fact, can "encourage and stimulate the generous-minded among the young, and make a character that is gently born, and a true lover of what is noble, ready to be possessed by excellence" (1179b7). As for teaching, "argument and teaching are not powerful with all people, but the soul of the student must first have been cultivated by means of habits for noble joy and noble hatred, like earth that is to nourish the seed" (1179b23).

This agricultural metaphor of the soul that must be prepared to receive the ethical seed also reveals to us that the main target, if not the only target, of this education for virtue is young people. We cite again this remarkable chapter:

> But it is difficult to get from youth up a right training for excellence if one has not been brought up under right laws; for to live temperately and hardily is not pleasant, to most people, especially when they are young. (1179b31)[17]

Childhood and youth thus appear to be the time of all dangers, but also the time in which educational intervention is still possible. Ingrained vice is, in fact, just as impossible to eradicate as entrenched virtue.

---

17. The part of the phrase at 1179b31, ἐκ νέου δ' ἀγωγῆς ὀρθῆς τυχεῖν πρὸς ἀρετὴν χαλεπὸν μὴ ὑπὸ τοιούτοις τραφέντα νόμοις, should literally mean this: "to receive from one's youth a correct education turned toward virtue is difficult for those who have not been nourished under laws of this kind," that is, that turn one toward virtue. Admirable flexibility of Greek syntax in general and Aristotelian syntax in particular . . .

One of the consequences, ultimately fairly important, of this way of thinking, and that readers of Aristotle have not missed, is his negative attitude toward childhood. Children are very often associated with animals[18] or madmen,[19] up to this statement, to us astonishing, but that many in the West have adopted as their own until the nineteenth century:

> There are many consequences of life that make people throw away life, such as disease, excessive pain, storms, so that it is clear that, if one were given a choice, not to be born at all would, as far at least as these reasons go, have been desirable. Further, the life we lead as children is not desirable, for no one in his senses would agree to return again to that. (*EE* 1.5, 1215b19ff.)

So, Aristotle is not taken in by the fable of infantile innocence and authenticity; he does not dream of eternal youth. But more important for us is that Aristotle sees in the child an irrational being (thus the parallel with animals) who, *for this very reason*, is not only amoral, but full of bad tendencies that are only going to get worse if one does not guard against that.[20] This attitude is important because it allows us to take another step toward understanding intemperance. If, in fact, people generally choose vice despite that fact that virtue would give them happiness, it's due to the bad habits acquired in childhood. As we know that repeated actions solidify into habits, and thus into virtues or vices, we understand that most people, not having been corrected in childhood, display vicious *habits*, even though these habits are contrary to their nature as rational beings. But since a child is an irrational being, he cannot really be intemperate. Aristotle thus recovers a part of the Socratic teaching (that the child is vicious because of ignorance) and Platonic (that it is the presence of an irrational part of the soul, from childhood, that makes vicious conduct possible).

---

18. The *Rhetoric* accordingly says that one does not feel honor and shame before children or animals (1.11, 1371a14, 2.6, 1384b24), and the *Ethics* repeatedly parallels children and animals.

19. Cf. *Eudemian Ethics* 1.3, 1214b29; *Politics* 7.1, 1323a32.

20. Cf. *Nicomachean Ethics* 3.15, 1119a34, a particularly interesting passage in that it develops two theses: first, the more or less spontaneous state of children is ἀκολαστία, in English translated as "naughtiness" when applied to children, but, second, the appellation is derived from the adult state, which we translate as *intemperance* or *self-indulgence*. This illustrates the fact that Aristotle defines things by their developed state.

As for the way that Aristotle means to give young people good habits that will become solidified into virtues, this cannot happen, as I have said, except "from outside them," as one of the passages cited above indicates: it is necessary to make them obey good laws. That is one of the decisive points for us as we examine the relationships between ethics and politics. After having vigorously recalled the impotence of ethical discourses for leading people to virtue, even that these discourses as we have seen have the goal not of "knowing what virtue is," but "to become good," Aristotle indicates the means, or at least the main way, of realizing the practical calling of ethics. But it is not *all* laws that can have a good ethical effect, only "just laws." Otherwise said, it is necessary to have a way to know which laws are just; when one has understood that such laws do not exist regularly and nonrandomly except in a correct constitution, one sees that political philosophy as a whole is meant to rush into the chasm opened by the ethical discourse that asks itself about its own efficiency. Politics thus becomes the strong arm of ethics.

But at the same time, we are able to resolve the second problem that we encountered in our analysis of Aristotle's ethical positions, that of the audience for the ethical treatises. If they are useless for the virtuous and have no effect on the vicious, and if, on the other hand, ethics has no effect unless one has *habituated* young people to virtue by continual obedience to good laws, then Richard Bodéüs is right:[21] the audience for the ethical treatises is the person who is in charge of the morality of others, to whom the scientific knowledge of virtue, vice, true friendship, and pleasure, is very useful. Certainly, it's a concern of the magistrate who is charged with applying these laws, but it is above all a concern of the legislator who makes or amends those laws. Thus, we are brought back to the question of the relationships between ethics and politics.

In an often-cited passage at the end of the first chapter of the *Nicomachean Ethics*, Aristotle explains that ethical instruction (which he calls in this passage, it is important to note, *politics*[22]) cannot concern young people because, contrary to mathematics for example, the study of ethics is not profitable except to those who already have some experience. "It

---

21. In his fundamental work, Richard Bodéüs, *Le Philosophe et la cité. Recherches sur les rapports entre morale et politique dans la pensée d'Aristote* (Paris: Les Belles Lettres, 1982), English translation by Jan Edward Garrett, *The Political Dimensions of Aristotle's "Ethics"* (Albany: State University of New York Press, 1993).

22. Cf. 1095a2: τῆς πολιτικῆς οὐκ ἔστιν οἰκεῖος ἀκροατὴς ὁ νέος, "A young man is not an appropriate auditor for political lectures."

makes no difference whether one is young in years or youthful in character" (1095a6); this instruction is useless both for the brainless as well as for the intemperate. But for "those who desire and act in accordance with a rational principle, knowledge about such matters will be of great benefit" (τοῖς δὲ κατὰ λόγον τὰς ὀρέξεις ποιουμένοις καὶ πράττουσι) (1.1, 1095a10, already cited). In my opinion, this expression can doubtless be applied to people who have decided to become virtuous and thus are interested in having some acquaintance with virtue. We have seen that they are few in number, even if they do exist. For reasons given above, this situation cannot be very frequent. There are, in fact, two kinds of people who submit their behavior to reason: those who are constrained by good laws and legislators, who, imposing this submission on others, must first apply it to themselves. What sort of legislator would he be, in fact, if he has not grasped the central role of virtue in the happiness of the city? Certainly, there have been vicious legislators, but the Aristotelian legislator ought to be a creator of virtue. And, we repeat, such a legislator needs knowledge especially of ethics.

Just like Plato, Aristotle makes the education of people a matter of politics, certainly in a more flexible way than Plato, since for him families remain in charge of the education of their children. But all the same, it is the city that has the last word in submitting everyone to the law. In the field of practical excellence, the game is played with three teammates. The philosopher, first: as he is excellent in theory but not in practice, he ought not rule because he is not the person who can do it best. But, in politics, neither can he do what he knows how to do best, that is, to know for the sake of knowing, because politics is a practical science that aims not only at knowledge. Thus, we must clarify his role in politics, if he has one. As for the magistrate, his excellence consists in making the city function well by applying the laws well. A problem arises here, that we do not yet have the means to resolve, that of the form that this excellence can take when the laws are bad. There is at last the legislator. The figure of the legislator is one of the most significant in the collective imagination of the Greeks, especially when it is a matter of heroes, often elevated subsequently to the rank of semi-divine beings, who found a city by giving it its first laws, that is, its first *constitution*, since a constitution is the system of laws of a city. The personality of the Aristotelian legislator is more modest, because the foundation of new cities was not very frequent in his day, at least (and we will come back to this) in the Greek cultural region. It's a matter of one or more men (if Aristotle does not say that women are excluded from this function by reason of their ethical inferiority, it is doubtless because that seems to him obvious), who ought to bring it about that the legislative system of their city will make its citizens happy. As the fundamental requirement for happiness is ethical virtue, that means that the legislator has, above all, an ethical function.

The Missed Birth of Ethics

Let us continue accepting, for the moment, the common idea that the two principle practical sciences are, according to Aristotle, politics and ethics, to which one sometimes adds economics, in taking this word in its etymological sense, which makes of it the science concerned with the administration of the family or the home, "domestic administration," if one prefers to speak Latin rather than Greek. Aristotle explains, with one of his usual etymological ploys, that one may go, by way of a small modification, from *ethos* (ἔθος), "habit," to *ēthos* (ἦθος), "character," from which is derived *ēthikos* (ἠθικός) (*EN* 2.1, 1103a17),[23] the association between *ethos* and *ēthos* having already been made by Plato (*Laws* 7, 792c). Ethical virtue is thus a virtue of character and at the same time a *habit*, which in a way repeats what was said about virtue as a *state*.

Is Aristotle then, as in many other domains, the founder of a new science, ethics, and of a new relation between kinds of knowledge, which simultaneously opposes and connects ethics and politics, and which was destined to continue until our time? In fact, the word "ethics" does not appear in Plato, although it is frequent in Aristotle. It is certain that the Stagirite is the first to have installed a separation both terminological and disciplinary between ethical questions and political questions.[24] But this separation has made room for a good many anachronisms. Thus, we must

---

23. The *Eudemian Ethics* makes the augmentation of the vowel correspond to "the augmentation of the habit" (ἀπὸ ἔθους ἔχει τὴν ἐπίδοσιν, 2.2, 1220b1). See the precious article by Paul Demont, "Note sur les premiers emplois de èthikos (ἠθικός) chez Aristote. Le sentiment d'amitié et les transactions de gré à gré," *Ktema. Civilisations de l'Orient, de la Grèce et de Rome* 5 (1998): 81–90.
24. Cf. Pierre Aubenque, "Politique et éthique chez Aristote," *Ktèma. Civilisations de l'Orient, de la Grèce et de Rome* 5 (1980): 211–221; Philippe Betbeder, "Éthique et politique selon Aristote," *Revue des Sciences Philosophiques et Théologiques* 54 (1970): 453–488.

be very careful if we ask to what extent Aristotle adopts positions that we would call "totalitarian" because they subordinate rights and duties of individuals to the purposes of the State. At the same time, we will see that the moralization of politics appears in very different ways in Aristotle and in modern theorists.

Concerning the ethical doctrine of Aristotle and the relations he makes between ethics and politics, questions on which the bibliography is immense, we will limit ourselves, besides the considerations developed above about happiness and virtue, to the following. Contrary to what the interpreters cited above in a note have claimed, it is necessary to say that the epoch of ethics did not arrive in the person of Aristotle, and that it would not arrive until the Hellenistic schools, Epicurean and Stoic, when the very word "politics" in its full sense will have lost, if not all meaning, in any case any real referent. In Aristotle, the predominance of politics in the practical domain, which he conveys by saying that politics is "architectonic," that is, that it directs the other practical science as the architect directs the workers,[25] is such that he asserts, for example in the first chapter of the *Nicomachean Ethics*, that his studies in ethics belong to politics.[26]

Ethics is a strange discipline, since it is posited by Aristotle with a certain degree of autonomy—that is shown by Aristotle's creation of a new appellation: *ēthikē* implies *technē*, "the ethical science, or discipline," for in Aristotle words reflect things, and at the same time this autonomy is denied, or at least strongly reduced, by the inclusion of ethics in politics. Can't we resolve this dilemma by declaring, as most interpreters until now have done, that ethical science is subordinated to political science, which Aristotle wanted to express by saying that politics is architectonic in the practical order? And, in fact, politics is in a dominant position in relation to ethics. That can be shown in two ways.

In the first place, there is this remarkable fact that any ethical position taken by an individual is never done outside politics. To be sure, there are particular situations that relate directly, or principally, to ethics, for example when an individual must choose a way of conducting his daily life: Should he respond to an insult? Should he beat his slave? But to the small degree that this person means to analyze his or her choices, it cannot be done without finding some political foundations and perspectives. Every

---

25. Cf. *Nicomachean Ethics* 1.1., 1094b4, 7.12, 1152b2.

26. Cf., for example, *Nicomachean Ethics* 1.13, 1102a12, "This examination (of virtue) belongs to politics"; cf. *Rhetoric* 1.2, 1356a26, which includes the study of character, as well as of the virtues, in politics; see also 4, 1359b10.

ethical question is ultimately political. I cited above the famous definition of virtue in the *Nicomachean Ethics* as the "happy medium," without, of course, developing this crucial point of Aristotelian ethics. Courage is the *mean* (τὸ μέσον) between cowardice and foolhardiness, which are two vices. This means that this *happy medium*, far from being a compromise, in order to be an excellence, has to be a kind of perfection, what Aristotle formulates by saying that "the happy medium is in a way an extreme" (τὸ μέσον εἶναί πως ἄκρον, *EN* 2.6, 1107a23).[27] But this mean, which Aristotle describes as a mean "relative to us" (πρὸς ἡμᾶς, 2.6, 1107a1) and not "in the thing itself" (κατ' αὐτὸ τὸ πρᾶγμα, 5, 1106a29) as six is the mean between ten and two, depends very much on the situation in which the subject is involved. Thus, the virtuous person shows his virtue in feeling the passion "at the right times, with reference to the right objects, toward the right people, with the right aim, and in the right way" (2.5, 1106b21).

We will see, often and from several directions, the omnipresence of the idea of relativity in Aristotelian politics. If we consider only a part of the formula just cited, "toward the right people," we grasp to what point, for Aristotle, the virtuous act, like every action and emotion of a subject, depends on the relationships that he or she entertains with his or her equals and unequals. The very idea that an ethical attitude must be the same in all circumstances and in regard to every human being has no place here: courage, loyalty, justice, but also friendship, anger, or pity, depend on our social relationships. They will not be the same if they involve another citizen, a woman, a child, a foreigner, a slave, but also a wise person or a vicious person. We will also have occasion to grasp how much the system of values that brings together the citizens of a city at a given moment depends on the colors of the constitution of this city. Because honesty, courage, and all the other virtues do not take the same form in an aristocratic regime as they do in an egalitarian city. Thus, it appears to us that ethics is either political or it isn't.

Thus—although we could offer many other examples—for the question of pleasure, which as we have seen is inevitable for someone who deals with ethics: "The study of pleasure and pain belongs to the province of the political philosopher" (*EN* 7.11, 1152b1). The pleasure that accompanies a virtuous act, for example a courageous act, is not the sensual pleasure we get from food or sex. The satisfaction that the courageous person senses of having acted as he ought, in appropriate

---

27. Cf. Michel Crubellier and Pierre Pellegrin, *Aristote. Le philosophe et les savoirs* (Paris: Seuil, 2017), 165ff.

conditions, in appropriate position, is, one may say, an "ethical pleasure," that is, a political one.[28] We will see repeatedly that Aristotelian politics is fundamentally eudaemonist and only life in a city can allow a happy life, or that, to put it another way, only *citizens* can pretend to complete happiness, which is accompanied by pleasure. For, as he says in the text that follows the one just cited from the *Nicomachean Ethics*, "most people say that happiness involves pleasure" (1152b6). That which is true for the citizen is also true for the city. That's why Aristotle can speak, in a closely similar sense, of the "virtuous city" (*Pol.* 7.4, 1326a9) and of the "happy city" (*Pol.* 7.1, 1323b30; 2, 1324a11). One rediscovers in this subsuming of ethics under politics one of the cardinal theoretical positions of Aristotle. It is the more developed figure or stage of a reality that gives sense, and thus explains, the less developed forms or stages of that reality: the adult explains the child. This agrees with Aristotelian teleology, which is opposed to the "mechanistic" explanations of the Presocratics for whom it is the generation of a reality that enable us to understand it. Thus, it is the excellence of a man who is free, Greek, adult, and virtuous that *defines* the virtue, while those of the woman, child, or slave are nothing but partial or degraded imitations. But this excellence of the free man is *political* even when it concerns individual actions. A virtue exercised by a man is not the same as the homonymous virtue exercised by a woman, a virtue is not the same when it concerns a man or a woman, a virtue must, furthermore, be in conformity with the laws, and thus with the constitution of the city in which it is exercised. Feminine, infantile, and servile virtues, on the other hand, are prepolitical virtues. Women, children, and slaves are, as we will see below, nonpolitical parts of the city.

The second way to show the domination of the political over the ethical was mentioned above, and we need to explain it a bit. The acqui-

---

28. I have always thought, in contrast to many, that the Epicurean conception of pleasure as the absence or suspension of pain is not so distant from the Aristotelian conception. In positing pleasure as a corollary of the activity, but also without excluding sensual pleasures, Aristotle provides a rich picture of pleasure that could have put Freud on the road to his idea of "sublimation," if he had read the relevant texts of Aristotle. Cf. *Nicomachean Ethics* 10.5, 1175a19: "Whether we choose life for the sake of pleasure or pleasure for the sake of life is a question we may dismiss for the present. For they seem to be bound up together and not to admit of separation, since without activity pleasure does not arise, and every activity is completed by pleasure." Cf. 10.5, 1175b32: "Pleasures are so close and so indistinguishable from activities that it admits of dispute whether the activity is not the same as the pleasure."

sition of virtue, obviously the central problem of ethics, is political. We have seen that virtue, exactly like vice, is a habitual state (*hexis*), that is, a state that, without being innate, becomes nevertheless consubstantial with the subject to whom it belongs: when it has the sense of *habitus* one would better say that such a habit is a "second nature." Aristotle clings to the idea that, as we have seen, would not have seemed strange in his day, according to which such a state is *acquired* by the repetition of actions that correspond to it: good actions, for example courageous actions, to acquire a habitual courageous state, bad actions that produce a vicious state. This habitual state will become a true virtue, in this case courage, when the performance of courageous acts become natural and agreeable to the subject. Thus, it is by obeying good laws, in our example those that prescribe courageous behavior, that one acquires virtue, at least *ethical* virtue. That legislation has as its goal that to make the citizens virtuous by making them acquire good habits is not presented by Aristotle as his own discovery, but as a common position. The *Nicomachean Ethics* declares that what actually happens in cities "witnesses" to the truth of this thesis (cf. 2.1, 1103b2). So, everything is in the hands of those who enforce the laws, and even more radically, of those who conceive, promulgate, and modify the laws. Obviously, this process of inculcating virtue has all the more chance of success if it is addressed to young people, and Aristotle does not seem to have been opposed to the idea that to make young people obey the laws, one use toward them some constraint.[29]

Besides the spontaneous tendency of people, and especially the young, to an excess of passion and uncontrolled pleasure, we must add a properly political cause of the massive presence of vice in the cities. We have seen, and we will see again several times, that the functioning of the city spreads virtue, and thus happiness, in the body of citizens, mainly by making citizens virtuous by continued obedience to good laws. But what about when the laws are bad, when, for example, they bless the despoiling of one sector of the population by another, encourage informers, establish discrimination on the basis of wealth? Aristotle explains the existence of bad laws by the fact that they correspond to unjust deviant constitutions: "Right forms of government will of necessity have just laws, and perverted forms of government will have unjust laws" (*Pol.* 3.11, 1282b11). Thus, it is doubtless possible to suppose that, for Aristotle, in the case of cities with deviant constitutions, the very functioning of the institutions causes

---

29. *Nicomachean Ethics* 10.10, 1179b31 and 1180a4, analyzed below.

the ethical state of the citizens to deteriorate. This is particularly visible in the worst sort of deviation, tyranny, which makes the subjects of the tyrant become mean, fearful, and stupid. But on the one hand this direction is not much explored by Aristotle, and, on the other hand, such an explanation only displaces the problem that it is meant to resolve. Why, in fact, are there so many vicious regimes? But that sort of analysis has the merit of placing the question of the acquisition and conservation of virtue right where it must be placed, that is, at the political level.

Thus, we understand that it would be very useful to the magistrate and legislator to have read the ethical treatises, even though that utility is less massive than one might think at the outset, as the appendix to the present chapter will demonstrate. I also put in evidence the differences in style of exposition between the ethical texts, which mainly *define* ideas like virtue, happiness, or friendship, and the political texts, which are largely prescriptive. We rediscover there the interpretation, in my opinion correct, of Richard Bodéüs, who was the first, to the best of my knowledge, to show that the major audience of the Aristotle's ethical treatises (but also the political treatises, as is less difficult to understand) is the legislator. How, in fact, will he make laws that are supposed to direct citizens toward virtue if he does not know what virtue in general is, and also, and perhaps above all, if he lacks the teaching of the *Ethics* about particular virtues, notably in what respect they are differentiated from neighboring notions. Thus, for example, how would one legally incite citizens to courage if the legislator confuses courage and foolhardiness? Isn't that one of the errors of the legislators who established the warrior constitutions like that of Sparta, which as we will see several times Aristotle thinks are bad? Politics will deal with ethics, then, as one expects an architectonic science will deal with a subordinate science.

Nevertheless, this image is false. Let's return to a point already considered in order to complete, qualify, and correct what has been said. We must note that politics is not architectonic for ethics in the same way as for other sciences, and that in any case Aristotle never says that politics is architectonic *for ethics*.[30] When Aristotle explains, in the *Nicomachean Ethics*, that strategy, economics, and rhetoric are subordinate to politics

---

30. He sometimes seems close to saying that, as at *Nicomachean Ethics* 6.8, 1141b22, where he remarks that for prudence (the supreme ethical virtue) there is an architectonic sort that can only be politics. But this passage conforms even more to what I intend to say in this chapter about the relationships between ethics and politics in that it affirms that "politics and prudence are the same state (ἕξις) but their essence is not the same" (1141b23, trans. following P. Pellegrin).

(1.1, 1094b3), we understand, in general if not in detail, what he means: the science (or art) of strategy, with its own body of rules and procedures, also has precise goals, all submitted to a principal goal, that of defeating the enemy in armed conflict. Thus, a particular maneuver may have as its intermediate goal that of weakening the enemy in dividing his forces, another for fooling him to make him engage his forces unwisely, but all of that for the sake of victory. To say that strategy is subordinate to politics, or that politics is architectonic in relation to strategy, is to say that "the goal of politics includes the goals of the other sciences" (1094b6), including strategy. In fact, it is for ultimately political goals that one seeks to win wars, and as I have just recalled, Aristotle is very critical of cities like Sparta, for which war and victory are supreme goals, because "war ought to be chosen for the sake of peace" (*Pol.* 7.14, 1333a35). This status of subordinate science is especially important in the case of economics, the science that is concerned with the management of the "house," that is, of the enlarged family, because it is necessary, precisely, to keep economics in its subordinate place so that the city not become a large family or an association dedicated to profit-making.

It is not the same for ethics. Ethics and politics, in fact, ultimately have the same object, virtue and human happiness, and, we will come back to this point, if politics sometimes has as its goal the happiness *of the city*, this at least accompanies and very often is identified with the happiness of the citizens. The same goes for the relationship between virtue and happiness, as we have seen, since the virtuous city is happy. That is at any rate what the *Nicomachean Ethics* recognizes after having declared that politics is architectonic. "Even if the good[31] is the same for a single person and for the city, that of the city seems at all events something greater and more complete both to attain and to preserve" (1094b7). To say that ethical and political discourse have the same object is a way of recognizing that they belong to the same science, and we have offered above reasons for which this science should be called "politics" rather than "ethics." To the extent that in the famous passage in which Aristotle writes that "politics uses the rest of the practical sciences, and it legislates as to what we are to do and what we are to abstain from" (1094b4), whether the term "practical" was added later or not,[32] it is ultimately not surprising that Aristotle does

---

31. Or "end"; it comes to the same thing for our purposes, and it is thus translated by Ross/Urmson.

32. Bywater suppresses it, as does Burnet, who sees it as a gloss by Aspasius.

not cite ethics as one of these "practical sciences." Although he does not fail to come back to this thesis, nevertheless not explicitly affirmed by Aristotle, that ethics is a practical discipline, it's not certain that in strict Aristotelian terms it would be a practical *science*. Finally, and contrary to what people like Pierre Aubenque or Philippe Betbeder imagine, for Aristotle ethics is not an autonomous science, because it is not a science at all. It is, at best, a point of view that a political scientist can adopt.[33]

Nevertheless, we must notice that even reduced to the status of "point of view," even condemned to impotence if it is deprived of the aid of politics and even partly useless to the legislator as the appendix below will show, ethics keeps a certain coherence and autonomy. This can be shown by three remarks. The first is that politics, as dominant as it is, keeps an *instrumental* role in relation to ethics and in relation to its ends. In a passage that we will have occasion to analyze more completely, Aristotle aims a somewhat sarcastic criticism at the Platonic city that can be called "happy" while its citizens are unhappy (*Pol.* 2.5, 1264b15ff.). A city that functions well with good laws cannot be for Aristotle an end in itself since the end of life in a city is the "happy life." All passages in Aristotle that say that "even if the good is the same for a single person and for the city, that of the city seems at all events something greater and more complete both to attain and to preserve, for though it is worthwhile to attain the end merely for one person, it is finer and more godlike to attain it for a nation or for cities" (*EN* 1.1, 1094b7, already quoted), must not in any case provide a basis for a "totalitarian" reading of Aristotle's position, which would say that individual ends ought to be sacrificed for the collective, the harmonious functioning of society. The end of the "virtuous city" is the happiness *of the citizens*, and it cannot be called "happy" unless the citizens are happy.

---

33. There is a passage in the *Eudemian Ethics* that simultaneously confirms and seems to contradict what I have just said: "The absolute good would be this—the end of the goods practicable for man. And this is the good that comes under the supreme of all the practical sciences, which is politics and economics and prudence, for these states of character differ from the others in the fact that they are supreme (whether they differ at all from one another must be discussed later on)" (1.8, 1218b11). That politics and ethics (here designated by the main ethical virtue, prudence) refer to the same state is what I have just now been trying to establish. But here economics also seems to be politics considered from a certain point of view and thus cannot be truly an autonomous science. Ethics studies the happiness of the individual, politics the happy life of the city, and economics that of the family. Such differences between the *Ethics* are not rare.

To the extent that there is a problem, abundantly treated by the commentators, of the articulation of the two happinesses recognized by Aristotle, contemplative happiness and practical happiness, it seems to me that we have found in the preceding remarks the way to escape from the notion, assuredly not Aristotle's, according to which these two approaches to happiness are mutually incompatible, which would present everyone with a choice. Ultimately it is because happiness is *first of all* an individual matter that contemplation and action can both be called happinesses, if not equally. It is up to each person to choose his path, and nothing prevents him from changing it according to the circumstances. If, on the other hand, in the practical domain the happiness of the city were above that of individuals, then the person who would choose contemplative happiness would have to justify his choice, and doubtless would have to make it compatible with the ends of the city. The city would also have the right to constrain him, as in the case of the philosopher of the *Republic* who is forced to go back down into the cave.

All of this reinforces the thesis that I have developed above, that politics is not really architectonic for ethics. We have seen that that is true first because ethics is not a science, or even an art like strategy or medicine. We now can grasp that, if it is true that in the case of an architectonic science, "the end of this science must include those of the others [i.e., those for which it is architectonic]" (*EN* 1.1, 1094b6), ethics is not in a relationship of this kind with politics.

The second remark is drawn from an Aristotelian thesis that will also be examined in greater depth later, that moral values, notably justice, depend on the constitution in place in each city. It is obvious that an aristocratic regime and an egalitarian regime would not promote the same virtues, nor would consider the same sort of man as a model for the other citizens. Nevertheless, it is still the case that there exist what one may call the "fundamentals" of ethics, and the virtuous individual is not mechanically dependent on the regime in which he lives. There are psychological states that are virtuous everywhere and others that are vicious everywhere. In fact,

> the excellence of the citizen must be relative to the constitution of which he is a member. If, then, there are many forms of government, it is evident that there is not one single excellence of the good citizen that is perfect excellence. But the good man, we say, is in accord with one virtue, namely, the complete virtue. (*Pol.* 3.4, 1276b30)

Perhaps Aristotle does express here the common opinion that he will feel the need of making clear, but like all the Greeks of his time, he has before his mind the example of Socrates pursuing civic virtue to the point where he opposed the legalities of his city. The question arises of knowing whether that, assuredly applied to perverted regimes like democracy and oligarchy, is also valid for correct regimes like aristocracy and the "polity."[34]

Finally, a last remark, there is in Aristotle a true philosophy of the subject that is closer than one generally thinks to modern moral philosophy. Catherine Dalimier has found it in the *Eudemian Ethics*, and I will summarize here the conclusions in the introduction of her translation of that treatise.[35] If we realize that there is no really good reason to doubt the authenticity of the *Eudemian Ethics*, we are forced to notice, as specialists on Aristotelian ethics have done, that it presents some differences from the *Nicomachean Ethics*. I'm not going to go through those differences here, I'm satisfied to offer my opinion, the same as that of C. Dalimier: in the *Eudemian Ethics* we have "an ethics that is the same—differently." It is better to quote Dalimier:

> While the *Nicomachean Ethics* calls attention in an appendix to the necessity of giving the support of the law to ethics and presents its research as the beginning of a more general investigation that can be called "politics," the *Eudemian Ethics* is explicitly addressed to the *private individual* who wants to achieve happiness (including the methodological and programmatic passages like 1.2) and ends, not on the necessity of establishing a constitution that will make the citizens happy, but on *kalokagathia*, presented as "perfect" individual excellence. (24, trans. A. Preus)

This "personalist" approach that characterizes the *Eudemian Ethics* can be found via three themes. First, in this work the most thorough analysis of individual responsibility is presented. To this point, we should reread *Eudemian Ethics* 2.6, which characterizes the virtuous or vicious

---

34. In my translation of the *Politics* I have translated the word *politeia*, when it designates not just a constitution in general, but the correct constitutional form that puts a large number of virtuous people in power, with the phrase "constitutional government." Here I am satisfied to use the Anglicized word, "polity."

35. Catherine Dalimier, trans., *Aristote, Éthique à Eudème* (Paris: GF-Flammarion, 2013).

act primarily by the fact that the person who does it is responsible, while the person whose actions are involuntary is not responsible. There is no contradiction there with the teaching of the *Nicomachean Ethics*, but a difference in emphasis that makes the *Eudemian Ethics* the closest approach in ancient moral speculation to the modern idea of the "moral subject."

Then there is *kalokagathia*. It is possible, even probable, that Dalimier is right in thinking that Aristotle understands the *kalokagathos*, a very important idea in Greek ideology of the classical era,[36] not as "beautiful and good," as the portmanteau *kalokagathos* means literally, but "good for the sake of the beautiful."[37] But what I want to emphasize is that *kalokagathia*, offered at the end of the *Eudemian Ethics* as "perfect excellence," is defined in *practical* terms (8.3, 1249b16ff.). But it's absolutely a personal, not political, excellence, since Aristotle characterizes it as a life consecrated to the "contemplation of god" (ἡ τοῦ θεοῦ θεωρία, 1249b17), which is the third theme that I want to discuss. Obviously, we should not give in to the temptation to think that we have here an allusion to contemplative activity like that which is in question at the end of the *Nicomachean Ethics*. In the *Eudemian Ethics*, that which marks the limits of the human is called god or the divine. This "divinization" to which the *Eudemian Ethics* appeals is not only completely *practical*, but it is also promised to the greatest number:

> For if the good life consists in what is due to fortune or nature, it would be something that many cannot hope for, since its acquisition is not in their power, nor attainable by their care or activity; but if it depends on the individual and his personal acts being of a certain character, then the supreme good would be both more general and more divine, more general because more would be able to possess it, more divine because happiness would then be the prize offered to those who make themselves and their acts of a certain character. (1.3, 1215a12, trans. J. Solomon)

---

36. For a famous historical analysis that is contrary to this one, see that of Werner Jaeger, who, in his famous *Paideia: The Ideals of Greek Culture* (Oxford: Oxford University Press, 1945), gives this idea an aristocratic origin. Cf. Felix Bourriot, *Kalos kagathos: d'un terme de propogande de sophists à une notion sociale et philosophique* (Hildesheim: Georg Olms, 1975).

37. Dalimier, *Aristote, Éthique à Eudème*, 38.

Let us quote Dalimier one last time:

> Doubtless ethical virtue can be perfected in the *polis* by the practice of calculating means and by the support of habituation, but it rests essentially on a possible private understanding of the good, *to kalon*. Ultimately, if the warrior faces dangers, if there are true friends, "it is because it is beautiful." (3.1, 1230a32)[38]

Aristotelian ethics is thus submerged into politics, but without abandoning its ambition of describing, or even permitting, the happiness of the individual person. It is politics that gives the legislator the means to bring about virtue, that promises happiness, in the city. But it is not politics that defines happiness. When he devotes himself to that task, Aristotle produces something that is perhaps the closest form to philosophy of the moral subject, something that one rarely finds before the modern era, except perhaps in an embryonic form that one habitually attributes to the Stoics. But it is not my intention to engage in this theoretical war of gods and giants in this place.

The *Politics*, a Split and Twilight Work

Thus, we will follow Richard Bodéüs on this fundamental point: dismissed from the political scene, the philosopher establishes himself solidly in the wings in the role of instructor of the political man in his "developed" form, that is, a legislator. But the legislator is confronted with two complementary but different tasks. In the first place he must affirm, and reaffirm when it has been forgotten, that the city has an ethical calling: "The true political man is also the person who is the most devoted to the study of virtue, since he wants to make his fellow citizens into people who are very respectful of the laws" (*EN* 1.13, 1102a8).

So, the legislator will read the ethical treatises and many parts of Aristotle's *Politics*. But to establish, or, often, to reestablish virtue at a strategic level, the legislator must possess, in addition to ethical knowledge, a profound understanding of social reality in its different forms. Thus, the *scientific* aspect, in the modern sense of "science," of the *Politics*. Because to establish a correct constitution, or to rectify an existent constitution—

---

38. Dalimier, *Aristote, Éthique à Eudème*, 41.

which is, as we will see, the situation most often met with—the legislator must be able to apply an impressive range of knowledge. In the first place, there are the already established scientific disciplines. Thus, medicine of Aristotle's day that we call by the rather vague term "Hippocratic" places a fundamental importance in the geography, hydrology, and meteorology of countries inhabited by ill people, which sums up the title of one of the most famous treatises of the Hippocratic Corpus, *Airs Waters Places*, a work no longer attributed to Hippocrates himself, but considered "Coan," that is, coming from the teachings of Hippocrates. In other words, the Aristotelian legislator, if he wants to be able to determine the location where a city has to be founded, to enlarge a city or to found a colony, must have a sufficiently advanced medical education. But it is also necessary that the legislator have an understanding of psychology, biology, geography, strategy, anthropology, and agronomy, without forgetting mathematics, meteorology, harmonics, and a good many other arts and sciences, with a massive amount of history. All that produces the first treatise of political science, which would remain for a long time without competition and doubtless is still without competition at its own level. Obviously, we will try to call attention to its most remarkable aspects. This kind of scientific breakthrough conforms to the program that Aristotle destines for the practical sciences, that is, to find practical application. All these analyses end in prescriptions and counsels addressed to the legislator.

This scientific aspect, in the modern sense of "science," of Aristotle's politics harmonizes fairly well with the whole group of passages that reveal simultaneously his ability to analyze political situations and to offer advice for those situations with a pragmatism that is sometimes frankly Machiavellian. But on the other hand, the entire politics of Aristotle, like that of Plato, rests on the distinction between correct and deviant regimes. Only correct regimes develop in the civic body the virtues that lead to happiness. For the city to fulfill its ethical role it must find ways to assure the correctness of the laws. When the laws do not play their role of making the citizens, especially young people, accustomed to good habits, they have to be changed. We will see in detail, great detail, in a later chapter, following the analysis provided by Jacques Brunschwig, why and how the laws must be repealed or modified. In any case submission to the laws should not be absolute nor do the citizens owe them blind obedience. Aristotelian politics is thus permeated with a radically *normative* function. As in Plato, it's a matter of knowing how to establish a city, if not "ideal," at least the best possible. Thus arises simultaneously the matter of the audience for Aristotle's ethical and political treatises, and the reasons, for modern readers, for the main tension in Aristotle's political philosophy as it is revealed in the *Politics*, and which, we may say, we will trace throughout our study.

In the *Politics* we find ourselves faced with a work incorrigibly divided between a *normative* aspect and an aspect that is *realist* or *positivist*. How can we understand this opposition? Is the *Politics* divided or pulled in opposite directions? We could evade the problem, like those commentators who, every time that they find themselves facing textual differences in Aristotle, try to explain them by the existence in these texts of distinct chronological layers. According to an interpretation that has had many partisans, book 1 would be a kind of general introduction mainly concerned with communities anterior to the city, principally the family considered in its different relations (master/slave, male/female, children, and patrimony); book 2 would be an examination of constitutions thought to be excellent, either those that have actually existed, or those that have been proposed by political theoreticians; book 3 would define, among other things, the citizen, the city, and the constitution; and books 7 and 8 study the characteristics of the best possible constitution and the education one must give to citizens. These five books, taken together, would thus constitute the normative side of the *Politics*. Books 4, 5, and 6, in that they provide the means to distinguish different kinds of constitutions, study the way in which these constitutions evolve and transform into each other, and explain how revolts occur and how one may prevent them, would be the positive side of Aristotle's political thought. This has led some editors, at least since the sixteenth century, to change the order of the books as given us by the manuscripts and to put books 7 and 8 after book 3.[39]

In the twentieth century some, taking another step, have found in the "normative" books a hint of Platonism and thus have not hesitated to give them an early date in Aristotle's career. Obviously, Werner Jaeger has provided the most forceful version of this thesis, in his usual manner, peremptory, ingenious, and based on a very close reading of the texts.[40] According

---

39. Cf. Antoine Scaïno da Salo, also a theoretician of handball and tennis, *In octo libros Aristotelis qui extant de Republica Quaestiones* (Rome: 1577). This ordering has been followed by a good many later commentators. Thus, for that which is still the best commentary on the work, the edition of William Lambert Newman, *The Politics of Aristotle*, 4 vols. (Oxford: Clarendon Press, 1887–1902), critical text with philological, historical, and philosophical commentary. This excellent work is nowhere near being surpassed.

to Jaeger, books 2, 3, 7, and 8 of the *Politics* form an old version, and thus closer to Platonism, into which books 4 through 6 were added later. One of the most convincing "proofs" in his eyes is to be found in the fact that the "realist" books quote the "idealist" books, but not the inverse. Jaeger also claims to have found "many mutual references" between books 2 and 3, on the one hand, and books 7 and 8, on the other, which would show the consistency of this group of "idealist" books. According to him, book 1 would be a later introduction taking up again themes (different kinds of power: those of master, husband, and father of the family), which he had treated in the lost dialogues, those too thought to be early in Aristotle's career. This passage in 3.6, 1278b30, seems to confirm this thesis: "There is no difficulty in distinguishing the various kinds of rule; they have been often defined already in our popular discussions (*exoterikoi*)." Jaeger goes much farther when he attributes to the "Original *Politics*" (*Urpolitik*) a kind of Platonic logic even in its method of exposition, namely, "logical division," and to the later "realist" sections an "immanent and biological" approach.[41] Jaeger is led to extremes that are the lot of all subsequent chronologists. Thus *Politics* 2, which represents for him the real introduction, would be the oldest, with the exception of the last chapter, which includes a list of legislators, which he would have added later . . .

The problem of the coexistence of different dimensions would then disappear, since it only reflects Aristotle's doctrinal evolution, and the present state of the text of the *Politics* would be explained by the cavalier way an editor would have assembled writings from different periods and functions, an event that would be far from unique in the annals of ancient editing. It seems that we must not only, when it is a matter of Aristotle's texts, refuse to throw ourselves into the arms of chronology, which is a refuge of ignorance (in fact one cannot rest these hypotheses on any objective data, for example stylistic, given that the texts of the corpus were not *edited* by Aristotle), but it is especially fertile to follow the more difficult path, in the case of the *Politics*, of keeping the manuscript order. This presumption, methodologically wise, in fact elucidates the absolute originality of the Aristotelian position among ancient political philosophers.

---

40. Jaeger is cited here following the second edition of the English translation of his book, more reliable than the German original because it was checked by its author: *Aristotle: Fundamentals of the History of His Development* (Oxford: Oxford University Press, 1948).

41. Jaeger, *Aristotle*, 270.

And ultimately that is for the most part what Jaeger does, despite every appearance. Because, though remaining a passionate chronologist, he refuses to attribute to any third person (Nicomachus or Theophrastus, for example) the insertion of the realist books in the middle of the "original *Politics*," but gives credit to Aristotle himself. According to Jaeger, at a late stage in his life and career Aristotle thought the two points of view, "idealist" and "realist," ought to function together, and that in a particularly remarkable form, since he would have, precisely, composed this "patchwork" by inserting realist texts between two families of idealist texts. It is a great shame that Jaeger did not set aside his chronological speculations, not because they are false, but because they belong to the realm of the undecidable, for he has grasped the rich complexity of the *Politics* better than many others. Prudence should have forbidden him to do more than register his preference for a construction that he presents as established, that makes the "idealist" or "normative" the oldest part in Aristotle's development.

To reaffirm the ethical goal of city life requires the "normative" analyses of the *Politics*, but to intervene in the unstable equilibrium of existing constitutions to give them, or make in them, the possibility of an ethical functioning, demands that the legislator have sufficiently mastered the objective areas of knowledge that Aristotle was the first to propose in the "realist" books of the *Politics*. That does not at all mean that we should read the *Politics* as if it were a modern book on the subject. There remain between books and even within certain books passages that seem to have come from different places and of which it is not absurd to think that they were written at different periods. But these discords are marginal, and most can be overcome. The question of the sort of unity that the *Politics* displays will be taken up again at the end of this book. Experience shows, and let us hope that we will demonstrate it in the following pages, that the *Politics* cannot efficiently perform its function of educating the legislator unless it walks on two legs, the normative and realist.

Let's go back to Aristotle's own historical situation. Perhaps it is not absurd to think that his status as a subject and his father's friendship with the king contributed to providing the philosopher with a situation *in retreat* from political life. Already Plato, taking account of the world contingencies of his time, was satisfied with trying to make kings into philosophers or even, as we have seen, to bring philosophers into contact with kings in order to advise them, if he couldn't make philosophers into royalty. The results at Syracuse were hardly conclusive. Furthermore, Athenian democracy did not please Aristotle any more than it charmed Plato.

But this historical circumstance magnifies, in a way, the strangeness noted at the beginning of the introduction, that Aristotle was the only philosopher to have attempted to think through that uniquely Greek and omnipresent phenomenon, the city. We know, since Hegel and his "owl of Minerva," which only flies at dusk, that it is only when historical situations have become completely developed that they can become completely thinkable, but in our case the dusk is decidedly very advanced. It is at the very least striking that Aristotle undertook to show that the city would be simultaneously the frame for the human psychological and ethical blossoming and the perfect and unsurpassable form of human society while he was the contemporary of the collapse of the world of cities, supplanted by the great Hellenistic empires that came out of Alexander's conquests, predecessors of Rome in the domination of the Mediterranean world. The *political* world in fact disappeared when the centralized and absolute power of the prince, begun by Philip II of Macedon and especially his son Alexander the Great, put an end to the cohabitation of more or less independent cities—small cities survived only thanks to alliances, sometimes forced, with more powerful cities—most of the time rivals, but sometimes allied in the face of shared dangers. Thus, the way was opened for the establishment of that autonomous moral science that inattentive readers have attributed to Aristotle. Freedom, exiled from the world at large, took refuge in inwardness. That's what Hegel describes as the moment of universal slavery whose most characteristic thought was Stoicism.

But Aristotle was, to some degree, not only a spectator but an actor in this story. He was, in fact, the tutor of Alexander the Great. It is remarkable, and has often been remarked, that Philip II, who began the process of burying Greek liberty, does not seem to have hesitated in giving his son a Greek education. The choice of Aristotle as tutor must have been the result of several factors. People as well known as Plato or Isocrates would doubtless not have been willing to go to live in Macedonia, and it was out of the question for Philip to send his son to Athens. Did the friendship between Nicomachus, Aristotle's father, and the kings of Macedonia play a role? In any case this instructional relationship did not last very long, and it involved very young participants, since Alexander, twenty-eight years younger than Aristotle, became king at the age of twenty.

Odd couple formed by "the greatest of conquerors and the greatest of philosophers," the student did not adopt the basic positions of his teacher. For Aristotle, in fact, not only is citizenship the condition and simultaneously the sign of human perfection, but this citizenship is, for reasons that we must examine in detail, the distinguishing mark of the Greek world. Alexander was, against the beliefs of his teacher, the one who put an end to the power of citizens and whose grand design was to blend all the people he had conquered into a single people, in the first place by biological fusion brought about by unions between Macedonians and Asians. To tell the truth this great project did not go farther than the recommendation that Alexander made to his officers to marry Persian women, as he had done himself. We should add that the relations between Aristotle and Alexander went seriously downhill to the point that the philosopher's safety was in danger, since Alexander had had Aristotle's nephew Callisthenes executed, apparently on the grounds that he was unwilling to prostrate himself before him. It's a notable anecdote in that the two concepts of power collide, that of the citizen who clearly would not prostrate himself before anyone, and that of the subject who lives in perpetual prostration. Perhaps the death of Alexander saved the life of Aristotle, but only for a short time, since he died a few months later.

Did Aristotle recognize the historical transformation that he had lived through? Did he think that the gesture of Alexander was just an unhappy and transitory episode in the history of Greek *politics*? Or was he rather conscious that he was waging difficult, even desperate combat? If "man is naturally a political animal," we may presume that Aristotle really believed that this "politicalness" could not be abolished, because in his view even Alexander did not have the means to overturn the course of nature. Werner Jaeger believed that he could hold that Aristotle had to take account of the political revolutions of his era in the lost dialogue, *Alexander, or On Colonization*. But this hypothesis is baseless. In any case it is *for us* that Aristotle's enterprise is tragic, because it is we who see, from the perspective of subsequent history, as a freely chosen project that could not avoid the death of that which it was trying to save. In any case, by founding his political philosophy firmly and exclusively on the city, Aristotle condemned himself to not have any real future. The *Politics* was not translated into Arabic, and although it was abundantly commented upon in Medieval Latin, it was in an equivocal way, since it was in a historical context totally different from that in which it had been written. There is a very interesting history of ideas there, but we will hardly touch on it here.[42]

---

42. See for example the interesting little book by Marcel Demongeot, *La Théorie du Régime Mixte chez saint Thomas d'Aquin* (Marseille: F. Carbonel, 1927), or his *Le meilleur régime politique selon saint Thomas* (Paris: André Blot, 1928).

Appendix to the First Chapter

The preceding somewhat scholarly exposition offers some rhetorical and pedagogical advantages since it does not allow the argument to be lost in the meanders of the numerous hermeneutic quarrels that feed upon the text of the *Politics*. But we need to be more exact on a number of points that have been the topic of discussion among interpreters.

Should not the great split between theoretical and practical sciences be seriously relativized? Isn't the theoretical autonomy that one attributes, on the basis of very few passages, to the *Politics*, artificial, and in any case due to later readers? We must mention here, without going into the details of their rich and subtle analyses, the attempt of at least two interpreters to subsume the political thought of Aristotle under his "metaphysics."[43] If there is any dependence between Aristotelian politics and metaphysics, it would be in the direction of politics borrowing its foundations from metaphysics, because no one could seriously dream of an Aristotelian metaphysics founded on political principles. Marx and Freud were still in the future. But we do not see Aristotle invoking principles that we could call "metaphysical" when he deduces the various propositions of his political philosophy. On the contrary, an "unmediated" reading (to the extent that that phrase is meaningful) of the *Politics* reveals a profound difference of content and style from those of the texts that comprise the *Metaphysics*. Thus, even the words used to express the great questions posed in the *Metaphysics* are remarkably absent from the *Politics*. It may seem to us somewhat ironical, but Aristotle doubtless does not see it that way, that when we find the word *ousia* in the *Politics*, it is in the sense well attested in Greek of "patrimony," and there is no indication allowing us to think that it means "substance, essence," though *ousia* is, in Aristotle's other treatises, the keystone of his ontology. It is completely obvious that from the moment that the ethical and political treatises of the Aristotelian corpus can be attributed to Aristotle, there can be no incompatibility between Aristotle's positions in politics and metaphysics. But there is no

---

43. Andreas Kamp, *Die politische Philosophie des Aristoteles und ihre metaphysichen Grundlagen. Wesenstheorie und Polisordnung* (Munich: 1985); Manfred Riedel, "Metaphysik und Politik bei Aristoteles," *Philosophisches Jahrbuch* 77 (1970): 1–14. Cf. the review of Kamp's book by Eckart Schütrumpf in *Gnomon* 61, no. 4 (1989): 293–296, and especially the solid refutation of the theses of Riedel and Kamp in Wolfgang Kullmann, *Aristoteles und die moderne Wissenschaft* (Stuttgart: Franz Steiner, 1998), 314–334.

dependence of either one on the other. Ultimately it is not surprising that the subtle and interesting works of people like Andreas Kamp and Manfred Riedel would be in a way an oxbow lake of Aristotle interpretation.

The problem of the status of the research carried on in the *Politics* needs to be rapidly summarized, but more than the relationships between the *Politics* and the *Metaphysics* it would be on the relations between the *Politics* and, if not the *Organon*, at least the logical procedures that are presented there that we must look at. From that point of view there are notable differences between the *Politics* and the *Ethics*, to which I will have to return.

In the *Prior* and especially the *Posterior Analytics*, Aristotle offers the criteria for scientificness at the same time as he provides the tools to produce it. Thus the necessity of a scientific proposition is guaranteed by the syllogistic form of the reasoning that establishes it, while the truth of the proposition flows from the fact that the syllogism in question is a scientific or demonstrative syllogism, that is, that it is not only valid but also in the first figure, constructed from true premises, prior to the conclusion and the cause of that conclusion. One of the principal questions posed by the interpreters who have initiated and developed the "biological turn," about which I will speak in the next chapter, is to know to what degree and in what form Aristotle resorts, in his most incontrovertible science, his zoological researches, to this restrictive procedure, the scientific syllogism. But the demonstrative syllogism (demonstration) is not the only procedure proposed in Aristotle's methodological books. Definition, division, and induction are some others. James Lennox has devoted a good deal of work to showing that the zoological works use logical procedures studied in the *Organon*.[44] Thus, to have red blood and wings are two characteristics that belong to the *essence* of the bird, and as such they are not demonstrated. But the fact of being a biped follows, and its necessity can be demonstrated.[45] But, paradoxically, it's in a methodological work, the

---

44. The most efficient way to access the work of Lennox is to use the collection of his essays, *Aristotle's Philosophy of Biology: Studies in the Origins of Life Science* (Cambridge: Cambridge University Press, 2001).

45. *Parts of Animals* 4.12, 693b5: "That the feet should be two in number is a matter of necessity. For a bird is essentially a sanguineous animal, and at the same time a winged animal, and no sanguineous animal has more than four points for motion. In birds, then, as in those other sanguineous animals that live and move upon the ground, the limbs attached to the trunk are four in number. But, while in all the rest

Posterior Analytics, that one must look for an example of a demonstrative syllogism relating to physical realities.[46]

The same goes for the *Politics*. The work is entirely hemmed in by an implicative or inferential structure; we will see the difference in a moment. Many of these arguments are presented in a form that could easily be put into syllogistic form, whether or not the two premises and conclusion are explicitly present in the text. We will see an example in the case of the analysis of the concept of "slave." Nevertheless, it's rather difficult to identify truly demonstrative syllogisms. The deductive arguments at work in the *Politics* serve different purposes. Sometimes it's a matter of establishing a thesis, as in the first lines of the *Politics*, which show that, from the fact that every community aims at a good and that the city is the supreme community, the good at which it aims is the most supreme good of all; sometimes Aristotle means to define the field of inquiry as at the beginning of book 3, where he shows that whoever wants to study "constitutions" must first define "city," and that

> since the city is a composite, like any other whole made up of many parts—these are the citizens, who compose it. It is evident, therefore, that we must begin by asking, who is a citizen, and what is the meaning of the term? (3.1, 1274b38)

But it can also be a matter of applying a general rule to a particular case, of the construction of a new concept or of a more precise definition of a concept badly understood, like that of "polity": "Now we must present our opinions about "polity." Its nature is, in fact, clearer now that we have defined oligarchy and democracy, because the "polity" is roughly a mixture of oligarchy and democracy" (4.8, 1293b31).

---

these four limbs consist of a pair of arms and a pair of legs, or of four legs as in quadrupeds, in birds the arms or forelegs are replaced by a pair of wings, and this is their distinctive character. For it is part of the substance of a bird that it shall be able to fly, and it is by the extension of the wings that this is made possible. Of all arrangements, then, the only possible and so the necessary one is that birds shall have two feet, for this with the wings will give them four points for motion." My choice is a little wicked, because the Aristotelian orthodoxy of this passage has been challenged; see the notes to my translation of the *Parties des animaux*.

46. Namely, the syllogism that shows that vines lose their leaves because they have large leaves, *Posterior Analytics* 2.16, 98b1.

To consider the question of the logical structure of the *Politics*, fortunately we have at our disposal a detailed study by Richard Bodéüs on the *premises* that we find in the text and that furnish us with material for our consideration.[47] There are points at which I do not agree with Bodéüs, including these two: Bodéüs considers only books 1, 3, 7, and 8 of the *Politics*, with the pretext that it is in these books above all that one finds the propositions that can serve as *premises* for the arguments, while "in Books 4 and 5 thought to be 'realist' (where the philosopher, one may say, observes more than he argues),"[48] these premises are rare. Bodéüs leaves aside books 2 and 6, which, according to him, have an average number of such premises. I suspect that that decision of Bodéüs, even if it is not entirely devoid of a textual basis, reveals above all what we may call a *prejudice* that we will discuss again below, according to which the text of the *Politics* is irremediably divided into "normative" and "realist" sections. Bodéüs would have been better off including books 4 and 5, where such premises are far from absent. The second point of disagreement bears on an audacious hypothesis proposed by Bodéüs, that it is by reading the *Politics* in reverse that we come closest to Aristotle's canonical demonstrative schema: in book 7 Aristotle would establish the best constitution; he then would show in book 3 that there are constitutions other than the best, in order, at last, in book 1, to show the specific difference between the city and other human societies. I cannot accept any such scheme, as everything that follows in the present volume will show in detail. Thus, I cannot accept that Aristotle waits until book 7 of the *Politics*, if we keep the traditional order of the books, to deal with the best constitution.

Another point that Bodéüs treats in considerable detail that I tend to find rather useless ends in a right conclusion. He remarks that the premises in the *Politics* take the form of propositions introduced by "since" (ἐπεί), while in the description of deductions in the *Analytics*, most of the syllogisms are generally introduced by "if" (εἰ). Let us take a short detour. There are two approaches to the syllogism; interpreters have not come to agree about them, perhaps because both are right, an

---

47. Richard Bodéüs, "Quelques prémisses de la réflexion aristotélicienne sur la cité" in *Politique et Philosophie chez Aristote. Recueil d'études* (Namur: Societé des Études Classiques, 1991), 89–127. A shorter version was published in Pierre Aubenque, ed., *Aristote politique. Études sur la "Politique" d'Aristote* (Paris: PUF, 1993).

48. Bodéüs, "Quelques prémisses de la réflexion aristotélicienne sur la cité," short version, 332.

indication of that being that Aristotle does not distinguish between them. According to an implicative conception of the syllogism ("if A, then B"), its necessity depends on the relationship between the two terms ("if the earth flies, it has wings," as the Stoics would put it), that is, one cannot have B false if A is true; according to an inferential conception, it is the necessity of the antecedent that leads to that of the consequent ("since A is true, then B is true": since this animal has red blood, it moves at four points). Doubtless one may say, as Bodéüs does, that "to say ἐπεί is . . . to refer to that which is acquired immediately or from the beginning."[49] But it seems to me more interesting to note that a distinction of this kind has no significance except in certain cases.

In a brilliant and subtle article, Catherine Dalimier[50] analyzes the difference between the two forms of necessary relation between terms, following Simplicius who, in his commentary on Aristotle's *De Caelo*, criticizes Alexander of Aphrodisias for having gone from an implicative to an inferential format while commenting on the analyses that Aristotle devotes to the special element of which the heavens are composed, that which the traditions have called the "quintessence." When Aristotle posits that "if there is a simple circular movement which is that of a simple body, then there is a simple body (an element) that is moved in a circle," Alexander understands: "since there is such a movement, there exists a celestial element." The argument as stated by Alexander and followed by a crowd of commentators would thus establish the *existence* of the quintessence, while the text of Aristotle only asserts the necessity of a *relationship* between two terms, circular movement and quintessence. Obviously, this does not prevent Aristotle from thinking that the quintessence exists. But, in a treatise of natural science like the *De Caelo*, what is at issue is important. Catherine Dalimier shows this very well, notably in what concerns the status of astronomy, a science at the crossroads of three great theoretical sciences: physics, mathematics, and theology.

On the other hand, one might think that the difference is not that crucial in texts of political philosophy, and I believe that is what Bodéüs means to say. In fact, in the *Politics*, in the great majority of cases the

---

49. Bodéüs, "Quelques prémisses de la réflexion aristotélicienne sur la cité," long version, 95.

50. Dalimier, "Les enjeux de la reformulation syllogistique chez les commentateurs grecs du *De Caelo* d'Aristote."

reality of the antecedent is a given: since the family is such and such, since the city is part of such and such a reality, since democracy reinforces such and such a tendency, and so forth. But the implicative form is not absent from the *Politics*, when it is a matter of putting an antecedent and a consequent in relation to each other independently of the existence of one or the other. Thus, in a famous comparison, in *Politics* 4.4, between the a priori construction of various species of animal and various constitutions (a text about which I have written a good deal, and to which I will return), Aristotle says that "if the number of necessary parts is in fact so many," then the number of their conjunctions will be the number of species of animal (1290b29). Similarly, in the same chapter: "if one posits that the soul is more fully a part of the living being than the body" (1291a24), then in the city also certain parts are more "parts" than others. It is not to be doubted that Aristotle is persuaded that officeholders with a properly political function and those whose function is purely technical are not equally parts of the city, as we will see again in detail. Nevertheless, he here wants to emphasize the necessity of a homology between the soul and the city. At the same time, a little farther along, at 1291a39, Aristotle explains that "if it is necessary that parts of this kind (deliberative and judicial) exist in cities, and exist in a good and just way," then it is necessary that cities be governed by citizens who have a particular form of virtue, political virtue. Aristotle does not rely on the affirmation of the existence of deliberative and judicial parts in this place either.

But the most important is to decide how Aristotle establishes the premises that serve as the basis for his exposition of his political philosophy. I will adopt here a nomenclature that is more immediate and approximate than that of Bodéüs, also with some differences. It seems to me, for example, that it is not necessary to give too much importance to propositions that Aristotle accepts because they are held to be true by most people. Thus, when Aristotle says that "we see" it's not always, or even most often, a matter of appeal to common experience, but a recognition of an obviousness. The first sentence of the *Politics*, already cited ("since every city, as we see, is a certain community," 1251a1), seems to me to have a status analogous to that of sense perception, on which Aristotle always asserted that the natural sciences are based. From that sort of perception follows a deduction that can be phrased in the form of several syllogisms and that aims to establish that the city is the "most supreme of all" communities. That sort of perception is not at all a judgment or opinion that some could share and others not. Most of the perceptions that serve as a basis for Aristotle's political arguments are drawn from the political experience or documentation of his time. That's how it is with the double premise that we find at *Politics* 6.7, 1321a5: "As there are four chief divisions of the common people, farmers, artisans, traders, laborers, so also there are four kinds of military forces—the cavalry, the heavy infantry, the light-armed troops, the navy." This is the result of an *observation*. Obviously, that does not prevent Aristotle from using the opinions supported by the unanimity or majority of people. Bodéüs cites the one that opens chapter 15 of book 7 of the *Politics*, that says that individually and collectively, people are all looking for the same thing, happiness. The same procedure occurs at 3.16, 1287b17: "no one doubts that the law would command and decide in the best manner whatever it could."

Bodéüs also correctly remarks that certain political premises rely on the competencies of specialists and cites, among other less convincing examples, the division of melodies into ethical, active, and enthusiastic (8.7, 1341b32). But there are two sorts of introductory propositions that interest me above all, those that are drawn from Aristotle's ethical speculation and those that depend on theses exterior to ethics and politics. Let us begin with these.

In the first place, there are the arguments that appeal to specific disciplines. Thus, when it is a matter of legislating about the age of marital unions, the legislator needs to know the period of fertility for men and women, because, as Aristotle says in *Politics* 7.16, 1335a6, those who ignored this information paid a price. It is worth quoting the passage:

> Almost all these objects may be secured by attention to one point. Since the time of generation is commonly limited within the age of seventy years in the case of a man, and of fifty in the case of a woman, the commencement of the union should conform to these periods. The union of male and female when too young is bad for the procreation of children; in all other animals the offspring of the young are small and ill-developed, and with a tendency to produce female children, and therefore also in man, as is proved by the fact that in those cities in which men and women are accustomed to marry young, the people are small and weak; in childbirth also younger women suffer more, and more of them die; some persons say that this was the meaning of the response once given to the Troezenians—the oracle really meant that many died because they married too young; it had nothing to do with the gathering of the harvest.

The oracle told the people of Troezen, Μὴ τέμνε νέαν ἄλοκα: "Don't plow a new (young) furrow," meaning, do not allow your girls to have intercourse too young. We notice here the appeal to observation of what happens in other animals, a relatively difficult observation to exploit because few animals have the same gestation time as human beings. This illustrates something said above, that the legislator needs to master a large number of areas of knowledge.

There is next and above all Aristotle's appeal to explanatory patterns normally used by other sciences, patterns that thus acquire a larger validity. We see a remarkable example by analyzing *Politics* 1.2, in which Aristotle explains the political character of man, but also the fact that human beings are the only ones to use language, in resorting to a teleological explanation that seems to gain its most complete expression only in biology. The basis of this explanation is that Nature gives to living beings the means to live at their best, that is, above all, for each species to survive everlastingly: for example, she gives wings to the bird and not to the fish. There is in this place something like a perspective of including politics in a natural science and therefore a danger for the distinction between theoretical and practical sciences. Thus, we must look at this question in detail. This will be done in the next chapter.

It is obviously difficult to draw precise conclusions from an examination from without, and therefore superficial. It seems nevertheless that these remarks have some force against the position of W. L. Newman,[51] for whom the *Politics* is rather a discussion among friends than a technical treatise. Newman uses the word "colloquial." Carlo Natali,[52] relying both on Newman and on articles cited by Bodéüs, also concludes that the *Politics* is a work directed, if not to the "public at large," then at least to a nonspecialist public. Ultimately none of Natali's three arguments carries the day. The character that one may call "literary" rather than "technical" that one finds in the *Politics* in comparison with treatises like the *Metaphysics* or *De Anima* is, in my opinion, very doubtful. On the one hand, there are in the *Politics* very technical passages (one might think of the last three chapters of book 4 or of the causes of revolt in book 5) and, on the other hand, because a treatise dealing with realities as concrete as the city, magistrates, and various regimes, takes on a falsely "easy" look compared

---

51. Newman, *The Politics of Aristotle*, vol. 4, xxxv–xxxix.

52. In a presentation on Aristotle's definition of "citizen" in a colloquium in Paris, in May 2015.

to speculations on being qua being. As for Natali's second argument, that the *Politics* does not employ a technical vocabulary in the way that the scholarly treatises do, it is debatable: the ideas of essence, actuality, and entelechy do not occur because there is no reason for deploying them, but words like "power," "city," "citizen," "constitution," "polity," "stasis," are indeed deployed in rigorously defined senses. Finally, the thesis that the *Politics* relies, in its deductions, on "endoxic"[53] premises is, ultimately, as we have seen, too partial to be true. As in other treatises, Aristotle relies on propositions, some of them surely endoxic, but many of them come from observation and others from disciplines whose scientific nature is not in doubt in Aristotle's eyes.

Now we must examine Aristotle's use of his ethical speculations in the *Politics*. There are citations of the ethical treatises in the *Politics*, although it is often difficult to decide whether it is a matter of an allusion to precise passages of the ethical writings as we have them.[54] From these references we can draw two conclusions, seemingly contradictory, and then a strongly remarkable appreciation for the relationships between Aristotle's ethics and politics.

The first conclusion is that political research depends on the results of ethical research or that, to put it in terms of Aristotelian epistemology, ethics is prior to politics *for us*.[55] That's not difficult to understand: if we

---

53. In his edition of the *Topics*, Jacques Brunschwig uses this term ("endoxales" in French) to designate premises constructed from "agreed upon ideas" (ἔνδοξα) by everyone or by most people. The word "endoxic" is used in English by, for example, Richard Kraut in "How to Justify Ethical Propositions: Aristotle's Method," in *The Blackwell Guide to Aristotle's Nicomachean Ethics*, ed. Richard Kraut (Oxford: Blackwell, 2006), 76–95, and discussed in detail by Dorothea Frede, "The Endoxon Mystique: What Endoxa Are and What They Are Not," available online at ancphil.lsa.umich.edu/-/downloads/osap/43-Frede.pdf.

54. *Politics* 2.2, 1261a31; 3.9, 1280a1; 12, 1282b20; 4.11, 1295a36; 7.13, 1332a8, 22. Certain assertions that one tends to consider as theses derived from common sense should doubtless be referred to the ethics. Thus at 4.11, 1295b4, a passage not counted by Bodéüs for this reason, we read, "it is admitted that moderation and the mean are best." Given what precedes this line, it is likely that this is an allusion to the doctrine of virtue as a mean (cf. 1295a37).

55. According to the Aristotelian doctrine of two priorities, "for us" and "per se" (or "naturally"), something to be discussed further below. What we have seen concerning the political roots of the virtues makes us think that ethics is not naturally prior to politics.

want to discover the conditions for actualizing a virtuous and happy city, we need to have fairly precise ideas about what virtue and happiness are, ideas that are studied in the *Ethics*, and the same goes for friendship, pleasure, and justice, and the various individual virtues. Thus, the difference between numerical equality and proportional equality as the *Nicomachean Ethics* develops it in its analysis of justice is absolutely indispensable in Aristotle's examination of political justice, as Aristotle recognizes in three of the references in the *Politics* to the *Ethics*, listed earlier in note 54.

But—and this is the second consequence of the study of references to the *Ethics* in the *Politics*—the *Politics* does not need the *Ethics* as we have it. The text of the *Politics* can in fact function, that is, deploy its conceptual apparatus and arrive at the prescriptions or advice addressed to the legislator with, one may say, its own means. Thus—and this demonstration can be made in every other case—we understand perfectly, starting only from the text of the *Politics*, what Aristotle means when he says that the partisans of democracy are in favor of a division of power according to numerical equality, while those of the oligarchy fight for proportional equality, without having to resort to the analyses of *Nicomachean Ethics* book 5. The subtle analyses of the *Ethics* of virtues as means, of courage for example as a mean between cowardice and foolhardiness, do not receive any allusion in the *Politics*, which proves that the legislator does not need them. As for the relationships between virtue and happiness, a crucial point in Aristotle's thought, as indeed for all the other Greek philosophers, the legislator would learn quite enough by reading *Politics* book 7. In fact, we find ourselves before an astounding fact: the statesman can play his prescriptive role perfectly with very limited access to the subtleties of the ethics, even if, obviously, a deep understanding of the subjects treated in the *Ethics* would not do the legislator any harm. But, on the other hand, as it is the legislator, creator of good laws, who allows ethics to achieve its principal end of making men good, we see that ethics has an absolute need of politics in that it presupposes the existence of the city to explain how virtue is acquired. It's not enough to say that one becomes virtuous by obeying good laws; you still have to know how to establish good laws, that is, how to install correct constitutions. But that is the very heart of the legislative calling.

To that we must add that there is between the *Politics* and the *Ethics* a remarkable difference of form. If we consider things in a very general way, the *Ethics* tries to *define* key ideas like virtue, friendship, pleasure, and so on. To do that, there are long definitional sequences. Thus, to define friendship, Aristotle, after having presented as usual the opinions of other philosophers, determines the proper characteristics of friendship, distinguishing the species, the difference between neighboring notions. But the analyses in the *Ethics* are not accompanied by prescriptions or recipes for how one may become virtuous, to experience a virtuous friendship, to arrive at an unmixed pleasure, and so forth. The *Politics*, on the other hand, contains plenty of definitions, for example that of "citizen," but the analyses of the different kinds of constitutions, their mode of conservation and ruin, all are directed toward practical applications to be put into effect by the legislator. In other words, the *Politics* completes the program of the *Ethics*, that of the *Nicomachean Ethics* for example, when Aristotle asserts there, in a passage already partially cited:

> Since the present inquiry does not aim at theoretical knowledge like the others (for we are inquiring not in order to know what excellence is, but in order to become good, since otherwise our inquiry would have been of no use), we must examine the nature of actions, namely, how we ought to do them. (2.2, 1103b26)

The *Ethics* claims that it is not a purely theoretical speculation, but aims at practice; but it's the *Politics*, especially the "realist" books, that permits putting the conceptual analyses of the *Ethics* into operation. In fact, it is necessary to endow the city with a correct constitution for the citizens to become virtuous and happy. Otherwise virtue would lead a quasi-clandestine existence, virtuous people being, like Socrates, a kind of pariah in their own city, with the dangers that ensue from that.

These very summary considerations on the forms of exposition of the *Ethics* and *Politics* reinforce the idea that it's a matter of one and the same enterprise, but reinforce it from an unexpected side: reduced to itself, Aristotle's *Ethics* simply cannot fulfill the program assigned to it. For that, it needs the *Politics*.

CHAPTER 2

A Biological Politics?

To say the least, studies of living things have a decisive place in Aristotle's philosophy. What has been called "the biological turn" has been one of the most important events in the domain of the history of ancient philosophy in the second half of the twentieth century. The expression, invented by our English-speaking colleagues, refers to a double movement that has profoundly revolutionized our reading of Aristotle. On the one hand, it's a matter of reintegrating Aristotle's biological corpus, one fourth of the extant texts of Aristotle, into *philosophy*, more precisely into his theoretical philosophy. The same concepts and expository methods are at work both within and without the biological works. Aristotle's biology is a *philosophical* biology, which in no way contradicts the fact, noted above, that a treatise like the *Parts of Animals* eminently belongs to the history of biology. On the other hand, in a movement that is reciprocal of the first and doubtless more important for our reading of Aristotle, scholars have noticed not only that the biological *use* of these concepts and expository and explanatory methods help us better appreciate their use in the logical or metaphysical works, but also that biology is in the background of texts that are not part of the zoological corpus, yet give these texts their true scope. That has been shown, for example, in the excellent edition of the treatise *On Generation and Corruption* by Marwan Rashed:[1] it's only when one realizes that Aristotle is thinking of living things that one re-

---

1. Marwan Rashed, *Aristote de la génération et la corruption* (Paris: Les Belles Lettres, 2005).

ally understands his analyses of growth, alteration, and mixture. Besides, one cannot really grasp the meaning of Aristotle's theory of causes if one has not read the *Parts of Animals*, nor of his theory of potentiality and actuality without turning to the *Generation of Animals*.

Is the politics also affected by the biological turn? From a certain point of view, that is impossible, because biology (a term that did not exist in Aristotle and had to wait for Lamarck to appear in French) is a part, indeed in several ways the principal part, of theoretical natural science, while politics is the architectonic science in the practical domain. Or more likely, if politics and biology overlap, it would be a matter of analogical relationships that don't really apply the same theoretical procedures in studies carried out in the two disciplines. And those relations do exist. Besides the organicist comparisons we find in the *Politics*—for example, that the parts composing a city should have the proportions they have just like the parts of a living organism do, or for another example, the good functioning of a city is comparable to the vital activity of a living organism in good health—Aristotle even proposes, in a famous passage in *Politics* 4.4, a combinatory method that is identical for constructing a priori various constitutions and various living species. But that is not enough to enable us to talk about an Aristotelian sociobiology, a sociobiologist being a person who looks at the study of the living world for concepts, methods, and models for understanding human social reality. One of the most important, and most contested, results of sociobiology is taking ethical and social values as nothing more than adaptive values that operate in disguise.[2]

However, in one of the most commented-upon chapters in the Aristotelian Corpus, *Politics* 1.2, Aristotle indeed seems to go beyond simple analogies. It is in this chapter that he establishes the famous thesis that "man is naturally a political animal." And it is even more striking that to do this he resorts to principles and methods that he usually uses in biology. In a more general way, if the city exists by nature, a necessary corollary of the fact that man is naturally a political animal, one might well ask why the study of the city does not fall within the study of natural entities, physics. And, above all, how should one understand the *political*

---

2. The bible of this movement that never stops dying and being reborn from its ashes remains the work of Edward O. Wilson, *On Human Nature* (Cambridge: Harvard University Press, 1978). This is a kind of simplified version of his great work *Sociobiology: The New Synthesis*, published by Harvard in 1975.

thesis that "man is naturally a political animal" when we know that, for example, in a notably famous passage in the *History of Animals*, Aristotle makes "political" a *biological* characteristic as one of the "ways of life" of animals that may be applied to other living things besides man?

Aristotle's Social Naturalism

The distinction that many interpreters have made between the partisans of the naturalness of social ties, including Aristotle, and conventionalists, among whom one normally counts some Sophists, is not as enlightening as one ordinarily thinks. Of course, some of the Sophists, the Skeptics, and doubtless others have been able to maintain that social rules as well as ethical values are conventional, but there has been a kind of consensus, at least since the layman's conception of the universe won out over the religious approach, as William K. C. Guthrie has very well demonstrated, relying on a text of Diodorus Siculus's *Historical Library*. In opposition to poetic and religious approaches, which would see the present state of human society as the effect of a fall or degradation from a previous "golden age," most thinkers adhered to an "evolutionary view of culture as the daughter of necessity," which can be found to be "identical in outline and in many of the details, in Aeschylus, Euripides, Critias, Protagoras, the Hippocratic *On Ancient Medicine*, and evidently the fifth-century source of the pre-history in Diodorus I.8."[3] In this chapter, in fact, Diodorus tells us that the first human beings

> led an undisciplined and bestial life, setting out one by one to secure their sustenance and taking for their food both the tenderest herbs and the fruits of wild trees. Then, since they were attacked by wild beasts, they came to each other's aid, being instructed by expediency, and when gathered together in this way by reason of their fear, they gradually came to recognize their mutual characteristics. And though the sounds which they made were at first unintelligible and indistinct, yet

---

3. William K. C. Guthrie, *A History of Greek Philosophy, Vol. II* (Cambridge: Cambridge University Press, 1965), 473. A good deal can be gained also from Guthrie, *In the Beginning: Some Greek Views on the Origin of Life and the Early State of Man* (London: Methuen & Co., 1957), already mentioned.

gradually they came to give articulation to their speech, and by agreeing with one another upon symbols for each thing which presented itself to them, made known among themselves the significance which was to be attached to each term. (Diod. Sic. 1.8, trans. Oldfather in Loeb)

All ancient authors who dealt with this question seem to have, more or less, come around to the idea that life without human association would be impossible or at least very difficult, putting in danger the survival of the human species. Thus, in all these approaches, social life and all that flows from it inevitably, like institutions and laws, base their necessity on two natural realities: the originally defenseless nature of human beings, and their needs. All writers, or nearly all, since it seems that only the Cynics, in antiquity, thought that society and social life were not natural. Diogenes of Sinope declared, according to Diogenes Laertius (6.44), that nature would offer human beings an "easy life" and that only the artificial needs that were created, like "honey cakes, perfumes, and things like that," forced them to accept technological and social means to obtain them.

Things are not always that neat, as Guthrie knows well. Take Plato for example. According to the myth of Protagoras in the dialogue that bears his name, society is not entirely the consequence of human needs and trial and error means to satisfy them. Humanity, finding itself lacking the natural advantages conferred on other animals, escapes from peril in two steps: in the first, Prometheus obtains for human beings techniques that palliate their natural lacks of thick skin, hooves, claws, speed, and so forth; then Zeus commands Hermes to give them the sentiments of shame and justice that make it possible for them to live in society, without which they could not survive. To say that it was these divine or semi-divine entities that gave these technical abilities and ethical values to human beings is the same as affirming that they were not gained from experience, and that brings the mythological story of the *Protagoras* closer to the Aristotelian position. Elsewhere Plato seems to align himself with what Guthrie describes as the common position. In the *Republic*, for example, he shows humans associating with each other because "each of us is not self-sufficient but has many needs" (2, 369b). People come together in a city because each one thinks, "this will be better for us," and that which "brings about the city is our need."

This common position shows us human beings *learning* at the same time from their situation and their needs, because those who were cold invented clothes, those who had problems digesting raw meat invented cooking, and above all, perceiving how vulnerable they were in their isolated condition, they formed communities. This ultimately looks like good sense, especially for people who, like us, are both the heirs of an empiricist tradition, much better informed than the ancients of the condition and reality of human societies called "prehistoric," and convinced, despite recent greatly disillusioning discoveries, that there really has been progress in human history. In opposing an approach of that kind, Aristotle risks looking like a simpleton, since he pretends that the reason for which human beings form families and cities is that they have an innate tendency to do that. Isn't that just like explaining the effects of opium by appealing to its dormitive power? It is appropriate therefore to show that Aristotle's theory is not as naïve as it appears, and that it is worth taking a better look at it, and to that end, we have to try to understand why Aristotle proposed a theory of the origin of society fundamentally different from that of all other philosophers. Why is Aristotle, who so much loves consensus, so opposed to everyone on such an important point?

Not that Aristotle denies any role to need in the establishment, and above all, in the development of human societies, as we will see. It will also be necessary to notice the points at which Aristotle separates himself from other thinkers, and thus where he does not separate himself. All the philosophers who followed Parmenides have accepted his thesis of the impossibility of going automatically from less complex states to more complex states, as the naïve Milesians had done, from chaotic elements to a cosmos whose very name implies the notion of order. As Diodorus Siculus says a bit before the text cited above, philosophers have given two main kinds of answer to the problem of the origin of the universe, but also to that of the human species and human society. For one group, the world has always existed as it is today, and for the others, it has come into being and been destroyed an infinite number of times, some of them thinking that these two events occur according to a determinate periodic cycle. Aristotle combines the two positions. He posits that species of animal have not evolved into their present form, or in a form followed by their present form, but in the case of the technology, cultural creations, and social institutions, he belongs to the group who believe in periodic cataclysms, but doubtless not periodically predetermined, taking humanity back to a primitive state, obliging mankind to recapitulate the route to culture.[4] Thus, Aristotle believes in the existence of human progress

---

4. Cf. *Metaphysics* 12.8, 1074b10; *Meteorologica* 1.3, 339b27; *De Caelo* 1.3, 270b19; *Politics* 7.10, 1329b25.

as he repeatedly indicates, and far from having nostalgia for the "golden age," he has no reverence for that which is ancient, and for him, men in their original condition resemble "mindless random individuals" (*Pol.* 2.8, 1269a6). In this history, human needs, which are interconnected, and also human ingenuity, obviously play a causative role.

The Origin of the Family and of the City

Taking account of human history does not necessarily lead to doing the work of a historian. At the beginning of the *Politics*, Aristotle presents a discussion that is not that of a historian, but does take a narrative form. This narrative indeed assigns a role to human needs, but they are not the determining explanatory factor. That's what happens in *Politics* 1.2, a passage that we will discuss at some length. Aristotle says that human beings necessarily form "at first" (πρῶτον, 1252a26) an association called "family" (or "house," as the Greek word οἰκία is often translated) for the sake of two main purposes, reproduction and "safety." After this first stage, Aristotle distinguishes his position from the common position presented above, because, if we look closely, we see that he in no way claims that it is *needs* that bring about the constitution of the family, in the sense that the family would be an *answer* to the needs of reproduction and mutual safety of human beings. Right from the start Aristotle situates things at a more fundamental level than that of human need or human will, since the two relationships that he gives as constitutive of the family (the relations between man and woman for the sake of reproduction and between master and slave for "safety") are described as the "necessary" relationships of people "who cannot exist without each other" (1252a26). That means that there was no prefamilial stage in human history. But that is not the case, as we will see, for the city.

From the case of reproduction, we grasp the way in which Aristotle will present his explanation. Reproducing oneself is not an action of "considered choice" (1252a28), people telling themselves that without offspring they have no chance of surviving, and thus choose to have children. Nor does Aristotle say that it is a kind of trick that Nature plays, using the attractiveness of sexual pleasure to achieve her ends, assuring the survival of the species. Human beings have "a tendency to leave behind them a being similar to themselves" (1252a29), and that is a biological characteristic, in the proper sense of the word, since it is common to all living things, even plants. Other Aristotelian passages give a true perspective on this doctrine. Thus, at *De Anima* 2.4, 415a26, we read that

> the acts in which the nutritive soul manifests itself are reproduction and the use of food, because for any living thing that has reached a normal development and which is unmutilated, and whose mode of generation is not spontaneous, the most natural act is the production of another like itself, an animal producing an animal, a plant a plant, in order that, as far as its nature allows, it may partake in the eternal and divine. That is the goal towards which all things strive, that for the sake of which they do whatsoever their nature renders possible.[5]

But it also happens that human beings can have babies when they want, thus according to a "considered choice," and even that their decision can be strictly regulated by the law in well-governed cities, both according to Plato and according to Aristotle, both of whom mean to control carefully the times and rhythms of births. Otherwise, in many cases, people have children because they need to rebuild the workforce, for example in their agricultural operations, and it is no less true that human beings also couple for the sake of pleasure, and that is probably true for some animals also. And, in fact, Aristotle means to take account of the combination of causes of the phenomena he studies, but those causes are of unequal importance.

The same goes for "safety," which Aristotle refers only to the relationship between master and slave. There too we find that the relationship serves to satisfy needs, at least those of the master, but here too, it is not this satisfaction that is the main explanation of the relationship in question. The domination of the master on the slave in natural slavery, but also the authority of husband over his wife, are only local applications of a hierarchical structure that includes "all nature" (1.5, 1254a31), whose functioning requires the cooperation of elements that are hierarchically ordered between each other and that extend even to nonnatural entities like harmony. The animal world reveals such relationships of natural subordination for the sake of safety of the groups in animal society, for example in bees. From these natural relationships, there results a common

---

5. Cf. *Generation of Animals* 2.1, 735a17, b24; 1.23, 731a24–b8; 3.10, 760a35.

task and, finally, each one finds a sort of blossoming of its own nature. This last characteristic permits Aristotle to say that in the case of *natural* slavery, the servile relationship is beneficial simultaneously to the master and to the slave. We will see later how to interpret that.

Aristotle affirms unambiguously that the family is a natural entity: "The family is an association established by nature for the supply of man's everyday wants" (1252b12). But here too this thesis is nothing less than obvious, to the extent that Aristotle really doesn't bother to prove it. The fact that it is constituted of natural relations, those of husband and wife, master and slave, seems to be the reason, not explicitly formulated, behind this naturalism. A very feeble reason, since Aristotle gives in the *Politics* examples of nonnatural entities made of natural parts, for example military alliances or economic unions, which are purely conventional although made from natural societies, that is, cities (3.9, 1280a34). It will be only after a long detour that we will really be able to deal with this problem and find a more solid basis for the naturalness of the family.

The next stage in the Aristotelian narrative is the village (κώμη). No appeal here to a "tendency to form villages." In fact, the village is formed next in the development of needs. When people want to satisfy needs that go beyond those of everyday life, those provided by the family, they bring together several families into a village. Villages in their turn have as their calling contribution to larger unities (cf. 1252b27). It seems, though the text is not very clear on this point, that the appearance of new needs brings about the village and not the other way around, but Aristotle says too little about the village that we can reject the idea that the village is a factor in the creation of new needs. Doubtless one may believe that both are true. Aristotle says of the village that it "seems to be a colony" of the family, the colony of a Greek city being its extension into foreign territory, founded by citizens of the original city and conserving the institutions and cults of the parent city, at least until the course of history decides otherwise.

The village is a "totally natural entity" (1252b16), as was the family, with a naturalness of the same kind but slightly different. In fact, Aristotle seems to maintain that the village is natural because it is composed of natural parts, that is, families, which are natural; we may hesitate about this claim because he gives very little space to a discussion of the village. Like the family, the village is supposedly natural because its parts are natural, not necessarily because its relationships are natural; as for the family, this is a rather feeble reason. Doubtless, we may think that if Aristotle does not establish more firmly the naturalness of the village, it's because the question doesn't interest him very much, and in a way, he is in a hurry to get on to the next step, that of the city (*polis*).

The last stage of this narrative is in fact the formation of the city or "political community" (κοινωνία πολιτική). Aristotle begins by proposing to explain the naturalness of the city by saying that, "if the earlier forms of society are natural, so is the city" (1252b30), and that is the only reason that commentators habitually remember. It's a demonstration that suffers from the same lack as has been indicated for the family and village. Needing a more radical reason, Aristotle immediately gives one, "for it is their end, and the nature of a thing is its end." A military alliance, on the other hand, is indeed a means used by cities to satisfy their need for security, but it is not at all the end or nature of the cities that participate. To put it another way, a city is an organic composite in which it is the whole that gives meaning to each of the parts. We find here again the famous Aristotelian doctrine of the two priorities noted above:[6] from the perspective of becoming, the parts come to be before the whole according to a "priority for us," but from the conceptual perspective it is the whole that is prior, a natural priority, because it is in relation to it that the parts have their function and thus are defined.

A passage in the *Nicomachean Ethics* seems to go against the *Politics* passage that we are considering. In 8.14, 1162a17, we read, "Man is naturally inclined to form couples—even more than to form cities, inasmuch as the household is earlier and more necessary than the city." The *Eudemian Ethics* expresses the same idea by saying that man is naturally "an economic animal" (7.10, 1242a23), that is, that he is naturally a member of a family. But obviously these passages express priority "for us," or chronological priority. As for the fact that the family would be "more necessary" than the city, Aristotle doubtless wants to say that before one may aspire to the "happy life" that is the objective aimed at by the city, it is necessary to live, which necessarily assumes the existence of the family. In our chapter 1.2 of the *Politics*, after having explained that the city is the end and nature of the communities that go to make it up, Aristotle writes, "Hence it is evident that the city is a creation of nature, and that man is by nature a political animal" (1253a1). The sentence is a little ambiguous in that it seems to imply that it is because the city exists by nature that man is a political animal, as some modern interpreters read it. We will have to come back to this question.

---

6. Among other passages, *Posterior Analytics* 1.2, 71b34.

For the moment, let us simply note that from the point of view of the individual person it is fundamentally because man has a political "instinct," that is, a tendency to live the life of a citizen, that the city is found to be the natural structure in which he can live the life of a citizen. He could not do that in any other association, even a natural one. This nearly inaugural chapter of the *Politics* does not mention any *natural* society that includes the city, putting the city in the position of the supreme political entity, which would be a kind of pleonasm, because what could be more *political* than the *polis*? This supreme or eminent position of the city was affirmed immediately in the first paragraph of the *Politics*: the city is "the highest (κυριωτάτη) of all and embraces all the rest" (1.1, 1252a5), which 1.2 repeats, saying that the city is a "complete community" (κοινωνία τέλειος, 1252b28). At least two things characterize the city or, if one likes, show by their presence that a human group has arrived at the level of the city. The first is that the community has achieved what Aristotle calls "nearly or complete self-sufficiency" (1252b28), an idea that will be clarified in the next chapter. The second is that the city allows its citizens to lead a "happy life," that is, to achieve happiness, the ethical end that they cannot achieve except in a city.

There is a great deal to say about Aristotle's idea of happiness, even if we limit ourselves to what concerns his political philosophy, but for now we need only make some general remarks. Happiness is a state of perfection that thus has a natural tendency to endure if nothing external prevents. Aristotle is not at the point of thinking, as the Stoics did, that nothing and nobody could tear away happiness from the sage, but we see that he is on the road to that point. The most important for our concerns about the city is that this perfection that is happiness can only come to a perfect person. Person or thing, since Aristotle speaks, as we have seen, of the "happy city." Aristotle will again take up the question of the identity and difference between the happiness of the individual and the happiness of the city in *Politics* book 7. "Perfect" means excellent or virtuous. Thus, it is the same for happiness as for virtue: Aristotle thinks that perfect happiness cannot belong completely to those who do not have perfect virtues, and if he does not say so explicitly for women and children, he has more to say in the case of slaves. We will see that in more detail when we talk about slavery. In any case, the happiness that slaves may gain is not political happiness, that of citizens of a city with good laws. As for animals, the two passages in the *Ethics* in which he refuses to grant them happiness[7] would be interesting to comment on, since it is because of the fact that, contrary to human beings, they do not participate at all in the divine that animals cannot be happy. Aristotle seems to accept the etymology, and doubtless the popular conception, of happiness: *eudaimonia* (εὐδαιμονία), the term translated by "happiness," is made up of the prefix *eu*, "good, correct," and a form derived from *daimon* (δαίμων), which generally designates a divinity of a lower rank than that of the gods, but in Aristotle the adjective δαιμόνιος is normally the synonym of θεῖος, "divine." Aristotle thus endorses the idea that happiness comes from a god, but from the god that is within us. This accords completely with the well-known Aristotelian doctrine that happiness "in the first and perfect sense" is, as the *Nicomachean Ethics* (10.8, 1178b7) says, contemplative happiness. Life lived according to ethical virtue is happy only "in a secondary degree" (1178a9).[8]

The passages that mention "happiness" (εὐδαιμονία) and the "happy life" (εὖ ζῆν) do not provide much of a clue to any difference in meaning between the two expressions. Aristotle seems to reserve the expression "happy life" for life in a city, and the word "happiness" for individuals, whether citizens or not, but with exceptions.[9] I leave it to those wiser than I to say more.

Let us return for a moment to the inhabitants of the city who are not citizens, women, children, slaves, to which we must add foreigners. There is a fundamental point there that we will find again, and about which we will speak more precisely, in that in a system that functions with hierarchically ordered parts, the excellence of each part is proportionate to its task. That is what is said in the very important passage (among others) *Politics* 1.13, one of the not very numerous passages in which Aristotle speaks of the relationship between women and men: in regard to "excellences of character all should partake of them, but only in such manner and degree as is required for the fulfillment of his or her

---

7. *Nicomachean Ethics* 10.8, 1178b23; *Eudemian Ethics* 1.7, 1217a24.

8. The question of the difference between contemplative happiness and active happiness is so important, and so difficult, that I will analyze the texts devoted to this question in a later chapter.

9. Thus, in *Politics* 3.9, 1281a1, where he writes, "A city is the union of families and villages in a perfect and self-sufficing life, by which we mean a happy and honorable life" (τὸ ζῆν εὐδαιμόνως καὶ καλῶς).

function" (1260a15). Thus, there would be a courage proper to a woman, which is not the "courage of a leader" but the "courage of a subordinate" (1260a23). We can take a further and crucial step, of which we will find again the effect later on, by remarking that this unequal attribution of excellences (virtues) is needed by Nature to accomplish the tasks that she assigns to members of various communities. And then another step: it is thus just and natural that inferiors work to achieve the blossoming, specifically happiness, of their superiors, even if it costs them some unpleasantness. Just and natural, that is, good and advantageous for all, we will come back to that in a more precise way, and more dramatic, in the case of slavery.

Another point about the relationships between the city and happiness. In order to show clearly that the city is the highest human society, Aristotle asserts that with the city a change in level is brought into operation. While other natural communities have the goal of satisfying needs, even if their appearance is not explained mainly by these needs, the city emerges from this horizon, because happiness is not on the level of "need." Certainly, members of a family can be happy, even if they don't live in a city. But this familial happiness belongs to those happinesses that I have just now spoken about that are incomplete because not political. And at the same time, the same goes for the virtues, which are for Aristotle, as for many other ancient philosophers, the main condition for happiness. The courage, temperance, justice that can occur in a family are only truncated versions of true courage, true temperance, and true justice, which can occur only in relationships among *citizens*. That shows us, again and in a more exact way, that politics is both the necessary condition for a true ethics—barbarians, for example, who live in families and tribes, do not have truly and completely ethical relationships, just as slaves doubtless do not experience true happiness—and the space where this ethics applies. In fact, happiness is, as the beginning of the *Nicomachean Ethics* reminds us, the goal of ethics. Ethics and politics have the same end, and this shows that they do not form two different sciences. In contrast, politics and strategy do not have the same end, even if the goal of the second is subordinated to the end of the first, which is architectonic for strategy.

The fact that the city in a way rises above the sphere of need doubtless does not prevent the city from being better than a village at satisfying certain needs of its members. Anyway, the city was founded on a logic of need. On this topic Aristotle provides a very nice description of the conjunction of the two processes. Fundamentally it is not because it would be useful that people merge several villages into one city, but because they have a natural political tendency. Similarly, it's not fundamentally because they are looking for sexual pleasure that animals engage in sexual intercourse, but because they have a natural tendency to reproduce themselves. But their *intention*, when they are looking for a partner, is obviously to have pleasure. Similarly, the intention of people founding a city was not to rise above the sphere of need: they found a city to live better (cf. 1252b30). But once the city has been founded, the citizens can obtain, as a *bonus*, access to a "happy life." This is a ruse of Nature that uses human need to lead people to bring about their natural tendencies, in this case their political tendency. People found the city that will bring them happiness when they do not yet have *any idea* of this happiness.

The explanatory order is thus as follows: endowed by nature with familial and political tendencies, man finds that it is also advantageous to obey this tendency. That is why one may think that it was utility that pushed human beings to make families and cities, as Aristotle says when he writes in the *Nicomachean Ethics*, reporting on the general opinion that is assuredly not his, "it is thought that the political community both came together originally and to endure for the sake of advantage (of its members)" (8.9, 1160a11). Similarly, we read in the lines preceding this passage that it is in view of the advantage of all that people join together to travel as a group. We have there precisely what Aristotle refuses to do, namely, to put all human associations on the same level, with various structural differences—the size of the group, the duration, and so on— but a group of travelers does not exist by nature, because man is not a "naturally traveling animal."

But we must not misinterpret what was said about the relationships between the city and happiness. It would, in fact, be equally false to understand that it is by living in a city that people *make the experience* of a happiness of which they previously had no idea. What Aristotle means to say, as our analysis of the last part of *Politics* 1.2 will show, is that it is because they have a natural capacity for complete happiness that people see themselves endowed by nature with a political tendency. Without a city, in fact, they cannot *actualize* this natural ability. But this explanatory pattern, which shows Nature providing living things with traits and tendencies that they are able to use to their advantage, is a characteristic of Aristotelian biology. As, furthermore, "political" is, as we have seen, a biological characteristic, we will have to turn to biology, as *Politics* 1.2 invites us to do. Only the reader versed in Aristotle's biology can elucidate the signification of that famous formula that makes man a "naturally political animal." So, we indeed have here an effect of the "biological turn" in our reading of the *Politics*.

"Man as a Political Animal in Aristotle"

In a 1980 article, translated into English in 1991 with this title, Wolfgang Kullmann has demonstrated this thesis and considerably advanced the interpretation of this crucial point of Aristotle's political philosophy.[10] He recalls correctly that "political" is one of the properties that Aristotle attributes to certain animals in his biological treatises. The *History of Animals*, in fact, when it divides animals into their various characteristics, calls "political" those animals that not only live together (in that respect political animals are differentiated from solitary animals), but also achieve a "common work," which differentiates them from animals that are simply gregarious and only live side by side. Thus, bees are political animals, while eagles are solitary, and sheep are only gregarious (*HA* 1.1, 488a2). Everything seems to encourage us to explain the "political" character of man in a way that one explains that a living thing is endowed by Nature with a determined characteristic. One finds then that the characteristic "political" not only does not enter into the definition of the species "man," and Kullmann correctly criticizes those who speak of "the definition of man as political animal," but, according to the *History of Animals*, it is not even a characteristic proper to man. As, on the other hand, we cannot think that man is political accidentally, in the sense that he could be political at some times and not at others, it remains that "political" is what Aristotelian terminology calls a "per se accident," that is, a property that really does belong per se to a subject, without being a part of its essence. In strict Aristotelian epistemological orthodoxy, per se accidents are the proper objects of scientific demonstration, which demonstrates neither essences nor accidental properties. At first sight, it would be necessary to think that the famous passage in *Politics* 1.2, 1253a7, means that man

---

10. Wolfgang Kullmann, "Der Mensch als politisches Lebewesen bei Aristoteles," *Hermes* 108, no. 4 (1980): 419–443, revised version 1998, 334–363; English translation in *A Companion to Aristotle's "Politics,"* ed. David Keyt and Fred D. Miller (Oxford: Blackwell, 1991), 94–117.

is "*more* political than any bee" and not that he is "political *rather than* any bee," the two senses being possible in Greek,[11] since bees are political too, but human beings are so to a superior degree.

The *History of Animals*, the longest Aristotelian treatise to come down to us, offers a group of observations about animals that has remained unequaled until the modern epoch. In it, animals are approached from four directions, "their ways of life, their activities, their character, and their parts" (1.1, 487a10), "political" being a way of life (487b32). What is called Aristotelian teleology notably consists of showing that Nature has, from all eternity, provided each living species with organs, functions, abilities, and relations with its environment such that the relationship between the advantages and disadvantages that it offers to each species gives that species a survival niche in which it can exist forever. To do this, Nature, says Aristotle, proceeds as when one gives a flute to the person who knows how to play it: she furnishes various living things with the physical, psychological, and behavioral instruments from which they are able to profit. Giving fins to a bird or lungs to a fish would be to give them something "in vain," but one of Aristotle's great teleological principles is precisely that "Nature does nothing in vain." Thus, on a point as precise as it is famous, human beings did not become intelligent by exercising their manual dexterity, as Anaxagoras thought, but they have hands because they alone are able to use them: "Now it is the opinion of Anaxagoras that the possession of these hands is the cause of man being the most intelligent. But it is more rational to suppose that man has hands because of his superior intelligence" (*PA* 4.10, 687a8).

Nothing prevents us, indeed on the contrary, of applying this pattern to politics. Responding, without naming it, to the myth of Protagoras who imagined that Prometheus first and then Zeus had to intervene to prevent human beings, lacking the means of survival, of becoming extinct, Aristotle, in the same passage of the *Parts of Animals* about the hand, shows that the hand is, in a way, many organs at the same time—talon, hoof, horn, spear, and sword (687b3)—and thus that Nature has provided human beings with a tool of survival that they can use, precisely because they are more intelligent than the other animals. Nature has not, contrary to the claims of the Protagoras myth, been forced to "correct" an early

---

11. The double sense of μᾶλλον was noted above in relation to a passage in Plato's *Statesman*.

defective version of a living species, because she has given to all from the start the means of surviving forever. The same should be true of the "political" characteristic. Eagles or sheep, in contrast, have no use of politics, because they would not be able to use that property, since they do not work in common with their fellows for a common goal.

It is neither experience, imitation, nor need that makes people political, but Nature who gives them this characteristic at birth because they are able to use it to fulfill their functions, first among them to survive as well as possible, and to use their abilities, of which the most complete would be their ability to be happy. Obviously, that does not mean that people have not learned their aptitude for politics, just as some birds have to learn to fly. But to learn, in this case, is not to acquire something new, but to actualize a potentiality already naturally present in the animal. We will see this explanatory pattern at work in the case of language.

In fact, after having shown that the real reason that the city is natural and man a political animal by nature, namely, that the city is, precisely, the *nature* of antecedent communities and individuals, at least free male individuals, who compose the city, Aristotle then goes into this "political animal" characteristic in a completely different way, through the analysis of language. Aristotle uses the same sort of reasoning that we have just presented: the city is natural because Nature makes nothing in vain, but she has given language to human beings, and language is made for presenting values, the advantageous, the good, the just, and their contraries. But having values like that in common is what makes a city, and also a family. It's not exactly a scientific demonstration here of the naturalness of the city (because it is not because people have ethical values that the city is natural), but what Aristotle calls, in the last chapter of the *Prior Analytics*, a "sign." Thus, following the example that he offers at 70a13, the fact that a woman is lactating is a "sign" that she gave birth, but it is not the cause, because it is not due to lactation that she gave birth. That people are ethical beings *shows* that city life is natural.

In the passage we are discussing, 1253a7–1253a19, the initial problem is that of communication between living beings, that is, of signification: Aristotle uses the word σημεῖον ("sign") at 1253a11. Animals—all or some of them, Aristotle is not precise about that here—experience pleasure and pain because they are endowed with sensation. Animals other than human beings, and here Aristotle probably means to limit his remark to *political animals* or at least gregarious animals, show to each other the pleasure and pain that they experience by their cries (their "voice," φωνή).[12] It is probable that this semantic need of animals comes from the fact that they live together, and that a solitary animal hardly needs to signify its pleasure or pain. Human beings also cry from pleasure and pain.[13] Cries thus serve all political animals, and gregarious animals too (1253a8), to express what one may call their "vital values."

But human beings can also talk, that is, they are able to express pragmatic values (advantageous and disadvantageous) and ethical values (just and unjust, good and bad). There too Aristotle may be contrasted to certain other philosophers who had something to say about the origin of language, whom we can see, following Guthrie, in Diodorus of Siculus a common and vulgarized version. According to this approach, widely shared even in our own time, it was necessity that pushed human beings to create a language in order to communicate with each other and thus assure their survival. This solution, falsely obvious, in fact poses more problems than it solves, because it runs up against the question of proceeding from simple to complex, a step that is vulnerable to the Parmenidean critique. This difficulty did not disappear with Aristotle, since, when they have encountered empiricist approaches like that of Condillac, linguists like Noam Chomsky have found it necessary to provide human beings with a "universal grammar" preceding all instruction.

Aristotle thus remains faithful both to his "eternalist" approach and to his teleological explanation of existence. As human beings are the only

---

12. "Whereas mere voice is but an indication of pleasure or pain, and is therefore found in animals (for their nature attains to the perception of pleasure and pain and the intimation of them to one another, and no further), the power of speech is intended to set forth the advantageous and disadvantageous, and therefore likewise the just and the unjust" (1253a10).

13. This is a matter of a general rule to which there are, as usual in Aristotle's zoology, some small exceptions. Staying with eagles, paradigmatically solitary animals, in *History of Animals* 9.32, 618b31, it is said that the "hare-killing" eagle is εὔφημος, "for it neither whimpers nor screams." *Euphemos* could mean either "keeps silent" or "makes sounds of good omen" (only). In contrast, the "mountain-stork eagle" "has all the bad qualities of the other species, and none of the good ones" (618b35). In some manuscripts it is called ὑπαιετός and in others γυπαιετός, "half-eagle" or "gyp-eagle"; "it is always hungry, and cries and whines" (619a3), though Aristotle does not tell us that this is in order to indicate its suffering to other animals. When Aristotle presents exceptions to his own rules, he shows us that he is giving us a true biology.

animals endowed with perception of ethical values—something that Aristotle expresses with an insistence that verges on pleonasm: "It is a *proper to* man that he *alone* has any sense of good and evil, of just and just, and the like" (1253a15)—they must have a means of mutually sharing them. This means is language. Thus, it seems that we are still in the frame of the teleological approach that Aristotle uses in biology and that, in the present instance, he applies to the human ethical and political values that are the basis for cities: because Nature gives organs and abilities to those who know how to use them, she furnishes human beings with the ability to speak, and not beasts, because human beings alone are able to use this ability, while beasts, because they do not have ethical values to communicate mutually, have enough with the cries for that which they want to express, namely, the vital values of what is agreeable and painful. Thus, Nature does nothing in vain.

In order to *incarnate*, in a way, the possibility of language, Nature has to dispose the human body in a certain way. To do that she has anticipated an intermediate level between the voice that human beings and many animals possess, and language: it is "speech" (διάλεκτος). What distinguishes "speech" from "voice" is not signification, since voice signifies, as our passage in the *Politics*[14] repeats, but the fact that it is composed of articulate sounds: "Speech is the articulation of voice by the tongue" (*HA* 4.9, 535a31). It cannot be totally trifling that Aristotle visibly hesitates on the question of knowing if only human beings are endowed with speech. Thus, in the *History of Animals*, he successively asserts that at least certain birds use speech (4.9, 536a21), then, a few lines later, that speech is "proper" to human beings (536b1), then finishes by finding in various animals, beyond the limits of the human species, "articulate sounds that one may consider as speech" (536b11). We see here again an attitude that we have already met, for example on the subject of happiness: speech is not *fully* possessed by any species other than human; in other animals, it is imperfect. It is not necessary to invent hypotheses about a text with distinct chronological layers.

But it seems that, in the case of speech, Nature's practice of giving tools only to those who know how to use them seems to be verified. She gives to human beings, beyond lungs and larynx that are necessary for production of voice, teeth and tongue that permit them to articulate

---

14. Cf. *De Anima* 2.8, 420b33: "voice is a sound with meaning, and is not the result of any impact of the breath as in coughing."

sounds. When, then, Aristotle writes in the *Generation of Animals,* "Voice is the material for language" (5.7, 786b21), it might be more precise to replace "language" with "speech." But obviously, in being the material for speech, voice is also material for language. Several passages in the *History of Animals* and *Parts of Animals* explain the matter: the human tongue is soft, sensitive, and large. One may notice, following Robert Bolton,[15] that as in all or most of the explanations bringing together a final cause and another cause, the material or moving cause associated with the final cause does not reveal a *necessary* connection, in that this arrangement of lips and teeth "is convenient" to permit the articulation of sounds, but other arrangements could have been used to obtain the same result; this is in fact the case in parrots, which have neither teeth nor lips but do have articulated speech.

The case of parrots also shows that there is a bit of "play" in Aristotle's teleological explanations, something that will not surprise any reader of the biological corpus. Because in their case Aristotle does not show that Nature does not give them speech in vain, since their articulated voice does not seem to respond to any function that cries alone could not have fulfilled. At the same time, the liver has no purpose, the triton is a sort of monster, many characteristics are harmful to those who have them, and so on. There are cases where certain animals prove capable of doing something that has no use to them, and that is true for parrots. Aristotle's entire natural philosophy, to the extent that it concerns the sublunary world, constructs propositions that are true "for the most part" and not "always." But this relative indeterminism is the most pronounced in the zoological branch of natural philosophy. This plasticity of teleological principles in a way brings zoology closer to the practical science of politics. In both areas of investigation, in any case, relationships that are brought to light have to accommodate a certain number of exceptions.

Thus, the situation is as follows: Nature gives living things other than human beings the *biological* means of speaking, speech, and of living in society, since certain animals have a political tendency. But only human beings use speech to communicate pragmatic and ethical values, and only human beings live in *political communities.* When Kullmann writes that

---

15. Robert Bolton, "The Material Cause: Matter and Explanation in Aristotle's Natural Science," in *Aristotelische Biologie. Intentionem, Methoden, Ergebnisse,* ed. W. Kullmann and S. Föllinger (Stuttgart: Franz Steiner, 1997), 97–124. I will refer more precisely to Bolton's theses below.

"the political impulse of man is genetically ingrained in him,"[16] he surely is right, but we must add this: there are two ways of being political, to live together and produce a common work, which is the way shared by all political animals, and to live together and produce a common work within a city, the manner proper to human beings. In fact, Aristotle says in the *Politics* that there is no city of animals, nor of slaves, "for they have no share in happiness or in a life based on choice" (3.9, 1280a32). All the same, there are two ways of articulating speech, the parrot way, in which words do not signify anything for them, or at least, no more than their cries, the other that of human beings whose speech signifies more than a simple cry would signify, namely, pleasure and pain, but also pragmatic and ethical values.

The last stage in Aristotle's argument comes at 1253a18, with a sentence that is ambiguous in Greek (ἡ δὲ τούτων κοινωνία ποιεῖ οἰκίαν καὶ πόλιν): literally, "the community of these makes a family and a city," but the "these" could refer to the shared values, or to the people who share those values. Newman,[17] followed by most interpreters, leans toward the first reading, because a community of people doesn't *make* a city, it *would be* a city, a rather weak argument, to tell the truth, and in any case this question is not important for us here. The passage at 1253a7 mentioned above should doubtless be understood, finally, as saying that man is "political *rather than* any bee," and not that man is "*more* political than any bee," because Aristotle distinguishes two senses, a basic sense and a full sense, of the word "political," so one should call "political" the individual who fulfills the conditions of the full sense, that is, to live in a city, *rather than* the one who lives only in a group, accomplishing a common task.

More precisely, Nature has given to human beings *human* speech in order to allow them to communicate to each other pragmatic and ethical values, and *human* politicalness to allow them to live a happy life. These values and this life are human specificities and cannot be considered as biological realities, that is, dependent on a causality that is ultimately organic. Between the politicalness of animals and that of human beings there is the entire machinery of deliberation and choice. We see this more generally in the way that Aristotle attributes to certain animals capacities that, at first sight, seem specifically human. That is the case with the pri-

---

16. Kullmann, "Man as a Political Animal in Aristotle," 99.

17. Newman, *The Politics of Aristotle*, vol. 2, note in the place cited.

mary intellectual virtue in ethics, prudence (φρόνησις): the *Nicomachean Ethics* tells us, in fact, that "some of the lower animals have prudence, those that are found to have a power of foresight with regard to their own life" (6.6, 1141a26). In an article devoted to animal prudence, Jean-Louis Labarrière provides a subtle analysis of the passages in which Aristotle attributes to certain animals not only prudence, but even those faculties that we know he elsewhere reserves to human beings, like thought (νόησις: cf. "dianoetic intelligence" at *HA* 8.1, 588a23), calculation (λογισμός), and even *logos* and wisdom, since in the *History of Animals* a kind of spider is called the "wisest" (σοφώτατον) (9.39, 623a8).[18] If one of the goals of Labarrière's article is to show that one must go beyond a simply metaphorical approach to animal prudence, nevertheless it remains that there is a strong demarcation separating animal prudence and human prudence: as animal prudence cannot rely on either judgment or deliberation, "it presides over no praxis."[19]

The prudence of animals is surely a proof of the excellence of Nature in that it demonstrates the adaptation of animals to their environments. Take, for example, *History of Animals* 9.29, 618ff., where Aristotle writes:

> The cuckoo seems to act with prudence in the disposal of its progeny; the fact is, the mother-cuckoo is quite conscious of her own cowardice and of the fact that she could never help her young one in an emergency; and so, for the security of the young one, she makes of him a suppositious child in an alien nest. The truth is, this bird is preeminent in the way of cowardice; it allows itself to be pecked at by little birds, and flies away from their attacks.

---

18. Jean-Louis Labarrière, "De la Phronèsis animale," in *Biologie, logique et métaphysique chez Aristote*, ed. Daniel Devereux and Pierre Pellegrin (Paris: CNRS, 1990), 405–428. Cf. this important passage from the *History of Animals*: "Just as in man we find skill, wisdom, and sagacity, so in certain animals there exists some other natural capacity akin to these. The truth of this statement will be the more clearly apprehended if we have regard to the phenomenon of childhood; for in children may be observed traces and seeds of what will one day be settled habits, though psychologically a child hardly differs for the time being from an animal, so that one is quite justified in saying that, as regards man and animals, certain psychical qualities are identical to one another, while others resemble, and others are analogous, to each other" (8.1, 588a29).

19. Labarrière, "De la Phronèsis animale," 415.

We should not allow ourselves to be fooled by the manner of expression in this passage; it could give the impression that the cuckoo, realizing that it would be unable to feed its young, adopts a "prudent" strategy to safeguard them. In fact, the situation is like in those passages where Aristotle seems to ascribe intentions to Nature. When, for example, he says that "the class of fish is prolific because Nature opposes the losses with the number" (*GA* 3.4, 755a31), that in no way means that Nature, having analyzed the situation and deliberated, has *decided* to compensate the large losses that fish experience from the actions of their predators by a greater fecundity. In fact, fecundity has been given to fish from all eternity according to the relationship between advantages and disadvantages discussed above. It's the same for the cuckoo: the disadvantage that consists of its "cowardice," a colorful and anthropocentric way to describe the biological character of the cuckoo, is compensated by its "prudent" behavior consisting of squatting in the nest of others.

Natural drives that assure the survival of an animal produce behaviors but not *actions* in the primary sense of that term, or to speak Greek, not *practice*. In Aristotelian terminology, an action (πρᾶξις) in the proper sense of the word is an act done voluntarily by a free subject, which has no other end than itself, contrary to a production (ποίησις) that has as its object a product.[20] Thus animals do not accomplish actions in the full sense of the word. For Aristotle, the properly human form of politicalness differs from animal politicalness by its *effectuation*. He certainly does not think of animals as mechanisms whose behaviors would be absolutely determined and predictable. Not only can animals learn, like the elephants that learned to bow before the Great King, but they can also deviate from the normal realization of their normal abilities like the little birds that, deprived of their parents, learn to sing the songs of other species.[21] Nevertheless it remains that this vital plasticity in no way blurs

---

20. See, for example, *Nicomachean Ethics* 6.5, 1140b6. I noted above the difficulty that Plato seems to have had in distinguishing between the ideas of action and production.

21. *History of Animals* 4.9, 536b14: "Of little birds, some sing a different note from the parent birds, if they have been removed from the nest and have heard other birds singing; and a mother nightingale has been observed to give lessons in singing to a young bird, thus suggesting that speech and voice are not identical by nature but can be artificially trained." As we have seen above, Aristotle sometimes attributes to certain animals "articulate sounds that one may consider to be speech" (*HA* 4.9, 536b11). He is thinking particularly of bird song, which he distinguishes from their cries. Perhaps we have there a lesser degree of articulation than in the case of parrots. For the elephants that bow, see *History of Animals* 9.46, 630b20.

the essential fact: living in a society that realizes a common work is, for bees, an innate vital characteristic that is indispensable to their survival and thus comes about automatically. It's one of the many examples of the Aristotelian thesis that "nature does not deliberate."[22] Animals do not produce political actions. But it is not the same for people. In our *Politics* 1.2, Aristotle makes an often-quoted remark that "a social instinct is implanted in all men by nature, and yet he who first founded a city was the greatest of benefactors" (1253a29). This remark is true both in general and for every individual city, each of which were in fact founded at a given time by one or several individuals. The foundation of the first city was assuredly a practical activity. But there is in contrast no bee that founded the first hive.

This can lead us to take part in an old quarrel. Eduard Meyer, at the beginning of a work dating from 1884,[23] claims that the analysis of the formation of the city from families and villages is only conceptual, not at all historical, because the city is the original form of human association, at least in the Greek world, and thus it could not have, for Aristotle, a historically prepolitical phase. Maurice Defourny thinks, on the contrary, that for Aristotle the organization of cities appeared only after a long period of time during which they did not exist yet,[24] and on this exact point he is right, as the last cited passage of the *Politics* shows, as well as other remarks in *Politics* 1.2: people at first lived dispersed, then monarchies appeared, then cities governed by kings, then, as Aristotle will say in later books, the two really existing constitutions in his time, namely, democracy and oligarchy, with some tyrannical interludes.[25]

But on the other hand, isn't Meyer right about the family? In fact, there is no prefamilial stage of human society, and in the case of the family we are much closer to animal nature than in that of the city. It is true that family solidarity rests on a binding affection that includes something biological, and Aristotle, like every Greek, was surely sensitive to the opposition between family and city such as that described in Sophocles's *Antigone*. But if one may think that Aristotle believes that human beings would rediscover the family *immediately* after each cataclysm,

---

22. Cf. *Physics* 2.8, 199b27; *Parts of Animals* 2.13, 657b1.

23. Eduard Meyer, *Geschichte des Altertums*, 5th ed. (Darmstadt: Wissenschaftliche Buchgesellschaft, 1953), I.1, 11ff.

24. Maurice Defourny, *Aristotle. Études sur la 'Politique'* (Paris: Beauchesne, 1932), 383ff.

25. Cf., for example, *Politics* 3.14, 1285b13; 3.15, 1286b8; 4.10, 1313a3.

the actualization of the human natural tendency to form a family differs greatly from the operation of animal impulses. That's what a passage of the *Eudemian Ethics* says, when Aristotle glosses the expression "economic animal," that is, "familial," which he applies to human beings, by writing that "man's unions are not . . . formed with any chance partner" (7.10, 1242a24), understanding this as a difference from other animals. There is among human beings a "community,"[26] and "a sort of justice, even if there is no city." The fact that rational calculation, that is, taking account of advantages and disadvantages, can also regulate human reproduction and the choice that one makes of one's slaves does not obliterate the fact that human beings have in themselves a tendency to reproduce independent of their reflective choice and a natural function of master (or slave). Rational calculation here plays the role of a cause associated with the essential cause (the innate tendency), as is also the case, as we have seen, with the attractiveness of sexual pleasure. Nevertheless, it remains that this associated cause contributes strongly to shape the human family. As for animals, they do not form families in the true sense. To put it another way, if one means to understand economics, in the etymological and Aristotelian sense of the word, as a science, which is entirely legitimate from Aristotle's point of view, one must rank it alongside politics among the *practical* sciences.[27] We should add that, as in the case of the city, the human family does not have the same form throughout the human species. Thus *Politics* 1.2 notes that the barbarians treat their women as slaves. Nevertheless, they form families. Animal societies do not experience such cultural variations.

All this permits us to take up again a question that was left to later. It's a matter of the interpretation of the sentence that says that "it is evident that the city exists by nature and that man is naturally a political animal" (1253a1). Some interpreters have thought that Aristotle meant to say that it is because the city is natural that man is naturally political.

---

26. Even if at *History of Animals* 8.1, 588b33, Aristotle says that certain animals terminate their "community" with their young once they are able to take care of themselves, the term "community" seems to be properly applied only to human associations. It's still the difference between the full sense and a derived and weaker sense.

27. Economics is doubtless, from Aristotle's point of view, and contrary to ethics, a "true" science that is not absorbed by politics, even if politics is architectonic in relation to economics. But we have seen above some hesitations, or at least one hesitation, by Aristotle on this point.

Possibly that is the case with Trevor Saunders, who, in his commented translation of the first two books of the *Politics*, understands the adjective "political" applied to man as meaning "fit for the state," "state" translating *polis*.[28] But it is more likely that man is political even if he does not live in a city, because the city, as natural as it is, is an artifact constructed by people, while it is not the city that makes these natural beings that are men. It is certain that people who have a political calling but have not had occasion to exercise it, would find such an occasion in becoming citizens of a city. But, on the other hand, as David Keyt notes,[29] it is not the fact that man has a natural tendency that entails that the city exists by nature. Keyt also remarks that it is not necessary that the product of a natural tendency itself exists by nature; thus, poetry or virtue are indeed the results of natural tendencies without themselves existing by nature. We have seen that the city is natural because it is the *telos* of prior communities like the family (1252b31). What neither Saunders nor Keyt has clearly seen is Aristotle's way of reasoning, as we have presented it in the preceding pages.

By nature, man has a political tendency, that is a tendency to lead, if nothing prevents—and God knows that there are many things that may prevent, beginning from ethical ineptitude for being a citizen, as is the case with barbarians—the life of a citizen. This life of a citizen is, in fact, advantageous for a person, notably in that it alone can assure him complete happiness. It therefore conforms to the Aristotelian conception of teleological Nature that this Nature gives people adequate means for realizing this natural tendency. This means is the city. That is enough to assure the naturalness of the city. Thus it is man, in that he confronts the project of becoming happy, who demands the city, just as fish, because they confront the task of surviving in water, call for natural means of moving easily in this medium, namely, fins. It's with this same explanatory schema that one can also really establish the naturalness of the family, a question that we have left hanging.

---

28. Trevor J. Saunders, *Aristotle Politics Books I and II* (Oxford: Clarendon Press, 1995), 69. Similarly, Richard Bodéüs translates *politikon* as "made for political community" in a passage cited above (*EN* 8.14, 1162a17) or "destined for the city" at 1.5, 1097b11. At 9.9, 1179b18, he even adds a capital letter "a being made for the City."

29. David Keyt, "Three Basic Theorems in Aristotle's *Politics*," in *A Companion to Aristotle's "Politics,"* ed. David Keyt and Fred D. Miller (Oxford: Blackwell, 1991), 126.

I have to make a brief remark here about my own vocabulary. I have been using the terms "man," "human being," and "person," to translate the same Greek word ἄνθρωπος, which, in contrast to the word ἀνήρ that designates a human male and is found at least five times in the *Politics*, is not applied specifically to human beings of the masculine sex. But to translate is not the same as establishing a biunivocal lexicon of the two languages. Aristotle affirms explicitly that there is no specific difference between male and female, and thus between man and woman, though there is indeed a relationship of contrariety between male and female, and a specific difference is a difference between contraries (cf. *Metaphysics* 10.9, 1058a31). Nevertheless, as we have seen and will see again, men are ethically superior to women, and I will come back in an appendix to the next chapter to the causes of that superiority. As we have also seen, feminine virtues are imperfect copies of masculine virtues. If we had to deal with this subject in its own right, we would doubtless be led to show that the difference between man and woman is not always described in the same way, because sometimes the differences are very large, and sometimes minimal.

Staying with the strict sense of the words, the famous phrase ὁ ἄνθρωπος φύσει πολιτικὸν ζῷον should be translated "the human being is a political animal by nature." If bees and ants are political animals, could one think that Aristotle would refuse that property to women? Well, even without an excessive dose of paradox, one must respond to that question in the affirmative. Women, in fact, cannot be concerned in the sort of politicalness of bees as we have identified that above, but, if they are political, it would be in the full sense that men are, that is, as members of a political community. But women are not members of a political community, or, as we will see more precisely in a later chapter what that means, they are not *political* parts of the political community. So, we should translate ἄνθρωπος as "man." When, on the other hand, Aristotle tells us that ἄνθρωποι have language in the full sense of the word, it is surely necessary to translate ἄνθρωποι by "human beings."

Our analysis of the natural character of the city and the politicalness of man in Aristotle is not without repercussions on his epistemology. We have, in fact, in this case the application in politics of an explanatory scheme from natural science, and particularly biology. But this explanatory scheme has, one may say, one foot in natural science and the other in practical science. Like the good mother that she is for living things, Nature gives to human beings language and to men the politicalness that they are able to use. And, from this point of view, the human political urge is part of what one may call the "biological toolbox" of men. Doubtless this trait is related to other natural human characteristics, like the fact that they are incapable of surviving alone, since Nature provides each living thing what it needs to survive. But this biological urge is actualized in a *practice*, that is, in actions that are not uniquely determined, or even principally, by what we would call laws of nature. As a result, if it is true as Aristotle says that it is the sharing of ethical values, and possibly pragmatic values, that *makes* a city, then the political urge of men does not automatically make them citizens, nor does it automatically establish a city. Nevertheless, they have a *political* character, including outside all cities, the same as they have feet, even if they do not walk. In fact, Aristotle makes clear at *Politics* 1.2, 1253a3, that "he who by nature and not by mere accident is without a city is either a wretch or above humanity."

This is not really a subversion of the great Aristotelian principle that different domains belong to different sciences, for it is not surprising that man, both a living thing and an ethical and political being, belongs to *both* biology and ethics. On the contrary, this great division is reaffirmed and, in a way refounded, and we must firmly resist the temptation to make of Aristotle an ancestor of sociobiology. Surely Aristotle thinks that if people were not able to use language to communicate their ethical values, Nature would not have given them the physical means to produce language, but language is not a cry continued by other means. Similarly, ethical values are not vital needs continued by other means, which is a basic thesis of all sociobiology, and at 1253a14, Aristotle carefully avoids describing the advantageous and disadvantageous, the just and unjust, as sophisticated forms of the pleasant and painful.[30] Similarly, at a more general level, there is no biological explanation of human ethical choices nor of the birth and history of cities. Nature is satisfied with giving that which is certainly not a small thing, the physical conditions necessary for ethical development in human beings and for the birth and history of cities. One of the consequences of that, well seen by Kullmann, is that as natural as it is, the city is not a natural *substance* (οὐσία), and Aristotle strongly resists the temptation to "naturalize" the city to the point where he would make of it a natural organism.

---

30. On the other hand, the just and unjust seem indeed to flow from the advantageous and disadvantageous: "The power of speech is intended to set forth the expedient and inexpedient, and *therefore likewise* (ὥστε καί) the just and the unjust" (1253a14).

CHAPTER 3

The Endangered Happiness of the City

The City Is Autonomous

We must never forget that foundation of Aristotelian political thought that is always present, even when Aristotle is engaged in analyses that seem to have put aside every idea of value and ethics: the city is the place of *complete* happiness and virtue. Virtue and happiness, as we have recalled, are related as means to end and appear in diverse forms. There is the virtue of a good husband or good wife, and thus a corresponding happiness. "Perhaps there is some element of value contained even in the mere state of being alive, provided that there is not too great an excess on the side of the hardships of life" (*Pol.* 3.6, 1278b25). But it is only with the status of citizen that a man can completely develop his potentialities and, to speak in Hegelian terms, be adequate to his concept. Hegel is in fact one of those who have thought most forcefully the twilight of politics that slightly precedes the tipping point into the era of interior freedom. We have already seen that a complete man will be courageous, moderate, and generous, and not in the way that a woman would be, or a child, or a man considered only as the head of a family. The same goes for freedom, which, still following the Hegelian tradition, we can consider as the decisive point of transformation after Aristotle. Far from exercising his freedom by liberating himself from the external world, as a Stoic sage would do, the Aristotelian citizen lives his freedom as a group of real rights guaranteed by his city. Nothing can constrain him or subjugate him unless his city intervenes, by way of the laws, to erect an obstacle. The citizen is free because his city is free. It seems that in the city of sages of Zeno, in contrast, the freedom of the citizens is primary and the origin of the organization of the city. Thus, one may think, though the testimonies are few, that it is because marriage ties are an attack on the natural freedom of the sage that the institution of marriage does not exist in Zeno's city. We situate ourselves today resolutely in a perspective of this kind, because the modern democratic State is called upon to furnish conditions favorable for the blossoming of each person or the means for families to pursue their own goals, primarily the well-being of their children.

Thus, we will have a better understanding of Aristotle's idea of the perfection of the citizen if we first grasp what makes the perfection of the city. Doubtless we can find in this process a resemblance with the procedure used by Plato in the *Republic*. But it's not because the city is more "legible" than the individual because it is larger that we begin with the city, but because it is prior. That point will be looked at again when we talk about the definitions of the city, the citizen, and the constitution. One of the main characteristics of a natural community is that it is self-sufficient, either completely, or to a large degree. That's what Aristotle calls αὐτάρκεια "autarky." This term, in Greek as in English, has an economic signification of the fact that, as the *Politics* puts it, "to have everything and lack nothing, that is autarky" (7.5, 1326b29). But the concept has, at least in Aristotle, a more developed sense, one that pertains to the description of a city. In this case too, there is a range of several senses of a term in relation to a fundamental sense, so that the autarky of different communities is relative. A family is called autarkic particularly if it can assure by itself the subsistence of its members. But a city is said to have "achieved the status of so to speak complete autarky" (*Pol.* 1.2, 1252b28), which means that it is not only economically independent, but that it also has what one may call political autarky. Aristotle is hardly effusive on this subject, but a passage in *Politics* 7 presents a clarifying distinction. Aristotle says there that a city that does not have sufficient population will not be autarkic, which can be understood in the normal sense of "autarkic" since a city with too few people cannot assure the subsistence of all its citizens. But he adds that a city with too many citizens "is indeed autarkic for indispensable things, like a tribe would be, but not as a city" (7.4, 1326b2ff.). The word "tribe," a slightly unhappy translation, I admit, of the word ἔθνος, designates a kind of community that can be numerically important, whose way of life is not necessarily "primitive" and possibly even very sophisticated, but not regulated by *political* rules, that is, by an ensemble of known laws all organized into a constitution. Certain Greeks of Aristotle's time lived in tribes, and that was the case with all the barbarians, unable as they were to arrive at a political level of social life. We will see the reasons below.

Two passages can help us understand what this political autarky includes, beyond economic self-sufficiency. At *Politics* 4.4, 1291a8ff., Aristotle proposes the following rationale: the city is autarkic, but "that which is a slave is not autarkic," therefore "it is impossible that something that is a slave by nature deserves to be called a city," which means that doubtless it could be a slave by accident, that is, provisionally, for example following a military defeat. One may suppose that, if this state of affairs lasts too long, the city would eventually lose its character of city. At *Politics* 2.2, 1261b11, it is said that the city is more autarkic than the family and the family than the individual. On the other hand, although the text does not say so, an association larger than a city, or a city that is not really a city because it has too large a population, as the text says explicitly, is, in relation to a real city, less autarkic (it does not have a so to speak "complete autarky"), that is, it enjoys an autarky in a way inferior because it is that of a tribe. Political autarky is thus characterized by independence vis-à-vis the external world, in which we see that economic self-sufficiency obviously plays an important role, but it is far from being sufficient.[1]

In fact, we must read the passage that says that the city is more autarkic than the family and the individual in parallel with the earlier passage in *Politics* 2, which criticizes the Socrates of Plato's *Republic* for saying that a city should try to be as much "one" as possible. Aristotle writes:

> Is it not obvious that a city may at length attain such a degree of unity as to be no longer a city?—since the nature of a city is to be a plurality, and in tending to greater unity, from being a city, it becomes a family, and from being a family, an individual; for the family may be said to be more one than the city, and the individual than the family. So that we ought not to attain this greatest unity even if we could, for it would be the destruction of the city. Again, a city is not made up

---

1. I wonder how Mogens H. Hansen, in *Polis and City-State: An Ancient Concept and Its Modern Equivalent* (Copenhagen: Munksgaard, 1998), could read Aristotle's *Politics* in a way that enabled him to write that "his (Aristotle's) concept of *autarkeia* has two aspects only: economic self-sufficiency . . . and demographic self-sufficiency" (81). Hansen notes correctly that Aristotle does not speak of *autonomia* in relation to the city, and he asserts that "the relationship between the concept of *polis* and that of *autonomia* should be rejected" (81). I'm not as sure as he is about that . . .

only of so many people, but of different kinds of people, for similars do not constitute a city. It is not like a military alliance. (2.2, 1261a16)

Thus, autarky does not presuppose homogeneity, but the harmonious articulation of *specifically* different parts. We may call that the organic integration of the components of the city and see, here too, the traces of Aristotelian social organicism that we noted above, and note that this too distinguishes Aristotle from Plato.

We need to recall here this difference: husband, wife, and slave, are parts of the family, and the family is a part of the city in an organic sense in that, as we saw above, the family achieves its telos, its *nature*, in the city. In a military alliance, in contrast, the city is a party to the alliance as a whole juxtaposed with others without being integrated into an organic unity. Thus, the alliance is not the telos of the city, but the city, or more precisely its preservation, is the telos of the alliance. The importance of size and proportion is relevant here. We saw that a city that grows too big ceases to be a city. That is also the case for a city that is too wealthy. These are examples of the disproportionate city that would be, Aristotle says, like an animal with a foot four cubits (six feet) long and the rest of the body two spans (sixteen inches) (5.3, 1302b36). This is another organicist metaphor.[2]

It seems to me that it is easy to understand what Aristotle means if one provides a brief gloss on the word "organic" used above. Although the words "autarky" and "autarkic" do not appear in the biological treatises,[3]

---

2. Does this conjunction of two theses, the first, in book 2, saying that the city is less unified than the family, and the other, in book 4, that the city is more autarkic than the family, offer grist for Jaeger's mill? The first thesis, located in an "idealist" context, does not in fact have the "organic" character of the second, located in a "realist" book. There are indeed two approaches, one organicist and the other not, but they coexist more than they oppose each other. They are both present in *Politics* 2: "This extreme unification of the city is clearly not good; for a family is more self-sufficient than an individual, and a city than a family" (2.2, 1261b10), which comes to saying that autarky requires diversity.

3. There is a remarkable exception at *Generation of Animals* 4.8, 776b5: "The part above the diaphragm is the part that controls life, while that below is concerned with nourishment and residual matter, in order that animals able to move about may contain within themselves nourishment enough to make them independent (τῆς τροφῆς αὐτάρκεια) when they move from one place to another" (trans. A. Platt).

perhaps we ought to include the idea of autarky in the list of concepts that connect Aristotle's biology to his politics. In fact, the living being illustrates rather well the idea of autarky in its various aspects: "economic," in the first place, as the *Generation of Animals* passage quoted in the note demonstrates, but also "political." For, as Georges Canguilhem writes,

> Biology must therefore first consider the living being as a meaningful being, and its individuality not as an object, but as a term within the order of values. To live is to spread out; it is to organize a milieu starting from a central reference point that cannot itself be referred to without losing its original meaning.[4]

The Greek world of cities is, in fact, an ensemble, a *collection*, of self-referring organisms, each bearing its own values, which depend very much on the current constitution in each city.

In fact, "autarkic" (αὐτάρκης) is often nearly a synonym of "perfect" (τέλειος). God, for example, is "first, eternal, and to the highest degree autarkic," and as he is in good condition (εὖ ἔχει), he is incorruptible and autarkic (cf. *Meta.* 14.4, 1091b16). To be a city in the full sense, a city thus needs to have an autarky that makes it *perfect*. In this state of perfection, in fact, it does not depend on the external world for anything: economically it can, by its own production rounded out by limited exchanges, assure its subsistence; politically, it is not subject to the laws of any other city or any other people; at the level of its spiritual life and its values, it has developed them according to its own genius, taking account of the nature of its constitution, its own history, and of its conception of its place in the world. There is there a major point of Aristotle's political philosophy that will be amply developed below; it rests on an idea that is very original in the history of political thought, that not all cities need to aim at the same sort of excellence, but that depends on the social and ethical status of its body of citizens.

Very soon in the course of our tour through Aristotle's politics we will see that in most cases real cities are unable to arrive at this state of autarky and thus to fulfill their principal ethical function, which is to

---

4. Georges Canguilhem, "Le vivant et son milieu," *La Connaissance de la vie* (Paris: Vrin, 1967), English translation by John Savage, "The Living and Its Milieu," Grey Room (Spring 2001): 21. I have always found in this famous article by Canguilhem a very Aristotelian basis. Cf. for example my introduction to the *Parties des animaux*, 2011.

make its citizens virtuous and happy. *And that is why political science is indispensable*, because it enables the philosopher to assist the legislator in making, or remaking, the city into a machine to produce happiness. But that can happen only when good laws are established, and those depend on a correct constitution, as we will see in detail.

Here too the Stoic sage takes the place of the city by pretending to be himself autarkic. But that is already beginning to germinate, even a little more than that, in Aristotle. In the first place, even if the beginning of book 7 of the *Politics* argues in favor of the involvement of the sage in the life of the city, I have recalled above that the possibility exists for a philosopher to lead a contemplative life liberated from almost any political involvement. Aristotle has no intention of forcing the philosopher to exercise power for the sake of the good of all as Plato does in the *Republic*. Actually, Aristotle has very little to say about the man who chooses the contemplative life to the detriment of an active life, and it is remarkable that he touches on this problem, rather than with reference to the philosopher leading a contemplative life in his ivory tower, in the form of the question of the exceptional man and how the city ought to make use of him. The exceptional man, quite like the contemplative philosopher, comes very close to the divine, and for that reason, tends to leave the political sphere, because there is no city of the gods. In fact, it's impossible, according to the *Nicomachean Ethics*, to imagine among the gods virtues like justice, courage, or liberality, precisely because they are not citizens. Justice: it would be ridiculous to suppose that the gods need to honor contracts; courage: it is difficult to imagine the gods facing dangers for the nobility of the deed; liberality is impossible for them because they have no one to give to (10.8, 1178b10). Similarly, a famous passage, already cited, from *Politics* 1.2, asserts that "the person who is outside the city . . . is either a wretch, or above humanity" (1253a3). But the most significant text for us is *Politics* 3.13, 1284a3. If an individual, and Aristotle adds "or a group of people," worth commenting upon,[5] has virtue so outstanding that it cannot be compared with that of the others (doubtless we should understand here, according to the logic of the addition of virtues proposed in 3.11[6]), then

---

5. If a group of citizens is alone truly virtuous in the city, it is just that that city should be an aristocracy. Doubtless Aristotle has in mind here a group that is both too small to form a political basis for an aristocracy and of a virtue too extraordinary.

6. See below, pp. 200ff.

he or they can no longer be regarded as part of the city, for justice will not be done to the superior, if he is reckoned only as the equal of those who are so far inferior to him in excellence and in political capacity. Such a man may truly be deemed a god among men.

People often think that Epicurus remembered this passage when he wrote, at the end of the *Letter to Menoeceus*, that the sage is "like a god among men." This presupposes that Epicurus had read the *Politics*.[7] But the difference between the two philosophers is striking. At the end of the chapter, Aristotle concludes that the only solution is to hand over permanent power in the city to such men. Because that would be the only way to give a *political treatment* to that sort of excellence. Epicurus, on the other hand, does not look for any political utility for that sort of superiority of the sage; he expects him to remain in his garden.

Man Is Not Only a Citizen

From what we have seen in the first chapter about Aristotelian ethics, we should at least retain the idea that the Greek concept of virtue is nearly unintelligible for people like us, formed as we are in the embrace of Judaism, whether in its "pure" form, or its Christian or Muslim form. That virtue is not only a *state*, but a natural and perfect state (I will come back to the conjunction of these two terms) that makes people happy, the great problem for ancient moralists, as we saw, was explaining the frequency of wickedness in the world. At least the ancient sage would find in virtue, if everything goes well, a stable and happy condition, not threatened by falling back into vice, because no one would be so crazy to bring about his own unhappiness. Or, to put it in other words, who would be crazy enough to give up on his nature, when he had put so much effort into liberating himself from everything that *denatured* him? The Christian saint, in contrast, as has often been stressed, cannot achieve virtue except *against* his sinful nature, and that is why one of the great theses of Christian preachers and directors of conscience is that human beings are unable to go against their nature alone, they cannot attain a

---

7. Perhaps Epicurus had read Plato's *Statesman* (303b) and *Republic* (6, 500c).

virtuous condition except by the grace of God, and even then only in a provisory and precarious manner. We need to hold on to the spirit of that opposition, even if expressed here very schematically.

This ethical position needs to be put into the more general frame of what has been called Greek naturalism, of which Aristotle offers a remarkable version. At the beginning, as always, there is Parmenides. The Aristotelian response to the Eleatic critique is that nature is an actuality of perfect, therefore eternal, being, because that which is perfect is not subject to corruption. As humanity makes up part of this nature, it participates in its perfection. This global perfection of nature both accommodates local imperfections (thus no individual animal is absolutely perfect) and tends toward a multitude of relative perfections, if we can use that expression. Each entity realizes its proper perfection in its proper place, which, in the case of the world of living things, for Aristotle natural beings par excellence, is found in the everlastingness of species, each of which shows its proper perfection by an integration of its vital functions and a kind of relationship with its environment that assure its everlasting survival. In fact, we know that Aristotle, when he set aside the question of the origin of the universe, was the first and perhaps the only one to replace the cosmogonies of his predecessors with a cosmology; his successors would reintroduce part of cosmogony in their speculations on the universe, even if, as we saw above, the process of ordering the cosmos had to be everlastingly repeated.

In ancient naturalism, equally in relation to ethics and politics, not only is it the case that the idea of a nature that is essentially flawed (not accidentally nor episodically) does not occur, but the idea of harmony wins out over that of conflict. Even if conflict, for example the conflict between the elements that compose the universe, constitutes the universe in that it assures the possibility of internal changes. The birth of philosophy doubtless contributed to the development of this idea of a pacified cosmos, divine conflicts having been tamed, and possibly that is, as Vernant thought, one of the effects of the city. We have here a conception of the insertion of human beings into the world that historically has been used several times, notably as an anti-Christian weapon, and sometimes anti-Semite. To the image of an *alienated* man cast by an angry God into a valley of tears, and stamping his infantile dependence by belief in absurdities, the Humanists, Romantics, and many others have opposed the representation of a Greek man *at home* in nature, and fundamentally a stranger to evil.

But it is obviously the transposition of this ancient image of the universe into political thought that particularly interests us. Then, the most obvious difficulty of ancient ethics stands out in clearer relief. There too the optimism of Jean-Pierre Vernant does not get away undamaged, because the Greeks invented a system, that of the city, which makes exist as citizens people who, in previous societies, would have been reduced to a silent obedience and who therefore find in the city the conditions of an ethical, affective, and intellectual blossoming that was previously impossible for them. And nevertheless, the history of cities is not only influenced by vice, but full of fraud, subversion, and crimes. I hope to show, and it is among my theses to which I am most committed, that Aristotle proposes a precise and strong response to this dilemma, common to ancient ethics and politics, in which he opposes all the other philosophers of antiquity. These other philosophers, in the first place Plato, but also the modern "anthropologists," a slightly ironical term by which Nicole Loraux refers to Vernant and those who think as he does, partisans of the "egalitarian consensus *polis*,"[8] in wanting to think of dissension and vice as kinds of pathology, were incapable of saving the ethico-political naturalism of the Ancients. It will be only after long detours that I will come back to this thesis.

Even if he shares, on the whole, the optimistic Greek vision of human nature and does not think of the present condition of human beings as the result of a "fall," Aristotle has no illusions. Since the perfect virtue is deployed in the political field, it's the same for vice, and when Aristotle speaks of "major crimes" (*Pol.* 2.7, 1267a13), he is not thinking of a sadistic villain, but of the tyrant. At the same time, he refuses the easy answer of making human wickedness a consequence of human unhappiness. Thus, he refutes the idea that need or scarcity makes people bad, and thus recognizes the black abysses of human perversity, an approach that is obviously more difficult to reconcile with the Greek conception of a good nature than with the Biblical image of human beings as sinners. And Aristotle makes fun of the naïve Phaleas of Chalcedon who, like all the "Rousseauists" of history, thought that equality would produce virtue by eliminating jealousy and resentment: "The equalization of property is one of the things that tend to prevent the citizens from quarreling. Not that the gain in this direction is very great" (*Pol.* 2.7, 1267a37); because nobody will be satisfied, because "the avarice of mankind is insatiable" (1267b1) due to the fact that "it is the nature of desire to be unlimited" (1267b30).

---

8. Nicole Loraux, *La Cité divisée. L'oubli dans la mémoire d'Athènes* (Paris: Payot et Rivages, 2005), 28.

By describing personal and political vice as the shadow of the infinite, Aristotle shows that he has not left the Greek consensus concerning the finite perfection of the cosmos. It is with the complete break from this consensus that Christianity would join perfection and infinity.

But before dealing with the question, as complex as it is crucial, of political conflict, and seeing Aristotle's perfectly original position on this point, it is indispensable to grasp that man, qua citizen, is at the center of a conflict that we may call one of qualification. The first chapter of the *Politics*, a crucial text to which I have called attention and will refer to again more than once, describes this situation in terms of different forms (or species) of *powers*. In the first place, there are forms of powers that are incompatible with each other: for example, no one can be a king and a citizen at the same time, except in that form of royalty in which the king is subject to the law. There is above all, and we will consecrate very long discussions to this question, the conflict between the groups of citizens that are candidates for political power. But there is also, according to Aristotle, a competition between powers in the same man. Because a man is not only a citizen. The genetic analysis of society in *Politics* 1.2 explains how people first form families, then villages, until arriving at the city, the last stage of *natural* human associations. The same man may find himself to be a citizen, but also a husband, a father, a master of slaves, a head of household, that is, he is at the center of a system of hierarchized different *powers*.

No one has thought that these different instances, described by Aristotle as powers, could peacefully cohabit. Thus Plato, having remarked that familial solidarities can enter into conflict with the goals of the city, had proposed a radical solution, that of suppressing the family. "Sexual communism" was certainly not, in his eyes, seen as meant to further the erotic blossoming of the citizens (although the *Republic* does anticipate sexual rewards for particularly brave soldiers, 5.460a), but to impede the recognition of family relationships. At the same time, in order that the guardians not be contaminated by the infamous life of peasants and artisans and by the ideology that accompanies it, the *Republic* establishes an absolutely tight division between the productive sphere and the citizen sphere by assigning to each of these people a *different nature*, relying on the idea of a difference in the nature of their souls, illustrated by the myth of the metals composing their souls. Although Plato does not say so in these words, the productive class of the perfect city of the *Republic* has a servile or quasi-servile status. Thus at 2.371e, in positing that auxiliary functions are fulfilled by people who are not distinguished by their intellectual qualities, but by their physical vigor that makes them able to accomplish tiresome tasks, Plato anticipates the description of the slave by Aristotle at *Politics* 1.5, 1254b27. The "Guardians" of the *Republic*, on the other hand, do not participate in commercial activities.

Aristotle's diagnosis is ultimately not very far from that of Plato, which is hardly surprising. Aristotle too thinks that the family and its productive activities are dangers for the political sphere. In examining the solutions that he proposes to resolve these problems, we are led to bring out in the open another tragic fact of his political philosophy. If one wants civic life to lead citizens to virtue, it is necessary to protect them from *economic* dangers, in both the ancient and modern senses of the term, that is, from the contamination by the force of family ties, and by the uncontrolled development of the productive and commercial sphere. To put it in other words, Aristotle wants to simultaneously conserve the family and its ties, and to limit the productive activity of the family and impede the familial and productive sphere from dictating its law to the citizen sphere. Aristotle must be the last to be intent on achieving such a project, because, as Karl Polanyi says, not only had exchanges and various forms of speculation become too important in his epoch, but especially because it was also Aristotle who was the first to understand this economic revolution. Thus, it was he who shows the almost unavoidable character of the danger that he wanted to make disappear.

"Aristotle Discovers the Economy"

That's the title of the article by Karl Polanyi that argues for this thesis, both surprising and stimulating.[9] It's easy to understand that the very idea of "economy" would be hard to locate in ancient societies, as we can see from the fact that modern languages have been forced to resort to a word that originally meant family administration to designate this fundamental human activity. "The prime reason," writes Polanyi, "for the absence of any concept of economy is the difficulty of identifying the economic process under conditions where it is embedded in noneconomic institutions."[10] The first of these institutions that make the economy visible

---

9. Karl Polanyi, "Aristotle Discovers the Economy," in *Trade and Market in the Early Empires: Economics in History and Theory*, ed. Karl Polanyi (New York: Free Press, 1957).
10. Polanyi, "Aristotle Discovers the Economy," 71.

is the *market*, which according to Polanyi, and contrary to what others have maintained, had hardly begun to exist in Greece in Aristotle's time. It was his analysis of different human communities that led Aristotle to bring out the fundamental concepts of the economy (exchange, price, use value, exchange value), but it is remarkable that the economy as he construes its structure is represented by him as a largely unnatural entity.

Polanyi, not at all an Aristotle specialist, has very well seen the essentials. For the Stagirite, a community (κοινωνία) is a group of people leading a common life regulated by exchange relations that are not egalitarian but are marked by friendship (φιλία) and achieve a certain degree of self-sufficiency (autarky), which brings it about that they do not have more than marginal dependency on external sources, or even none. We have already seen that this covers the concept of autarky when it is applied to the city. But here, in the case of prepolitical natural communities, it is a matter of economic autarky, something that Aristotle attributes to "tribes." Now we must see in what respect wealth is, from a certain point of view, indispensable, while, from another perspective, it can be fatal for a city.

At the beginning of Aristotle's analysis there is, as always, nature. It is natural that a community, itself natural, procures and conserves the means of its subsistence. The famous table of different human ways of life in *Politics* 1.8, one of the more literary and even poetic passages of the work, explains this diversity, both for animals and for human beings, by the diversity of "nutrients," that is, of edible things in a given environment, but also, in the case of human beings, of the ways of acquiring them. Nomads, peasants, thieves, fishermen, hunters, all have natural ways of life that may make people autarkic, and Aristotle clarifies that they resort to neither exchange (ἀλλαγή) nor to sale (καπηλική), whose intervention would in fact pose the question of the naturalness of the community that engaged in it. It is interesting to note that, in Aristotle's classification, he does not go directly from the "pure" types of ways of life to varieties relying on exchange, but there is an intermediate step of composite ways of life: when peasants do not succeed in being autarkic, Aristotle says, they can also be hunters, and so forth. Should we then understand that a way of life resulting from the combination of two natural ways of life is itself natural? Aristotle says only that those who adopt it live "agreeably" (*Pol.* 1.8, 1256b3). Thus, there is an art of acquisition of useful goods in the natural community (1.8, 1256b26) and, in the preceding lines, Aristotle also includes the art of war when this is intended to procure slaves, which corresponds to hunting applied to animals. For the family has a natural need of slaves.

It is when exchanges intervene in the process of acquisition that the situation changes, and this is the occasion where Aristotle "invents the economy." Aristotle's well-known thesis is the following: there are two natural realities, the first is that, according to the situations, particularly according to the environment in which they live, human beings are not provided with the same goods, the second is that communities grow. Exchanges thus appear necessarily, "of wine for wheat" (1257a27), and Aristotle says explicitly that this exchange is not contrary to nature, "because" it only completes the natural autarky of the communities (1257a29). This natural exchange can take a rather developed form and include money, and on this topic Aristotle in fact lays the foundation of that which would become political economy by distinguishing use value from exchange value, both natural, because they are based on the nature of the objects exchanged. When one wears a shoe, to return to the example of chapter 1.8, one makes natural use of the shoe in that it is "according to its proper usage"; when one exchanges the shoe for wheat, one uses the shoe as a shoe but not according to its proper use, because the shoe "was not made for the purpose of barter" (1257a13). Use value and exchange value are thus both natural, on the condition, for the second, that it has a natural basis, that is, that it is related to a need. But when one throws the shoe at the face of the president of the United States, one is not using it "qua shoe." But if the natural exchange considers the shoe "qua shoe," it is because the characteristics of the shoe are considered in the exchange, which permits setting a fair price. One, in a way, puts a foot in the right shoe. If a shoe is sold at an exorbitant price because it belonged to someone famous or because it was the one thrown at the president, the shoe is no longer exchanged "qua shoe." Exchange for money in such conditions is no longer natural.

It's in *Nicomachean Ethics* 5 that Aristotle deals most completely with the problem of exchange when he asks how a builder and a shoemaker can exchange their products at their fair value. It is very remarkable that these analyses are found in chapters devoted to justice. In fact, justice is the virtue that, because in its developed form[11] it is the basis for life in the city, is in a way the matrix of all the other virtues. Aristotle's major preoccupation is that exchange not make a dent in political life. In order for exchange to occur and be fair, it is necessary that a common measure

---

11. There is also a justice in prepolitical relationships, for example, between husband and wife.

be established between houses and shoes, which is expressible thanks to the introduction of money. But the true basis of evaluation of things exchanged is *need* (χρεία) and money is only a "kind of conventional substitute for need" (*EN* 5.5, 1133a28). So, there is nothing unnatural in all that and the natural art of acquisition finds its complement in natural exchange, including that by way of money. The passage to the unnatural, as conceived by Aristotle, is both clear in its general outlines and difficult to work out exactly in detail.

Clear, but, by Aristotle's own admission, difficult to identify, because the unnatural technique that he is going to characterize and condemn, "chrematistics," follows without a break the natural technique of acquisition. It is hard to tell when Aristotle stops talking about natural exchange and when he starts talking about "chrematistics."[12] The word χρηματιστική is a bizarre word formed on the term χρήματα, which means goods that one needs but before Aristotle took on the meaning of "sum of money, fortune, inheritance." Chrematistics is born when exchange is exercised in one's own interest for the sake of profit. That rests on a postulate largely shared, according to Aristotle, with his contemporaries, and very well expressed by Solon, great legislator and eminent sage who wrote in one of his poems a passage that Aristotle cites: "No bound for riches has been fixed for man" (*Pol.* 1.8, 1256a32). Aristotle is absolutely opposed to this way of seeing things, but there has not been enough notice of the angle of his attack. At the end of *Politics* 1.8, he asserts that in the art of acquisition, "as in all other arts," there is a limit, because the tools are not unlimited either in number or size. But "wealth is a set of all the instruments used by families and cities" (1256b36). Although it could give the illusion, chrematistics is thus not an art (τέχνη), but an imitation. We recognize there a Platonic problematic, doubtless even Socratic. Art, according to the various definitions that Aristotle provides for it, is a set of procedures pursuing an end relying on rational patterns and universal ideas, and which determines the condition of the person who achieves the process. If a technique takes its own operation as an end, it falls into indeterminacy since if one makes shoes to make shoes and not to wear them or to exchange them for things one needs, there is in fact no reason to stop making them.

---

12. One of the difficulties of chapters 1.8 and 9 of the *Politics* comes from the fact that Aristotle sometimes uses χρημαστιστική, understanding τέχνη, in a positive sense for the natural art of acquisition.

As we saw above about vice, we have again here the local application of a general Aristotelian position, this one shared with many other ancient thinkers, which devalues the infinite and the unlimited. Just as the world is both finite and perfect, two adjectives that sometimes, but not always, translate the same Greek word, *teleios* (τέλειος), so the city marks the natural limit of the practical sphere. Therefore, one must not, within the city, make autonomous those practices that ought to remain in the service of the city, whether they are or are not within the family. The acquisition of wealth by the intermediary of production and natural exchange is a part of these practices, just as is the art of war. Because, if it becomes autonomous, exchange no longer sets limits, and similarly, if the goal of social life is making war, the city has no reason to be at peace. That is why Aristotle considers it politically disastrous that the art of war, with all the virtues that go with it, above all courage, sets its activity as the common goal of a city, as was, for example the case with Sparta.[13] One should not allow a city to become poor or weak, but also not allow it to become a plutocracy or a city dreaming only of its conquests.

This search for measure underlies Aristotle's entire practical philosophy. Thus, ethical virtue is defined as a *mean*; we will see that the best constitution is defined as a *middle* one. We will also see how much such positions are very far from a soft centrism. As for chrematistics, not only does it engage men in an endless unnatural quest, but also it rests on an illusion that is paradigmatic too, in that it takes the means as the goal. The chrematistic way of proceeding is to make a profit from exchange (1.9, 1257b4),[14] and as that is done by way of money, one might conclude that money is the true wealth, although it has only purely conventional value and thus is at the mercy of a change of convention. Aristotle reminds us of how false was the wealth of Midas, who died of hunger while sitting on a pile of gold (1257b10). The speculator who tries to make his fortune grow as much as possible will find himself in violation of natural balance. In a general way, that balance excludes the infinite, as well as in the universe taken as a whole as in one of its parts. Aristotle demonstrates that in *De Caelo* 1.5–7.

The principle of sufficiency—which brings it about that Nature gives to each living thing a vital and ecological niche in which it can survive

---

13. Cf. *Politics* 2.9, 1271b2.

14. Cf. the case of Thales's monopoly and the two senses of "speculation," *Politics* 1.11, 1259a6; see also below, p. 112.

forever—plants and animals partaking in specific and not individual eternity is also part of the Aristotelian answer to Parmenides. As Polanyi correctly remarks, Aristotle does not accept the principle of scarcity that condemns human beings not only to technical inventions meant to make up for their natural weaknesses and to an endless extension of exploitation of the environment, but also to a permanent confrontation with groups of human beings other than their own. Thus, Polanyi supports, here too, what I said about Aristotle separating himself from the Greek consensus and coming nearer, in a way, to the Cynic positions noted above. The speculator cannot be virtuous, so it would be contrary to the principles of a well-governed city to have its citizens involved in speculation, and it ought not even allow a speculator to be a citizen.

Thus, we find here again, according to the same point of view noticed above, but in a new aspect, the tragic figure of Aristotle's philosophy. Thinker of the city while having educated the one who overturned the city, he made autarky the condition and criterion of perfection not only political but also human at the moment when the era of great empires was beginning. But Aristotle also was present at the shipwreck of the civic ideal on another front. He lived, in fact, in the period when economics lost its etymological anchor, which made it familial administration. We will also see that his concept of slavery as a family reality did not correspond with the majority practice of his time. Here too he is in the first line against himself, since he was the first to have the thought that would gnaw at, and finally overturn, the civic ideal that he made the goal of human life.

One may well ask whether Aristotle was so naïve that he thought that it was enough to keep commercial activities and those who engaged in them well apart from the centers of power in the city, in refusing citizenship to those dealing with money, and physically separating the mercantile agora from the political agora, in order to contain the development of a merchant economy. In any case, the remarkable distrust of economic activities, even natural ones, that Aristotle shows is doubtless no match for such a heavyweight historical movement. In fact, we have seen that he considered the boundary between the natural art of acquisition and chrematistics as not well marked, although normally the distinction between natural and unnatural domains is clear. Certainly, it belongs to the head of a family, who often is also a citizen, to occupy himself with the administration of the house and his inheritance, but, in a famous passage of the *Politics*, Aristotle advises, for that decisive part of household administration that is the governing of slaves, for those who can to "have stewards who attend to their households while they occupy themselves with philosophy or with politics" (1.7, 1255b35). But the fact that the head of family, in developing and consolidating the patrimony of the family, his natural function, might find himself, without noticing it, stepping into the speculator's shoes, makes natural economics itself something daunting. On this point too, it would thus be the philosopher who could furnish useful instruction.

What allows us to talk of "tragic" is that when we read Aristotle's analyses of chrematistics we are struck with the necessary, or anyway hard to avoid, character of the process that leads to chrematistics:

> When the use of coin had once been discovered, out of the barter of necessary articles arose the other art of wealth-getting (chrematistic), namely, retail trade; which was at first probably a simple matter, but became more complicated as soon as men learned by experience whence and by what exchanges the greatest profit might be made. (1.9, 1257a41)

All the more difficult to avoid in that Aristotle recognizes ineradicable human perversity. But the Greeks have also taught us that tragic heroes confront necessity, not just the accidents of life.

Familial Counterfeits of Political Power

Aristotle's recommendation to pass on to a functionary the task of directing slaves should not deceive us. He does not think that political life, or philosophical life, requires disengagement from the life of the head of a family. On the contrary, leading a family is one of the natural attributes of the man who possesses, or at least can possess, an excellence for that, alongside his excellence as citizen. He also possesses the excellence of administration of an estate, even if he is not the one who labors and reaps, because familial administration is architectonic in relation to the art of the cultivator.[15] Here the problem of the function of *Politics* 1.11 arises. It's a chapter that adopts a practical viewpoint and whose second sentence is decisive, but anything but clear. I have translated it this way:

---

15. Cf. *Nicomachean Ethics* 1.1, 1094a14.

"In all subjects like this one [i.e., acquisition and running an estate], the theory is liberal, but experience submits to necessity" (1258b10). Certain commentators, not the worst, understand that the theory is appropriate for free men, and the practice is in the domain of "necessities," which would be a way of designating the sphere of execution, notably servile. But it is difficult to think that Aristotle wrote this chapter for slaves. Another dispute, one about authenticity, also weighs on the reading of this chapter. It claims to continue the analysis of chrematistic presented in the previous chapters, but now it distinguishes three kinds instead of the previous two. As for the specialized vocabulary found in this chapter, it appears rarely, or not at all, elsewhere, but possibly that's because Aristotle does not treat these subjects in the rest of the *Politics*.

In this chapter, Aristotle indicates that the good master of the house will be recognized in three areas, which are given as subdivisions of chrematistic. The first is agriculture, which is divided into livestock and cultivation; the second is exchange, which is subdivided into trade by sea (itself divided into three parts), lending at interest, and employing salaried workers (itself divided into two forms); the third the nonagricultural exploitation of the earth, for example mines and quarries. Finally, it is in this chapter that Aristotle talks about monopoly, notably the one that was established by Thales of Miletus. To show people who make a big deal out of money-making that philosophy is not useless, Thales, using astronomical knowledge to foresee that there would be a large crop of olives, put deposits on all the olive presses in Miletus and Cos, and then rented them out at whatever price he wanted. Totally improbable story, we have to say . . .

In fact, we must grant great importance to this chapter both for what it is and for what it is not. It is Aristotelian, or anyway does not contain anything un-Aristotelian, and it completes the program announced at the beginning of chapter 8: "Let us now inquire into property generally, and into the art of getting wealth, in accordance with our usual method" (1256a1). So, if it was a successor who inserted it into this place in the *Politics*, that successor had to be a well-informed disciple. But this chapter does not deal with the subjects that it enumerates; it simply refers to treatises by specialists, of whom it gives two names, the agricultural writers Chares of Paros and Apollodorus of Lemnos. Remarkably it also says "a collection ought to be made of the scattered accounts of methods that have brought success in business to certain individuals" (1.11, 1259a3), somewhat in the way that the members of the Lyceum gathered constitutions of different peoples. We may conclude that, for Aristotle, all these sources of knowledge allow one not only to be a good administrator of an estate but also to become wealthy, including in some ways that are more or less dishonest; they are included in what the legislator ought to learn from the philosopher of the Lyceum.

Two remarks on this topic. In the first place, it is established in this chapter that the citizen, since that is who we are talking about, ought also to be an excellent head of a family. The Platonic philosopher king and even the Guardian of the *Republic* cannot make that claim, since the Platonic city abolished the family, at least for the Guardians, even though from the fact that he has knowledge of everything, the Platonic philosopher is in principle an excellent administrator. In the second place, knowledge, or at least some of the knowledge acquired by the Aristotelian legislator, is axiomatically neutral. It's up to him to use it ethically. We will see this very important perspective again later on.

Aristotle is definitely not a Platonist. The upper levels do not abolish the lower levels. There is a virtue, and thus a happiness, of father and husband, just as one may enjoy friendships of different kinds, as we will see. The only unacceptable thing would be to act like a *pater familias* while exercising one's function as a citizen, because the city is not a big family. On this point too, Aristotle is in direct opposition to Plato, as the philosopher of differences against the philosopher of unity. That is what, we repeat, appears with a singular force in the chapter, as short as it is crucial, which begins Aristotle's *Politics*. Modern interpreters agree in seeing in this chapter an anti-Platonic polemic, not limited to criticizing Plato himself.[16]

Thus, Aristotle feels the need of beginning his presentation of his political philosophy with a distinction between different kinds of *power*. It is not the same thing to exercise the power of a king over his subjects, of a head of family over his wife and children, of a master over his slave. But the kind of power that interests Aristotle the most is that of a "statesman" (πολιτικός), political power. The power that some citizens exercise over other citizens in the name of the laws of the city: "There is a power

---

16. "Those who think that to be a statesman, king, head of family, and master of a slave are the same thing" (*Pol.* 1.1, 1252a7) refers to Plato, who in the *Statesman* proposes "seeing the statesman like a king, a master of slaves, and a head of family, these terms referring to one and the same thing" (258e), and to Xenophon (*Economics* 13.5: "The person who can teach the art of military command can obviously also teach the art of being a good master, and the person who can teach the art of being a good master can also teach that of being a good king").

in virtue of which one commands people of the same kind as himself, that is, free. That is what we call political power" (3.4, 1277b7).[17] If the very concept of power includes ideas like that of hierarchy, inequality, and dissymmetry (even if consensual, codified, or provisional), and if the principle foundation of political life is equality between citizens, the very expression "political power" is an oxymoron. We can, relying on this inaugural chapter of the *Politics*, at least characterize what political power is not, in calling attention to the deviant forms that have been thought up by certain theoreticians or practiced by certain peoples or cities.

I have already said, and we will come back to this in detail below, that there are in the *Politics* several types of kingship, of which one is one sort of correct constitution. That is not the one that appears in *Politics* 1.1, but doubtless the regime that was common among the barbarians or in archaic Greece. Even if it is not tyrannical, this kind of kingship is the precise opposite of the political state, in that it does not have citizens, but subjects, and the will of the sovereign is above the laws. In fact, this kind of power is hardly different from despotic power, in taking the word "despotic" in its etymological sense, that is, "concerning the master of slaves." For reasons that we will see below, the barbarians of Asia were adapted to this kind of government, because, although intelligent, their lack of courage directed all their relationships so that they tied themselves to a form of slavery. Thus, their conjugal relationships are "the association of a female slave with a male slave" (1.2, 1252b7). The barbarians of cold regions are unable to form societies beyond tribal because of their stupidity, another idea that we will revisit.

According to the widespread idea of power denounced in *Politics* 7.2, any power, to the extent that it allows some human beings to dominate others, would be essentially despotic. If that were the case, it would be necessary for citizens to give up their goal of virtue and happiness, because the virtues of master and slave, when they are virtuous, are not complete virtues, and the same goes for their happiness. Aristotle is obviously not against the master and slave exercising their functions in an excellent way, but that excellence is not political excellence. It belongs to the familial sphere, since natural slavery is a relationship internal to the family.

All the counterfeits of political power that we have found in the preceding pages are thus powers that ought to be limited to the family. I will have occasion to show that all the constitutional deviations—tyranny,

---

17. Cf. *Politics* 1.7, 1255b20: "Political power is applied to people who are free and equal."

oligarchy, and democracy—actually adopt prepolitical positions, and we will find that again when we talk about revolts. If the city were a big family, the relationships of the governed to the governors and of the governed among each other would fall equally outside political relationships. First, because it is not appropriate for the governors to care for the governed in the way that parents care for their children. The child is in fact "undeveloped" (1.13, 1260a31), a state incompatible with that of a citizen. But the most pernicious remains that such a form of power assimilates citizens to brothers. In that case, in fact, one gets the impression that all the requisites of a political life are present together, since each one has for his fellow citizens the feelings of friendship and good will that make good cities, as we will see when we talk about the political function of friendship. Plato pushed this family concept of the city very far, to the point where he imagined fooling the citizens into thinking that they all descended from the same ancestor. But if what we said above is correct, it is necessary that a man leave the family sphere and enter the political sphere if he is to blossom ethically and achieve happiness. But the parental temptation is always present, much more than other forms of power, because no one loves being a subject or a slave, while many would love to be either parent or child.

The essential of this first chapter of the *Politics* is perhaps that according to Aristotle the different forms of power that are mentioned are different *specifically*, or "in form" (εἴδει), and not "according to larger or smaller number" (1252a9). We have to note here a terminological dissonance with other treatises of the Aristotelian Corpus. In the biological treatises, specific difference is in fact identified with difference according to the more and the less. Thus, in *Parts of Animals* 1.4, Aristotle puts into the same genus (γένος) that which differs by "degree, that is, the more and the less" (644a16), for example the length of wings of birds, while the genera differ by analogical difference, for example the feather and the scale are different kinds of protection for animals. But the doctrine is identical, and we even have here a good example of the same theoretical structure in different domains, natural science and politics.

We confirm again[18] that the terms *genos* (γένος) and *eidos* (εἶδος) do not designate fixed levels of generality, and that the same goes for analogy. Thus, in the *Parts of Animals*, at 2.8 653b35, fish-spine and cartilage are

---

18. I put a lot of work into this in my book *La Classification des animaux chez Aristote* (Paris: Les Belles Lettres, 1982), English translation by Anthony Preus, *Aristotle's Classification of Animals* (Berkeley: University of California Press, 1987).

offered as analogues to bone, while at 2.9, 655a33, Aristotle writes that "cartilage and bone have the same nature with a difference of degree," which makes of them forms of the same genus. When it's a question of studying the "genus" of rigid parts by which the bodies of certain animals are held upright, bone and cartilage differ according to the more and the less, the one being, for example, harder than the other, and they are thus "species" of the same "genus," "hard parts." When Aristotle means to establish how, in animals as different as mammals and fish, Nature resorts to different strategies to maintain the organism with rigid parts, then the fish-spine is analogous to bone. In the first case, one shows that bone and cartilage are different while they are fundamentally the same, in the second, that they are the same while being fundamentally different. In our passage of the *Politics* it is otherness that is being stressed. In fact, it is a matter of affirming that political power and despotic power, for example, both of which may have a *natural* form, are not simply variations of the same reality, which would differ only in respect to secondary or accidental characteristics. If, to mark this difference, which would be more analogous than specific, according to what we have said, Aristotle does not use the word "analogy," it is for a "technical" reason. When he compares species, genus, and analogy in the biological treatises, it is in fact to compare different sorts of *unity*. To say that two entities, animals or parts, are one in species is to show that they are closer than two entities that are generically one. Thus, analogical unity is a weaker form of unity. But in order to function, an analogy has to have four terms: bone and fish-spine are, from a certain point of view, the same thing because bone is to the rabbit as fish-spine is to the carp. But in the context of our chapter of the *Politics*, one cannot resort to a structure of this kind.

Aristotle Is Proslavery

We have already seen that Aristotle was the only writer in antiquity to have attempted to think through that reality that I have called "invasive" in the body of society, slavery. Slavery is a universal practice that was only very recently replaced by other forms of exploitation of man by man. Those recent forms are possibly more humane, and surely more profitable, than the practice they have replaced. Historical anthropology has discovered the presence of slaves even in stateless societies.[19] No matter what form it takes, there are three essential characteristics that define slavery per se: a slave is a forced laborer who is a *property* of his master; he or she is *merchandise*, that is, purchased and usually but not always resold; and he or she is an *outsider* to the people who shelter him or her. The fact that these three characteristics can be found, fairly clearly, in the Aristotelian concept of a "natural slave" shows that despite the important differences between the sort of slavery defended by Aristotle and the sort of slavery that was in fact practiced in his day, when he justifies the use of natural slaves, he is well and truly proslavery. At the same time, even if, as we said earlier, the Greeks were incapable of thinking of a world without slaves,[20] Aristotle's *Politics* shows clearly that in his day the legitimacy of slavery was the subject of debate.

We have first to notice that Aristotle does not at all offer us an analysis either objective or axiological of the slavery current in his day. As a result, once we have read his "treatise on slavery" in *Politics* 1, we still don't know what he thought about slavery as it was practiced in his day, which forms are more acceptable, and which less, how one ought to make use of slaves,[21] and so on. It's not that Aristotle is unaware of the problems that one would have to consider if one were to treat slavery for its own sake. A study of that kind would call for distinctions between several kinds of slaves (3.4, 1277a37), like the studies of constitutions demand distinctions between their species.

In an article devoted to slavery in Aristotle,[22] Malcolm Schofield makes the original and pertinent remark, that *Politics* 1.3–7 does not give us an independent analysis of slavery, but a supporting study intended to shed light on something other than the nature and properties of the slavery relation. We have seen that one of the underlying notions for

---

19. See the work of Harris Memel-Fotê, *L'esclavage dans les sociétés lignagères de la forêt ivoirienne (XVIIe–XXe siècles)* (Abidjan: Éditions CERAP, IRD, 2007).

20. One possible exception could be Alcidamas of Elea. Cf. R. Goulet, ed., *Dictionnaire des philosophes antiques*, vol. 1 (Paris: CNRS, 1989), 104–105.

21. The *Economica* in the Aristotelian Corpus deals slightly with this last point, but the work is not by Aristotle.

22. Malcolm Schofield, "Ideology and Philosophy in Aristotle's Theory of Slavery," in *Aristotles Politik. Akten des XI. Symposium Aristotelicum*, ed. G. Patzig (Göttingen: Vandenhoech & Ruprecht, 1990), 1–27.

any Aristotelian political consideration was that of "political power," a paradoxical form where power is exercised on equals. But slavery is the opposite of this *political* power, because it is the exercise of absolute power of one party over another. Slavery in the *Politics* would thus be a kind of theoretical foil for the essential question of the work, that of *political power*.[23] Finally, although it seemed to me evident that Aristotle's position on slavery was essentially *ideological*, in the Marxist sense of the term, M. Schofield objects, in the cited essay, to my position that Aristotle's doctrine does not fulfill all the conditions for being ideological, because, he says, it is not enough for a theory, representation, or idea, to be in a false relationship with reality to the benefit of social group to qualify it as ideological. It is also necessary that this mental construction is not supported by rational arguments for the people who adhere to it. But Aristotle's theory of slavery is founded on the internal requirements of Aristotle's philosophy.

Possibly the disagreement is mainly verbal, but in any case, what must be retained is that in fact Aristotle's theory of slavery is profoundly consistent with the rest of his philosophy, particularly his ethics and politics, even if—and Schofield insists on this point—this theory is sometimes difficult to square with other Aristotelian positions. Thus, he says, it is impossible to describe the same individual as a human being and as an ensouled tool. And in fact, as we will soon see, Aristotle often situates himself at the frontier that separates the conception of the slave as a human being and the conception that makes of the slave an animal or something subhuman. But he does not cross that frontier.

We can make another preliminary remark. When he deals with the power relations that constitute the family, Aristotle says very little about the relationships between wives and their husbands (to the point that analyses that make of Aristotle a phallocrat are irremediably hypothetical), even less about the relationships of father to his children, and so to speak nothing about the power of a mother over her own children.

---

23. An opposed opinion: the introductory sentence of Nicholas Smith's essay, "Aristotle's Theory of Natural Slavery," in *A Companion to Aristotle's Politics*, ed. David Keyt and Fred D. Miller (Oxford: Blackwell, 1991), devoted to slavery in Aristotle: "In Book I of the *Politics*, Aristotle develops a theory of natural slavery that is intended to serve two purposes: to secure the morality of enslaving certain human beings and to provide a foundation for the uses of slaves that he advocates in later books" (142). I agree with Schofield, and not Smith, on this point.

There are at least two explanations of this. One is that slavery constituted in Aristotle's day a "significant" subject, confirmed by the fact that there existed a debate about its legitimacy. Despite the gynocratic utopias like that of Aristophanes, there does not seem to have been a debate about the justice of the power of the husband over his wife and children. The other is that of Schofield: slavery requires a fairly developed analysis because it is the opposite and foil of political power. After all, why not accept both explanations?

In a well-known essay, Victor Goldschmidt[24] shows that, far from starting from observing the reality of slavery, Aristotle, in the first book of the *Politics*, first constructs the concept of the slave (in chapter 4) before asking himself, at the beginning of chapter 5, "if there is or is not someone who would be thus by nature" (1254a17). It's in the following chapter that Aristotle turns to the debate carried on in his day about the legitimacy of slavery, before asking himself, in chapter 7, whether there is a "science of mastery" that a master ought to possess in order to be a master. Finally, Aristotle returns to slavery in the last chapter of book 1 when he asks himself about the *virtue* of each of the members of the various relationships of subordination that constitute the family, that is, the relationship between husband and wife, father and child, master and slave. Furthermore, in another procedure unusual for him, Aristotle does not begin with a presentation of the various opinions of his predecessors on the problem at hand, although he has recognized, in chapter 6, that such opinions exist. This difference from his habitual practice is a kind of confirmation that Aristotle does not intend to pose for himself the problem of slavery nor to treat it in the same way as those that he really addresses to himself, something that tends to support Malcolm Schofield's point of view.

Even before the construction of the concept of a slave, Aristotle first clears the theoretical space of this concept, starting from the constitutive relations within the family. Chapter 3 takes up the results of the preceding chapter, about which we have already said quite a lot, in which he posited that the most elementary natural society, the family (οἰκία), exists for the sake of satisfying two fundamental needs, reproduction and security. But

---

24. Victor Goldschmidt, "La théorie aristotélicienne de l'esclavage et sa méthode," *Zetesis. Album Amicorum (Mélanges E. De Strycker)* (Antwerp: De Nederlansch Boekhandel, 1973), 147–163. Reprinted in *Écrits*, vol. 1: *Études de philosophie anciennes* (Paris: Vrin, 1984), 63–79.

"security" (σωτηρία) presupposes cooperation between one who commands and one who obeys commands, by nature, and reading chapter 2, we get the impression that the only hierarchical relationship that counts toward security is that between master and slave (cf. 1252a30–34). It's evident that in reality there are many other factors that contribute to security, but, once again, in giving an account of the birth of the city, Aristotle does not undertake to do the work of a historian any more than he describes a historical-social reality. Clearing the theoretical space for the concept of a slave is exactly that, not *describing* the elements that could contribute to the security of the family, which are necessarily diverse and disparate, but showing that nature, which "does nothing in vain," has anticipated a special relationship to satisfy this need. Of course, a man may also use his power over his wife for the sake of the security of the family, and that happens in most cases. But that is an accidental "utilization" of the wife, since Nature intends one agent for one function.[25] The same goes for the situation in which a master has children with one of his slaves or a free woman has a child with a slave.[26] It is not part of the function of a natural slave to have children with her master or his mistress.

Within this relationship of natural dependency that contributes to mutual security, and which he already calls a relationship of master and slave (1252a32, 34), Aristotle will progressively give content to this idea of "slave." Lines 1.2, 1252a30–34, explain that mastery and slavery are natural if they are based on natural abilities, distinct and complementary. The power of the master, when he is a natural master, comes to the person who is naturally able to "anticipate in thought" tasks that the slave is naturally able to carry out. From this *natural* complementarity derives one of the most important properties of the relationship between master and slave, a property that is the consequence of the naturalness of this relationship and at the same time reveals this naturalness, namely, that servitude is advantageous to both parties.

The subversion of this hierarchy is thus harmful to both parties. In a comparison full of meaning, Aristotle establishes an analogy between the relationship between master and slave and that between soul and

---

25. Cf. *Politics* 1.2, 1252b4. Sometimes Aristotle says the opposite: cf. *Parts of Animals* 2.16, 659b35, but both positions may be reconciled.

26. The city is sometimes obligated to legitimize such relationships when there is a shortage of citizens, as Aristotle notes at 3.5, 1278a29.

body. In the latter case, the passionate part of the soul, which is very dependent on the states and impressions of the body, can dominate or be equal to the intellectual part; but Aristotle says, "This equality or reversal is harmful to both parts" (1254b9). This is not directly transposable to the relationship between master and slave. It is necessary to understand why, despite appearances, there cannot be a reversal of roles between them. Assuredly the slave cannot take the place of the master because he does not have the ability to schedule the work to be done. As for the master, he is certainly not unable to carry out the tasks to be done, but doing them would be potentially harmful to him, for several reasons of unequal importance. In the first place, that would entice the master to be neglectful of the activities that ought to be his, political and philosophical, as we have seen; it would risk having bad ethical effects on him, to the extent that it is true that virtue is born from practice (cf. *Pol.* 8.2, 1337b11–14). But no one is more conscious than Aristotle of the influence of the way of life of a person on his ideology: to act as a "base artisan"[27] is to adopt very quickly the values of a base artisan, rely on those values in one's political practice, and support a mercantilist practice of power.

But above all we must remember the connection that Aristotle establishes between the relationship between master and slave and the goals of nature, as we will do again on the crucial point of common advantage between master and slave. The relationship of servitude is a structure that nature has destined for the "security" of the family, and it is not good that a function would be performed by something not naturally destined to perform it, or that a natural capacity remains unused. A passage from book 3 of the *Politics* is instructive on this point of view (3.4, 1277b3), even if its interpretation is debated. Concerning manual tasks, Aristotle says,

> The good man and the statesman and the good citizen ought not to learn the crafts of inferiors except for their own occasional use; if they habitually practice them, there will cease to be a distinction between master and slave.

Doubtless this means that when, for example, one tinkers for immediate needs or for pleasure, the distinction between master and slave no

---

27. In my translation of the *Politics* I translated βάναυσος as "artisan," or "base artisan"; I discuss this term in more detail below.

longer applies.[28] But at that point we are fairly far from the "security" of the family. An activity is thus not naturally servile per se, except when it is inserted into the relationship between a natural master and a natural slave in view of a certain end, namely, security. Thus, by definition a natural master cannot have a servile activity. Aristotle says so very clearly: "Many apparently servile tasks are an honor to the free young people by whom they are performed, for actions do not differ as honorable or dishonorable in themselves so much as in the end and final cause" (7.14, 1333a7).

In a general way, for Aristotle, someone who would be forced to perform laborious tasks because he has been captured and sold as a slave, for example, would not thereby become a natural slave.

The text of *Politics* 1.4, in which Aristotle constructs the concept of "slave," is not easy to understand precisely. This construction occurs in several steps. The slave is first defined there as an ensouled instrument that is part of the necessary goods for family life. At the end of this passage Aristotle asserts that slavery is necessary because looms do not weave by themselves, nor do lyres play music by themselves. Aristotle seems to adopt the position shared by all proslavery writers that consists of presenting slavery as a necessary evil, but that is an illusion. One would have to understand nothing of the Aristotelian approach to maintain, as some have done, that one could imagine that for Aristotle, even as a contrary-to-fact conditional, there could be alternatives to slavery, certain technical inventions making possible, if not suppressing, at least reducing recourse to slavery.[29] But even in a completely automated society there would nevertheless remain, according to Aristotle, natural masters and natural slaves, both having in the servile relationship an interest not only economic, but, as we will see, ethical.

---

28. The interpretation of lines 1277b6–7 is contested. Many interpreters, including Thomas Aquinas, Vettori, Lambin, Richards, understand: "for otherwise there will result an absence of all distinction between master and slave" (following Tricot's translation). These interpreters make the preceding phrase into a parenthesis and attach οὐ γὰρ ἔτι directly to μανθάνειν. But the interpretation that I have adopted in my translation, and it is not mine alone, seems better to me, if only grammatically: when a freeman tinkers for his enjoyment and personal use, there is neither master nor slave any longer.

29. Cf. the remark by Jean Aubonnet in his translation of the *Politics*, *Aristote, La Politique* (Paris: La Belles Lettres, 1960), vol. 1, in a note to the passage in question: "Only Aristotle in the fourth century BC seems to have imagined that the solution to the problem of manual labor and slavery lies in the development of machines" (114).

This first, instrumental, approach to slavery is so inadequate, if not fallacious, that Aristotle immediately adds an analysis that denies to the slave the status of instrument in the proper sense of the word. To do that he uses an argument that can be formalized into two syllogisms: (1a) "The object of property is an instrument for the sake of supporting life" (1253b31). (1b) "The slave is an ensouled object of property" (1253b32), (1c, conclusion understood) "The slave is an instrument for the sake of supporting life." (2a = 1c), (2b) "Life is an action (*praxis*)" (1254a7); (2c) "Therefore the slave is an assistant among those contributing to action" (1254a8). As, among other things, Aristotle in this chapter contrasts production and *praxis*, thus refusing to make the slave an instrument of production, one could conclude from that, wrongly, that for him the slave was what one calls a "domestic," devoted to "household" tasks.[30] In fact, Aristotle's position is much stranger than that, at least for people today.

As has been indicated already, action (πρᾶξις) and production (ποίησις) differ in that that latter produces "something other than its own usage" and this is a matter, Aristotle says, of a *specific* difference (1254a5), and thus their instruments differ in the same way. For example, a shuttle is an instrument of production, while from a coat one gets no product but its own use. What Aristotle calls κτήματα (possessions), the goods that allow living one's life within the family, are all, he says, in the active class. And the slave is among them. This quasi-biological approach to the slave is strange, to be sure, in that the slave is characterized as a *part* of the master, "an ensouled part, separated from his body" (1255b11)—separated, yes, but all the same a part, a living part. Note that this strongly (re)integrates the slave into the family, whose other constitutive relationships also demonstrate this characteristic of vital fusion, as much the conjugal relationship in which the two partners are "a single flesh," and the relationship of parents to their children who are "flesh of their flesh." The slave is thus a *practical* agent, not a productive one, because he is part, as an organ (it's better to translate ὄργανον as "organ" than as "instrument"), of the life of his master. Like all the other members of the family he or she is, like them, in a sense a member of one body. That does not at all mean that the slave cannot have a productive function: one's hand too can have one while remaining a part of the body, and it is probable that

---

30. Jacques Brunschwig, in "L'esclavage chez Aristote," *Cahiers philosophiques* (1979), maintained this, before he changed his mind.

"safety," as Aristotle understands it, assumes that slaves would take charge of several productive tasks.

So then, what about the *possession* of the natural slave by his master, since the fact that a slave being the property of another person is one of the characteristics that define slavery? Well, from this point of view too, Aristotle's natural slavery is real slavery. At 1.4, 1254a14, he says that "one who naturally does not belong to himself, but is the man of another, is a natural slave; and that person is another's man who, while being a man, is an object of property."

He repeats this at 1.5, 1254b21, when he says that the slave "is one who belongs to another." Aristotle's precise expression is very interesting: "he is a slave by nature who, potentially, belongs to another (and that is why he belongs in fact to another)." Doubtless we must understand it this way: "to belong to another" is a defining characteristic—at least if it is not the very definition—of a slave, even before he or she actually belongs to someone. The one who is born a natural slave anticipates belonging to another, a belonging that will allow him to realize his or her true nature.

In fact, this "object of property" is not only closely united with his owner, but his owner cannot do without him without losing his status as head of a family. One may wonder, in that case, if it is possible for a master to *sell* his slave, one of the essential prerogatives of the master in actual systems of slavery. Obviously, there is the case of an insubordinate and vicious slave that the master wants to get rid of, but then it's not a matter of a natural slave. It seems that, from Aristotle's point of view, someone who is naturally a *good* master will not easily separate himself from his slave. In any case he would not do it for the sake of financial gain, as was practiced in the slave system that existed in Greece. Nevertheless, it is still the case that when Aristotle insists that the slave is a *separated* part of his master, he keeps the possibility of selling him. In any case Aristotle refers to the commercialization of slaves, by way of an allusion to the slave market where one might find "well-born" people if slavery rested solely on force (1.6, 1255a28), and if he does not enlarge on this topic, that is doubtless an additional proof that it is not his intention to explore the question of slavery per se, and in any case he would not approach it either as a historian or as a sociologist.

Thus, there are two conditions that must be fulfilled for the existence of natural slavery. On the one hand, it is necessary that both master and slave "deserve" their status (1.6, 1255b14; 7.14, 1333b40), and we will see below what that means in the case of the slave. We know ever since

Politics 1.2 that someone who is able to "anticipate in thought" would not be a natural slave. But obviously it could happen that such a person would be enslaved in the actual Greek system, based as it is on the hazards of capture in wartime. On the other hand, it is necessary that there be between master and slave a "community of life" (1.13, 1260a40), which would not exist, for example, with salaried workers, and could not be found except within the family, since it would only be there that this "fusion" would be possible.

At 3.5, 1278a11, Aristotle proposes this distinction: "Among the necessary people are slaves who serve individuals, and artisans and laborers who serve the community." Additional proof that Aristotle is not describing here a historical reality, since this division does not account for the attested social practice of public slaves.[31] The immediately following passage at 1.13 just cited goes farther, since Aristotle says there that the free worker lives a kind of "partial slavery" (1260b1), and he makes this surprising remark, the artisan "only attains excellence in proportion as he becomes a slave" (1260a40). That means that, when he is in fact in a position of collaboration with someone who plans for him, the worker has, finally, the status of a slave—even if it is to a lesser degree, since he misses having that kind of intimacy established between master and slave creating what Aristotle talks of as *friendship* in their case[32]—which confers on him a *virtue* that he cannot possess when he is not in that servile state. All of that means that for Aristotle it is better to be a slave than a free manual laborer, because, qua slave, he experiences enduringly an excellence in participating in a natural task in which the free worker is involved only during the time of his work. But in himself, the manual laborer is not capable of "practicing virtue" (3.5, 1278a20). And the fact that manual labor may bring wealth ("most workers are wealthy," 3.5, 1278a24), does not make any difference in Aristotle's eyes; just the opposite, because this sort of rich person, unworthy of liberty, unduly demanding participation in power in the city, would constitute a politically dangerous pressure group, which would tend to establish and maintain a plutocracy.

---

31. But this question is addressed in *Politics* book 7. On the question of public slaves, see the hard-hitting work of Paulin Ismard, *La démocratie contre les experts. Les esclaves publics en Grèce anciennes* (Paris: Seuil, 2015), to which I will refer below on another point.

32. Cf. *Politics* 1.6, 1255b13, and *Nicomachean Ethics* 8.14, 1161b5: "Qua slave one cannot have friendship for him, but only qua man."

It does indeed seem that many of the slaves in ancient Greece were owned by heads of families and a good many of those were occupied with tasks within the home; it may be that historical facts of this kind led astray Jacques Brunschwig. But that does not make Aristotelian familial slavery a description of a historical situation. If we needed to find a historical example, it would rather be what certain anthropologists have called "lineage slavery."[33] Undermining historical theses of the Marxist stripe, which saw in the simultaneous birth of antagonistic social classes and a governmental apparatus regulating society for the benefit of the dominant classes, the origin of real oppression, their works have, in fact, shown that there exist in stateless societies this extreme form of human exploitation of other humans, slavery. Foreigners, having been captured or, more often, sold by their people of origin as a penalty, are attributed to lineages that use them as workers while keeping them outside normal lineage relations. Their servile status is marked in several ways that prevent their being confused with other forms of dependency: they do not have access to legitimate matrimonial unions—which does not at all mean that their sexual unions, including those outside their own class, are not tolerated, which gives them, among other things, the possibility of having offspring; they carry symbolic names recalling their servitude; they are excluded from political and religious life; they incur specific punishments that are generally dishonoring; after their death their bodies are not treated the same nor buried in the same places as those of free persons. In such a system, slaves are a small proportion of the population in comparison with free persons,[34] which prevents slavery from creating a major source of tension in the society where it occurs. Furthermore, lineage slavery sets in motion a process of assimilation of slaves into the lineages that own them, and the descendants of slaves can be integrated into these lineages

---

33. Cf., among recent publications, the reference work by Memel-Fotê, *L'esclavage dans les sociétés lignagères de la forêt ivoirienne*. For a classic discussion of lineage slavery in Africa, see Suzanne Miers and Igor Kopytoff, eds., *Slavery in Africa: Historical and Anthropological Perspectives* (Madison: University of Wisconsin Press, 1979), 179ff.

34. Memel-Fotê reports that in 1904 slaves represented, according to colonial statistics, between 2.5 and 4.8 percent of the total population of Adjukru people (Lower Ivory Coast), a relatively high percentage in comparison with other lineage societies located in the interior of the country (435).

by entering into a legitimate matrimonial union forbidden to their parents or grandparents.[35]

It bears repeating that such a lineage slavery, even if it seems "softer" than certain forms of the servile condition in the slavery mode of production, is a true slavery, that is, a social system in which one takes by force human beings reduced to the condition of merchandise in order to confiscate the product of their work. Even Aristotle recognizes that the slavery that he calls "natural" rests on force: "The legitimate art of acquiring slaves . . . belongs to the art of war or of hunting" (1.7, 1255b37). The legislator should even take measures so that citizens will be able "to make themselves masters by way of war on those who deserve to be slaves" (7.14, 1333b37). In fact, the differences between the historical reality of lineage slavery and the natural slavery defended by Aristotle are more instructive than their similarities. The main difference is that, in the lineage system, it is because there is no state apparatus that can organize and control the phenomenon that slavery develops within lineages, while in Aristotle's system slavery is *held outside the state apparatus*, for a very good reason, still the same, that the relationship of power between master and slave does not derive from political power, which is fundamentally a power exercised by and on equals. Despotic power is specifically distinct from political power, as we have seen, and is deployed within the family.[36] A second difference is that in Aristotelian slavery, even if the descendants

---

35. This is a fundamental point in several respects. Thus, in slave systems in state-governed societies, historians have noticed the great difficulty that masters have had to assure the reproduction of their slaves by natural growth. Thus, the necessity for slave systems to engage continually in wars of capture, and the difficulty that these systems encounter when, as was the case for the American South in the nineteenth century, the sources of replacement dry up. (Cf. Claude Meillassoux, *The Anthropology of Slavery* [Chicago: University of Chicago Press, 1991], part 3, chapter 5: "To Buy or to Breed?"). Lineage slavery seems not to have encountered this problem, which can cause astonishing theoretical confusions. Thus, in an epoch-making book on slavery in Africa, edited by Suzanne Miers and Igor Kopytoff, the editors believe that they can assert that the peculiarity of African domestic slavery is that it extends to individuals who do not belong to a lineage relationship of dependence to which women and children of the lineage are generally subject (22–24). Were Miers and Kopytoff aware that they were adopting an anti-Aristotelian, indeed *Platonic* position?

36. Thus, it is doubtful that Aristotle could imagine public slaves as participating in a natural slave relationship.

of slaves are also called to be integrated into a lineage, as free members, integration takes place on the basis of *ethical* criteria, and not as a result of time lapse alone. We will see however that this distinction, when one looks at it closely, loses its edge.

Once he has constructed the concept of the slave, as a human being attached to his master with whom he collaborates in the common task of "safety," Aristotle asserts that there are people who correspond with this concept. From that comes that the debate, which actually happened in his day, as he himself reports, on which the legitimacy of slavery would, in principle, be decided: "Hence, where the relation of master and slave between them is natural they are friends and have a common interest, but where it rests merely on convention and force the reverse is true" (1.6, 1255b13).

It is necessary to distinguish clearly the characteristics that bring it about that an individual *deserves* the status of slave. These characteristics are, on the one hand, natural and not tied to circumstances, since people who are slaves by nature are so "since birth" (1.5, 1254a23) and not, for example, as a consequence of imprudence, when one has allowed oneself to be captured by pirates, or an offense, when one is sold as a slave to repay debts. They are, rather, based on psychological traits, in the Aristotelian sense of "psychological," that is, those translated by *ethical* properties. Let us look at several passages in *Politics* book 1.

In a text that looks very "tough" to us, Aristotle says that "in terms of usefulness" there is hardly any difference between slaves and domestic animals (1.5, 1254b24). On the other hand, there is one at the rational level, in that animals "cannot even apprehend reason, but obey their passions" (1.5, 1254b23).[37] As for the natural slave—and this text does seem to provide this characteristic as a distinctive trait of the natural slave—"he participates in only enough reason that he can apprehend it (in his master), but does not have it himself" (1.5, 1254b22).[38] To appreciate the implication

---

37. There is an important variation in the manuscripts at 1254b23: I adopt the reading best established paleographically, λόγου, and not λόγῳ, which would mean "animals, though perceiving, do not obey reason but their passions" (Ross, Dreizehnter), which in aligning slaves with animals would destroy the opposition that Aristotle means to address between them.

38. Could we draw the conclusion from this that slaves who are not natural slaves could, in certain cases, not have reason enough to share, which would justify Plato's position? It seems probable to me that for Aristotle only the *natural* servile condition

of this difficult passage, one that would deserve extensive commentary, it is necessary to remember one of Aristotle's habitual theoretical practices, which consists of mobilizing only enough conceptual apparatus necessary for the topic at hand. Several times in the *Politics* Aristotle refers to a summary description of the human soul, something that has led certain scholars to assign these texts to an early date when Aristotle had not yet constructed the complex psychology of his "maturity."[39] That slaves "do not possess reason" should be understood with all the more nuance in view of the fact that Aristotle formally says the opposite in chapter 13: "Those who say that slaves do not have reason, and recommend that one use only the imperative voice with them, are mistaken" (1260b5), a criticism directed at Plato (cf. *Laws* 6.777e).

Entirely human as he is, the slave is no less an incomplete being, from an intellectual and ethical point of view. It's the same for all members of the family who are in a subordinate position, that is, the wife, child, and slave, who "possess the various parts of the soul (i.e., the same as those possessed by an adult free male), but they possess them differently" (1.13, 1260a10). That means that they indeed possess the rational part of the soul, proper to human beings, but minus certain functions that are present in the perfect human being and with certain other functions otherwise directed or in a less developed state than in the adult free male. Thus, fundamental point, "the slave is totally deprived of the faculty of deliberation, the woman has it but without authority, the child has it but imperfectly" (1.13, 1260a12). All these subordinates thus have a share in the ethical virtues, but not in "complete ethical virtue" (1.13, 1260a17), which can only belong to citizens. Thus, there is a temperance, a courage, and a justice proper to the slave as there are proper to the woman (1.13, 1260a20); as we have seen, these virtues have been given to them so that they may be able to accomplish excellently the tasks assigned to them.

All that poses the formidable problem of the slave's virtue. Aristotle in fact recognizes that not only does the slave have a virtue in the

---

implies reason. A nonnatural slave could very well be provided with reason (one thinks of Plato reduced to slavery after his capture), but he does not enter into the rational relationship with his master here described by Aristotle. As I have said, in this case there is no natural servile relationship. This is perhaps an additional attempt by Aristotle to show that natural slavery does not rest exclusively on force.

39. Cf., for example, the famous book by François Nuyens, *L'Évolution de la psychologie d'Aristote* (Louvain: Éditions de l'Institut Supérieur de Philosophie, 1973), 197.

sense in which a horse well adapted to its task is said to have a virtue (an excellence), even if it is indeed a virtue of this kind that he assigns to the slave when he says that the slave "does not need more than a bit of virtue, just enough not to be inadequate for his task" (1.13, 1260a35). Aristotle also attributes to slaves an *ethical* virtue. But how is that possible in someone to whom he refuses the faculty of deliberation? There is here an important difference between the slave and other subordinates. In fact, the child has an "imperfect" faculty of deliberation and the woman has one "without authority," which allows them to develop ethical virtue, even if the supreme form remains inaccessible to them. But someone who is unable to deliberate is unable to choose (cf. *EN* 3.2, 1112a15: choice presupposes deliberation). How then would the slave participate in ethical life? It is, basically, what Aristotle recognizes when he declares that slaves have no share in happiness, the end of ethical life: there are no cities of slaves or of animals "because they do not participate in happiness nor in life guided by reflective choice" (3.9, 1280a32, a passage already cited).

Aristotle is going to get out of this difficulty by using, without saying so, the doctrine of the fusion of master and slave. He maintains two theses: first, that the slave, qua part of the master, does not participate in reason except to the degree that he perceives it in his master, and second, that the relationship between master and slave is analogous to that between soul and body.[40] This last position is better understood when one remembers that "the power of the soul on the body is a magisterial (despotic) power" (1.5, 1254b4). Like every ethical being, the slave indeed submits his desires to the control of reason, but *to the reason of his master*. To obey the reason of his master is ultimately to obey the "admonitions" of his master (cf. 1.13, 1260b6), and it is in this sense that "the master ought to be the cause of the virtue of the slave" (1.13, 1260b3). In terms of deliberation, not being able to deliberate himself, the slave is not able to choose, notably, what is good for himself. Thus, it is necessary that someone do it for him. But we have to say a bit more about the slave's inability to deliberate, and to that end consider a too often neglected aspect of Aristotle's theory of slavery.

---

40. "The relation between master and slave is the same as that between soul and body, worker and his tool" (*EE* 7.9, 1241b17); "the same thing is advantageous for the whole and for the part, the body and soul, and the slave is a part of his master" (*Pol.* 1.6, 1255b10).

Among everything that legitimates natural slavery in Aristotle's eyes the most fundamental is doubtless the very order of nature, where one finds again the teleological explanatory schema that we noticed above. Free citizens, and we must add those who are virtuous and thus fully deserve the name of citizens, cannot live their life as citizens without being liberated from economic functions that would deprive them of *leisure*. This idea of "leisure" (σχολή) plays an important role in that it is a sign of political excellence, a bit like the way that pleasure is a sign of ethical excellence. We have seen that when a person acts well, but with displeasure, when, for example, someone gives up vicious conduct but painfully because he would like very much to . . . , that person is not virtuous. The virtuous person should do good deeds with pleasure, and this aspect of the virtuous action is so important that Aristotle, as we have seen, goes so far as to say, "the whole concern both of excellence and of political science is with pleasures and pains" (*EN* 2.2, 1105a10, passage already cited). At the same time, when citizens lead a life of leisure, it is possible for them to achieve that for which the city exists, namely, "the happy life." The life of leisure, in fact, is not for the sake of anything but itself, and that is why, according to Aristotle, possibly in reaction to Platonic analyses, leisure is not a game, a game being an activity that aims at something like a mixture of pleasure and relaxation or a neutral state. Leisure is also not inactivity.

But leisure has a price:

> Many necessities of life have to be supplied before we can have leisure. Therefore, a city must be temperate and brave, and be able to endure: for truly, as the proverb says, "There is no leisure for slaves," and those who cannot face danger like men are the slaves of any invader. (*Pol.* 7.15, 1334a18)

Part of that price must be paid by the citizens themselves, for example by making war to maintain the city as an autarkic entity. But nature has foreseen making slaves pay the larger share of this price. Slavery is thus legitimated from the moment that there exist human beings who are physically and ethically destined for tasks that would prevent the citizens from having a life of leisure if they had to achieve those tasks themselves. But such beings exist and will always exist. In a famous chapter of the *Politics* (7.7), Aristotle offers a theory of climates that is anything but original. The idea that the climate of a place shapes the character of the people who inhabit it seems to have been shared by many Greeks, and we find versions both in Plato and in the Hippocratic treatise *Airs Waters Places*.

Aristotle maintains, as if it were a *fact*, that neither the barbarians of "Europe," living in cold regions, who are courageous but stupid, nor the barbarians of "Asia," clever but cowardly and servile, can lead the life of citizens. I would like to make two remarks about this passage. In the first place, Aristotle writes that "the tribes of cold regions and (καί) Europe" are stupid and courageous; this can be taken in three ways: The most improbable takes the καί as a simple conjunction implying that it is about tribes in cold regions and also those of Europe. Newman understands "the tribes of cold regions and especially those of Europe," while I understand rather "the tribes of cold regions, that is, those of Europe." The work of Hecataeus of Miletus on the "description of the earth" distinguishes three continents: Europe, Asia, and Libya, a division taken up by Herodotus and Strabo, which means that we can take it as dominant. It definitely seems that Aristotle accepts it, since he writes in the *History of Animals*: "As a general rule, wild animals are at their wildest in Asia, at their boldest in Europe, and most diverse in form in Libya; in fact, there is an old saying, 'Always something fresh in Libya'" (8.28, 606b17).

But here Aristotle seems rather to adopt a division that seems at first sight to be that of the Hippocratic treatise *Airs Waters Places*, which distinguishes Europe and Asia to the extent that he opposes these two regions to the Greek territory, a division that is more applicable to the problem that preoccupies Aristotle, that of the ethical qualities of the people concerned and their relationship to political life. In any case, it seems that Europe, which goes from Spain on the east to modern Ukraine, was located by the ancients to the north of the lands habited by the "race of Hellenes" (*Pol.* 7.7, 1327b29), and Asia, which included Egypt and Libya, to the south. Thus, in *Politics* 7.7, there is this division: Europe/cold/north, Asia/hot/south, Greek lands/medium temperature/middle of the world.

In a very useful work on the subject we are discussing here (and on many others), Jean-François Staszak thinks that the fact that Aristotle puts forward this theory of climates without any justification shows that he takes up "a theory developed elsewhere and sufficiently accepted that it would not be a matter for debate . . . , sufficiently known that it would not be necessary to elaborate on it. . . . We will see below that this theory is in fact a direct borrowing from the Hippocratic teaching."[41] But

---

41. Jean-François Staszak, *La géographie avant la géographie. Le climat chez Aristote et Hippocrate* (Paris: L'Harmattan, 1995), 96.

what Aristotle proposes is not what we find in *Airs Waters Places*. If we take the example of the cowardice of Asians, we see that the Hippocratic treatise indeed assigns to it a climatic origin, but not on the ground that the Asiatic climate is hot, but because it does not present great variations in temperature. But it is these contrasts that provide energy and passion. Furthermore, the Hippocratic author sees another cause for the softness and cowardice of Asians in the "laws" imposed on life in despotic regimes (XVI.1-3). But ultimately, J.-F. Staszak, who knows the Hippocratic theories of climate, as the second part of his book demonstrates, probably is right: it is enough for Aristotle to "know" that the Asians, who live in hot regions, are cowardly, as, so to speak, everyone knows. From that cowardice comes their inaptitude for political life.

On the other hand, it is necessary to note that the causal relation between climatic heat and psychological dispositions is more suggested than explicitly asserted: Aristotle simply says that "the tribes of cold regions, that is, Europe, are full of spirit" (1327b23). But doubtless that's how it is for Aristotle. Can we conciliate this climatic psychology with Aristotle's physiological doctrines that show us rather that spirited animals have warm blood and that fear is rather associated with cold?[42] Yes, if we follow *Problemata* that explains that "human beings have a natural tendency that counteracts the effect of locality and season, for if both had the same tendency they would soon be destroyed" (14.16, 910a39). And the author of this *Problem*, who is perhaps not Aristotle himself but surely an Aristotelian, gives additional explanations: the inhabitants of hot countries have porous bodies, allowing their internal heat to escape to the outside, while the inhabitants of cold countries have more compact flesh

---

42. Cf. *Parts of Animals* 2.1, 650b27-651a4: "Fear chills the body, so that in animals whose heart contains so watery a mixture the way is prepared for the operation of this emotion. For water is congealed by cold. This also explains why bloodless animals are, as a general rule, more timorous than such as have blood, so that they remain motionless, when frightened, and discharge their secretions, and in some instances change color. Such animals, on the other hand, as have thick and abundant fibers in their blood, are of a more earthy nature, and of a choleric temperament, and liable to bursts of passion. For anger is productive of heat; and solids, when they have been made hot, give off more heat than fluids. The fibers, therefore, being earthy and solid, are turned into so many hot embers in the blood and cause ebullition in the fits of passion. This explains why bulls and boars are so choleric and so passionate. For their blood is exceedingly rich in fibers, and the bull's at any rate coagulates more rapidly than that of any other animal" (trans. Ogle).

under the influence of the external cold, and this impedes the escape of the internal heat.[43]

My second remark is that this system is not isometric with the opposition between Greeks and barbarians as some, including me, have concluded too quickly. In fact, Aristotle says: "There are also similar differences in the different tribes in Greece; for some of them are of a one-sided nature, and are intelligent or courageous only, while in others there is a happy combination of both qualities" (1327b34).

Lacking additional information from Aristotle, we can only construct hypotheses. As I have recalled above, not all the Greeks lived in cities, but some lived in "tribes." Possibly Aristotle thought that some Greeks possessed some *natural* qualities indispensable for living a political life, but doubtless they were insufficient. It certainly seems to be what "one-sided nature" would mean.[44] If that is the case, it would seem logical that Aristotle would attribute this condition to the same climatic causes that affect barbarians. But then would these Greeks deserve to be natural slaves? Is this about Greeks living in Asia Minor and in Italy? But remarkable cities flourished in those territories. Is it about Greeks living in hilly places where the climate could be different from that of the plains? Or, a hypothesis that seems the most attractive to me, is it about Greek tribes that, for various historical reasons, had not yet attained to city life, a situation to which *Politics* 1 alludes in talking about the one who was the first to establish a city (1.2, 1253a30)?

However that may be, the message is clear: neither courage nor intelligence is enough to save one from being enslaved. Thus, only the Greeks, and even those among them who were the people of the center of the world, could hope to be able to live in a city. The Aristotelian doctrine of natural slavery thus is found to be inscribed in the image of the universe, also Aristotelian. The organization of the world presented to us in this chapter of *Politics* 7 demonstrates that in arranging human beings incapable of living in a city around the periphery of the Greek world, Mother Nature has created a kind of reservoir of natural slaves for

---

43. A passage in the *Generation of Animals* seems to contradict what I propose here. We read: "The bodies of animals are colder when the environment happens to become so" (2.4, 738a18). But this is about the influence on procreation of the variations of temperature according to the seasons in the same territory and not about the relation between a hot or cold nature of an animal and the climate where it lives.

44. "One-sided" translates μονόκωλον, literally "one-legged."

the Greeks. Although the Aristotelian analysis does not formally establish that slaves ought to be non-Greeks, and, as we have just seen, there are probably even some Greeks that deserve to be enslaved in view of their one-sided nature, we see that Nature, in her great wisdom, by means of the climatic system tends to make natural slaves primarily of barbarians, thus restoring to Aristotelian slavery one of the characteristics of all slavery, that of reducing to servitude foreigners, as we noted at the beginning.[45]

This chapter 7 of book 7 of the *Politics* invites at least two important remarks to clarify our approach to the Aristotelian theory of slavery. First, one may think that, once separated from their original climatic conditions, a stupid or coward slave would gradually lose these characteristics, if not himself, then in any case his descendants. Thus, we rediscover in Aristotle's theory one of the characteristics of lineage slavery, its calling to integrate the descendants of slaves into a lineage after a certain lapse of time. Second, when Aristotle writes that Asians "have an intelligent and subtle soul," we must certainly take these words in their full sense. After all Aristotle was not at all ignorant of the scientific and technological accomplishments of certain barbarian peoples, at the same time as the collective memory of the Greeks was full of the remembrance of their military exploits.[46] In any case this shows that the natural slave is not necessarily destined to this condition by virtue of his stupidity, something that *Politics* 1 could readily suggest. This book, in fact, creates an image of the slave as a big baby unable to rule himself, somewhat in the way that triumphant colonial ideology made of "the native" a carefree big baby, a lazy simpleton. *Politics* 7.7 leads us to complete that image.

It also allows us to say more about the inability to deliberate that characterizes the slave, that which sanctions his ethical inferiority and

---

45. There is a very interesting passage on this matter at *Politics* 1.6: the people who say that those are slaves who are captured by force do not want to accept the consequences of this position (someone who is "well born" could be a slave), and add that this rule applies only to barbarians. Aristotle comments, "In using this language they really mean the natural slave . . . , for it must be admitted that some are slaves everywhere, others nowhere" (1255a30).

46. It's difficult to say what Aristotle means by "barbarians of Asia." Were the Egyptians included in this group, those to whom he attributed the invention of mathematics? As for the bravery of the Medes and Persians, on the one hand it was not enough to enable them to conquer the Greeks, and on the other it illustrates the approximate character of climatic determinism that brings it about that, for example, some soldiers may love warfare, including some Asians . . .

legitimizes domination by his master. In fact, technical deliberation, the ability to determine the means to an end, is not the same as ethical deliberation, which is not satisfied with determining means only but also arranges the totality of those means for the realization of an ethical good. It's one thing to be able to deliberate concerning the best way to win a war, and quite another to have the virtuous deliberation of the courageous, which acts for the sake of a good, an end dictated by virtue itself.[47] The slave is incapable of this second kind of deliberation, without counting that he may also be unable, due to stupidity, to carry out technical deliberation. The coward deserves to be a slave, but also the imbecile. Aristotle does not tell us which one deserves it the most.

And by the same token we understand much better what makes a man a natural master. *Politics* 1.7 is a short chapter, too often neglected, in which the question is raised whether there is a science of being a master. This chapter too begins with a summary of opinions, and the text does not tell us whether these opinions were held by someone or whether they were thought up by Aristotle himself. The opinion that comes second in the text is that one can be taught to be slave, and thus also to be a master. Thus, at Syracuse, Aristotle says, slaves were taught how to do the various tasks that would be assigned to them, for example cooking. But that's an abuse of language, since it's one thing to teach someone how to do something, and quite another to teach how to *be* something. Hence the first opinion: "The master is not called a master because of what he knows, but because he is of a certain character, and the same applies to the slave and to the free person" (1255b20). At the end of the chapter Aristotle adopts a position that looks like a mediation between these opinions, but that in fact leans strongly toward the first opinion, saying that if there is a science of the master, "this science is not anything great or wonderful" (1255b33), an assertion immediately followed by the recommendation that one appoint a steward to supervise the slaves if one can.

More exactly therefore, one is a master because of one's natural virtue, not because of some particular bit of knowledge. *Ethical* virtue is not taught, unlike intellectual virtue, but is born from the repetition of virtuous actions, as we have already seen in a previous chapter. At the same time, as the first chapter of *Nicomachean Ethics* 2, among other texts, explains, although virtue is not taught, it is learned by practice, as is the

---

47. Cf. *Nicomachean Ethics* 3.7, 1115b20: "The end of every activity is conformity to the corresponding state (ἕξις)."

case also for various arts, since it is "by building that we become builders" (1103a33) and furthermore, "the act of building well makes good builders, the act of building badly makes bad builders" (1103b10). The major goal of this chapter is to show that one does not naturally possess virtue as one naturally possesses the sense of sight, but "we are naturally made to acquire the virtues, and we achieve that through habituation" (1103a24).

To what extent is all that applicable to the case of the master? Obviously, one is a master because one is courageous and not because one has taken a course on courage, and especially because one knows how to deliberate and choose, which presupposes that one has the supreme ethical virtue, "prudence" (φρόνησις). But the virtue of the master that enables him to direct his slaves in an excellent manner, is that learned by practice? Doubtless it is, although Aristotle does not say so explicitly. Thus, one is born a master, but at the same time it is necessary to become one. One can learn how to exercise one's function as a master just as, as I said above, a bird can learn to fly. But one no more learns to *be* a master than a bird learns how to be a flying animal. Is it the same for the slave? We have seen that Aristotle says explicitly that one is born a slave, of course, if it's a matter of natural slavery. At the same time, it is just as true that a slave can improve himself, better fulfill his function as slave, with practice and time. But, in his case, we come back to the pattern outlined above: it is only by the direction, particularly the admonitions, of his master, that the slave can develop his virtue. We cite again the well-known formula: "The master must be the cause of the virtue of the slave" (*Pol.* 1.13, 1260b3). We thus see again the same lack of symmetry between master and slave: to develop his virtue as a good master, the master obviously needs to have a slave, but it is not the slave who develops the virtue of his master, while it is the master who, by reasoning, deliberating, and deciding for the slave, creates the virtue in the slave.

There remains a crucial point, one that I dare to think that everyone until now has gotten wrong, which is to understand the meaning of the position that the servile relationship exists in the interest of both parties. In fact, all the commentators have taken it that the slave would have an interest in his servile condition because left to his own devices he would not survive, somewhat as we agree to recognize for infants. But for Aristotle it's the master who cannot live his life as master without his slave. He admits without difficulty that the relationship between master and slave advantages the master "and only accidentally advantages the slave" (3.6, 1278b35), while the father wields his power "essentially" (3.6, 1278b39) for the benefit of his child. And Aristotle adds, "If, in fact, the slave were to disappear, it is impossible that the power of the master persist" (3.6, 1278b36). But what about for the slave? When M. Schofield, in agreement with nearly all interpreters, writes that "they (slaves) need someone else to deliberate on their behalf if they are to survive," he supports a thesis that if it were true would be in contradiction to other Aristotelian positions.[48] It's enough to read on in *Politics* 1.5 to see that Aristotle says there, as it is better for the body to be ruled by the soul, and bad for both that the body rule, at the same time it is better for animals to be ruled by man, which brings it about that "tame animals have a better nature than wild animals, and it is better for all to be ruled by man, for it is thus that they find their safety (σωτηρία)" (1.5, 1254b10). Note that Aristotle does not limit his comment to tame and domesticated animals, but he says that for the others also, that is for wild animals, it is better to be ruled by man. But it would seem that for wild animals, the less that man meddles in their existence, the better off they are. Furthermore, it is not true that domestic animals need humans to be able to survive, as the *History of Animals* tells us, "Wherever a race of animals is found domesticated, the same is always found in a wild condition: as we find to be the case with horses, cattle, pigs, men, sheep, goats, and dogs" (1.1, 488a30).[49]

And in any case, from what we have just seen, it is absolutely impossible to argue that Aristotle believed that the people of the East, although fundamentally natural slaves, were incapable of surviving on their own, since they had been doing it very well for a long time.

The solution to this problem is both simple and for us strange. It has already been summarized above on the matter of happiness, when we saw that the blossoming of an inferior occurred for him when he worked for the happiness of his natural superior. We can say this another way. The degree of perfection of an animal and that which is good for it can be understood according to two scales. From the point of view of the animal itself, that is better that makes it easier to lead its life, to nourish itself, to develop, to reproduce, to escape from danger, and so on. But there is

---

48. Schofield, "Ideology and Philosophy in Aristotle's Theory of Slavery," 14.

49. In this first chapter of the *History of Animals*, Aristotle actually proposes two contradictory approaches (and he recognizes that they are) since a few lines earlier he says that some species are always wild or always tame. Thus, human beings and mules are always domesticated. But the thesis proposed here is also that of the *Parts of Animals* (cf. 1.3, 643b5).

also a perfection relative to animals, which is measured by their degree of resemblance to the most perfect among them, the human being. In fact, Aristotle says that human beings are "the animals most in conformity with nature" (*IA* 4, 706a19; cf. 5, 706b10). From this fact, from the point of view of Nature in general, what is the best is what provides the best being with some advantage. We can therefore say that for an animal to serve human ends is better by nature than to serve one's own ends, from two points of view: from the point of view of the "user," it is natural for human beings to use the tools that they find in nature, particularly animals, to satisfy their needs, and from the point of view of Nature in general, and not the nature of the individual animal. That's what permits Aristotle to say that it is better for a wild animal to serve human ends. The same goes for slaves.

The fact that the inferior is naturally the tool of the superior, as is the case for the natural slave, has several consequences. First, there are degrees of naturalness that bring it about that human ends are "more natural" than the ends of other animals, and the ends of the ethically virtuous man are "more natural" than those of his slave. We can analyze the brief statements at 1254b22–24 this way: animals do not have reason, but they can have behavior that is in a sense rational when they obey the rational orders of men. We have seen that the same goes for slaves, except that they have a kind of reason by delegation. This rational conduct because of another is thus "more natural" than the conduct adopted by the slave on his own initiative. Consequently, this double norm of perfection, in relation to oneself and in relation to Nature in general, clarifies the famous passage in the *Politics* often interpreted as revealing in Aristotle a "providentialist" position: "Plants exist for animals and animals for man" (1.8, 1256b16). It is natural for a tiger to eat people, and from this fact, *from the point of view of the nature of the tiger*, "people exist for tigers." But from the point of view of the nature of human beings, and from the point of view of Nature as a whole, in which human beings are "more conformed to nature" than tigers, tigers exist for human beings.

That allows us, finally, to return, better equipped, to the problem of *safety*. It seems doubtful that Aristotle could maintain that human beings naturally made for slavery need masters to survive, like children, for example, need their parents. After all, as I have already said, the barbarians, who are naturally servile (cf. 1.2, 1252b6; 7.7, 1327b28), survive very well. What is saved in the servile relationship is the community of master and slave, and that is advantageous for both parties. For the master, the advantage is not difficult to see, because without a slave he cannot lead life as a master, that is, thanks to leisure, develop his ethical faculties. For the slave, the advantage that he finds is that of participating, thanks to abilities that he does not possess himself (the master's reason in a way lends them to him, and especially full and complete ethical virtue), to a task whose realization is beyond his own excellence. Hence this slight correction to the thesis that slaves have no access to happiness: "No one assigns to a slave a share in happiness—unless he assigns to him also a share in human life" (*EN* 10.6, 1177a8); the "life" in question ought without doubt be understood as the ethical life of a freeman. But in the servile relationship, the slave shares in this life in an indirect way, by way of his master, of whom he is a tool (organ). The same goes for the relationships, intimately connected to each other as we will see, between justice and friendship. We saw above that Aristotle claims that "there are reciprocal advantage and friendship between a slave and his master" when they have this relationship naturally (1.6, 1255b13). But we are far from the true friendship as we will define it later in this chapter. That's why the *Eudemian Ethics* is laudably circumspect when it says that between master and slave "there is no relationship of friendship nor of justice, but an analogue of these" (7.10, 1242a30).

Let us return briefly to the reasons that Aristotle gives for preserving the family and not dissolving it into the body politic as Plato did, at least the Plato of the *Republic*. There are two kinds. Book 2 of the *Politics*, in the chapters devoted to the critique of the Platonic cities, that of the *Republic*, and then that of the *Laws*, give reasons that we can call "economic": the community of women, so-called, as that of possessions, would provoke such difficulties that their intended purpose, making the city happy, could not be achieved except at the cost of the unhappiness of everyone.[50] Thus, in outline, the Aristotelian fundamental critique of every sort of totalitarianism, a doctrine that claims to create collective happiness from the sum of individual unhappinesses. Aristotle never stops reaffirming the isomorphism that he sees between city and citizen: in the happy city, happy citizens; in the virtuous city, virtuous citizens. But the basic reason for preserving the family is, as we have seen, that it rests on *natural* desires of human beings, and one cannot suppress nature by decree.

---

50. Cf. *Politics* 2.5, 1264b17: "The whole cannot be happy unless most, or all, or some of its parts enjoy happiness."

The acquisition and management of wealth such as slaves are thus two practices that are familial, that is, prepolitical, that the legislator ought to know for at least one fundamental reason: Aristotle does not think that the citizen ought to have a tabula rasa of other social relationships, so it is necessary that the citizen make correct usage of his position as master of a house. To ensure that, it is necessary that the legislator know how to set the limits that will prevent intrafamilial relationships from going outside their sphere and outside their natural condition. In the case of wealth and slavery, when they depart from their natural location, the family, they will have the effect of destroying the city. In one case, if the city posits as its goal the accumulation of wealth, it would thereby establish an oligarchy, that is, as I have said, a plutocracy, which, when it follows its own tendency will finish, as we will see, in tyranny; in the second case, if slavery is developed to the point where people who are not naturally destined for slavery are enslaved, that too gives birth to tyranny.

It is not only in relation to the family that the civic space ought to situate itself and affirm its preeminence. There are also a certain number of associations that rest on religious, local, social bases, which extend from religious brotherhoods to sporting clubs, through age groups and instructional institutions. In reality, the perpetually renewed and perpetually contested attempt of the city to impose its law on that which is not the city has been one of the most serious recurrent problems faced by the city. But Aristotle founds all communities on the affective forces that he sums up under the one heading *philia*, usually translated "friendship." Among other passages, consider this one from the *Politics*:

> Such a community [i.e., a city] can only be established among those who live in the same place and intermarry. Hence there arise in cities family connections, brotherhoods, common sacrifices, amusements which draw men together. But these are created by friendship, for to choose to live together is friendship. The end of the city is the good life, and these are the means toward it. (3.9, 1280b35)

There we have from Aristotle a remarkable political recycling of the pleasure contributed by the various associations to which each citizen belongs. We should, for several reasons, say a bit more about this notion of friendship. We often see from historians the image of the city as a kind of men's club united by bonds of friendship, even of love, a haven of civic equality snatched from the tumult of the world. Certainly, we could get that idea from reading Vernant. On the other hand, we could ask ourselves whether friendship does not open the possibility of a contradiction with one of the cardinal theses of Aristotelian politics in which the city is the major natural association, and thus that the political tie is that which includes all the others. Friendship, as we will see later in detail, makes justice useless by superseding it, but justice is the foundation virtue of political community. So just as the family implements prepolitical relations, could friendship trace the outlines of a *natural* relationship that is "suprapolitical"?

"Friendship is the greatest of goods for cities."

Books 8 and 9 of the *Nicomachean Ethics* and book 7 of the *Eudemian Ethics* deal with φιλία, a term generally translated "friendship," and related ideas, because it is a matter of a subject nearly obligatory in ancient ethical thought, as was also the case for pleasure. In fact, Aristotle refers *philia* to ethics, and via ethics to politics, right at the beginning of his treatment of the idea in the *Nicomachean Ethics*, tearing *philia* away from the field of natural philosophy.[51] As it happens, some Presocratic philosophers had described affinities between the realities constituting the universe in terms of "friendship." The most famous of these was Empedocles, who made of *philia* one of the two fundamental cosmic forces, the one that tends to bring together into more complex systems the constituents of the universe. Actually Empedocles doubtless did not use the word *philia*, a term invented in the time of Plato, but rather talked of *philotēs* (φιλότης), the word that we have in extant quotations of Empedocles, while *philia*

---

51. Cf. τὰ φυσικά at *Nicomachean Ethics* 8.1, 1155b8, and the passage that precedes it: "Not a few things about friendship are matters of disagreement. Some define it as a kind of likeness and say like people are friends, whence come sayings 'like to like,' 'birds of feather flock together,' and so on; others on the contrary say, 'potter hates potter.' Some inquire more deeply and in a more scientific fashion, Euripides saying that 'parched earth loves the rain, and stately heaven when filled with rain loves to fall to earth,' and Heraclitus that 'it is what opposes that helps' and 'from different notes come the fairest harmony' and 'all things are produced through strife,' while Empedocles, as well as others, expresses the opposite view that like aims at like. The scientific problems we may leave alone (for they do not belong to the present inquiry); let us examine those which are human and involve character and emotion" (8.1, 1155a32).

is found in the accounts and summaries of his teaching by Aristotle and his commentators. We must note Aristotle's somewhat mocking tone as he talks about the confused character, even ridiculous, of these old systems. Perhaps he also captures the spirit of Plato's *Lysis* where a detour is made to the question of whether likes or opposites go best together. The matter of the relationships between *philia* and natural philosophy will come up again below. Once again, Aristotle reaffirms his basic position that theoretical sciences and practical sciences are separate.

What interests us is obviously the relationships between *philia* and politics, relationships that we can bring together in the idea of "political friendship" (πολιτικὴ φίλια), something that has been the subject of an interesting debate between interpreters of Aristotle's philosophy. That *philia* has a particular tie to politics is obvious even in a cursory reading of the *Politics*. Aristotle even asserts that this tie is necessary when he writes that "political community presupposes *philia*" (*Pol.* 4.11, 1295b13). In fact, if *philia*, confined to the ethical-political sphere, has a characteristic of particular importance for us, it is that it operates on the same field as justice,[52] while it subverts justice. The major problem that justice must resolve, when one considers it as a basic virtue from the political point of view, is to determine what is owed to each person. We will see more exactly below how Aristotle means to attribute to each one the part that he may claim, but we can already say that the basic rule of that distribution is to give to each according to his political merit, that is, in relation to what he contributes to the city. Thus, two men who contribute equally to the good functioning of the institutions of the city ought to receive equal shares. In a well-functioning constitution, everyone, or nearly everyone, would find equitable the way that rewards are distributed, not only material goods but especially a share in the authority and power in the city as well as the symbolic gratifications attached to them.

But the relationship of friendship is thus shaped that if I have a friend, I would accept, even wish, that he should receive more than his share, including to my detriment, and I would even find pleasure in that voluntary dispossessing. If that kind of feeling of generosity spreads throughout the civic body, relationships between citizens will be more relaxed, less conflicted, and the city will have less fear of revolts. In fact, a citizen who feels himself to be a "friend" of his fellow citizens will

---

52. "Friendship and justice relate to the same things and are revealed between the same persons" (*EN* 8.9, 1159b25).

no longer function on the basis of his own personal interests, but will demonstrate benevolence toward his fellow citizens, *because it is them*, to paraphrase Montaigne's famous formula. Aristotle expresses this in an unexpected way in the *Nicomachean Ethics*:

> But equality does not seem to take the same form in acts of justice and in friendship; for in acts of justice what is equal in the primary sense is that which is in proportion to merit, while quantitative equality is secondary, but in friendship quantitative equality is primary and proportion to merit secondary. (8.8, 1158b29)

Aristotle illustrates these considerations by saying that friendship between people who are too unequal (rich and poor, king and subjects, god and men) is impossible or very difficult. But what this passage also says is that I can agree to divide goods, whether material or spiritual, into two equal parts with my friend, even if I would be justified in demanding a division proportional to our respective merits that would be to my advantage and that would be *properly speaking* just. On the other hand, Aristotle does not seem to consider the situation in which only one of the parties cedes. The reason for that is that *philia* presupposes reciprocity, and we will see more precisely in what way, below. Few of the Greeks who thought about city life would have disagreed with Aristotle's assertion that "friendship is the greatest of goods for the city" (*Pol.* 2.4, 1262b7).

But, since politics represents the supreme activity and includes all human practical thought and activity, some have wanted to see in the expression "political friendship," which does not appear very often in the *Nicomachean Ethics*—a little more often in the *Eudemian Ethics*—the supreme form of friendship. That is John Cooper's interpretation in his contribution to the 1987 Symposium Aristotelicum devoted to the *Politics*.[53] According to Cooper, the "common good" whose pursuit is, for Aristotle, the sign that the city is good, presupposes that the citizens accomplish some common work, but also, and perhaps above all, that each one find in himself the generosity necessary to complete this common work without expecting an immediate personal profit. But only *philia*, or *philia* more than anything else, brings it about that each one takes pleasure in placing the satisfaction

---

53. John Cooper, "Political Animals and Civic Friendship," in *Aristoteles 'Politik.' Akten des XI. Symposium Aristotelicum*, ed G. Patzig (Göttingen: Vandenhoech & Ruprecht, 1990), 220–241; Julia Annas's response is on 242–248.

of his friend before his own. That would make the excellent city a club of generous men, and for Aristotle generosity is an eminently political virtue. I would now like to show why we must reject that interpretation.

Let us begin (we won't make a habit of it) with sociolinguistic considerations. Although the word *philia* was a recent coinage in Aristotle's day, the word *philos* (φίλος) is old. Some, like Gustave Glotz,[54] relying on the fact that in Homer φίλος sometimes has a possessive sense (the phrase φίλα γούνατα, "his knees," is often cited) concludes that this adjective is applied to whatever belongs most to the subject, that is, Glotz thought, to the members of the lineage of the possessor. For Émile Benveniste, on the other hand, in his famous *Vocabulaire des institutions indo-européennes*,[55] the word *philos* refers essentially to hospitality relationships, that is, relations with foreigners. If, then, my *philos* par excellence is the guest that I receive according to the rules of hospitality, the sentiment that I devote to him, *philotēs* (φιλότης), ancestor of *philia*, has more to do with the social and contractual sphere than with the biological and symbiotic interdependencies of the family. Certainly, *philos* sometimes has a purely possessive sense, but that does not prevent Benveniste from being generally right. As for φίλα γούνατα, Benveniste connects that expression to a greeting ritual in which an infant is placed on the knees of the father or grandfather who thus recognizes it as a member of the community. By situating itself alongside contracts and institutions, ancient friendship, and thus also Aristotelian friendship, thus does not only concern intimacy, but locates itself within the bounds of the political.

Aristotle calls *philiai* (plural of *philia*) relationships very different from each other: paternal, maternal, filial, and conjugal love, mutual feelings experienced by members of cultural and religious associations, among others, but also fellow travelers and the like. It is difficult to say which of the ties that we characterize as obviously erotic are considered by Aristotle as kinds of *philia*. Certainly, the relation between husband and wife is a kind of *philia* though it includes sexual relations. I tend to think the same goes for homosexual relations between lover and beloved, at least when they are not passionate, since *philia* is not *eros*. But if one looks at the examples given in the *Ethics*, one can see that intrafamilial relations are given a very important place. Thus, in a passage of the *Nicomachean*

---

54. Gustave Glotz, *La solidaritéde la famille dans le droit criminal en Grèce* (Paris: Albert Fontemoing, 1904).

55. Émile Benveniste, *Vocabulaire des institution indo-européens* (Paris: Éditions de Minuit, 1969).

Ethics that will provide us a little later with a starting point, Aristotle gives four descriptions of *philia*, illustrating two by the relationship between mother and child; the two others are not illustrated, but they could easily apply to familial relations.

That also makes the *philia politically* interesting, since, as we have seen, the relations between the familial sphere and the political sphere constitute one of the major problems of Aristotle's political philosophy. The political philosopher, and consequently the legislator, necessarily are confronted, sooner or later, with this problem: How to mobilize the instinctive energy that individuals invest in their family ties to the service of the city, or, at least, prevent it from endangering political relationships? How to prevent a citizen from being a father before being citizen, and from using the fraction of *political* power that he holds qua citizen for the benefit of his son? The answer to that question is easy as long as it stays at the general level: to prevent dangers of that kind, it is necessary to inculcate in citizens what Aristotle calls *political virtue*, a crucial concept of Aristotle's political philosophy, though he turns out to be desperately laconic about it. We cannot avoid returning to it later.

But *philia* operates at the level of the family just as much as in the city. The origin of the city, as described by Aristotle, demonstrates this particularly well. The first form of political community is kingship, because it is a kind of politicization of the family. That's a beginning of politics, when the patriarch, who can be a kind of prepolitical king, accepts whether he likes it or not to submit to laws. One of the driving causes of the movement from the patriarchal to the political is precisely *philia*, since it is because they are attached to the king by relationships of filial love that his subjects accept him as king. For a *political* king should be, at least to some degree, accepted as king by his subjects who are already citizens. At this point they conceive the city as a big family. At the same time the difficulty that commentators have in deciding whether *philia* falls on the family side or the contractual side also bears witness to the ubiquity of *philia*. Thus J. Cooper figures that "civic friendship is just an extension to a whole city of the kinds of psychological bonds that tie together a family and make possible this immediate participation of each family-member in the good of the others."[56] This thesis, which reminds one a bit of that of Miers and Kopytoff noted above, on the subject of slavery, seems to consider the familial form of *philia* as the most developed and perfect form of friendship. We can think that familial *philia* is the most "basic,"

---

56. Cooper, "Political Animals and Civic Friendship," 236.

and for that reason, that it is the origin of other forms of *philia*, and in that sense, as we will see below, Cooper is right. But it cannot be a matter of a thesis proposed by Aristotle, and Cooper does not claim that it is, because for Aristotle, in all domains derived, extended, or weaker forms get their meaning only by relation to the perfect form. But for him the familial form of *philia* is far from being the perfect form.

Obviously, it is not enough to say that *philia* is a feeling of disinterested and altruistic affection that one has for someone without it taking the form of a passion, and thus irrational. There is more to it, as the beginning of *Rhetoric* 2.4 says:

> We may describe friendly feeling (*philia*) toward anyone as wishing for that person what you believe to be good things, not for yourself, but for him, and bringing about these things as much as possible. A friend is one who loves and is loved in return. Those who think they feel this way toward each other think themselves friends. (2.4, 1380b35)

That *philia* presupposes a kind of reciprocity is expressed more precisely in the passage in the *Nicomachean Ethics* whose study was announced above:

> For men think a friend is (i) one who wishes and does what is good, or seems so, for the sake of his friend, (ii) or one who wishes his friend to exist and live, for his sake; which mothers do to their children, and friends who have come into conflict. (iii) And others think a friend is one who lives with and has the same tastes as another, (iv) or one who grieves and rejoices with his friend; and this too is found in mothers most of all. It is by some one of these characteristics that friendship too[57] is defined. (9.4, 1166a2–10)

We no longer read this chapter in the same way since 1924 and the publication of Hans von Arnim, *Die drei aristotelischen Ethiken*.[58] Von Arnim thinks that by comparing the parallel passages in the *Eudemian*

---

57. This "too" is explained by what precedes: Aristotle is in the process of making a parallel between the feelings that go with *philia* and those that one experiences for one's self.

58. Hans von Arnim, *Die drei aristotelischen Ethiken* (Vienna: Hölder-Pichler-Tempsky, 1924).

Ethics and the *Magna Moralia* he can show that this chapter refers to definitions of *philia* given in the Academy by Speusippus and Xenocrates. On the other hand, it is clear to anyone who reads the sections in Aristotle's *Ethics* devoted to *philia* that the four[59] criteria given here do not constitute an exhaustive list. But above all, von Arnim finds a difference between the first two definitions that insist on the anti-egotism of *philia* and the latter two (or three) ones that assert that altruistic sentiments are not enough to make a relationship a *philia*, since it is also necessary to share the values and even life with one's *philos*. Perhaps this second position refers to the difference that Aristotle makes between *philia* and *eunoia*, since "well-wishing" (εὔνοια), examined right after *philia* in the *Nicomachean Ethics*, requires neither reciprocity nor sharing. So, there are not four (or five) definitions[60] of *philia* offered in this passage, but two.

Thus we find in this passage the two sides of the definition given in the *Rhetoric*, but in a way opposed to each other, flagged by their attribution to different people: on the one side, to feel *philia* for someone is to wish him well regarding his own interest; on the other side, "others" characterize *philia* by the sharing with friends of tastes, values, sentiments, and even their life. This is not a matter of two opposed and incompatible concepts, since one can easily imagine that someone lives with another whom he considers as his friend, sharing many things with him, all the time wishing for this friend every possible good "for the love of his friend himself." We have here rather two descriptions that put the accent on different characteristics, disinterested altruism in the one case, sharing in the other.

At the same time, I tend to think that Aristotle has not only juxtaposed two equally valid approaches to *philia*, but that that juxtaposition reveals a critique, possibly even a virulent critique, of the conception of *philia* as a disinterested altruistic sentiment. The two examples given in support of this first description of *philia* show that. As for the second example, that of friends who are angry at each other but don't hate each other to the point that they wish evil for the other, perhaps we should go as far as A. Gauthier and J.-Y. Jolif and see in it a bit of polemical irony:

---

59. Or five, since usually "lives with and has the same tastes" is read as two criteria. I follow J. Tricot in counting four here.

60. Cf. the word ὁρίζονται at 1166a10, which clearly does not have the strong technical sense of Aristotelian definition.

Aristotle would like to criticize "those who see in disinterest the essence of friendship," to the point of mocking them, because for them "the (angry) friend cannot avoid wanting good for his friend, and he won't get any benefit from it, not even in sharing the joy with his friend, because he doesn't want to see him anymore."[61] Thus the true *philos*, according to this definition, is the one who is angry, because, not hoping for anything in return from his friend, he loves in a totally disinterested way . . . The last two characteristics of *philia* provided by this passage would thus constitute a sort of critique of the first two. And the first example of the first description of *philia* clarifies Aristotle's intentions. The *philia* of the mother and her offspring is not at all a reciprocal relation: the mother wishes, in the context of high infant mortality, a long and good life for the infant to which she has given birth, very likely without expecting anything in return. In this example and that of the angry friends that follows it the relationship of *philia* thus does not produce a community between friends. In fact, it's more a matter of well-wishing than of *philia*. Through the second polemical example, and the very arrangement of his list of characteristics of *philia*, Aristotle means to reduce the importance of disinterest in *philia* and support that it presupposes that even if one is not paid back, at least that *philia* involves the sharing of something between friends.[62] Furthermore, in the previous book Aristotle had affirmed that "nothing characterizes *philia* more than living together (τὸ συζῆν)" (8.5, 1157b19).

Thus, it seems that there is at least a progression in the characterizations of *philia*, the people of the second group completing the definition of the people of the first. With, perhaps, a biting critique of those who suppose that the essential attribute of *philia* is disinterest and unilaterality, and thus a promotion of the approach to *philia* as a sharing of tastes and life. The last example in the passage demands a certain subtleness to be appreciated. It too appeals to the relation between mother and child, but it is no longer a matter of wishing well for the child, but of *sharing* with it pains and joys (τὸν συναλγοῦντα καὶ συγχαίροντα τῷ φίλῳ, 1166a7). Even if the child does not have any greater share in the relation of *philia*

---

61. René Antoine Gauthier and Jean-Yves Jolif, *Aristote. L'éthique à Nicomaque* (Louvain: Publications universitaires, 1959), vol. 3, 727.

62. Cf. *Nicomachean Ethics* 8.9, 1159b31: "The proverb 'everything is in common between friends' (κοινὰ τὰ φίλων) tells the truth, because friendship is community."

than in the first example (because its mother can suffer and rejoice in its pains and joys without the child being aware of it), the situation of the mother has changed in that in this example *philia* establishes a community between her and her child.

Richard Bodéüs seems to think that this chapter is entirely critical.[63] Aristotle would be in fact intending to show that these forms of *philia* proposed by the Platonists are ultimately feelings that the subject feels for himself, and thus would not be true *philiai*. Bodéüs is more right than he thinks. Because that is indeed the thesis that Aristotle develops in this chapter: if one wants to understand what *philia* is, one has also to understand "whence it comes" (ἐκ . . . ἐληλυθέναι, 1166a2). But it comes from the sentiments that each one feels toward himself. We saw that the list at the beginning of the chapter maintains that the true characteristics of *philia* are also to be sought in the two last characteristics and that it is necessary to make that agree with altruistic well-wishing. But the proof that that is true is that these last characteristics are also those sentiments that a good man feels toward himself. Aristotle shows that in the passage that follows, and sometimes in a way that surprises us. Thus, for the person who thinks that to be a friend to someone is to live with him, or wish to live with him, the idea is derived from the fact that the sage loves to live in his own company, that is, by remembering past joys and indulging himself by hoping for future goods. But we know that the virtuous man "is the measure of all things," and it is precisely this chapter that says so (9.4, 1166a12). That makes this group of four (or five) attitudes that can find themselves validated as possible attitudes of a virtuous man to also be applied "to other men to the extent that they believe themselves to be" virtuous men (1166a11).

We can conclude from all that that this chapter, far from being simply doxographical and polemical, very well reflects Aristotle's own thoughts about *philia*. The analysis of bad people that closes the chapter confirms this. There is no true *philia* between bad people, not only because they do not feel any joy between each other as Aristotle says at 8.4, 1157a19, but because they do not love themselves.[64] A striking picture of *philia* as a projection to others of what the good man feels for himself. That is an

---

63. Cf. his notes to his translation of the *Nicomachean Ethics* published by GF-1Flammarion.

64. Cf. 1166b17: "having nothing lovable in them they have no feeling of love to themselves."

angle of attack neglected by interpreters who are more concerned with the differences between active and contemplative lives. Because, after all, nothing obliges the sage from going outside himself. We will see that Aristotle takes up this idea of an active life in which the subject does not go outside himself in the context of the city, in *Politics* book 7.

If *philia* is essentially simultaneously a devotion to the other and a desire to "live together" while sharing values and sentiments, there is a great temptation to think that *philia* would achieve a certain completion if only in one way or another it could be the tie between the citizens of the same city, since the city is "the perfect community."[65] Thus we arrive at political *philia*.

Political Friendship and Ideology

As I have said, in the *Nicomachean Ethics* the expression "political friendship" does not occur often. We will look at the *Eudemian Ethics* in a bit. There are, in the first place, passages where this expression appears, but in fact they are not talking about political *philia*, or it is not clear what they are talking about. Thus at 9.1, 1163b32, Aristotle says:

> In all *philiai* between those different in kind [doubtless we must understand: when one *philos* has one sort of *philia* and the other another sort of *philia*], proportion equalizes the parties and preserves the friendship, for example even in the political form of "*philia*" the shoemaker gets a return for his shoes in proportion to their worth.

I think that many interpreters have, perhaps mistakenly, understood "*philia*," and that one should perhaps understand "community." Even if the reading "*philia*" should be adopted, the passage means nothing except the fact that there is *philia* in the city and that, when the proportionality is destroyed, this *philia* is also destroyed, without necessarily drawing the conclusion that there exists a *philia* whose characteristic is being "political."

The same goes for the passage in the *Nicomachean Ethics* where we read that "like-mindedness seems to be political *philia*, as they say" (9.6, 1167b2), and the parallel passage in *Eudemian Ethics* 7.7, 1241a32. Here

---

65. Cf. *Pol.* 1.2, 1252b28, where, we recall, τέλειος qualifies κοινωνία and not πόλις.

too, to say that like-mindedness (*homonoia*) is political *philia* is not to say that there exists a political *philia*—on the contrary, it is to say that when it is applied to the political community, *philia* becomes *homonoia*.

The last passage in the *Nicomachean Ethics* that mentions political *philia*:

> Every form of friendship, then, involves association, as has been said. One might, however, mark off from the rest both the friendship of kindred and that of comrades. Those of fellow-citizens [*politikai*], fellow-tribesmen, fellow-travelers, and the like are more like friendships of association; for they seem to rest on a sort of contract. (8.12, 1161b13)

A passage like this is far from creating a space for political *philia* of the sort that people like John Cooper dream about, but it does teach us something important, at least if we interpret it following Gauthier and Jolif.

They maintain, in fact—contrary to a reading, notably Thomistic, that claims that the passage is talking only about communal *philiai* while separating out *philiai* of families and those of friends, doubtless from childhood—that *philiai* of families and between childhood friends are an *exception* to the general rule according to which every *philia* occurs in a community. Obviously that reading does not go without difficulties, since it is contrary to several of Aristotle's usual theses. According to that interpretation the family and associations of comrades would not in fact be communities, but in the *Politics*, especially, the family is always presented as a community. It would therefore be necessary to conclude that we have here a more precise sense of "community" as signifying a group of people united by a contract (ὁμολογία, 1161b15), something that the family surely is not.[66] In addition, according to Aristotle's usual teaching, cities and tribes are natural realities, while here they rest on a contract, in contrast to the family. We recall that one of the reasons for the naturalness of the city, in *Politics* 1.2, is that it comes from families, themselves natural. In fact, Aristotle has no intention in this place to contrast that which is natural to that which is conventional, but that which is regulated by rules, for example a constitution, to that which remains uncodified, like family relations, thus contrasting the natural with rules

---

66. Not all the difficulties are not resolved however, for example, concerning tribal friendships.

and the natural without rules. Because for Aristotle the domains of the natural and the regulated are not disjoint sets. He would come to the assistance of Émile Benveniste, whose contractualist interpretation of *philia* was noted above. But the quoted passage, far from characterizing a kind of *philia* as "political," says simply that *philiai* established in cities—note the plural form: "*philiai* political, tribal, etc."—but also among members of a tribe or companions on a voyage, and so forth, are, or can be, of a contractual nature.

That's enough about political *philia* in the *Nicomachean Ethics*. Later we will come to the *Eudemian Ethics*, not because it exhibits real differences from its *Nicomachean* sister, but because it will open a totally unexpected perspective on political *philia*.

It's not only the case that the passages cited from the *Nicomachean Ethics* do not establish firmly—that's the least one can say—that there is for Aristotle a political *philia* carrying a special status, but they actually give powerful reasons to think the opposite. The *Nicomachean Ethics* in fact introduces two well-known distinctions between different kinds of *philia*. Aristotle differentiates the concept along two axes: first by the difference in *eidos* of the objects of *philia*,[67] according to whether they are chosen for virtue, for pleasure, or for utility; and next according to whether the *philia* takes place between equal or unequal persons. We notice two points. First, that of these two divisions each introduces a hierarchy: "perfect" *philia* is *philia* according to virtue, and that according to pleasure is closer to it than that according to utility; and *philia* between equals is better than that between unequals, perfect *philia* being that between equals. That is yet another example of the exemplary and explanatory status of perfect conditions in relation to imperfect conditions. Nevertheless, it remains that all the imperfect forms of *philia* are truly *philiai*. Next, and this goes along with what we have just said, *philiai* based on virtue also have the characteristics, at least some of them, of *philiai* based on pleasure and utility. In fact, it is not at all surprising, for anyone who knows a bit of Aristotelian ethics, that virtuous friends would find their friendship both pleasant and useful.

But it seems obvious that community *philiai* are *philiai* of utility, or in some cases, of pleasure, but are not perfect *philiai*. They would therefore not have the characteristics of perfect *philia*, for example *duration*, as 8.8

---

67. "The objects of *philia* differ among them according to species (form)" (*EN* 8.3, 1156a6).

explains, for as soon as the utility or the pleasure ends, the friendship is definitely in danger of ending. Virtue, however, as we have seen, is durable, so that friendship based on virtue is also durable. But above all, according to Aristotle, perfect *philia*, that which is based on virtue and is between equals, can include very few people—in fact, most of the time, two men. Thus, at *Nicomachean Ethics* 8.7, 1158a10: one cannot have perfect *philia* for more than one person "just as one cannot be in love with (ἐρᾶν) several people at once, for love is a sort of excess, and it is the nature of such only to be felt toward one person,"[68] which is repeated in 9.10.

It would be a good idea to give some notice to the question of the number of friends, because the way that Aristotle deals with it gives the partisans of the political friendship as the supreme friendship evidence to support their position. The passage that interests us is in the second part of *Nicomachean Ethics* 9.10 (1170b32–1171a20). Aristotle here defends the idea that the number of friends should not be *disproportionate*. As is also the case for the number of people to constitute a city (a comparison that is not innocuous in this place), set between ten and one hundred thousand, two numbers obviously disproportionate. The idea expressed by Aristotle that the number of friends "is presumably not a single number, but anything that falls between fixed points" (1170b32), seems to me to indicate that the number varies according to the type of friendship under consideration. The comradeship among young people can include a larger number than a love affair. And for a relationship to be a friendship, it must be reciprocal (1171a4). It is noteworthy that this is, at the end of the day, the criterion that Aristotle hangs on to, rather than that of disinterest: after all, Aristotle could very well have said that the number of friends is limited by our capacity to be disinterested toward a limited number of people. That confirms what we said above. And it reminds us of an aspect of friendship that we must not forget: friendship is a *personal* relationship, as Julia Annas strongly emphasizes in her critique of John Cooper's essay.

---

68. In this passage of the *Nicomachean Ethics*, the "excess" (1158a12) is generally connected to "love" only. But in this place *philia* is also found to be described as an excess, and that which is said above about the opposition between *philia* and passion needs to be completed. Perfect *philia* is excessive because, in its domain, it is not surpassed by anything, but, to speak in Freudian terms, passion is on the side of Thanatos because, besides being extreme, it deprives the passionate person of self-mastery, which *philia* does not do. This confirms again the idea that *philia*, no matter how excessive it may be, is not destructive of the self, since it is fundamentally an avatar of self-love.

From all of that, and especially from the personal character of friendship, it follows that one cannot have a great number of friends. How then should we understand what Aristotle writes at the end of the chapter? Here's the passage:

> Those who have many friends and mix intimately with them all are thought to be no one's friend, except in the way proper to fellow-citizens, and such people are also called obsequious. In the way proper to fellow-citizens, indeed, it is possible to be the friend of many and yet not be obsequious but a genuinely good man; but one cannot have with many people the friendship based on virtue and on the character of our friends themselves, and we must be content if we find even a few such. (1171a15)

If then it is true that friendship of citizens with each other can, contrary to the other forms of friendship, involve many people, it is because it is not a friendship based on virtue, or even on a personal relationship. All of that is a way of saying that political friendship is a friendship based on utility, which drastically undermines the pretentions of those who think that *philia* reaches its highest form in its political form. *Philia* gains in extension what it loses in value.

Nevertheless, even if it is not a perfect *philia*, there is no doubt that for Aristotle *philia* is very useful for cities. Thus, at *Nicomachean Ethics* 8.1, 1155a22, we read:

> Friendship seems to hold cities together (συνέχειν), and lawgivers care for it more than for justice, for concord seems to be something like friendship, and this they aim at most of all, and expel faction as their worst enemy; and when men are friends they have no need of justice, while when they are just they need friendship as well, and the truest form of justice is thought to be a friendly (φιλικός) quality.

To be treated justly by one's fellow citizens surely brings satisfaction, but it is not this satisfaction that friends look for, and feel. In *philia* one can find oneself disadvantaged from the point of view of the laws of justice, that is, one may be treated *unequally* by fellow citizens who are naturally one's equals, and still find pleasure in that. Aristotle's break with the physical approach to *philia* is thus complete. *Philia* does not arise from a physical speculation, not only because it would then be the object of theoretical knowledge, but also because those who Aristotle calls the "Physiologists" thought of *philia* as a balance between elements, while for Aristotle it is not, because it is justice that assures balance, and *philia*, precisely, is not justice.

Thus, *philia* does better than justice, of which the *Politics* never stops repeating that in the relationships between citizens, that is what allows the city to really function as a city, because *philia* does the inverse of justice, and that is why "legislators care more about it than for justice." *Philia* is not, strictly speaking, described by Aristotle as a virtue, but we can assume that it is accompanied, like the virtues and particularly justice, with pleasure. And in fact, there is nothing that a legislator can wish for better than that the city would be made up of citizens so generous toward each other that they would not be bothered about injustices that their fellow citizens might commit toward them. These fellow citizens would be disposed—in the sense in which when one has a virtue one is disposed in a certain way—to concord, *homonoia*. We will see that this ideal is impossible to achieve.

Of course the passage quoted above reflects opinions of people other than Aristotle, but there is not a shadow of doubt that he too thinks that justice ought to be at least tempered by *philia*, lest it become a coldly legal relationship that would not ensure a true *tie* between citizens. We will take up this question again when it is a matter of the opposition between the "ethical" and the "legal." Although it is not the perfectly virtuous *philia*, which is not really possible except between two good men, political *philia*, although remaining in its domain of *philia* based on interest, can, if it frees a least some of the citizens from the obligation of justice, not by leading them to injustice in a habitual sense, but in letting them rise above themselves, profoundly change the nature of the political relationships between citizens. By its political and social consequences, it would in a way prevail over perfect *philia*, which, because it's about two men, has little political significance. It is this hope that the *Eudemian Ethics* obliterates.

The *Eudemian Ethics* has more to say than the *Nicomachean Ethics* on the subject of political *philia*. It does not at all invalidate the results of the *Nicomachean Ethics*; although it does not at all place political *philia* at the top of the scale of *philiai*, the *Eudemian Ethics* does open new perspectives; when we say this, we do not rely on any hypothesis about the relative chronology of the two *Ethics*, nor do we derive any evidence for any such hypothesis.

The *Eudemian Ethics* offers, in book 7, many more occurrences of the expression πολιτικὴ φιλία than the *Nicomachean Ethics*. In the *Eudemian Ethics* Aristotle really addresses the question of political *philia*, especially its ambiguous character, which in my opinion is not at all the case in the *Nicomachean Ethics*. If we exclude the passage 7, 1241a32, noted above as parallel to *Nicomachean Ethics* 1167b2, we find seven occurrences of πολιτικὴ φιλία in *Eudemian Ethics* 7.10.

This chapter asserts explicitly, as the *Nicomachean Ethics* does not, that political *philia* belongs to the class of *philiai* based on interest (1242a6). This to the point that Aristotle quotes the saying "Athens no longer recognizes Megara," doubtless because the interests of Athens no longer coincide with those of Megara, "nor do citizens recognize each other, when they are no longer useful to one another; their friendship is temporary, for the exchange of goods" (10, 1242b25). We cannot more completely distinguish the political *philia* from the supreme form of *philia*: based on utility, it is short and precarious. But this political *philia* seems to take measures to reduce this inconvenience, by trying to establish a relationship of equality between the people who are concerned. Here's the passage:

> There is here, too, the relation of ruler and ruled that is neither the natural relation, nor that involved in kingship, but each is a ruler and ruled in turn; nor is it either's purpose to act with the beneficence of a god, but that he may share equally in the good and in service. Civic friendship looks toward equality. (1242b27)

That the political relationship between individuals, who are obviously citizens, might not be a "natural relationship" ought not be misunderstood: Aristotle is not denying that this relationship, which is indeed a power relation since certain ones rule and others are ruled, would be natural. At least that is the case, as we will see later in detail, in well-governed cities. But what Aristotle means here is that this relationship does not have the immediate and quasi-biological naturalness of the relations between husband and wife, father and children, master and slave, king and subjects. Neither is political friendship as it is here described as disinterested and benevolent as that of the gods, either the difficult relationship they may have to one another or the one they may have with human beings. This passage shows clearly that to proclaim that the citizens are also friends is to recognize a fundamental identity among them, and thus to make the power relation more acceptable, or less unacceptable, to the subordinate parties. This operates above all in the constitutions in which there is alternation in power, in a way the canonical variety of political power.[69] The *philia* that is thought to exist between citizens then functions like a reaffirmation of their fundamental equality. We thus rediscover here, vested with a political function, the characteristic of *philia* that is to treat equally people who are in fact unequal.

In the description that is given of it here, political *philia* thus seems to be a subversion of justice, since it treats at least one of the friends unjustly, namely, the one who accepts receiving less than his due. In contrast, by positing an equality among citizens, it imitates perfect *philia*, although differentiated in certain essential points. We will see that this political *philia* fills, and in a more efficient way, the role of justice in the maintenance of political community.

But the *Eudemian Ethics* reveals another aspect of political *philia* that is in a way opposed to the preceding aspect. Aristotle shows this by means of the opposition between friendship as a "legal contract" and as "ethical friendship." We find the same doctrine in the *Nicomachean Ethics* at 8.13, 1162b23, 25, but in a less developed form. Aristotle compares legal relations to ethical relations on the one side, and written laws to unwritten laws on the other, opposing the rigidity of the legal contract, which demands strict execution of its clauses, notably in terms of the date of execution, to the flexibility of an ethical agreement that, taking account of the affective relationships between the parties to the agreement, "is more liberal in terms of the time of payment, while continuing to keep the character of a contract" (1162b27). The *Eudemian Ethics* goes farther in explaining that political *philia* can take two forms, moving from one to the other, making it much less interesting for a city. Here are the passages:

> There are two kinds of political friendship, the legal one and the ethical one. And political friendship considers equality and transaction just as buyers and sellers do. . . . When, then, it is based on a contract, this friendship is also legal; on the other hand, when partners rely on each other, it tends to be an ethical

---

69. Cf. *Politics* 1.1, 1252a1: "When, according to the rules of the political science, the citizens rule and are ruled in turn," and 3.4, 1277b27: "But there is a rule of another kind, which is exercised over freemen and equals by birth," passage already cited.

friendship, that between comrades. This is why it is in this kind of friendship[70] that one finds most recrimination, the reason for that being that it is not a natural friendship: other kinds of friendship are based either on utility or on excellence, but in this case people want both: they have a utility relationship but make it an ethical relationship, just as between good men, which means that they don't have recourse to law under the pretext of trusting each other. (1242b31–1243a2)

And Aristotle mentions this remarkable example: "In some places the law forbids lawsuits for voluntary transactions between those who associate as friends" (1243a8).

Ultimately a very obscure passage. Why isn't political friendship natural? Catherine Dalimier, in her notes to her translation, thinks that that means that it belongs to two distinct kinds that are both natural, the legal relation and the ethical relation, and I think she is right. Like the *Nicomachean Ethics*, what this passage teaches us is that one must not mix kinds. Once citizens have chosen ethical friendship, which keeps from perfect friendship that essential characteristic of situating itself outside justice, one asks of those citizens to draw the consequences and give up having recourse to the courts for deciding their cases. Otherwise, they need only hold to the letter of the law. But they can't change the rules in the middle of the game. What seems to me new in comparison with the *Nicomachean Ethics* is the assertion, somewhat subliminal, that this double game is nearly impossible. Because what the *Eudemian Ethics* tells us is that this kind of generous friendship cannot exist between citizens, and that those who want "both"—legal relationships when that suits them, and ethical relationships when they need them—at best are deluding themselves, at worst fooling everyone else. It seems Aristotle knows Aesop's fable about "the bat and the weasel," which becomes in Jean de la Fontaine "the bat and the two weasels": "I'm a bird, look at my wings! . . . I'm a mouse, long live the rats!" *Philia* based on generosity is certainly possible in the perfect form of friendship between two virtuous men, and doubtless also within the nuclear family, but no one would agree to be injured repeatedly

---

70. The ταύτῃ at 1242b3 seems to me to refer to the political friendship that is the subject of the passage and not to the friendship between comrades (ἑταιρική), which wouldn't make sense.

by a great number of one's fellow citizens. It seems, according to what Aristotle says, that it is generally the lender who insists on the terms of the contract, while the debtor appeals to the benevolence expected among friends. Aristotle recommends a law that requires a choice between being friends or not: those who have declared that they are friends can no longer go to court. Perhaps Aristotle was laughing up his sleeve at the proposal that a law oblige citizens to decide whether they will stick to the law or call each other friends . . .

Aristotle thus shows us that friendly relations between citizens, encouraging them toward mutual generosity, are very useful to the city and that it is for good reason that legislators "care about it more than for justice," but that it would easily be the origin of "recriminations" (cf. τὰ ἐγκλήματα, 1243a12). Why, then, recommend developing *philia* among citizens if, instead of making their relationships "more fluid" as people think it would do, it would create conflicts in their relationships? It occurs to me[71] that in political *philia* we find ourselves face to face with an ideological concept, in the Marxist sense. If we actually succeed in inculcating in citizens the idea that, ultimately, they are friends, and that that friendship assures them a basic equality, they will cling more strongly to the existing constitution in their city, including people who are dominated. In cities where there is alternating power, it's simply a matter of getting those governed to be patient until they come to exercise the magistracies. But such regimes are in fact rare, and, as we will see again in the next chapter, even in Athens the "real" power was beyond the grasp of the common people. In cities where the constitution prevents certain citizens from having all or some of the offices, inculcating that idea is both more difficult and more urgent. It would make domination much easier. Furthermore, the false equality installed by friendship serves to reduce not only the political impatience of the governed, but doubtless also the economic frustrations of the poorest.

So, I will take up again here the words of my essay on political *philia* cited in the note. Essentially, in my opinion political friendship is a myth served up to the citizens for the greater advantage of the current

---

71. By bringing together the passage in the *Eudemian Ethics* and Freud's *Civilization and Its Discontents* as I have explained in my essay, "De la *philia* politique chez Aristote. Malaise dans la cité?" in M. Crubellier, A. Jaulin, and P. Pellegrin, *Philia/Dike, Aspects du lien social et politique in Grèce anciennes* (Louvain-la-Neuve: Peeters, 2018). I have often more or less copied sections from that essay in these pages on *philia*.

constitution. By inculcating in certain citizens, or really in all of them, the idea that strict justice can be superseded by an ethical sympathy between them, the legislator lies to them for their own good. We will see below that Aristotle does not have many scruples about resorting to a political lie in order to make the city function well, for example by making it out that certain members of the civic body may be citizens although they have no actual power at all; this deception is aimed at preventing people from being hostile to the constitution (*Pol.* 3.5, 1278a38).

To begin the study of the relationships between citizens by looking at "political friendship" before justice is surely putting the cart before the horse. We will see, in fact, that the *Politics*, but also the ethical treatises, exert extraordinary efforts to define the justice relationships without which there would not be a political community. The justice in question, which ensures that each one receive, in the matter of goods and power, that which he deserves to receive, is in no way an ethical ideal in the Kantian sense, but a form of relationship that preserves the interests of the people that it includes.[72] It's still necessary to persuade the parties concerned that what justice provides them is indeed what they ought to get, although people tend to "want more." But the analyses that Aristotle presents concerning the role of friendship in the city demonstrate two things: First, that the city would not function really well unless the citizens not only agree to surrender, to the profit of their fellow citizens, advantages that strict justice would give them the right to possess, but secondly, to take pleasure in that, because that is an essential characteristic of friendship. The citizens are then more than virtuous since, if it is true that the virtuous person enjoys doing good, nothing obliges him to renounce his rights. Citizens find this pleasure of friendship outside the law, because one cannot enforce *philia* by decree, but it is not against the law. And then a fundamental point for us, friendship is something that prepolitical communities, especially the family, bequeath to the city. The suprapolitical would thus be the direct heir of the prepolitical. In this sense J. Cooper is right to grant familial *philia* a privileged place in the development of all *philia*. We can go farther in that direction.

---

72. Cf. *Nicomachean Ethics* 8.9, 1160a4ff.: from the point of view of justice it is better to defraud a fellow citizen than a friend, to fail to help a stranger than a brother, strike any random person rather than one's father. Obviously, Kant never claimed anything like that . . .

Nicomachean Ethics 8.9–11 proposes a comparison between different kinds of human associations and different political regimes (constitutions) with different kinds of friendship. In chapter 10, leading up to chapter 11, Aristotle proposes a different relationship that seems to run contrary to one of the fundamental principles of his political philosophy, pointed out above. In this chapter 10, Aristotle lays out the "resemblances" that are "like models" (ὁμοιώματα δ'αὐτῶν καὶ οἶον παραδείγματα, 1160b22) between different constitutions correct as well as deviant (we will soon see what that means), and the relations that exist in the family. Thus the relationship between a father and his children is of the royal variety, and of the tyrannical variety if, as is the case in Persia, the father treats his children like slaves; the relationship between husband and wife resembles an aristocracy, and an oligarchy when it is flawed because the husband "extends his domination over everything" (1160b35); the relationship between brothers may resemble either a polity, called "timocracy" in this passage, or a democracy. There is some fluctuation in the characterization of the relationship between master and slave, which is both tyrannical and natural. In fact, this passage does not call into question the specific difference that exists between the powers at work in the family and political power, since it's a matter of similarities introduced by Aristotle with a warning when he says that they are "like models." In chapter 11, Aristotle goes farther in showing that, reciprocally, each constitution employs a *philia* that resembles that of one of the prepolitical relationships. Thus, the friendship that is characteristic of a timocratic regime resembles that which exists between brothers.

We thus learn, in this context, that political friendship takes a particular form in each kind of constitution. As chapter 9 showed us that the friendship that exists between members of a family or an organization more restricted than the city would be stronger than the friendship between citizens,[73] we realize that political friendship, in the specific form that it takes in a given city, is only a dim reflection of a prepolitical form of friendship. Although it occurs in the supreme community, political friendship is decidedly not the supreme friendship. Consequently, the problem of the strength of prepolitical solidarities that led Plato to suppress the family remains. But Aristotle's fundamental idea about the relationship between friendship and the city still has him in opposition to Plato. The enjoyment of life that attaches to various relationships that

---

73. Cf. *Nicomachean Ethics* 8.9, 1159b35ff.

exist between citizens—those that belong to the family and to all kinds of religious, athletic, and local associations, as we have seen—from the moment that this enjoyment moves away from frenzied passion, it is, we would say, the creator of a social tie. That's a fundamental position identical to one that Freud would take: if one reinforces *philia*, or Eros for Freud, one also reinforces the cohesion of the city; Freud would say that we thus consolidate the barrier against the death instincts.

Possibly we find there again, in a form belonging to the practical domain, a fundamental thesis of Aristotelian philosophy. In fact, just as the difference between the role of the philosopher and that of the legislator reflects a distinction between sciences of two different kinds, so too we see at work here a typical Aristotelian philosophical move. Here too we can invoke the shades of Coleridge: there are two ways of thinking that are, once again, exemplified by Plato and Aristotle. According to the first, the progress of thought, especially its movement toward more and more rigorous forms, happens by rejecting as deceptive the previous forms. "Previous" should be understood in two ways. First, it is necessary to reject everything, or almost everything, that has been thought by earlier philosophers. We rediscover that practice of the tabula rasa in people like Descartes. Aristotle, on the other hand, thinks that each one brings his own contribution to the discovery of truth, with the exception of those who have taken an entirely mistaken road. But the rejection of the "previous" also attacks the forms of knowledge that are not considered to be scientific or philosophical. The most important example would be that of sense perception. The entire Western scientific tradition, at least in the natural sciences, has been built on the Platonic *rejection* of sense perception, considering it an obstacle to thought. Aristotle, on the contrary, believes that there is true perceptual knowledge, one might even say perceptual thought, and our senses in fact teach us about the world as it is.[74]

Similarly, for collective life we find yet again this difference between Plato and Aristotle. Aristotle is aware of the danger of nonpolitical goals pursued by citizens to the detriment of their life as citizens. That's how it would go for those who give in to the desire to become rich. But it is not

---

74. Thus, on the crucial problem of the organization of sensible data into coherent representations, for example, by the fact that sense impressions are compared to each other, situated in space or endowed with movement, Plato makes thought intervene, while Aristotle figures that the senses themselves are capable of that work. Aristotle proposes the ideas of "common sensible" and "common sense" to do that.

a good idea for the city to separate citizens from their previous affections, because in developing those, in a very strong form, they develop benevolence and selflessness and thus contribute to making them good citizens. Prepolitical does not necessarily mean antipolitical, and friendship is a notable example. By developing the various forms of *philia* among the citizens, prepolitical communities are a factor in *politicizing* these citizens.

A Few Words about Women and, Again, about Slaves

The analysis of Aristotle's "sexism" has become, especially in the last twenty years of the twentieth century and above all in American academic circles, something of a literary genre. But it is remarkable that the studies devoted to this issue have been based almost exclusively on the way in which Aristotle thought about the *biological* inferiority of women to men, particularly through their roles in procreation. In that respect the relationships between men and women are only a special case of the relationships between female and male. But there is almost nothing on the ethical and political inferiority of women, essentially because Aristotle says very little on this matter.

So it is not a bad idea for us to look a bit at what has been written in this area—an Aristotelian way of proceeding, to tell the truth—and especially at a book by Sophia M. Connell, who has studied Aristotle's views on the relationships between the sexes,[75] and at an article by Marguerite Deslauriers about the virtues of slaves and women.[76] S. Connell is all the more effective in her denunciations of the excesses, and especially the errors, of feminist critiques of Aristotle, in that she has no intention of clearing him of the charge of sexism, as (male) interpreters of my generation have tried to do. One may "contextualize" all one likes, it nevertheless remains that Aristotle is sexist. The core of Connell's work bears on Aristotle's theory of the generation of living things, almost exclusively based on the *Generation of Animals*. She shows that, despite the fact that the male role is outrageously overvalued, it is nevertheless false to claim that Aristotle

---

75. Sophia M. Connell, *Aristotle on Female Animals: A Study of the "Generation of Animals"* (Cambridge: Cambridge University Press, 2016).

76. Marguerite Deslauriers, "Aristotle on the Virtues of Slaves and Women," *Oxford Studies in Ancient Philosophy* 25 (2003): 213–223.

conceives the female as lesser or as an absence (infertile male, less hot, less developed, etc.). Far from being a "privation of maleness," the female has a really *genetic* role proper to her. But Connell reminds us that there are two facts that one cannot avoid: we do not know the reasons for Aristotle's sexism, and we cannot simply put together the fairly large number of passages in which Aristotle explains the subordinate role of females in procreation and the passages—to tell the truth, *the* passage, or at most two passages—in which he takes the side of defending the ethical inferiority of women. For that we can turn to M. Deslauriers.

In *Politics* 1.13, the passage that tells us the most about the ethical inferiority of women, they are compared to slaves and children. Of these latter, one may simply say that they have the faculties and virtues of men, but they are not yet developed. It seems that Aristotle implicitly thinks only of boys when he says that they have the faculty of deliberation, "but not developed" (1260a14). One of the roles of the city would be precisely of watching over that development to ensure that it occurs correctly. The solution proposed for slaves, that is, that they deliberate by way of the deliberation of their master, seems not applicable to women because this solution is made possible by the fact that the slave is a part of his master (we analyzed this thesis above). M. Deslauriers shows us that that won't work for women. There remains the puzzle that these free human beings, women, are refused citizenship and made subservient to other free human beings, men.

Two passages cited by Deslauriers can help us. The first is *Politics* 1.12, 1259b4ff., which describes the relationship between men and women in terms of *power*, but apparently in a somewhat self-contradictory way:

> In most cases in which the power is political the citizens rule and are ruled by turns, for the idea of a political power implies that the natures of the citizens are equal, and do not differ at all. Nevertheless, when one rules and the other is ruled the former endeavors to create a difference of outward forms and names and titles of respect. . . . The relation of the male to the female is always of this kind.

To tell the truth, there are two ways to read this passage, with very different consequences. One can take it as a comparison between political power, which can take on various aspects, but which tends to rest on an alternation of power, and marital power, which excludes this alternation.

But one may also understand that Aristotle here counts marital power among the political powers, with this characteristic, that it excludes alternation. Deslauriers adopts the second reading. But if marital power is to be *political*, it would have to be in a very weak or metaphorical sense, since one of the foundations of Aristotle's political thought, reaffirmed from the first chapter of the *Politics*, is that there is a difference in kind between marital and political powers. Nevertheless, it remains that political power and marital power are both powers that free people exert over free people.

The second passage, more interesting for us, is in *Nicomachean Ethics* 8.10. We already mentioned it, but it deserves closer attention. In this chapter that is part of the study of friendship and that sets up a parallel between different kinds of friendship and different regimes, Aristotle establishes also a parallel between political regimes and familiar relationships, and indeed still in terms of power. But with what words of caution! We quote it again: "One may find resemblances to the constitutions and, as it were, patterns of them even in households" (1160b22). That does not bring into question the specific difference between political power and familial power, and one may even say that in its very mode of expression this passage confirms Aristotle's usual doctrine on the kinds of differences that we talked about above. The word ὁμοίωμα can in fact be considered as nearly a synonym of "analogy," and that is indeed what Aristotle is talking about, since he says:

> The association of husband and wife seems to be aristocratic; for the man rules in accordance with merit, and in those matters in which a man should rule, but the matters that befit a woman he hands over to her. If the man rules in everything, he transforms the relationship into oligarchy. (1160b32)

What is an aristocracy? It is a regime in which the power is entrusted to a minority of people because of their virtue. The other members of the city, who are formally excluded from citizenship or accorded partial or even purely verbal citizenship (deception to which we have already alluded), need to obey without really participating in power. Oligarchy is a deviant form of aristocracy, in which the power is indeed passed to a minority, but no longer on the criterion of virtue but in general on that of wealth. The comparison with the conjugal relation is therefore very enlightening on what Aristotle thinks about marriage. When it functions well, that is, when it is according to (his) nature, the husband exercises power by reason of the fact that he has a virtue that the wife does not have. Doubtless that is above all the deliberative virtue mentioned in 1.13. Thus, the wife does not have a place analogous to that of a *citizen*, but we have the following analogy: that which the citizen is to the non-citizen inhabitant (or to the quasi-citizen) in an aristocracy, the husband is to the wife when their relation is as it should be. However, when the husband tries to supplant his wife and decide everything, particularly the "feminine" part of household administration, we have a deviant form of the conjugal relation.

When the conjugal relation, which is of the aristocratic type when it functions well, deviates, it is not surprising that Aristotle finds a resemblance with the deviant form of aristocracy, namely, oligarchy. Like every deviant constitution, an oligarchy is a regime that functions in the interest of the class of oligarchs and not for the "common advantage." We will have a good deal to say, with many details, about this criterion of the distinction between correct and deviant constitutions. It means that a functioning oligarchy does not develop virtue in the body of citizens and in those who could become citizens if they were to acquire more virtue. But when the husband takes over from his wife those tasks that are naturally hers, he simultaneously prevents his wife from exercising *and developing* her excellence, and he performs those actions for which he does not have excellence. So, we are really in the same condition as that which describes a deviant constitution; the oligarchs too not only prevent the development of virtue in their fellow citizens, but they themselves rule without the political excellence that they would need in order to govern for the sake of the common advantage.

And Aristotle drives in the same nail with the following sentence: "Sometimes, however, women rule, because they are heiresses; so their rule is not by virtue of excellence but due to wealth and power, as in oligarchies" (1161a1).

From all that, it follows that Aristotle never affirms the equality of the sexes. To be sure, conjugal power is, like political power, an example of power exercised over free people, and this is why one must not treat one's wife as a slave, as barbarians do. But that which makes the absolute originality of political power is that it is exercised on people who are also *equal*, which is not the case for marital power.

For what we are concerned about here, the inferiority of women, derives principally from their inferiority in deliberation. "Women possess the faculty of deliberation, but without authority" (*Pol.* 1.13, 1260a12).

One would be presumptuous or lying if one pretended to have a complete understanding of this assertion. Nevertheless, we may propose the following hypotheses. The ethical inferiority of women certainly has, according to Aristotle, a physical basis, and ultimately it comes from the fact that the female embryo lacks the heat from which everything is derived: that females do not produce semen but "menses," that females are generally weaker than males, but, we must remember, with exceptions and remarkable variations according to different species of animals.[77] We don't know how Aristotle decided that the deliberative inferiority of women flowed from their physical inferiority, as S. Connell correctly points out. But what we know is that this is the result:

> On Aristotle's view, the deliberative faculty in women operates only in a particular domain, the household, which exists for the sake of another domain, the city. Because the household is for the sake of the city, the city is better than the household, and hence the rule of the former is without authority relative to the rule of the latter.[78]

But the fact that the husband exercises his power in a more worthy and more crucial domain, that of the city, does not give him the competence to arrange the household.

The introduction of teleology into the explanation of the inferiority of women is, finally, the best we can do. It is necessary, once again, to apply the rule according to which Nature gives to each agent the appropriate means for accomplishing its task, for the good of all. The family is necessary for the city, that is its end. Husband and wife are each endowed with the sort of deliberative capacity that is appropriate for their function, and any encroachment of either on the territory of the other endangers the whole. The ethical inferiority of women, we must remember, is not accompanied by any intellectual inferiority, but rather denies them deliberation "with authority," that is, at least, deliberation at the level of civic affairs. But without that inferiority, which goes along with the fulfillment by women of their functions, there would not be a city.

---

77. Cf. *History of Animals* 9.1, 608a33: "All females are less courageous than males, except in the bear and the panther."

78. Deslauriers, "Aristotle on the Virtues of Slaves and Women," 229.

As for slaves, everything said above is about *natural* slavery, which is one of the relationships that constitute the family. Along with many others, I have insisted that this slavery is so different from the slavery actually practiced in Greek cities in that time that the text of *Politics* 1 cannot give us any information about Aristotle's opinion concerning actual slavery. Nevertheless, there is in the *Politics* room for another sort of slavery that does not rely, or not only relies, on the head of a family, but on the city. Thus in 7.10 we read:

> The very best thing of all would be that the farmers should be slaves taken from among men who are not all of the same race and not spirited, for if they have no spirit they will be better suited for their work, and there will be no danger of their making a revolution. The next best thing would be that they should be barbarian country people, and of a like inferior nature; some of them should be the slaves of individuals, and employed on the private estates of men of property, the remainder should be a common property and employed on the common land. (1330a25)

Here it is no longer the kind of perfection in which the slave can pretend to be an organ of his master, but of the well-understood interest of the city with a correct constitution. To pretend that this text is of Platonic manufacture, because old, as many interpreters have done, does not fundamentally change things. What we have to think is that there coexist two approaches to slavery in Aristotle. It's a coexistence without contradiction, because what is said about natural slavery in book 1 in no way implies that Aristotle was opposed to slavery as he saw it practiced all around him. The city has needs that the family does not, and vice versa, and thus the tools adapted for responding to these needs are different. The only question that really matters to us, without being able to know at what points Aristotle thought the slavery of his time needed reform, is this: is the slavery needed by the excellent city also natural?

Doubtless Aristotle would respond to this question in a positive way, for the following reasons. The excellent city would make slaves only of people who are unable to behave as free men and women. And, just like domestic slaves, they would find a sort of perfection in participating, to the extent of their ability, in the realization of a work that is beyond them, that of making the city function by relieving citizens from onerous and degrading tasks. The only thing that the public slave would lack would be the union with his master from which flows the "community of life" that Aristotle talks about. In the case of the domestic slave, as we saw, his master can say that he is one of his organs, even if he exists separately. Can one say of the public slave that he or she is like an arm, or hand, separated from the city? Lacking texts, it is hard to decide whether Aristotle personified the city to such an extent that he could adopt a position like that. We will see below that he does come to consider the people, at least metaphorically, as "a kind of single human being with many feet, many hands, and many sense organs" (*Pol.* 3.11, 1281b6). In any case, Aristotle very likely thinks that the situation of a domestic slave, if his master is not a villain of course, is preferable to that of the public slave. Not for the same reason, as we have seen, that makes Aristotle prefer the condition of the slave to that of the day-laborer, because the laborer does not have the "advantages" of the slave except when he works under the orders of a master, but, doubtless, because public slaves are like the wandering limbs of Empedocles's zoogony, in search of a body.[79]

---

79. Cf. *Physics* 2.8, 198b32, with Simplicius's commentary 371.33ff. DK31B61.

CHAPTER 4

Citizen, City, Constitution

The Citizen and Power

It is time to put to the test the dichotomy stated above between normative and realist politics, and we can begin, as does Aristotle himself, by paying attention to the concept of "citizen," obviously central in his political philosophy. We have seen that the good citizen is characterized by his ethical virtue, which alone can make the city the place for happiness. But to understand what a good citizen is, one must first know what a citizen is or who is a citizen. But each city would give a different answer to the question, "Who is a citizen?" It's worth noting that this question, if we take the books of the *Politics* in the order transmitted by tradition, is not taken up at the beginning. In book 1, the city is taken as an enveloping community, but the notion of "citizen" does not even appear. In book 2, it is the main topic, at least quantitatively, of the *Politics* that come onto the stage, specifically the *constitution*, and more precisely, "the best constitution of all" (2.1, 1260b28). But as it's a matter of examining constitutions that have really existed or been imagined by political theoreticians, the very idea of a constitution is not defined, and that of a citizen even less.

The definition machine starts up in *Politics* 3. In fact, we can't begin on the question of a constitution until "city" is defined: "He who would inquire into the essence and attributes of various kinds of constitution must first of all determine what a city is" (3.1, 1274b32).

The question was left hanging until now, as even the phraseology of the question that Aristotle poses at the start of book 3 shows: τί ποτέ ἐστιν ἡ πόλις, "What, finally, is a *polis*?" or "What, exactly, is a *polis*?"

No sooner is this question posed than Aristotle finds three immediate justifications. There is, in the first place, a problem that is in fact very urgent, and historically recurring, knowing who "performed a certain act"—the city, the party in power, the tyrant (3.1, 12174b35)—and thus who is responsible at the time. Is the French Republic responsible for the laws and decrees of the Vichy government? Next, it is indeed the city that concerns the action of the legislator: "And the legislator or statesman is concerned entirely with the city" (3.1, 1274b36). With this simple remark, Aristotle recognizes that it is indeed the legislator to whom he addresses the *Politics*. Finally, "The constitution is an arrangement of the inhabitants of the city" (1274b38). Later, Aristotle will even say that the constitution is "a kind of life for a city" (4.11, 1295a40), which confirms that one must define the city before studying constitutional problems.

But it is impossible to understand what a city really is if one has not already answered a preliminary question: "Who is a citizen, and what is the meaning of the term?" (1275a1). In fact, the city is a whole composed of parts, and these parts are citizens: ἡ γὰρ πόλις πολιτῶν τι πλῆθός ἐστιν, "The city is a certain quantity of citizens" (1274b41). At first glance that definition looks sketchy and inexact, because the city is composed of a good many other things besides citizens, but, we will see, that is a *politically* correct definition: what makes a *polis* be a *polis* is its citizens (πολῖται, plural of πολίτης).

This order of exposition, that proposes studying the citizen before the city, and the city before the constitution, is an order that one might call "pedagogical," but it is neither *scientific* nor *natural* in that it does not start from the most basic to go toward that of which it is the basis. For even if it is because he is political by nature that a man may be a citizen, it is nevertheless true that, as *Politics* 1.2 says, the city is prior to each citizen, and it is because a human community is regulated by a certain type of system of laws, that is, by a constitution, that it is a city, and not because it is a city that it has a constitution. In any case these three realities, the constitution, the city, and the citizen, are closely related to each other, for as we will emphasize many times, it is in function of its constitution that is, as we will see, its *form*, that a city confers citizenship on certain men and not on others. That is anyway the proper and main objective of the *Politics*, the constitution, to which leads off, fairly quickly, book 3. The *Politics* never abandons this objective.

This path doubtless finds solid support in the common consciousness of the Greeks, to the extent that we can discern what that consciousness was. The great divide by which the Greeks defined themselves, between Greeks and barbarians, was translated politically into an opposition between citizens and subjects. And Aristotle never contradicts the generally accepted belief that citizenship is a natural property of human beings worthy of the name, that is, males, Greeks (at least some of them, as we have seen, since not all Greeks lived in cities), free, and not too evil. To all these characteristics, citizenship adds another, that of *equality*. Since political power is the power that allows governing equals, the Greek city definitely installed that unusual kind of government that rests on the equality of rights between governors and governed when they are citizens in the same city. When Claude Mossé writes concerning the Athenian democracy that "it remains that it was the first time in history that such a principle of equality in freedom of speech and equality before the law was formulated, that privileges based on birth or wealth were negated,"[1] she is certainly right. From that point of view, the Greeks are indeed the ancestors of our democracies, which pretend to put into effect power of that kind. It would seem that *Politics* 1.2 starts by trying to base that common conception on reason, but Aristotle drops that project in order to investigate the prepolitical community that the family is.

The final characteristic of the citizen, in this common approach of citizenship, is that to be a citizen is to obey written *laws*, known by all and applying to all. The city and the constitution, by reference to the laws, are grasped together with the citizen. In fact, the constitution is both the set of laws of a city and a system of government in which it is the law that has the last word. Even monarchy, when it is the form of government of a *city* in the true sense, is one of the correct constitutions because the king exerts his power under the aegis of the law, while oriental monarchies are essentially despotic because the monarch is above the law.

In other words, if we had only book 1[2] of Aristotle's *Politics*, there would be no difficulty in putting Aristotle into the grand tradition from Plato to Vernant that says that citizenship is part of the essence of man. In fact, Aristotle's formula "man is naturally a political animal" is often interpreted this way; we have tried to decode it above. From this *essential*

---

1. Claude Mossé, *Politique et société en Grèce ancienne. Le 'modèle' athénien* (Paris: Flammarion, 1995), 11.
2. We may add books 2, 6, and 7, but not book 3, which, although reputed "normative," does not adopt this generalized viewpoint.

point of view, a man has rights that frame his citizenship: if one denies him freedom or the right of giving his opinion by his vote on civic affairs, one has deprived him of part of his essence.³ His "Dasein," to use a terminology much later than Aristotle, then does not correspond to his concept. We're right in the middle of normative politics, in which citizenship is the culmination of humanness, because a human being has not fully developed his concept until he is a citizen, and reciprocally, the human being who has "political virtue" deserves in the highest degree to be a citizen; that virtue is the excellence that allows him to govern and be governed for the sake of common advantage. We will soon explain all of that.

It is truly astonishing that the great majority of interpreters who have claimed to distinguish different levels and dates in Aristotle's *Politics* have classified book 3, without much hesitation, among the "normative" or "idealist" texts. Yet right from the start this book propels us into *realist* politics. It's not only a matter of knowing who deserves to be a citizen, but what it is that actually makes one man a citizen and another not. Later, it will doubtless be one of the principle tasks of a good legislator, enlightened by the philosopher, to make the concept and reality coincide by bringing it about that actual citizens be the sort of people who deserve to be citizens. But *Politics* 3 defines the citizen as the one "who participates in a judiciary function or a magistracy" (3.1, 1275a22), in short, who shares in *political power*. That this is a matter of a purely political criterion and pertains to a realist politics can be clearly seen, among other things, in the answer that Aristotle gives to the question of knowing whether one must consider as real citizens those who are so unjustly (3.2, 1276a1). Aristotle's answer is clear and direct: just as a person who performs as a magistrate is a magistrate, no matter how he obtained this function, one who participates in deliberative and judicial power, no matter how, including fraudulently, is a citizen. Whether we like it or not, from the moment that we decide that a community under consideration is a city, there will be people who do not deserve to be

---

3. A very important prerogative for citizens, both in Athens and elsewhere, was the ability to address a court, for example, to register a plea. A metic had to have a "patron" to do it in his name. But it was actually the participation in the assembly and in the courts that best characterized a citizen. The proof of that is that when a citizen was punished with *atimia* after a serious crime, these were the rights that he lost, even though he kept his citizenship and was able to transmit it to his sons.

citizens, but who nevertheless are, because they participate in political power (cf. 3.2, 1276a2–5).

The main consequent of all this is that the status of citizen is eminently unstable and variable. And that in two ways. First, as Aristotle repeats several times, a particular individual would be a citizen in a democracy and not in an oligarchy. But the life of cities such as he has described it to us is anything but a long tranquil river, in that it has a background of an endless struggle of antagonistic groups with demands (as we will see in detail below) for which Aristotle generally recognizes a certain legitimacy. Constitutional change is thus not, or not fundamentally or always, a pathological phenomenon, a "feverish episode," although that can be the case. A constitution is a provisional manifestation of a provisional balance of power, for, as Aristotle says loudly and clearly, even if it is in this instance about slavery, "the winner always wins by virtue of some good" (*Pol.* 1.6, 1255a15). But constitutional change is a profound and radical change. Thus, the question that Aristotle posed at the beginning of *Politics* 3, whether the government of a city is bound by the decisions and engagements of the preceding government, has an answer that is also clear: if the constitution is the same, yes, if it has changed, no. A change of constitutions, by reorganizing political power, makes and unmakes citizens, because such-and-such who was a citizen is no longer one after a change in constitution, while such-and-such who was not previously becomes one. The change in constitution modifies the civic body from the point of view of quantity, in that the number of those who can be citizens varies from one constitution to another, and from the point of view of quality, since the *criteria* of citizenship vary. It's not the same thing, as it happens, to base citizenship on liberty, on wealth, or on warlike virtue.

The civic body may also vary, without a change in the constitution, for another reason, noted by Aristotle. The most interesting case is that where the city is forced to give citizenship to foreigners or even to slaves due to the "lack of people" (ὀλιγανθρωπία), for example as a consequence of wars that have been costly in human lives:

> They make such people citizens because of the dearth of legitimate citizens (for they introduce this sort of legislation owing to the lack of population); so when the number of citizens increases, first the children of a male or a female slave are excluded, then those whose mothers only are citizens, and at

last the right of citizenship is confined to those whose fathers and mothers are both citizens. (3.5, 1278a29)[4]

Thus, there is a long way between ideal and reality. Doubtless it is in agreement with the essence of a free and virtuous Greek to be also a citizen. But in reality, a citizen is a man who ought, *with right from a certain point of view*, defend his citizenship that has been contested, *with right from another point of view*. That's an essential point, which it seems that very few people have seen, and that we are going to discuss at some length. By asking about the relationship between those who are in fact citizens and those who deserve to be citizens, *Politics* 3 functions as a kind of turning point between realism and normativity.

But the status of "citizen" undergoes another kind of variation even within the city at a given moment. Nothing describes that situation better than George Orwell's wisecrack that all men are equal, but some are more equal than others. In all cities, in fact, even in the most democratic, the whole set of powers was not conferred on all the citizens. Thus, in the paragon of all democracies, Athens, the executive power generally belonged to the notables, while all free men participated in monitoring the magistrates at the end of their term.[5] Also, Aristotle's definition according to which the citizen is the person who participates "in a judicial function and a magistracy" (3.1, 127522) is accompanied by an important condition. The magistracy that defines the citizen is, as Aristotle says, of "unlimited duration" (1275a26). It thus refers more to a status than to a function, and that is why it is normally not considered a magistracy. In the same way, today, we would hesitate to say that citizens who have the right to vote are "political men and women." One may readily attribute the character

---

4. As at Argos, where they were forced to give citizenship to *perioikoi* (5.3, 1303a6). *Perioikoi* are literally those who "live around"; only in certain places was it properly applied to serfs (Laconia, the Argolid, Crete, for example). But Aristotle sometimes uses it as a quasi-synonym for "slave" (e.g., 2.9, 1269b3; 7.9, 1329a26). To reinforce a democracy, the leaders often reinforce the people by adding to them illegitimate offspring or children with only one citizen parent (cf. 6.4, 1319b8). Aristotle presents that as a well-known procedure, and thus doubtless fairly frequent.

5. Aristotle mentions this at 3.11, 1281b32. In Crete, where there was a much-respected constitution, although "less elaborate" than that of Sparta (2.10, 1271b21), all the citizens participated in the assembly, but its only power was that of ratifying the proposals of the elders and Cosmi.

of "magistrate" to a *strategos* ("general"), for example, or to the person who is in charge of public finances, or any other citizen invested with a legislative or judicial executive function, and not to the members of the assembly of the people, or, in modern democracies, to voters. But Aristotle says that we must go contrary to that common usage, for the assembly, which also serves a judicial function for important matters, is the real source of power: these people are "all powerful" (1275a28). A magistracy is called, in Greek, an *archē*, which is also the term that designates power in the most fundamental sense, and *archē*, we must not forget, also means "foundation, principle," but also "origin, beginning." We must also keep in mind that the verb *archein*, "to exercise power," is applied especially to a power, or an authority, that is the object of rules and consensus, and is far from being an arbitrary power based only on force. The exercise of power based on force is designated by the verb *kratein*.

The citizen recognized as such in his city, and thus in his constitution, is the custodian and principle source of power. This means that we must complete the definition of the citizen as a member of the assembly and of courts:

> But still, our definition of a citizen admits of correction. For under the other forms of constitution (than democracy) a member of the assembly and of a jury-court is not a "magistrate" without restriction, but a magistrate defined according to his office. Either all of them or some among them are assigned deliberative and judicial duties either in all matters or in certain matters. (3.1, 1275b13)

The form does not matter much: if the assembly is reduced to a role of representation, if it doesn't even exist anymore, and the powers that are those of the assembly and courts in a democracy are transferred to certain defined magistracies, returning to certain of them for more or less a long time, then that which defines the citizen in the full sense is that access to these magistracies. Because that's where the power is: the citizen is "he who has the ability to participate in deliberative or judicial power" (1275b18).[6] We notice that almost surreptitiously, at the end of

---

6. We need to note the word "participate" (κοινωνεῖν, i.e., to exercise in common), which shows that even in minority regimes citizenship is a function shared among equals. Constitutional monarchy thus appears to be a limiting case.

the chapter, Aristotle reformulates his definition of "citizen," since "the one who participates in a judicial function and a magistracy" becomes "one who has the capacity of participating in a deliberative or judicial power." Such a definition includes a limitation that needs to be measured.[7]

Statements of this kind do not show that Aristotle intends to contest the paradigmatic character of popular regimes, even if he sees their weaknesses. With democracy, and even more with polity, we are completely within *political* territory, while the other constitutions have kept something of the prepolitical. In any case that is what etymology itself shows, and is what Aristotle says: "When the many administer the city for the common interest, the government is called by the generic name—a polity" (3.7, 1279a37), which in a way amounts to saying that the polity is *the* constitution par excellence. That question will come up again, a little later, when we confront democracy and oligarchy. It is obviously in the interest of every city to have the "people" as numerous as possible, even if this people does not partake in power, but as the group of people who adhere to the constitution, or at least who are not hostile to it. Aristotle even envisages the case where it has been brought about that if some members of the civic body are citizens, but don't have any power, this *deception* (Aristotle's word, ἀπάτη) is intended to prevent people being hostile to the constitution (3.5, 1278a38). It's even the case that a whole chapter of the *Politics*, 4.13, is devoted to "pretexts for fooling the people," with "fooling" translating the verb σοφίζεσθαι (1297a15).[8] So Plato does not have a monopoly on political lies. In cities such as Aristotle analyzes them, but also in actual cities recounted to us by history, one may be more or less a citizen. That applies to the beginning of *Politics* 3, which has the reputation of being the foundation of a normative politics. It certainly looks like normativity blended with realism . . .

Nevertheless, there remains a question that Aristotle puts on the back burner, if we may put it that way, that of the content, and thus of the extent, of the power of deliberation and judgment that characterizes

---

7. Do we need to take account of the terminological hesitation between "judicial function *and* magistracy," and "deliberative *or* judicial power"? Newman says that "magistracy" is wider and includes "judicial function" ("judicial function and *more generally* magistracy"). In fact, there is a third formulation, "judge and member of the assembly," or the reverse. One should doubtless understand that citizenship can be defined at a minimum by one of these powers, and that in democratic regimes these powers belong to the assembly itself.

8. Literally, "do as the sophists." The passage tells us of the pretexts used "in the *politeiai*," which may be understood either as "in the polities" or "in the constitutions."

the citizen. Does citizen deliberation extend to the laws, with the power of making, unmaking, or modifying the laws? Because when, starting at book 3, chapter 10, of the *Politics*, Aristotle asks himself the question that is politically crucial, "What ought to be sovereign in the city? (τί δεῖ τὸ κύριον εἶναι τῆς πόλεως)" (1281a11), it definitely seems that this sovereign power includes legislative power in the modern sense. And, clearly, the answer to this question depends on the constitution under consideration. It's a question that becomes especially urgent in the case of a government of the mass of people.

Considering the sequence of topics in *Politics* 3 does better than many learned commentaries. We will have to stop at several of the stages.

Aristotle's realism, which leads him to define the citizen by the power invested in him, and not citizenship as an essential property of free Greeks, confronts conceptions no less realist. In chapter 2, Aristotle attacks, ironically as we have seen, the idea of citizenship that Athens had given a particularly crude shape, that established that a citizen was a man born to two citizen parents. That obviously leads to an infinite regress, since the parents would have to have two citizen parents, who themselves . . . This concept, according to Aristotle, mixes levels. Since the *polis* is *political*, that sounds in Greek ears like evidence that its foundation, citizenship (*politeia*), cannot be a matter of genetics. This critique of a way of conferring citizenship that must have been fairly common (in this chapter, we have seen that Aristotle attributes it not to Athens but to Larissa) ends by putting the question of defining the citizen directly into *politics* in the strict sense. On the contrary, Plato, both in the *Republic* and in the *Laws*, pushes the analysis of the city as a family as far as it can go, including the most fantastic aspects of Athenian ideology, although he recognizes them as lies. Here too it is one of the effects of the confusion of human communities as Aristotle criticizes it from the first lines of the *Politics*. Thus, when Socrates tells the members of the city of the *Republic* that they are born from the earth and are thus brothers and sisters, he recognizes that it is a lie (3.414b–c), a "noble lie," useful for assuring the loyalty of the citizens.

Aristotle directs at this genetic definition of citizenship two very remarkable criticisms.[9] The first relies on the authority of Gorgias, who,

---

9. Aristotle calls it "an immediate political definition" (3.2, 1275b25). The expression used by Aristotle, πολιτικῶς καὶ ταχέως, has gotten various interpretations, when it has not been simply emended. But if the meaning of πολιτικῶς is not certain, the word ταχέως (which must not be corrected to παχέως, "summarily") clearly indicates something done in haste, not constructed, immediate.

according to Aristotle's text, was partly puzzled, partly ironical (3.2, 1275b27) when faced with this definition, and said that "just as mortars are made by mortar-makers, so Larissans are made by demiurges, who are Larissan-makers." There are two wordplays here: "demiurges" means "artisans," but also in some cities, doubtless including Larissa, a demiurge is the name for a magistrate; λαρισοποιός etymologically means both "maker of Larissans" but also a potter that makes Larissan pots, a famous specialization of the city. The meaning of Gorgias's jest is clear: it is due to a law, that is, to a *political* decision of the citizens, that the genetic definition of the citizen was installed. The second critique, in Aristotle's usual manner, consists in saying that the definition of the citizen, in order to escape the infinite regress of the genetic definition, ought to be something that applies to the first citizens, who can thus transmit that quality to their descendants. Thus, the current definition is ultimately based on Aristotle's definition . . .

The following chapter completes this movement of politicization by continuing the critique of the usual definitions, now not of "citizen" but of "city." Starting by taking up again the problem of the identity of the city over time after a change of regime, Aristotle then goes on to a criticism of this other received idea, following the one that says that citizens are the children of citizens, that the city is a group of people who live in the same place. He shows that this thesis is doubly false, because it can happen that the civic body of a city can be separated into several bits geographically distinct without that putting an end to the city, and conversely, that people can live together without making a city. Thus, the Peloponnesus is not a city, nor is Babylon, even though surrounded by walls. At the same time, it is not racial community that makes a city. That problem will be taken up again when Aristotle studies seditions, because ethnic homogeneity is a stabilizing factor in cities, but it is not a necessity for the existence of a city. At *Politics* 5.3, 1303a25, we read, "Another cause of revolution is difference of races (τὸ μὴ ὁμόφυλον) as long as the citizens have not acquired a common spirit (literally, do not breathe together)," which assumes that they can *become* ὁμόφυλον. Finally, like any composite entity (Aristotle offers the example of a piece of music), a city is defined by its *form*, and its form is its constitution. In a way, by the end of this chapter, Aristotle has completed his reductive process, going from city to citizen to constitution, because, we repeat, it is indeed the constitution that says who is a citizen—the same individual, if for example he is poor, would be a citizen in a democracy, but not in an oligarchy—and it is the constitution that gives form to the city. Incidentally, Aristotle notes that he is leaving until later the answer to a question that is very important to him, that of the size of the city, because one constitution cannot govern too great a number of citizens (cf. 3.3, 1276a30).[10] That is a problem that we have already seen when we looked at the question of the autarky of the city.

Aristotle is quite aware that the city is not just a political reality in that some of the conditions for its existence do not derive from the political sphere, even if they are necessary for the city. The city would not exist "unless, also, the people live in one and the same place and unless they intermarry" (3.9, 1280b35, passage already cited). All of that concerns the material conditions for the city. But the form that makes a city out of this human material is the constitution. We find here again the dichotomy that runs through, especially, the entire Aristotelian biology, that brings it about that the form of the animal and the material conditions without which that form could not be realized work together. In this same *Politics* 3.9 Aristotle also mentions associations like commercial agreements and military alliances that cannot pretend to be cities because, among other things, they are looking out only for the immediate profit of their members and not virtue and happiness. This passage has strongly contributed to convincing interpreters that book 3 is "normative."

It's rather a matter of an indirect approach to politics: show everything that the city is not, or not essentially, to explain what it is. By placing itself irremediably into politics, the rest of book 3, from chapter 4 to chapter 18 (the last), deals alternately with two kinds of problems. The first is related to the ethical content of life in the city. Aristotle reminds us several times of the ethical goal of political life, since it is for the sake of virtuous actions and happiness that the city exists. The second turns on the various forms of constitutions. But there is a sort of intersection between these two groups of passages that forms one of the foundations of Aristotelian political philosophy. That consists of the study of the variation of values, especially justice, in different constitutions. The way that Aristotle proceeds in recognizing what we have said very briefly above, that all these approaches have something valuable, represents in fact a major turning point in this philosophy. In any case constitutional diversity is presented as the background condition for Aristotelian theorizing.

---

10. This passage sends us to "the examination of this difficulty on another occasion," which may well be 7.4, 1326a8ff. That is evidence that the books of the *Politics* are not as disjointed as is sometimes said and that book 7 is perhaps not as ancient as some have thought . . .

Excellence Is Plural

To begin with, for the ancient Greeks the diversity of kinds of constitution was a fact of life. Isocrates figured that "there are only three kinds of constitution: Oligarchy, Democracy, and Monarchy" (*Panathenaic* 132), while Aeschines writes that "everyone agrees that there are three constitutions for man, tyranny, oligarchy, and democracy" (*Against Timarchus* 4). And in fact, the Greek cultural region was made up of cities, some of them democratic, some oligarchic, others monarchies more or less tyrannical, without forgetting that some Greek populations also lived in "tribes" and not in cities, as we have already seen.[11] This diversity is made apparent in very different texts, from tragedies to historical accounts.[12] It is difficult to decide whether this constitutional diversity seemed normal or surprising, even scandalous, in Greek eyes. In any case it gave theoreticians of politics plenty to think about. Some of the classifications of different kinds of constitutions seem to have had a discernable influence on Aristotle, possibly that of Herodotus,[13] but especially those of Plato who, in the *Republic* (544a), distinguishes the best regime (monarchy or aristocracy), timocracy, oligarchy, democracy, and tyranny, and in the *Statesman* (291d) and *Laws* (712c) gives the following list: monarchy, tyranny, aristocracy, oligarchy, democracy. The Platonic analysis is based on a difference of value between the constitutions—thus, in the *Republic* classification, the worst regime is the vicious form of the best, since tyranny is a depraved monarchy—and on the possibility that constitutions have of going from one form to another. This transformation, according to Plato, follows a necessary sequence, since one always goes from timocracy to oligarchy, from oligarchy to democracy, and so on.

One sees how much, from the point of view of content, Aristotle relies on Plato. But he distances himself on several points. We will see, for

---

11. Cf. Raoul Lonis, *La cité dans le monde grec* (Paris: Nathan, 1994): "In some regions the Greeks chose to live as an *ethnos* (tribe). It's a form of organization in which populations live scattered in villages (*komai*) without a real urban center" (21). The word "chose" should receive further explanation.

12. See the well-documented book by Jacqueline Bordes, *Politeia dans la pensée grecque jusqu'à Aristote* (Paris: Les Belles Lettres, 1982).

13. *History* 3.80ff. Otanes speaks against the idea of monarchy and defends popular government; Megabyzus criticizes both tyranny and popular government—he would prefer an oligarchy (3.81.1).

example, that he strongly critiques the idea that there is a single sequence in the transformation of constitutions. But above all, there is in Aristotle an idea that is so novel that it has remained more or less hidden until today: constitutional excellence is plural. That is an idea that cannot be integrated into the Platonic system. A passage in the *Nicomachean Ethics* has been badly interpreted, even by the best commentators.[14] We read there, "There is just one constitution that is everywhere the best" (5.7, 1135a5). Aristotle does not at all want to say that, notably from the fact of the political nature of human beings, there is for all cities one single form of constitution that would be completely natural, the same for all. The "everywhere" has a distributive sense, and in this passage it means that in each particular case, for a given city at a given moment, there is just one constitutional form that is naturally the best, or, to look at the superlative another way that is *excellent*, and this rule is valid everywhere. Thus, there are for Aristotle several correct constitutions, and the distinction between correct and deviant constitutions is certainly the, or one of the, cornerstones of the edifice that Aristotle constructs beginning in *Politics* book 2. At the same time, since nothing is ever simple in Aristotle, we will have occasion to see that those who give an absolute value to "everywhere" are, in a way, not completely wrong . . .

A constitution is called "correct" if it directs a city for the sake of *common advantage* (τὸ κοινῇ συμφέρον[15]), while a deviant constitution aims at the particular advantage of a group or an individual. This idea of common advantage may be difficult to grasp and needs to be made more precise, since that of individual advantage seems clearer; still, common advantage is not entirely obscure. The city whose laws regulate the civic body in a way that bring it about that the citizens become virtuous, or more virtuous, or do not lose their virtue, functions for the advantage of all the citizens. For virtue is to the advantage of all, since it is the main condition for happiness. Thus, we understand why the three great types of deviant constitution are tyranny, oligarchy, and democracy, which are deviants of, respectively, monarchy, aristocracy, and polity. In fact, tyranny obviously has the goal of enriching and pleasing the tyrant, oligarchy functions for the profit of the rich, and democracy for the profit of the

---

14. For example, in the famous edition of the *Nicomachean Ethics* by René Antoine Gauthier and Jean-Yves Jolif.

15. Cf. *Politics* 3.3, 1276a13; 6, 1278b22, 1279a17; 12, 1282b17.

mass of poor people. What Aristotle calls "democracy" is a demagogical[16] regime in which the masses despoil and oppress the wealthy. What he calls "polity" is also, as we have seen, named by the word that means "constitution," and sometimes has the general sense of "political life" or "life of the city" and is, in addition, the word translated by "Republic" in the title of Plato's great dialogue; for Aristotle, it is a popular regime that, far from being demagogic, governs for the sake of the common good. This simple description of the various constitutions shows that the polity represents the culmination of a movement of enlargement, that is to say, as I have noted above, that it is the most "political" of constitutions, which confers on it, as we will see again, a leading place among the correct constitutions.

There is a property of correct constitutions that is both the cause and effect of the fact of governing for the sake of common advantage, and it will gain, in the following pages, a decisive importance. At *Politics* 3.6, 1279a17, Aristotle writes that "all the constitutions that aim at the common advantage are found to be correct in accord with absolute justice," the deviant forms being constitutions that rest on a partial conception of justice, that is, they function according to what seems just to one person or one social group.

From a certain perspective, all the correct constitutions are excellent, because excellence depends on the ethical-political state of the city under consideration, and more precisely, of the body of its citizens. Aristotle repeats several times that monarchy is natural, that is, excellent, for a city that is still in its infancy, because at that time there are few virtuous people (cf. 3.15, 1286b8). If a man, either alone or with members of his lineage, finds himself to be more advanced than the others on the road to virtue, it is just and conformable to nature to confide in him power in the city, and it would be unjust and contrary to nature to confide it to others. Aristotle notes that this kind of city is still close to a family or

---

16. For Plato, too, democracy is a regime that we would today call "populist." But the philosophers are in that respect going against common usage: Athens boasted that it was democratic. Thus, in the speech of Pericles reported by Thucydides, the *politeia* of Athens is a *democratia*. In 3.82.8, Thucydides gives his own version of the deviation in aristocracy and democracy: when *pleonexia* (greed) takes over from justice and mutual advantage, then the leaders on both sides "used specious names, the one party professing to uphold the constitutional equality of the many, the other the wisdom of the aristocracy" (πλήθους τε ἰσονομίας πολιτικῆς καὶ ἀριστοκρατίας σώφρονος), which gives us two bad regimes.

a tribe (cf. 1.2, 1252b19). The Greeks were quite conscious that this sort of regime has something archaic about it, and that is why they made the gods live under a king, says Aristotle, because "they represent the gods in their image" (1252b2). There is an assumed premise there, doubtless because it is obvious in Aristotle's eyes that the gods lead an "archaic" life, closer to the heroic past than to the political present. But the king, in a kingdom that is a correct constitution, is a *political* king, that is, not only is he subject to laws, without which the city would not live under a constitution (thus Aristotle hesitates to count tyranny, a regime in which the laws are not sovereign, in the number of constitutions[17]), but also, he has taken on the goal of the virtue, and thus the happiness, of the citizens. But by developing virtue among the citizens, he produces men who, because they have become virtuous, deserve to participate in power and thus to constitute an *aristocracy*. That means that a monarchy that functions well digs its own grave. Obviously, this process has to stop at a given time. One may think that it is when the city has become a *polity*, since then it is ruled by a correct constitution and involves the greatest possible number of citizens.

In this Aristotelian schema of plural excellence, the passage from monarchy to aristocracy happens because a certain limited but sufficient number of subjects of the king have become sufficiently politically virtuous that it would be *just* for him to share power with them. And the first to notice this new situation ought to be the king himself. But the passage in which Aristotle describes the movement from monarchy to aristocracy does not exactly say that, and is interesting from more than one point of view. At 3.15, 1286b12, we read: "When many persons equal in virtue arose, no longer enduring the preeminence of one, they desired to have a commonwealth, and set up a 'new' constitution."[18]

The phrase "equal in virtue" is doubtless understood "equal to the king," but also perhaps "equal to each other." It is not certain that this virtue would be immediately ethical virtue, and even less certainly political virtue, a notion we will try to elucidate below. At 1286b10, it is said that

---

17. "Tyranny is a monarchy that exercises on the political community a despotic power" (3.8, 1279b16); tyranny is the regime "that is most distant from a constitution" (4.2, 1289b2).

18. Perhaps it is not necessary to understand the word "new," but rather that people did not have the impression that they were living under a constitution while they were subjects of a king. Thus, Aristotle conceives of the king as a tyrant; see preceding note.

"because of their beneficence some were made kings," but it is probable that they did not lose their beneficence from the fact that virtue arose among their subjects. The reaction of the subjects thus seems to resemble the sentiment that one notices among children when they grow up and no longer accept the authority of their parents rather than an ethical conduct. Thus it seems to me—but this is very hypothetical—that the "virtue" that provokes their impatience is something like a maturity that they have acquired and that makes the paternal care of the king unbearable. But it is also possible that the future aristocrats would be helped by their development of certain virtues, like courage, which lead them to defy the royal power. In any case, more than a royal beneficence that would lead the king to abandon his power, the change comes from the revolt of the dominated. We will see that Aristotle gives a general form to this idea that it is due to the initiative of the dominated that history progresses. Such a description makes the succession of the monarchical regime much more "open." However that may be, we must note for the moment that excellence sometimes takes devious routes to establish itself, even though we might at first glance imagine that the virtue of the king and that of the future aristocrats would be enough to assure the passage from monarchy to aristocracy.

In fact, there are two ways to leave monarchy behind. The "good" way would be if the king recognizes that he ought to share power with others who have become sufficiently virtuous, and that he ought to establish an aristocracy. But the other way, which must have happened often in the history of Greek cities, is that kingship is replaced by a deviant regime, under two main forms: either a tyrant succeeds a king, who could be a king himself who has fallen into vice and excess, or a regime with a larger basis, but oppressive, succeeds the king, for example an oligarchy. And that is what the next part of the text tells us: "But when the citizens deteriorated and enriched themselves out of the public treasury, wealth became the path to honor, and so oligarchies naturally grew up" (1286b14); but it seems that the beginning of this change started in the direction of aristocracy (since the revolutionaries were virtuous people) and then later they "deteriorated." The situation described in this passage in the *Politics* is thus in a way a mixture of two paths. There is indeed a movement of virtuous people, "people equal in virtue," as Aristotle says, which should produce an aristocracy, but it seems that the transition has been, on the one hand, initiated by reasons other than the love of virtue, and on the other, capable of leading to a conflicted and troubled situation, which is, in short, what Aristotle and others have called *sedition* (στάσις). Thus, we see already, and we will have occasion to lay out the reasons for this, that sometimes sedition may be an improving process.

To exercise the function of citizen for the sake of the common advantage, whether it is a matter of governing in the strict sense, that is the exercise of a magistracy, or simply to participate in political life, in fact presupposes that the citizens be virtuous. And more precisely, that they have what Aristotle calls "political virtue," an idea already mentioned, one of the Aristotelian concepts for which Aristotle's reticence seems proportional to their theoretical importance. To establish any kind of constitution, whether correct or deviant, is above all to decide the criteria for assigning political rights, that is, according to what modalities some would have access more or less extensive than others to political power, and all the material and symbolic advantages attached to that power. The legislator who means to establish, maintain, or restore a correct constitution thus must pay attention above all that no one have access to citizenship, that is, as the beginning of *Politics* 3 has established, to power, if he is not endowed with enough political virtue. Aristotle is even more precise, when he says that power ought to be attributed proportionally to the degree of political virtue possessed by each one:

> Our conclusion, then, is that political community exists for the sake of noble actions, and not of living together. Hence, those who contribute most to such a community have a greater share in it than those who have the same or a greater freedom or nobility of birth but are inferior to them in political excellence. (*Pol.* 3.9, 1281a4, partially already cited)[19]

This is why Aristotle devotes *Politics* 3.5 to the problem that we have already noted, that of the exclusion of artisans from political power. "The excellent city will not make the artisan a citizen" (1278a8), and, as the sentence continues, if the artisan, in such a city, is a citizen, then political

---

19. One might perhaps convey an immediate reading of this passage by considering that Aristotle here claims only that virtuous citizens live their political life more fully than those who bring other characteristics. But this passage is included in a set of chapters that deal with the claims of different classes to the exercise of power. In any case the excellent city gives more power to an individual or a class to the extent that he or they possess political virtue.

virtue (Aristotle says "the virtue of the citizen," πολίτου ἀρετή 1278a9), which was in question in the previous chapter, would not apply to every citizen, and thus the city would not be "excellent," which is another way of saying that its constitution is not correct. The artisan is in fact incapable of political virtue, since the goal of his existence is not the common advantage, but the use and growth of his inheritance. The *banausos*, the word translated by "artisan," seems originally to designate someone whose activity is related to fire. In fact, the word is perhaps more interesting for what it does not designate than for what it does: the *banausos* is neither a peasant, nor a sailor, nor a warrior. The artisan is at best an economic man, at worst a chrematistic man, the worst being the more frequent. He therefore cannot be made political. That is why, as I have already noted, I have sometime translated the word *banausos* as "base artisan."

This question of political virtue is so crucial that I must devote a section to it, which can be done by making a sort of commentary on a chapter of the *Politics* as important as it is misunderstood, book 3, chapter 4.

Ethical Virtue and Political Virtue

This chapter asks whether the virtue of "the good man," that is, the ethical virtue of a virtuous man, is identical or not with the virtue, or it would be better to say, the "excellence" of the citizen. This text has disconcerted interpreters because it seems to maintain opposing theses, but until recently there has been a kind of agreement to see in it Aristotle taking a "realist" position, according to which, since it would be utopian to think that all the citizens of a city could be ethically virtuous, it would be good to recognize that one can be a good citizen at the same time as having some vices. Thus, one would have in this text one of the sources of the recurring question in moral and political philosophy of the relationship between the two domains. Thus, in a passage to which it will be necessary to return, Aristotle says that, to choose a general, it is necessary to take into account "experience more than virtue" (5.9, 1309b5), which seems to solidify the divorce between ethical virtue and political excellence. Furthermore, this common reading gives an additional stab wound to the "normative" character of *Politics* 3.

In order to avoid a mistaken interpretation of a passage, one has to grasp first its goal and its architecture. It is not the goal of the chapter to proceed to a conceptual analysis that would allow distinguishing between ethical virtue and political virtue, for example by bringing into evidence the political dimensions of individual virtues. Not only is it the case, and Aristotle is one of those who have shown this the best, that courage or justice differ whether they are examined from an individual or collective perspective, but in fact they change their shape according to the regime; this is so true that one may not be courageous in the same way in a warrior aristocracy that prizes the individual exploit and in a popular regime that figures that true courage is to keep one's place in battle order,[20] and it is also true that the same actions are not considered equally just in these two kinds of regimes. But the question that Aristotle asks himself in this chapter is the *political* question of knowing whether one can be a good citizen while being personally vicious, and reciprocally, whether ethical excellence guarantees political excellence. Thus, what interests him in this chapter are the actual virtues of the citizen, even if the results of his consideration do have some effect on the very definition of the ethical virtues.

The second aspect that must be grasped concerns the organization of this chapter. It does not present a single argument, but rather examines in order various theses.[21] In fact it is important to see that there is a turning point precisely at 1276b35. Before that point Aristotle presents a conception of the relations between ethical and political virtues that is actually quite realistic, without illusion about human nature. He there develops a comparison between the citizen of a city and a sailor on a boat (and a member of a choir, an example that I leave aside), which leads him to say that the excellence of a citizen, another way of saying "political virtue," is the ability to work for the safeguard of the constitution of the city. This political virtue would thus not be the same in all constitutions. But as, he says, ethical virtue is the same for all, a thesis that he does not bother to defend, one can be a good citizen without having ethical virtue (1276b34). One may say that that's a good thing, since otherwise very few cities would function correctly. It is difficult to understand why commentators have generally not seen that this position cannot at all be Aristotle's. Of course,

---

20. From the institutional side, no longer ethical, Aristotle examines both how certain weapons are more convenient for certain regimes and which military measures each ought to take in order to survive. Cf. 6.7, 1321a5–26: in places where conditions lend themselves to cavalry "the natural conditions are present for the establishment of a strong oligarchy," where it is the heavy infantry of hoplites, it corresponds to a less rigorous oligarchy, while light infantry and navy are the popular weapons.

21. At 1276b36, Aristotle uses the verb διαπορεῖν to announce arguments pro and con.

as we will see in more detail, the political philosopher needs to instruct the legislator on the means of making constitutions endure, including deviant constitutions, but that's not the only goal of political virtue. This position cannot however be Aristotle's, especially because it eliminates all reference to the good, that is, to virtue and happiness, and thus does not tie political virtue to the ethical goal of the city.

The excellence of the sailor, like that of the citizen, is double. A rower, for example, has a proper (ἴδιος, 1276b25) excellence, which is to row well, and an excellence common to all sailors, rowers, and others, which is to participate in the safety of navigation. It's the same (ὁμοίως, 1276b27) for citizens. Most likely one can understand that each citizen can have his proper virtues (be courageous, temperate, etc.) that can be exercised in relation to his functions in the city, but that there is another "definition" (λόγος, 1276b24) of one's virtue, which is to make one excellent in the preservation of the constitution of the city. The first excellence (row well) is called by Aristotle "the most precise" (ἀκριβέστατος, 1276b24), which doubtless should be understood as signifying "best adapted" to the person concerned, this word being approximately repeated by ἴδιος, "special," in the next line. The general virtues, both for the sailor and for the citizen, are in a way "more vague." But they are nonetheless more important than the special virtues, which are subordinate to them. In fact, there would be little point in knowing how to row well in a boat that will sink, or to be temperate in a city that will be obliterated.

Nevertheless, there is a limit to the comparison between the rower and the citizen. Even if the excellence that enables the rower to contribute to the safety of the boat is more important than his rowing ability, that ability does not endanger the boat. It goes differently in the city. According to Aristotle, ethical virtue is in fact unique: "the good man, *we say* (φαμέν) is such in accord with a unitary virtue" (1276b33), a thesis that appears so obvious to Aristotle that, as I have said, he does not feel the need to prove it. But political virtue, whose common goal is the conservation of the constitution, will often run contrary to ethical virtue. In an oligarchy, for example, it would be ethically virtuous to be generous to the poor person who has stolen something, while that doesn't work at all for the preservation of an oligarchical constitution. In deviant constitutions, one may even say that political excellence often demands ethical vice—thus a good democrat ought to be expert at plundering the wealthy—and there are also many cases in which a virtuous man would be a poor citizen, as in the case of generosity mentioned above. To put it in Aristotelian terms, Socrates was accused of lacking political virtue, though he certainly did not lack ethical virtue. But what about in correct constitutions?

Thus there is at 1276b35 a turning point in this chapter where Aristotle adopts both a new method and a new point of view. The new method is *diaporematic* (cf. διαπορούντας at 1276b36[22]) and the research is directed *from the point of view of the excellent constitution* (περὶ τῆς ἀρίστης πολιτείας, 1276b37). In other words, the initial question becomes, "In an excellent constitution must the excellent citizen also be ethically excellent?" This question is examined by way of two opposed theses. From this confrontation, Aristotle, as he often does, will take a position that borrows from both sides, and that will be his own thesis.

For partisans, not identified by Aristotle, of the first thesis, it is impossible that all the citizens be ethically virtuous. Doubtless those who take this position view it as an obvious common opinion. But we are dealing with an excellent constitution: "All must have the excellence of the good citizen, for it must be the case within a perfect city" (1277a1). The argument continues a bit, admittedly in a rather tangled way. In an excellent constitution, all the citizens must be excellent. But that is not ethical excellence, it is political excellence. Since the citizens are different from each other, they do not have the same political virtue. So, when Aristotle writes that "the excellence of the good citizen must belong to all" (1277a1), this "all" is distributive, so that we must understand that each citizen will have an individual excellence that can be called "political." That is why, nine lines later, Aristotle can assert that "the excellence of the citizens cannot possibly be the same" (1277a10).[23] Concretely, that seems to me to say that in an excellent constitution, this citizen will be a courageous soldier, that citizen an excellent judge, and each one will make political use of his virtue, his courage in the one case, his justice in the other. That would not prevent them from having ethical defects,

---

22. Cf., for example, Bonitz's *Index Aristotelicus* 187b11. H. Bonitz, *Index Aristotelicus*, second edition (Graz: Akademische Druck- U. Verlagsanstalt, 1955).

23. The argument is not constructed very clearly: Aristotle introduces at 1277a5, not "a further thrust," as Newman says, but an important premise—the citizens are not identical; therefore they cannot have the same excellence—which he had in a way already expressed at 1276b38 ("the citizens cannot all be alike").

for example to lie occasionally, be a bit envious, or somewhat excessive in their physical pleasures.

This thesis, which resembles that which was presented at the beginning of the chapter, is not well founded because, according to the presupposition of the present argument, it is supposed *to be applied in an excellent constitution*. Such a constitution in fact must develop the virtue of the citizens and, without that virtue, they would not be happy, and the city would have failed to achieve its goal. In an excellent constitution, ethical virtue and political virtue proceed together. The "realist" position, that of the beginning of the chapter, is thus shown to be inconsistent when it is located in an excellent constitution, and since that is what Aristotle does, his position cannot be simply that which people usually ascribe to him, that of decoupling ethics and politics.

An attempt to save this realist approach is proposed at 1277a13ff. There would be certain citizens who would be excellent both ethically and politically, and would be the rulers, and others who can claim only political excellence, in this case excellence as the governed. This solution, adopted above all in monarchical or minority regimes, sometimes takes an extreme form, noted here by Aristotle, when an education of rulers is given from the start to those who are destined to rule. When Jason said, "He felt hungry when he was not a tyrant" (1277a24), he meant that for him not to rule was very painful. But this solution is ultimately verbal, since it calls citizens people who are not really citizens. It's better to return to the actual definition of correct constitutions: when only one man is virtuous, meaning that he possesses complete virtue, ethical and political, we have kingship; when a small group are virtuous, an aristocracy, and when many are, a polity.

The second thesis, presented at 1277a25–29, that is, very briefly, posits two forms of political excellence, one that of the ruler, the other that of the ruled. The virtuous man then has the virtue of one who commands, since he possesses prudence (φρόνησις), which is simultaneously the supreme ethical virtue and that which enables making good decisions at the right time. Aristotle reminds us a little later that it is the essential virtue of the ruler. On the other hand, the good citizen *of the excellent city* will have both excellences, that of the ruler and that of the ruled. Hence this absurd conclusion: the good citizen has a more complete excellence than the ethically virtuous ruler, since he also has the excellence of the ruled, which the ruler does not have. Thus, certain virtuous men would not make good citizens, although they have prudence.

Following this, Aristotle reminds us of the aspect that appears to be crucial in the two theses: the first so much increases the difference between the ruler and the ruled (they ought not be educated in the same way) that it opens a way to a kind of despotism; the second posits that political excellence includes the excellence of commanding and the excellence of obeying, which means that the excellence of the commander is not sufficient to make an excellent citizen.

The solution to this diaporematic examination proceeds by Aristotle reminding us of his theory of different powers. In the case of marital, paternal, and masterly powers, roles do not change. It is thus useless, and even unnatural, to teach someone who is to become a master how to fulfill servile tasks. Aristotle does however notice exceptions to this rule, as we saw.[24] For the rest, it is better to quote:

> But there is a power of another kind, which one exercises over those who are similar to him, that is to say free; we call this power "political," which the ruler must learn by obeying, as he would learn the duties of a general of cavalry by being under the orders of a general of cavalry, or the duties of a general of infantry by being under the orders of a general of infantry, and by having had the command of a regiment and of a company. This is why it has been rightly said that he who has never learned to obey cannot be a good commander. The excellence of the two, ruler and ruled, is not the same, and the excellence of the good citizen is to be able to rule and to be ruled, and the excellence proper to the citizen is to know the rule applied to free men in both senses. And it is also the excellence of the virtuous man to be capable of both. (3.4, 1277b7)

And, a few lines farther on, Aristotle reaffirms the difference between ruler and ruled by reintroducing prudence:

> Prudence is the only excellence peculiar to the ruler; it would seem that all other excellences must equally belong to ruler and ruled. The excellence of the ruled is certainly not prudence, but only true opinion. (3.4, 1277b25)

---

24. Cf. p. 122 n.28.

Such passages overturn the common reading, represented notably by Newman,[25] according to which only the ruler is ethically excellent, the ruled being politically excellent, but without possessing complete virtue, that is, prudence.

I think that the only interpretation that reconciles all the theses endorsed by Aristotle is the following: It is all the more likely that Aristotle would be of the opinion that the command and obedience ought to succeed each other temporally given that he thinks that young people are unable to be ethically virtuous.[26] But our chapter is not arguing in favor of a gerontocracy. It is the excellent citizens themselves who, he says, should take turns commanding excellently and obeying excellently. But if the virtue of obedience is part of the total excellence of an excellent citizen, he needs to exercise it from time to time. When he exercises it, he is in the situation described by Aristotle as that of someone who does not exercise his prudence, but rather regulates himself on the basis of *true opinion*. Doubtless that means that at that time the citizen adopts an attitude of reasoned adherence to the decisions of the city. In a later chapter Aristotle is more explicit:

> And a citizen is one who shares in governing and being governed. He differs under different constitutions, but in the best constitution he is one who is able and chooses (προαιρούμενος) to be governed and to govern with a view to the life of excellence. (3.13, 1283b42)

According to the famous Aristotelian example, which he remarkably repeats at the end of our chapter, the governed citizen obeys the governor as the flute-maker orders his behavior according to the instructions of the flute-player.

However, it is necessary that we take this technical comparison with a grain of salt. In the first place, the flute-maker and the flute-player are not thought to exchange positions, unless, accidentally, the maker also plays the flute. In the second place, the flute-player would not be a better flute-player if he also knew how to make flutes, while the governor becomes a

---

25. Cf. 1.234ff. and appendix B. Newman remarks that Aristotle deals with two opinions, the first that political virtue implies ethical virtue, or at least effaces ethical vice, and Newman cites Thucydides (2.42.3), who says that courage in the service of one's country "effaces the bad committed in private affairs"; the second is that of Socrates, for whom one cannot be a good citizen unless one is ethically good (Newman cites Xenophon *Mem.* 4.2.11).

26. Cf. *Nicomachean Ethics* 1.3, 1095a3; 6.8, 1142a15.

better governor having been governed. Aristotle even says that he *learns* to govern by being governed. We should remember that there are cases, exceptional, in which Aristotle thinks that the virtuous man ought never obey in the city. Thus, for the one who is "preeminent in excellence" (3.13, 1284b28): to command such a man "would be as if mankind should claim to rule over Zeus, by dividing offices. The only alternative is that all should happily obey such a ruler, according to what seems to be the order of nature" (3.13, 1284b30). But are we still talking about politics?

Aristotle's position on the relationships between the excellence of the citizen and ethical virtue is, in the final analysis, not at all what it is normally said to be. It is the opposite of a commonsense position, of compromise and ethical resignation, since Aristotle ultimately maintains that a good citizen in a city with an excellent constitution ought to be ethically excellent. We should also note that when he sums up the road covered by *Politics* book 3 in its last chapter, Aristotle does not adopt a "centrist" position: "We showed at the commencement of our inquiry that the excellence of the good man is necessarily the same as the excellence of the citizen of the excellent city" (3.18, 1288a37).

When he governs, an excellent citizen must possess complete ethical virtue, *prudence*. He also has the possibility, and the duty, to obey the laws and the magistrates in an excellent fashion. But his ability of obeying well does not abolish his ability to command well. In addition to what it contributes to the fundamental question of the relationship between ethical and political virtue, this chapter offers an interesting contribution to the definition of political power, the invisible and always-present framework, as I said at the beginning, of Aristotle's political philosophy. In fact, it is the doctrine that Aristotle reaffirms since the first book of the *Politics*, that there is a difference of form (or species) between commanding and being commanded (cf. 1.13, 1259b37). This difference reflects the difference that exists between the protagonists of the power relation, because the husband differs from the wife, and the master from the slave. In fact, the power of the master over his slave or that of the husband over his wife introduces this sort of difference.[27] In the political power that is established in a city

---

27. It's a matter of a specific difference other than that which exists between the forms of power themselves. Aristotle asserts, in fact, that there is no specific difference between male and female (cf. *Met.* 10.9, 1058a31), while he doubtless believes that the powers of the husband, and of the master, differ specifically. Thus, man and woman do not differ specifically qua living beings, but they differ specifically in that one commands and the other obeys, naturally, because to command and to be commanded naturally are specifically different. Specific difference is at least as variable as species itself.

with an excellent constitution, each citizen may receive contrary attributes, particularly since he may both command and obey. For specific difference is the difference between contraries.

We may take a further step by raising an additional difficulty. As we saw, in the case of natural slavery, there is a hierarchy, itself natural, between master and slave. This is true of all natural powers, except political power. A citizen is not, in fact, naturally superior to another citizen. In a way, this power is even conventional in that it rests on legislative prescriptions of the current constitution, which sets who should govern, how, and for how long a time. We nevertheless have some reason to think that Aristotle would have trouble not thinking of political power as a *natural* power. Possibly the study, impossible to carry out satisfactorily here, of *political obedience* would help us to clarify a bit this enigma that represents, as I said at the beginning, the idea of political power, that is, of power over equals. As Athenian democracy, for example, actually functioned, as well as in Aristotle's analyses in the *Politics*, it's a matter of voluntary obedience. The obedience of a wife to her husband, and even more, that of a slave to his master could indeed be voluntary, but based, we may say, on a fundamental coercion. There were authoritarian means, even violent means, to force the slave to obedience and a wife to her duties. When a citizen has committed a crime that the law finds incompatible with his status as a citizen (for example, when he has damaged the city by not reimbursing the city for a debt that he has contracted in the name of the city), he is *excluded*, completely or partially, from political relations. This is *atimia*, which we discussed above.[28] Obviously excluding the slave from the servile relationship won't work as a punishment . . .[29]

One of the shortcomings of traditional interpretations is not to distinguish, in *Politics* 3.4–5, the passages in which Aristotle is talking about excellent cities from those in which it is a matter of cities that are not excellent, and those where the matter of excellence is not taken into account. It is certain that the legislator, whose most frequent task (as we will see in detail shortly) is to *repair* deviant constitutions, will most often work in the situation where the citizens are not virtuous. Let us take a

---

28. Cf. p. 174 n.3.

29. Wives have an intermediate position in that one might exclude them from the conjugal relationship by repudiation. Since Athenian marriages involved complex interfamilial relationships, divorces appear to have been relatively rare; see Louis Cohn-Haft, "Divorce in Classical Athens," *Journal of Hellenic Studies* 115 (1995): 1–14.

look at a well-known example. Aristotle, as we have already said, does not want to give political rights to artisans:

> The best form of city will not admit artisans to citizenship; but if they are admitted, then our definition of the excellence of a citizen will not apply to every citizen, nor to every freeman as such, but only to those who are freed from necessary service. (3.5, 1278a8, passage partially cited above)

Cities that give artisans access to magistracies thus find themselves in the situation described at the beginning of chapter 4, before the diaporematic analysis. It is important to notice that Aristotle does not seem to cast doubt on the fact that, in an imperfect situation, there does indeed exist a political excellence, and that it is defined by the ability of preserving the current constitution, that is, the deviant constitution. But artisans could do that, and do it well, that is, they could assist in establishing and maintaining a constitution with the mercantile orientation that corresponds to their class interests, and thus their ideology. We will find again and study in detail this "functional" conception of constitutional excellence, as well as its relationships with its ethical consequences.

As we will see at the proper time, the ability of maintaining the current constitution is one of the competencies that the legislator ought to acquire. Thus, this ability is also desirable in the citizen. This is all the more the case, as we will see in detail below, since *revolution* is not the kind of constitutional change that Aristotle prefers.

A New Shape for Constitutional Excellence: Mixture

What good would it do Aristotle to adopt extremist positions, like that which demands that every citizen of the excellent city be an ethically virtuous person, if the result would be that he would fail to achieve what is doubtless his major goal, to give the legislator the means to realize excellence *in reality*? Could Aristotle believe for an instant that a city composed entirely of "good men" could be founded and continue to exist? The solution to this problem would be that legislators would found only monarchies or aristocratic cities with a very limited civic body composed of virtuous people. And Aristotle never stops asserting that kingship and aristocracy would be the correct constitution, and even *from a certain point of view*, that of excellence, that they are correct constitutions par excellence (cf. *Pol.* 4.2, 1289a31). Thus, it is necessary to reaffirm once again, and once and for all, that the best solution—and are there others?—for establishing a city that functions well and assures the happiness of its citizens is to limit power to virtuous men.

This universal rule has as a consequence, as I said above, that the "everywhere" of the *Nicomachean Ethics* passage that says that "there is just one constitution that would everywhere be the best" (5.7, 1135a5) has also an absolute sense: everywhere aristocracy, meaning that the virtuous people are in power, is the best regime. Nevertheless, Aristotle is quite conscious of the fact that monarchical regimes, or regimes with a very restricted number of governing persons, belong in the past,[30] and that the development of rhetoric had changed the rules of the political game (cf. 5.5, 1305a12), distancing the cities a little farther from their patriarchal origins. On the other hand, Aristotle notices that popular regimes are more stable than others, and he explains that by the fact that "no dissension worthy of the name arises among the people against themselves" (5.1, 1302a12). He often recalls that a constitution is in danger if it has that mass opposed to it (cf. 3.11, 1281b28), and often enough in the *Politics* he offers advice and furnishes recipes for conciliating the masses. We will see, in fact, that trying to make regimes stable is one of the main goals of the legislator. We can see very well that Aristotle does not cling to the idea that the realization of political and ethical perfection of men will necessarily occur by the creation of cities governed by a minority of "prudent" individuals, or just one, in the case of kingship. In this sense, his declaration, more or less introductory to his study of constitutions in which he places among correct constitutions a popular form, the polity, alongside kingship and aristocracy, shows that he has not resigned himself to confining excellence to a few minority regimes.

But from the political point of view, that which distinguishes the prudent person from the imprudent is the ability to deliberate well to make good decisions. Before seeing how Aristotle comes to distributing to the mass of citizens the prudence that makes good men, we must try to characterize more precisely what prudence is from the point of view of the constitution. To do that we must detour by way of the difficult Book 6, chapters 7 and 8 of the *Nicomachean Ethics*, which deal with

---

30. "At the present time, there are no longer royalties, and if any do appear, they are rather tyrannical monarchies" (5.10, 1313a3).

the relationships between prudence and politics. Aristotle maintains that political excellence is the culmination of prudence. He calls the highest kind of prudence "legislative," whereas the kind of prudence that "is related to particulars is known by the general name 'political,' this has to do with action and deliberation, for a decree is a thing to be carried out in the form of an individual act" (1141b25). Commentators have seen here a difference between that which one would later call "legislative" and "executive" powers, so that in his French translation of the *Nicomachean Ethics*, Richard Bodéüs translates πρακτική as "executive." And Aristotle writes that the first kind is "architectonic," while the second concerns people who work like "manual laborers" (1141b29). Beyond the many difficulties of detail that it presents, this passage collides with an essential aporia. If, in fact, the legislator is immersed in the sphere of the universal and if the politician who executes is nothing but a worker limited to the sphere of the particular and does not understand what he is doing, both of them lack a characteristic of prudence, namely, by definition, of conjoining universal to particular. Because prudence consists essentially, after deliberation in the soul of the prudent person, knowing how to apply the rules and general concepts to particular situations.

Here is the reading of this passage that seems to me to be the most interesting. Legislative prudence, which, like all prudence, must combine universal and particular, produces what are called "practical syllogisms,"[31] which have as universal premises the general analyses of political philosophy (the political nature of man, the happy life as a human destiny, etc.) and as minor premises the ethical and sociohistorical characteristics of the people to whom one must give laws (the number of virtuous people, geographical, climatic, and economic situation of the city, etc.), the result (the "conclusion") consisting of specified laws, adapted to the people under consideration. Executive prudence starts from these laws, taking into account the circumstances, and produces decrees that allow settling situations that escape from the precise application of the law due to its generality, "because no decree can be universal" (*Pol.* 4.4, 1292a36). At the end of *Politics* 4.4, Aristotle characterizes extreme democracy by its inverting the order between laws and decrees: while "the law ought to be supreme over all, and the magistracies judge of particulars in accord with the constitution" (1292a33),[32] in the most extreme democracy "decrees

---

31. Cf. *Nicomachean Ethics* 6.12, 1144a31, and *Movement of Animals* 7.
32. This remark confirms my reading of *Nicomachean Ethics* 6.7–8.

supersede the laws. This is brought about by the demagogues" (1292a16). Thus, this sort of democracy is near tyranny: "The spirit of both is the same, and they alike exercise a despotic rule over the better citizens. The decrees of the one correspond to the edicts of the tyrant" (1292a19).

In other words, the second prudence starts where the first one ends. Thus, the two prudences distinguished together in the *Nicomachean Ethics* passage constitute complete prudence. In fact, without the deliberation of practical prudence, legislative prudence would not achieve the "practical end," which is the decree (1141b27). That is not to say that the ruler must possess the set of both prudences, particularly legislative prudence, while it is certain that he must have practical prudence. We will have to come back to this point when we look more closely at the respective statuses of ruler and legislator. What is certain is that the problem remains of the attribution of prudence, even if only "practical," to a mass of citizens.

There is a chapter, one of the most profound, and for modern readers one of the strangest, of the *Politics*, which aims at taking up this challenge; it is book 3, chapter 11, which defends the idea that the best government is that of the masses. The perspective of this chapter is essentially ethical, and it is not any random popular mass that is in question, since certain mobs are like savage beasts and are absolutely without any ethical value (cf. 1281b15ff.). The doctrine here presented comes to the aid, so to speak, of the conclusion of 3.4, where it is said that there is no good citizen who lacks ethical virtue, relying on a very original and entirely operational conception of ethical virtue as far as it relates to the problem under consideration.

The first lines of this chapter deserve a quick textual review:

> Many of these questions may be reserved for another occasion. The principle that the multitude ought to be in power rather than the few best people might seem to offer a solution that may involve some difficulties, but is likely to contain some truth. For the many, of whom each individual is not a good man, when they meet together may be better than the few good, if regarded not individually but collectively, just as a feast to which many contribute is better than a dinner provided out of a single purse. For each individual among the many has a share of excellence and practical wisdom, and when they meet together, just as they become in a manner one man, who has

many feet, and hands, and senses, so too with regard to their character and thought. (1281a39)

The "solution"[33] here proposed concerns the question of the preceding chapter, which was of knowing "what ought to be the supreme power (τì δεῖ τὸ κύριον) in the city" (3.10, 1281a11). And Aristotle furnishes as an additional sign of this superiority of the mass over each individual even if excellent, the case of works of art, asserting, without appearing to need to justify it, that the aesthetic judgment of the many is better than that of any individual, because "some judge one part, others another" (3.11, 1281b9). Not only do the people make a body, but Aristotle even provides it with a kind of subjectivity.[34]

A comparison presented in this chapter, at 3.11, 1281b35, focuses on the precise character of this superiority of the popular mass over the elite, including the "ethical elite." Aristotle writes, "Just as impure food when mixed with what is pure sometimes makes the entire mass more wholesome than a small quantity of pure would be," the same goes for the people of the masses, "combined with the better class they are useful to the city." In order for this alchemy to function, it is thus necessary that there be in the heart of this mass of people some individuals of great virtue who serve in a way as a leavening, the popular mass being useful to the city because it possesses "a quite good enough perception" of situations. The earlier part of this chapter permits us to think that Aristotle means that the analysis of the situation by a large number of people would not suffer from the limitations of an analysis carried out by one individual. That is why it is necessary to have the members of the popular mass participate in deliberative functions, and also judicial functions, which also have a deliberative character—remember the trial of Socrates. The idea that the judgment of the crowd on works of art is superior to that of the expert goes against our common conception of art, but we will grasp without difficulty the idea that deliberation is better to the extent that it includes more people.

---

33. To take λύεσθαι (1281a41) as meaning "refute," with some, including Bonitz, seems impossible: just the presence of the word ἀπορία gives it its usual sense of "resolve a difficulty."

34. On collective subjectivity, cf. 1282a34: "For the power does not reside in the juryman, or counselor, or member of the assembly, of which the aforesaid individuals are only parts or members."

We have to take the food analogy seriously, because in the case of nutrition as in the case of the political regime we have a double description, and double access, to excellence. Just as the diet that is made only of the purest food is excellent, and even, one may say, the most excellent of all diets, so the city all the citizens of which are individually ethically virtuous would be the best of all excellent cities. But there is another form of excellence, both nutritionally and politically: the *mixture* of a pure food with a more abundant impure food, provided that it is not toxic, provides an excellent nutritional regime, just as the mixture of several ethically excellent individuals with a mass not made up of ethically excellent individuals, but still not vile and bestial, would result in an excellent city.

If, then, there is an ethical virtue, and, as Aristotle specifies, an intelligence (διάνοια) of the mass, then an excellent popular constitution is possible in which the conditions that Aristotle sets for the attribution of citizenship, that is, ethical excellence, are satisfied. But Aristotelian realism is not far behind these ethical, and thus normative, considerations: that the masses ultimately present the ethical characteristics that make it worthy of participating in a city with a correct constitution is, we may say, fortunate, because if the masses do not participate in power, the city will be "full of enemies" (1281b30). So this is an elegant way to introduce a form of popular regime into the list of correct constitutions, which up to now has included only kingship and aristocracy. If in political judgment as in aesthetic judgment the citizens are "one man," then one may attribute total political virtue to the masses: people who are minimally virtuous are better than people who are extremely virtuous, "not individually, but collectively" (1281b2).

But Aristotle places two conditions. The first is that everything that resembles sole exercise of power, what Aristotle calls (1281b26) "the highest magistracies," must be forbidden to the masses. That is what Athens did, as Aristotle recalls, citing Solon (1281b32). The second important restriction is that in the case of a popular regime it must have good laws and they must be absolutely sovereign, with the magistrates intervening only in cases where the laws are too general to be applied. Here we find again the typical situation in which practical prudence must be exercised, starting from general rules, in this case the laws, to particular cases. The citizens of an excellent city can thus share in "ethical and intellectual qualities" (1281b7) that, even if they are not possessed completely by each individual, do allow putting into operation the necessary ethical virtue that is required to be an excellent citizen, according to 3.4. Finally, we note that this kind of "general virtue" only superficially resembles what modern political thinkers, particularly Rousseau, call the "general will." To be exact, the virtue of the mass, according to Aristotle, is an *ethical* virtue, which presupposes that each citizen has personally at least the traces of moral value and that by *adding* their virtues, the general will, on the other hand, is based on the *neutralization* of their particular *interests*.

If we read *Politics* 3.11 in the light of the distinctions made in the *Nicomachean Ethics* 6.7–8, we see that the collective prudence of the mass will be "political," that is, practical, rather than legislative, since it does not help to make laws. But that was also the case of the good man and of the citizen in the condition of obedience, in 3.4, since both submit to laws that they did not make: the politically prudent citizen by deliberating on the means necessary to apply the laws, the obedient citizen carrying out the result of this deliberation in which he has confidence. Neither one is involved in legislative prudence. The domain concerned with the deliberation of citizens is, in fact, strictly limited and framed by the laws. Thus, we understand what Aristotle meant by the last form of his definition of citizen as "he who has the ability to participate in deliberative or judicial power." This deliberation is not the legislative deliberation of citizens in a democracy that makes laws, as was the case in Athens, and as occurs in modern democracies where popular assemblies have legislative power. As for the institution of laws, that rests in the hands of exceptionally virtuous people. The same for their modification; this kind of intervention would be the privilege of the Aristotelian legislator.

The result of *Politics* 3.11 thus has two aspects. On the one hand, this chapter establishes the possibility of a constitution that is simultaneously popular and correct. But, on the other hand, it does not offer an answer to the question posed in chapter 10, namely, what or who should be sovereign in the city.[35] In fact chapter 11 is far from giving sovereign power to the people. If, as many think, Aristotle sketches a portrait of the polity in this chapter, then this polity would be hard to think of as a really popular regime, because it lacks essential attributes from the fact that Aristotle posits two principal limitations on a possible sovereign power by the masses: first, the people would not have access to the highest magistracies; second, they would not make laws. In actual

---

35. This is seen very well by Antoine Léandri, "L'aporie de la souveraineté," in *Aristote politique. Études sur la Politique d'Aristote*, ed. Pierre Aubenque (Paris: PUF, 1993), 315–339.

popular regimes, like the Athenian democracy, the first condition was often met, but not the second. The polity sketched for us in *Politics* 3.11, if that is what it is, would thus need a source of power outside the people to make the law, but especially to modify it. In other words, it would need a legislator, whose essential role, as we will see, is to modify the law for the adaptation of the constitution, principally in two directions: it is necessary to change the law when the evolution of the people has brought it about that the constitution is no longer precisely adapted to them, and also it is necessary to change the law to defend the constitution against internal and external enemies.

But *Politics* 3.11 nevertheless marks an essential step in the Aristotelian analysis of constitutions in that it introduces a new form of an excellent constitution, that of an *excellent mixture*, all of whose components are not themselves excellent. Far from applying only to the popular constitution, this analysis applies to all correct constitutions. Because it is not only the popular constitutions that can be excellent because they correspond, in dietetics, to the diet that is not made up entirely of pure food. We will consider in detail below the question of the constitutional mixture, but I would like now to illustrate this new form of the excellence of constitutions from the example of those correct, and thus excellent, constitutions, kingship and aristocracy, which would in principle owe none of their excellence to a mixture.

Thus, in the long analysis of monarchy that runs through several chapters of *Politics* 3, after having recalled that the true kingship, the regime in which the king has power by virtue of his ethical superiority and governs for the common advantage of his subjects, is definitely one of the correct constitutions, Aristotle limits the excellence in two parameters. First, as we have said, monarchy is characteristic of a certain epoch in which the benefits of education have not yet been felt, and consequently virtue is not yet very widespread. In fact, good education is as much ethical as intellectual. When things have changed, monarchy is no longer justifiable: "Where men are alike and equal, it is neither expedient nor just that one man should be lord of all" (3.17, 1288a1). But also, and especially, Aristotle, having taken into account the various species and varieties of the realities that he has examined, his trademark approach, shows that this regime, no matter how correct it may be, contains the seeds of degeneration. Among the monarchies some, which do not present all the characteristics of the pure form of kingship, deserve nevertheless to be called "kingship." In fact, there are two extreme forms: at one extreme, the royal family or king governs the city as the head of the family governs the family (this is "absolute monarchy," παμβασιλεία), at the other extreme, monarchy of the Laconian type, which is a kind of perpetual office of the general (*strategos*), which can be reserved for a lineage: "Most of the others lie in a region between (μεταξύ) them, having less power than the absolute, and more than the Laconian" (3.15, 1285b35). That amounts to saying that the other forms of monarchy are mixtures of the two extreme forms.

At 3.15, 1286a5, Aristotle explains that one may leave aside the other forms, because absolute monarchy is both "a form of constitution" and it presents the characteristics of monarchy in a purer state than the others. To say that it is "a form of constitution" is to underline, in a subliminal way, that it is tangential to two realities that are not *political*, the family on the one side, tyranny on the other.[36] Nevertheless it remains that the legislator has more of a toehold on the mixed forms. And we understand well that when in chapter 3.15, Aristotle underlines the advantages, but also the inconveniences, of monarchy, he is thinking about the mixed forms. Among the inconveniences he cites the fact that an individual person can be corrupted more easily than the mass of people, that hereditary succession does not ensure that virtue will succeed virtue. He also repeats that the mass, even if composed of people who are not very virtuous, would make better decisions than the king alone, no matter how virtuous he may be (15, 1286a30). Also, it is necessary to take precautions to prevent the king from becoming a tyrant, among which would be giving him a military force that would be effective against those of individuals and of factions, but not on that of the totality of the people.[37]

In this last requirement we also grasp how tangled with each other are the two aspects of Aristotelian politics as they are presented in the

---

36. Cf. *Politics* 4.10, 1295a17: "There is a third kind of tyranny, which is the most typical form, and is the counterpart of the absolute monarchy."

37. There is a third characteristic that also darkens the image of monarchy, namely, that the form subject to the laws is badly characterized. Cf. 3.16, 1287a3: "The so-called kingship according to law, as I have already remarked, is not a form of government, for under all governments as, for example, in a democracy or aristocracy, there may be a general holding office for life, and one person is often made supreme over the administration of a state." That this monarchy "is not a form of government" means that it is not a form among the others, because many magistrates in many constitutions are endowed with this kind of power over everything under the authority of the law. In a sense, therefore, monarchy is nowhere because it is everywhere.

Politics. There is nothing more "realist," in fact, than this anticipation of measuring the armed force that will allow the king to dominate factions, without acquiring the power that would enable him to become a tyrant. But one may also read here an important principle that belongs to the "normative" side. To say, in fact, that the people ought, in every way, to remain the strongest, is to recognize that every regime that does not have the people on its side is bad, either because it is perverted, or because it is unstable. But we know, ever since *Politics* 3.11, that the people, provided that it has not become a villainous mass (which could happen sometimes, for example under the influence of demagogues), is in a way the original font of political virtue. Aristotle seems to prefer to correct popular regimes rather than overturn them. Basically, the fact that, as we will see, extreme democracies tend to wind up in tyrannies is fortunate, because tyrannies can be overturned, at least overturned more easily than popular regimes . . .

We must notice that in the distinction that Aristotle is using, the different kinds of kingships are regimes that actually existed in the heroic age: kingships Laconian, barbarian, and those of the aesymnetes.[38] Doubtless several actual monarchies of his day were instantiations of these types, even perhaps absolute monarchy, which is a kind of ideal type. It's only later that Aristotle uses an a priori method of construction of all possible cases of constitutions, before any empirical verification. That means, if we take the text literally, that Aristotle thought that the actual kingships were correct constitutions, even if they were more or less distant from pure kingship, at least until they degenerated. That is an important difference from Plato, in that Aristotle intends to propose reforms that are actually feasible. That is why, taking account of the historical circumstances of his time, after his analysis of monarchy, he deals only so to speak with the two constitutions that are more or less the only ones present in the Hellenic region, democracy and oligarchy. We will see more exactly the reasons that Aristotle gives for that situation. That amounts to recognizing, on the one hand, that monarchies no longer existed except in the form of tyrannies, regimes largely irremediable from a *political* perspective, and rather unstable,[39] and on the other hand, that the Greek world is populated

---

38. In the Homeric poems the aesymnetes were those who organized festivals, but the name is often applied to magistrates endowed with the most extensive powers, either for a specific task, or for life.

39. Cf. *Politics* 5.12, 1315b11ff.: Tyrannies that last are those where the tyrant does not act like a tyrant.

very largely by deviant constitutions. With his usual political brilliance, Aristotle proposes analyzing constitutional excellence and deviation as the effect of provisional combinations of forces. That orients us in the direction of that which is perhaps one of the most revolutionary ideas of Aristotelian politics.

The same thing happens for aristocracies, but in a way that is still more explicit. In *Politics* 4.7, Aristotle begins his study by positing a definition of aristocracy:

> The term "aristocracy" is rightly applied to the form of government that is described in the first part of our treatise; for the government (πολιτεία) of the absolutely best men in terms of virtue and not merely of people who are good relative to some hypothesis is the only one that deserves to be called an aristocracy. (1293b3)

The next sentence draws the principle consequence of this status of a "pure" aristocracy: "*Only* in this city are the good man and the good citizen one and the same person absolutely." That confirms what was said above, that the only constitution that would be excellent without having recourse to a mixture would be the aristocracy with, doubtless, monarchy as the limiting case.

But there are forms of oligarchies and democracies that one could also call "aristocracies" because, beyond their particular criteria for the attribution of power (freedom for democracies, wealth for the oligarchies), they also add virtue. Thus, Carthage attributes power according to three criteria ("wealth, virtue, and the people"); Sparta does so according to two criteria, "democracy and virtue." But Aristotle goes farther:

> ... especially these two, I mean the people and oligarchy. For to combine these is the endeavor of polities; and most of the so-called aristocracies have the same aim. In fact, this (τούτῳ) is the basis of the difference between aristocracies and what we call polities, and is the reason why some are less stable and others more so. For those that lean more toward oligarchy are called aristocracies, those that lean toward the masses are called polities. (5.7, 1307a10)

At 1307a13 τούτῳ refers to the proportion of the mixture between oligarchy and democracy. We will analyze in detail below this Aristotelian definition of "polity" as a mixture of oligarchy and democracy. In other words, one can give the name "aristocracies" to polities that are more minority governments than popular. We are thus immersed in the constitutional mixture without leaving correctness because aristocracies are correct constitutions.

Aristotle's *Politics* presents its analyses by means, among other things, of breaks. We have seen that the major one of those was that which distinguished books reputed to be normative (1, 2, 3, 7, and 8) from those called realist (4, 5, 6). Another break is important for us here: we find, in fact, that until book 3, chapter 7, Aristotle is mainly interested in correct constitutions and does not consider deviant constitutions except in relation to correct constitutions. Thus, we have seen that the difficult chapter 4 did not make sense until we understood that it was considering the case of the excellent city. We have also seen that chapter 6 asserts strongly that correct constitutions, which seek the common advantage, are organized according to "absolute justice." But in chapter 8, Aristotle undertakes the examination of democracy and oligarchy and, from that moment on, all his analyses, never forgetting the difference between correct and deviant constitutions, are carried out either on deviant constitutions, or on the movement from correct constitutions to deviant constitutions, or from deviant constitutions to correct constitutions. Thus, the large central bloc of the *Politics*, including the last ten chapters of book 3, plus books 4 through 6, are a kind of "treatise of deviations and how to get out of them." The most certain indication of this turning point is perhaps that from 3.8 on, Aristotle abandons the point of view of "absolute justice."

But the action of the legislator, as codified from the beginning of *Politics* 3 on, consists of making him look for an excellent constitution by working on deviant constitutions; that is a sign that the kind of excellence in question is the one considered in 3.11, which is the result of the mixture of the collective virtue of the masses with the individual virtue of several virtuous men; this becomes the principle goal of the work. That continues until the end of book 6. And, obviously, the legislator can very well deal with pure constitutions, whether in the case of correct constitutions or deviant constitutions. But in fact, these constitutions don't concern him very much. In the case of pure deviations (extreme democracies, oligarchies, and tyrannies), these are often beyond repair, and most of them can be overturned only by force, which is not at all the task of the legislator. Happily, as we will see very soon, these regimes don't usually last very long. Thus, deviant constitutions are for very much the most part mixed constitutions. As for pure correct constitutions, the legislator generally cannot establish them except by rectifying an "impure" form, that is, a mixture. Doubtless it would be somewhat more useful to *preserve* such constitutions, for example by purging a pure aristocracy from oligarchical ferment. But normally, the perfect virtue of aristocrats ought to be a sufficient protection. It thus remains that the legislator most often has to deal with mixed constitutions, whether correct or deviant.

Nevertheless, it remains that pure correct constitutions are doubtless the most desirable goal for the legislator. Possibly Aristotle has in view pure correct constitutions when, in passages that I will analyze in detail below, he speaks of the constitution "of our wishes." But this goal more or less cancels itself out since Aristotle at the same time posits that the most desirable constitution is the polity, if only because it is more stable than the others, all the time recognizing that such a correct popular constitution is not *in fact* likely to exist in a pure form, and it is even in order to construct a popular constitution based on the virtue of its citizens that Aristotle introduces a new form of constitutional excellence, the excellence of the mixture.

Class Struggle: Danger and Safety for Cities

Now we must examine in more detail the thesis to which we called attention above, that a constitution sanctions the provisional condition of a relationship of forces. For Aristotle the body of citizens, real citizens, that is, those who have political rights recognized by the constitution, or potential citizens, that is, those claiming these rights of which they have been deprived, is not composed simply of individuals, but of groups. Although the term is not entirely adequate, we may call these groups "classes," because they define themselves by their status, their demands, and their common ideological positions. Each of these classes demand political power, that is, control of the constitution, but what makes Aristotle's analysis so original is that he asserts on the one hand that this demand rests on a biased analysis of the situation, but on the other hand, these demands are, at least in part, justified. But before undertaking a closer look at Aristotle's subtle analyses, we must note a fact, doubtless too obvious to have been taken into account by the commentators, but one which bears both on the course of our reading of the *Politics* and also on our ultimate appreciation of Aristotle's political philosophy.

It would be better to "embody" these reflections in the two kinds of constitution that Aristotle has in mind, democracy and oligarchy. In every city with a little development there are at least a democratic party and an oligarchic party that aspire to give, or keep, a constitution for the city that leans in its direction. This is true even in cities with a correct constitution. An aristocracy, for example, is a constitution in which a minority class of virtuous people exercises power, but that does not prevent their existing in its heart an oligarchical (or democratic) party that asks for nothing more than tilting the relationship of forces in its favor. Even in a "pure" aristocracy that succeeds in reserving citizenship to a very restricted number of virtuous men, we may imagine that these people exist, potentially good citizens who are deprived of that status, and who desire the death of the current constitution.

But first it is necessary to define precisely the real basis on which these classes formed themselves, which is what is done in *Politics* 3.8. In most cases, in fact, the people of modest means are numerous and there is a small number of well-off individuals; of course, one may imagine (helped by etymology) a city in which the people of modest means are in the minority but are in power because they have available the means to accomplish, for example with external support, an "oligarchical" regime. But in fact, says Aristotle, the number of people in power in an oligarchy or a democracy is an accidental property (3.8, 1279b35), because the true criterion of belonging to a class is the scale of the available resources.[40] It is this availability that in fact determines the ideological positions adopted by the various classes, not the number of their members. This is very important to notice, because it shows that Aristotle intends to go beyond the descriptive stage in order to adopt a scientific attitude, that is, one that offers knowledge of causes. We will see that Aristotle describes the various attitudes of the different classes in *ethical* terms, since their divergence

---

40. Number is not however absent in the definition of a democracy, in that a regime cannot be called democratic if it puts a small minority into power; cf. 4.4.1290b9: "The government is not a democracy in which the freemen, being few in number, rule over the many who are not free, as at Apollonia on the Ionian Gulf, and at Thera . . . nor when the rich have the government because they exceed in number." This text is difficult to interpret, since Athens was certainly considered a democracy, although a minority of citizens ruled a large servile and foreign population. These "freemen" must thus be "those of full citizen-birth," as Newman puts it, and, therefore, the "not free" would be potential citizens, who would in fact be citizens in a democracy, those in question above.

bears on their conception of *justice*. Thus, we must not forget that these ethical positions have a social basis. In the final analysis, what determines the *political* attitude of a social group in the struggle for power in the city is what a Marxist would call its location in relation to production. But Aristotle expresses it in political terms: control of the constitution allows a dominant group to perpetuate, and, if it can, accentuate its manner of control of economic resources and the real and symbolical advantages that are attached to political power that the group thinks it deserves.

In fact, Aristotle several times describes the basic divergence that opposes democracy and oligarchy to each other, in slightly different terms, but without any change in doctrine. In *Politics* 3.9, 1280a11ff., it is said that democrats and oligarchs differ on the meaning of "the just" (τὸ δίκαιον), the first thinking that it is "the equal" and the second "the unequal." That means that for those who support democracy, power ought to be distributed in equal parts to each individual, provided that he has been recognized as a citizen in the city under consideration, while for the partisans of oligarchy, the parts of power ought to be distributed proportionally to the merit of the individuals. For oligarchs, merit is measured by wealth. The critique that Aristotle aims at these two conceptions—namely, that in the name of equality or inequality in one respect, these believe that they are equal in everything, the others unequal in everything—shows what he would count as a good analysis. There exist among citizens both equality and inequality, and the legislator must take that into account. For it is not a political life if one does not recognize the fundamental equality of all citizens, and political power, as we have seen several times, is power exercised on equals. But it is also necessary that quality be accounted for, because, as Aristotle says in 3.12: "And therefore, the well-born, or free-born, or rich, may with good reason claim office; for holders of offices must be freemen and taxpayers; a city can be no more composed entirely of poor men than entirely of slaves" (1283a16).

This last sentence deserves a few remarks. Aristotle in no way assimilates poor people to slaves, for the two cases are radically different. Why there cannot be a city of slaves has already been indicated: slaves lack the *ethical* characteristics that must belong to the citizen. And Aristotle compares them, on this point, to animals: they are not capable of "reflective choice," and are thus incapable of happiness (cf. *Pol.* 3.9, 1280a32, cited above). Every slave is thus unable to be a citizen. Many poor men, on the other hand, are able, but if there are no riches in the city it would be impossible to actualize some of the necessary conditions for the exercise of citizenship, notably leisure. We will find below, when we are looking at *Politics* book 7, this difference between essential characteristics and the characteristics necessary for the city.

In book 5.1, 1301a25ff., Aristotle, referring to what he had said "above," which seems to refer to the passage in book 3 that we have been talking about, repeats that the difference between democrats and oligarchs comes from the fact that the first think that they are equal in everything, and the second unequal in everything, making it more explicit: the first "because they are similarly free, believe that they are absolutely equal" (1301a30), the others "because they are unequal in wealth posit that in principle they are absolutely unequal" (1301a32). But Aristotle brings both positions under a formally identical thesis: "Everyone agrees that justice is proportional equality (κατ' ἀναλογίαν)" (1301a26). Probably one must understand that the position of the democrats can also satisfy this principle, which doubtless means that according to them one ought to distribute power proportionally to liberty, that is, equally among free people, since numerical quality is just a particular case of proportional equality. For, a little later (1301b29), declaring that he is developing the same thesis as at the beginning of the chapter, Aristotle develops his analysis. Equality has two senses, numerical and proportional; the first the one that democrats want to use in distributing power, the second is chosen by the oligarchs, the two positions subsumed under the following thesis: "People agree that the absolutely just is the just according to merit (κατ' ἀξίαν)" (1301b36). This last expression corresponds to the "proportional equality" that was just in question, but one must notice that here it has a bizarre resonance. To distribute power "according to merit" has a resonance so *aristocratic* that it is difficult to attribute this position to everybody. We must also notice that in 6.2, 1317b3, Aristotle asserts that the democratic concept of justice is "that each one have an equal part and not according to his merit." Careful readers of Aristotle know that it is better not to try to reconcile by force statements that differ in their mode of expression, when they are doctrinally convergent. It is necessary to understand that democrats locate merit in liberty, which assures to citizens a fundamental equality, and oligarchs locate it in fortunes. One can also understand that democrats and oligarchs are *formally* in agreement in saying that the distribution of power ought to be done according to equality, but their concepts of equality are not the same.

Doubtless a passage in the *Nicomachean Ethics* expresses the "canonical" form of this doctrine best:

All men agree that what is just in distribution must be according to merit in some sense, though they do not all specify the same sort of merit, but democrats identify it with the status of freeman, supporters of oligarchy with wealth (or with noble birth), and supporters of aristocracy with excellence. (5.3, 1131a25)

As this passage is not especially concerned with the distribution of *power* in the city, it does not foreground a fundamental point, namely, that this situation of opposition in the competing concepts of justice and equality applies to cities with a deviant constitution because, in excellent cities, the attribution of power is done according to "political virtue." And, in fact, we have seen that Aristotle asserts that correct constitutions are ruled "according to absolute justice" (3.6, 1279a17), which means that, since they are not based on a unilateral conception of justice, as are democracy and oligarchy, the division of power would not be difficult, at least to the extent that they are not deviant.

Experience shows that democratic regimes do not generally hold to the simple affirmation of equality, but have a tendency to exploit the wealthy by making them support common expenses, for example those related to war, and by making them support less prosperous citizens, as was the case in "extreme democracies." Aristotle gives this name to democracies where demagogues have become important; for example, poor people are paid to attend the assembly. As for oligarchical cities, the dominant class there has obviously the tendency to favor the accumulation of wealth. Two principle political dangers threaten them: on the one hand that they demand too high a property qualification for office, shutting out a large majority of the population (cf. 4.5, 1292a39), on the other hand members of the dominant class simply reject political life in order to devote themselves to private affairs (cf. 4.14, 1298b17). This last danger also threatens certain democracies whose social base is composed of peasants with moderate means, who have no desire to leave their rural residences to go to the city where assemblies are held, and do not have the leisure to participate in political life (cf. 4.6, 1292b27).

One can hardly say that Aristotle clings to illusions about human nature, and we see that by at least three things. In the first place, he shows us citizens whose ethical convictions are determined by their class membership and class interests. The divergent descriptions of justice are nothing but a smokescreen behind which people find "just" whatever tends to go in their interest. Next, we notice that the social and political practice of citizens, in terms of the acquisition of power, of legislations, of division of goods, depends on their economic status. Finally, and above all, the Aristotelian text shows us unambiguously a tyrannical trend as much among democrats as among partisans of oligarchy. In fact, each class has a tendency—and we get the impression that Aristotle regards it as largely conscious—of appropriating to oneself all powers to the point that one puts oneself above the laws, that is to say, to go beyond the political sphere. For example: when in *Politics* 4.6 he reviews several kinds of democracy and of oligarchy, Aristotle considers one of them a rather "rigorous" form of oligarchy, the one in which the rulers have much inherited wealth and are thus few in number. They are aware of their power, but they do not fall into *hybris*:

> Since they are more powerful, they believe themselves worthy of more power; that is why they themselves choose people of other social categories whom they bring into the government, but since they are not strong enough to govern without laws, they establish the law to favor themselves. (1293a23)

Aristotle suggests, it seems, that if they were stronger, they would go around the laws and put in place a tyrannical constitution for their own benefit. And Aristotle is well aware of the risk of leaving the political field, which he expresses by a comparison with fine art: if a painter excessively emphasizes the aquiline or snub character of a nose that he is painting, the representation will end by no longer having the form of a nose,

> which is also what happens in various constitutions. For an oligarchy or a democracy can exist in an acceptable form although very far from that of an excellent organization. But if one increases excessively one of these tendencies, first one will have a worse constitution, and finally, no constitution at all. (5.9, 1309b30)

In other words, in politics, virtue and moderation are the daughters of necessity.

That brings us to an entirely crucial conclusion: if, according to Aristotle, all cities, at least those with a deviant constitution, that is, the great majority of them, do not all end up governed by groups unconstrained by laws, that is, in a tyrannical way, it is not because the people in power are a little bit virtuous, nor because they have the political intelligence to realize that too much power destroys power (it is the legislator educated by the philosopher who can make this sort of analysis), but because their power in the city is counterbalanced and thus limited by the ability to resist the power of other social classes. But in themselves deviant constitutions have a tendency on their own to become more deviant, becoming more and more demagogic and exploitative in the case of democratic constitutions, and more and more restrictive and authoritarian in the case of oligarchic constitutions. That is what Aristotle expresses very clearly when he says that deviant constitutions are "despotic" (3.6, 1279a21). The end point of these processes would be, as Aristotle often notes, the installation of a tyranny, that is, the end of political life.[41]

If, on the one hand, historical reality is composed of groups at war with each other in order to take power and everything that flows from that, each one taking advantage of the weaknesses of the others in order to impose absolute domination, and if, on the other hand, Aristotle really aimed at helping to actualize cities with an excellent constitution, don't we need to think, like most commentators have done, that Aristotle is the philosopher who compromises with the evils of the world and the lesser of evils? Oh well, that reading is false, and even in his passages of glistening realism, the distinction, highly normative, between correct and deviant constitutions remains more relevant than ever. But this distinction takes, under the influence of the analyses we have reported on above, a very unexpected shape, one that in my opinion represents the most extreme point, the Land's End, of the Aristotelian political philosophy, which we will see is as novel as it is banal.

In the passages where he opposes the democratic to the oligarchic conceptions of justice, for example in *Politics* 3.9 cited above, Aristotle brings to each of these conceptions a double judgment, of which only one branch is generally taken into account by interpreters. The first of these branches is that these conceptions are unilateral: each of the two parties comes to

---

41. Let us read once more the remarkable passage 3.15, 1286b14ff., which describes the movement of deviation starting from monarchy: "As men became worse and began to profit out of the community, then reasonably oligarchies arose: for they made wealth honorable. And from oligarchies they first changed to tyrannies, and from tyrannies to democracy; for by constantly putting the government into fewer hands because of base love of gain, they made the multitude stronger, so that it attacked the oligarchs, and democracies came into existence."

"a particular conception of justice" (1280a9) but neither speaks of "the principle of absolute justice in its entirety" (1280a10). Thus, both parties are wrong. But the second branch, which is in fact the first if we follow the order of the text, not only gives the Aristotelian approach its proper character, but it helps us understand "absolute justice in its entirety (πᾶν τὸ κυρίως δίκαιον)." When, in fact, Aristotle writes about the partisans of democracy and of oligarchy that "all arrive at a certain conception of the just, but do not get beyond a certain point," that amounts to recognizing that, if they are not totally right, since they do not reach "absolute justice in its entirety," they are not completely wrong, or, to recall Aristotle's spatial metaphor, they are on the road, that is, they are on the right track, or at least they are not on an irremediably wrong track.

The unilateral approach to justice by both democrats and oligarchs thus means that both parties are wrong. The democrats, because they are equal in terms of liberty, believe themselves equal in everything, and thus worthy of equally acceding to all the power functions of the city. There is a dispute between interpreters about the exact significance of the word "liberty (ἐλευθερίᾳ)" (1280a24). Newman is certainly right to interpret it as "of free birth," in opposition to slaves, but doubtless it is necessary to understand that this term designates more precisely free *citizens*, and Newman himself notes that, in Greek literature, "free" is sometimes opposed to "foreigner." These people equal in respect to liberty are those whom Aristotle elsewhere calls "incontestably citizens" (cf. 4.4, 1292a1). The other interpretation, proposed for example by Jules Tricot, takes "liberty" in the sense of "political liberty." But doesn't that, so far as our study is concerned, come to the same thing?

The democrats reasoned thus: those who should be citizens and participate in power are those who are born from free citizen parents, which puts them on an equal footing. And in fact, on what other criterion than birth could such an ideology be based, since it does not aim at conferring the status of citizen according to any merit or talent? As for the partisans of oligarchy, Aristotle is more precise. They figure that they are, and are in fact, unequal in terms of wealth. But in a commercial transaction, "it would not be just that the person who paid one mina should have the same share of a hundred minae, whether of the principal or of the profit, as he who paid the remaining ninety-nine" (1280a28). And Aristotle draws the conclusion that if the city were a community formed in order to accumulate wealth, the partisans of oligarchy would be completely right:

"For if men met and associated out of regard to wealth only, their share in the state would be proportioned to their property, and the oligarchical doctrine would carry the day" (3.9, 1280a25).

In other words, both parties have prepolitical positions. For the oligarchs, Aristotle says so explicitly when he describes them as people who make of the city a market zone in which the State would intervene only to ensure that the rules of fair commerce are respected. Thus, they forget that the real purpose of the city is the happy life by way of noble actions, something that this same chapter, 3.9, repeats in the following sentence (1280a31), and they remain at the level of the family, which is, among other things, the location for the investment of inheritance. But the same goes for the democrats. They too remain at the level of the family, to which one in fact belongs by birth. We noted above that the idea of a citizenship based on the sharing of ethical-political values, independently of blood relationships, seems to have been an idea largely foreign to the Greeks. But we have seen that Aristotle retreated a bit in relation to the birthright, because even though he thinks that good men tend to be the parents of good men, everything that precedes this passage in book 3 shows that birth alone does not qualify a man for citizenship; he must also have a certain amount of "political virtue."

Let us look again at the first part of the sentence, on which commentators have hardly said anything: "All men cling to justice of some kind, but their conceptions are imperfect, and they do not express the whole idea" (1280a9–10). *Politics* 3.13 is doubtless clearest on this question. In a way even neater than 3.9, it asserts that of "those who claim power all, in a way, do so justly, but not all do it absolutely justly" (1283a30). The qualities in whose name they can claim a share in power are wealth, freedom, nobility, virtue, numbers. Aristotle's basic idea is that all these qualities are advantages that those who possess them may *justly* propose when demanding power, or a share in power. Thus, when he writes that "people of better lineage are more truly citizens than those without lineage" (1283a34), he seems simply to be reporting the opinion of a part of the city, what one may call the patrician prejudices of some. Probably Aristotle himself thinks that even if the nobility are not absolutely better than the others, at least nobility is a sufficient ground for seeking power. We also have to notice the miscellaneous character of this list of various pretexts for exercising power, since among the criteria proposed, which are partial and ultimately apolitical or prepolitical, virtue slips in. Either

Aristotle means this term in a very general sense of "excellence" in whatever domain, or, much more likely, he's talking about political excellence, the only criterion that provides a justified right to power. That means that, in the heart of a city with a deviant constitution, there are citizens who carry properly political values, who therefore, if they could, would establish in their city a correct constitution. More precisely, these people, who are like the pure food of *Politics* 3.11, would establish an aristocracy by conveying the power to themselves, or a polity by playing the role of the leavening in a mixture with the sufficiently virtuous mass. At the same time, reciprocally, we have seen that an aristocracy can shelter in its breast an oligarchic (or democratic) party like the worm in the apple.

Everything is, in fact, a matter of the relationship of forces, and Aristotle marks clearly the unstable character of these relationships, because there can always arise a man or a group richer than the richest, more noble than the most noble, and, as we have seen how that is possible, more virtuous than the virtuous, who will demand power. Not only does Aristotle recognize that power comes to the strongest at a given moment, but he maintains that, at least in a certain way, this is *just*. I have already cited the passage in *Politics* 1 in which, speaking of slavery, Aristotle recognizes that "the winner always wins on the basis of some good" (*Pol.* 1.6, 1255a15). In any case he remarks, "No doubt at all in determining who ought to rule in each of the above-mentioned forms of government" (3.13, 1283b4). Everybody can see what man or group is strongest. In this equilibrium of terror, in which each group measures its forces, a very important place is occupied by the "many" (οἱ πλείους, 1283a40) because the many have a tendency to be the strongest. Thus, at the end of the day, the important advice that Aristotle addresses to oligarchies, if they want to survive, is to "share the government with the many (τῷ πλήθει)" (6.7, 1321a26).

How then should we understand this mixture of ethical considerations turning on justice and of a Machiavellian conception that recognizes that it is finally the strength of a class that decides the distribution of power? Possibly by making two comments on this notion of justice, one ethical, the other political. It would belong to the Stoics to totally extricate virtue from external circumstances, but that is not (yet) the position adopted by Aristotle, for whom the virtuous man, who is also a citizen, must have the means for exercising his virtue, that is, give him worldly efficacy. One may say that these means allow him to "keep up his position" as a virtuous man. A very clear example given by Aristotle: How can one exercise liberality if one is very poor?[42] Although like all ancient moralists he argues in favor of the autonomy of the sage, who becomes godlike,[43] we have the impression, in reading the *Ethics* and *Politics* that Aristotle does not see the poor as bearers of an ethical message about detachment relative to the external world, but as people whose condition makes them potentially vicious.[44] Unless he is totally vicious, a man who is not virtuous but provided with means is doubtless, in Aristotle's eyes, more interesting, if not *ethically*, at least *politically* than someone inclined to be virtuous, but without means. By adopting that sort of position, Aristotle does not cause surprise among Greek thinkers; it is rather those who hold the opposite position who seem scandalous, the Cynics, for example, who claimed to find human actualization in the life of a dog, and the Stoics, who argued that even a person who is poor, ill, or tortured can be virtuous and happy.

In fact, very poor people cannot be *politicized*. But neither can the rich and powerful, to the extent that they refuse to submit themselves to the power of their fellow citizens. Aristotle explains this in this remarkable passage:

> Those who have too much of the goods of fortune: strength, wealth, friends, and the like, are neither willing nor able to submit to authority. The evil begins at home: for when they are boys, by reason of the luxury in which they are brought up, they never learn, even at school, the habit of obedience. On the other hand, the very poor, who are in the opposite

---

42. To be sure, the *Nicomachean Ethics* explains that liberality is not measured by the monetary value of what one gives, but "by the state of the giver, and this is relative to the giver's substance" (4.1, 1120b8); furthermore, "It is not easy for the liberal man to be rich" (1120b14). But to give something in a right way, you must have something to give . . .

43. One thinks of the very famous formula at *Nicomachean Ethics* 10.7, 1177b33, where he bids us "make ourselves immortal."

44. We have to distinguish, despite a terminological fluidity that does not surprise us coming from Aristotle, between several designations that are not equivalent for people who are not rich. The expression "middle people" (οἱ μέσοι), sometimes translated "middle class," especially describes a *political* reality by grouping together people who are "equal and similar" (4.11, 1295b25), those to whom par excellence political power is attributed. But it seems that the ἄποροι, which is better translated "those of modest means" than "poor" as is often done, need to be distinguished from the πένητες, a word that designates those who are destitute.

extreme, are too degraded. So that the one class cannot obey, and can only rule despotically; the other knows not how to command but only to obey like slaves. Thus arises a city, not of freemen, but of masters and slaves, the one despising, the other envying; and nothing can be more fatal to friendship and good fellowship in states than this. (4.11, 1295b13)

As for the political argument that the dominant class dominates *justly*, on the other hand, it is certainly not properly Aristotelian, but it is Aristotle who has provided the most developed version. It rests on the fundamental thesis of his politics that the laws are relative to the constitution and not the reverse.[45] But the law defines the just, the unjust, and that which is neither one nor the other. That means, for example, that the same law could be just in a democracy and unjust in an oligarchy. This is not a matter of the relativism that the Skeptics, Sextus Empiricus, for example, used to critique the idea that there are natural values. Far from saying that different laws are just as good as each other and that it is a matter of indifference whether one chooses one rather than the other, Aristotle, as in the case of constitutions, proposes that, on a given subject, there is just one law that is correct at a given time in a given city, namely, the law that is most compatible with the correct constitution that suits that city. As we will see below, the harmonization of constitutions and laws is one of the great problems posed to the legislator. A constitution produces its own particular norms of justice. Behind all that we will find a fundamental faith in nature. Except an enterprise proven to be perverse, like that of a tyrant who takes power in a city against the interests of all for the sake of his own purely personal goals, it is because of its natural characteristics (external givens such as geographical position, climate, resources of the territory), the ethical conditions of the people (the presence of virtuous people), and historical events, that such-and-such a regime arises for such-and-such a people. If, then, a particular part is, at a given moment, stronger than another, that reflects an objective situation that one ought not, except in extreme cases, think of as totally arbitrary. For Aristotle, everything that is real is rational.

---

45. "The laws are, and ought to be, framed with a view to the constitution, and not the constitution to the laws" (4.1, 1289a13). Plato had already held this position: *Laws* 4, 714b: there are as many legislations as there are constitutions.

But once again that does not abolish the distinction between correct and deviant constitutions. Oligarchic justice, which would be out of place anywhere than in an oligarchic constitution, is certainly "a determinate conception of justice," but it is not "justice par excellence as a whole." Correct constitutions, on the contrary, are, as we have seen, ruled by "justice par excellence as a whole," because they aim to achieve the common advantage. But what is needed in order to aim at the common advantage? Necessarily a *virtue*, in fact, "political virtue," a virtue that is simultaneously specific to this city and all-encompassing, in that the other virtues would not allow political actors to choose the common advantage in their city. Thus courage, which is incontestably a virtue, would not be sufficient to establish a correct constitution, as is shown by the case of all the warrior cities.[46] Consequently, once he has recognized the unilateral justice of democratic and oligarchic claims, and has also recognized that they would have the *right* to organize a value system, and thus also a system of laws based on those values, Aristotle nevertheless reminds us what is unsatisfactory about these systems. They are imperfect, even to the point of caricature: that is explained in *Politics* 3.10 in showing that justice in the narrowly legal sense of the term can be ethically and politically unacceptable. For example:

> If the poor . . . because they are more in number, divide among themselves the property of the rich—is not this unjust? No, by heaven (will be the reply), for the supreme authority justly willed it. But if this is not extreme injustice, what is? (1281a14)

From a strictly legal point of view, even the violent acts of the tyrant would be just (3.10, 1281a21). If we remember what was said about the tyrannical tendency inherent in every deviant constitution and that, as we saw, only the resistance of the classes that are not in power is able to contain it, we realize that such a justice, no matter how legal, *destroys the city*, or to use a very meaningful popular expression, it saws off the branch on which the constitution rests. The branch in question would be political life and the citizenship that makes it up. If the citizens are dispossessed, if

---

46. Aristotle has this interesting expression: at Sparta, the system of laws "exists in relation to a part of virtue, the warrior virtue" (2.9, 1271b1). Political virtue is thus described here, at least negatively, as "complete" virtue.

most people are forever excluded from civic life, and if this situation lasts a long time, there would no longer be a possible city, no constitution, no laws, no justice. This chapter goes very far, since even "good men" or the "most virtuous person" are criticized if they alone hold on to power, and, it is necessary to understand, if they do not govern according to political virtue. What is there to guarantee, for example, that the "most virtuous" man, once in power, will not become the plaything of his passions? We should remember that *Politics* 3.10 precedes the chapter that establishes the superiority of the power in which the mass of people is associated.

Hence this fundamental difference, which is neither more nor less than that which exists between correct constitutions and deviant constitutions: correct constitutions have the effect of spreading virtue through the body of citizens, which deviant constitutions do not do. That is a very important consequence in the case of monarchy, namely, that by contributing to the emergence of virtuous citizens, the king will find that he has produced the conditions for the termination of monarchy by favoring its transformation into an aristocracy. The same goes for aristocracy vis-à-vis polity. But we have seen, and will see again, that even in correct constitutions things often happen less peacefully.

The Laws and Justice

We have to return to a question that to say it is fundamental is the least one can say. It is that of laws and justice, beginning with justice. It wasn't Aristotle who put justice into the middle of discussions of virtue. It is enough to read Plato's *Republic*, or the myth of Protagoras in the dialogue named for him, to see that, as I have said above, justice is the "mother of all virtues." We have to see whether Aristotle's theory of justice, to which he devotes *Nicomachean Ethics* book 5, which is also book 4 of the *Eudemian Ethics*, functions in the *Politics*, a work in which justice is of course often at issue. Obviously, we have to see what aspects of this very difficult *Nicomachean Ethics* 5 would be useful to us in understanding the *Politics*.

On this point, too, Plato seems to be the philosopher of unity, while Aristotle is the philosopher of distinctions. For Plato, there is one kind of justice, which remains the same even when applied to different realities, the individual soul and the city for example. Aristotle, however, begins by declaring that justice "is said in several senses," as is injustice

(*EN* 5.1, 1129a26), more precisely in two senses. We thus have here a "homonymy," in the Aristotelian sense. If his predecessors did not notice this, says Aristotle, it's because this homonymy is not as obvious as that which exists for the word *kleis*, which designates simultaneously a key and the shoulder blade. But the text clearly puts justice and key / shoulder blade into the same category. But that is very difficult, because the homonymy affecting "justice" is much *softer* than that which applies to *kleis*. In fact there are two kinds of justice called homonyms: according to the first, justice is conformity with the law, according to the second, justice is what introduces, consolidates, or restores equality among the members of a society,[47] which has been habitually designated with the name of "general justice" (justice is the legal) and "particular justice" (justice is the equal). But particular justice is a part of general justice,[48] which creates a relationship between the two that is much closer than simple homonymy.

There is an important point there for us. After having declared that the two kinds of justice are homonyms (without using this word, but saying that "justice is said in several senses" and comparing it to the key / shoulder blade example, Aristotle alludes clearly to his doctrine of homonymy) the passage goes on to say the contrary. At 1130a32, Aristotle writes, "Evidently, therefore, there is apart from injustice in the wide sense another, particular, injustice that shares the name and nature of the first, because its definition falls within the same genus, for the force of both lies in a relation to others." Commentators tend to see this change as a correction (R. Bodéüs says that Aristotle "rectifies" what he had said above), although it is rather a complete about-face. We know, in fact, from the very beginning of the Corpus Aristotelicum, if one accepts the traditional

---

47. At 1129a26, Gauthier and Jolif are certainly right in following Ramsauer and reading "it seems that 'injustice' is said in several senses," and not "it seems that 'justice' and 'injustice' are said in several senses," because Aristotle establishes the polysemy of "justice" starting from that of "injustice." He therefore cannot affirm the polysemy of justice at the beginning of the argument. The unjust man, who is doubtless easier to characterize than the just man, is either the one who violates the law, or the one who takes more than he ought, that is, "who lacks equality." The arguments of the one who would like to suppress, that is, "who lacks equality," are strong but not decisive.

48. What Aristotle asserts is that particular injustice is a part of general injustice (5.2, 1130a33; 1130b14). Just as it has been concluded that there are two sorts of justice from the fact that there are two sorts of injustice, one may also conclude that general justice and particular justice have the same relationship between them as the corresponding injustices.

ordering that stems from the edition by Andronicus of Rhodes, that is, from *Categories* chapter 1, that homonymy and synonymy are absolutely opposed to each other in that the first is nothing but a false identity, as the example of *kleis* shows, while the second presupposes some common nature. Thus "man" and "cow" are synonyms, in the Aristotelian sense of course, because both partake of the nature of "animal." The various forms of justice, and the various forms of injustice, cannot be simultaneously both homonymous and synonymous.

Let us set this question aside for the moment in order to take it up again later, and begin now with particular justice. It too gets its definition from that of "injustice." But if injustice in general is that which violates the law, injustice according to particular injustice is that which violates equality in order to have more than it ought.[49] The demonstration of the fact that this injustice would be a part of general injustice can be seen very well in the examples given from 1130a16 and following, which are exceptionally enlightening. Legal injustice lurks behind all the vices: the coward who abandons his comrades in battle and the hot-tempered individual who strikes his fellow citizens are both unjust because they violate the law. The adulterer too is legally unjust because his intemperance causes him to violate the law. But, says Aristotle, if someone commits adultery in the hope of gain and making money by it (doubtless by having sex with a rich person who will compensate him, while the intemperate individual is, in contrast, prepared to ruin himself financially in order to satisfy his lust), that individual is *also* unjust in terms of particular injustice (2, 1130a24), because he satisfies, regardless, eventually, his lust, his desire to have more than he ought. It's that "also" that allows Aristotle to include particular injustice in general legal injustice. It's going to be the same for justice.

Particular justice is divided into several sorts, and that is one of the difficult issues in book 5, notably on the question of whether there are two or three sorts of particular justice, but that's not what interests us here. For us, the essential is understanding that there are two approaches to just distribution, and thus two conceptions of equality and inequality. The first, which Aristotle examines second, posits a numerical equality that means that a one-to-one exchange would be just, for example the two parties should receive and give as much as one another. The more important problem that is then posed is how to determine the equality

---

49. At 1129a32 I take the expression ὁ πλεονέκτης καὶ ἄνισος as a hendiadys: "The person who violates equality in attempting to have more than he ought" and not "the person who takes more than he ought and goes against equality."

of heterogeneous objects, not only (to use Aristotle examples) between a house and a pair of shoes but between the services that can be contributed by a peasant and a physician. Then Aristotle introduces an analysis of money, distinguishing between use value and exchange value, which is also presented in *Politics* book 1. We must emphasize that for Aristotle this kind of justice that defines justice by arithmetic equality is fundamentally apolitical, even if it is brought about between the citizens of a city. Apolitical also means "non-ethical" since the ethical is political and the city has a political goal. Thus: "It makes no difference whether a good man has defrauded a bad man or a bad man a good one, nor whether it is a good or bad man who has committed adultery." (5.4, 1132a2).

Then, in the justice that Aristotle calls "corrective," when equality has been violated, "the judge reestablishes equality" (1132a24), which is relatively easy in the case where the injustice relates to money or to goods that can be evaluated by the same standard, which would generally be financial. In contrast, things are more complicated in the case of wounding, adultery, and other harms of this kind. Aristotle proposes on this topic subtle analyses that show, for example, the pernicious character of *lex talionis*, and with those deft distinctions that I have said are Aristotle's trademark. Thus, corrective justice does not take the same form with the relation involving consenting participants, as in a commercial contract, and nonconsenting people, these cases divided into clandestine acts, like adultery, and violent acts, like murder.

The other type of equality, and thus of particular justice, which Aristotle analyzes before the one we have just now been talking about, is done according to "that proportion that the mathematicians call geometrical" (5.3, 1131b12), that is, one that establishes an equality of relations. This justice is called "distributive" (Aristotle talks of the "just in distribution," τὸ ἐν διανομῇ δίκαιον, 5.3, 1131b10[50]) in that it is meant to regularize "the distribution of honors, riches, or other advantages" (5.2, 1130b31). The principle of this justice is that each one ought to receive in proportion to what he brings to the community, which is generally a city. There is a general tendency to think that this distributive justice is essentially political in that it concerns only or principally the assignment of magistracies, that is, the division of power. But the passage quoted above shows that it is also concerned with wealth, for, as the *Politics* says, "it would

---

50. At 1131a25, Aristotle talks of the "just in sharing" (τὸ δίκαιον ἐν τοῖς νομαῖς). We must never forget that when one speaks of the law, the first sense of *nomos* is "that which is conveyed as a share."

not be just that he who paid one mina should have the same share of a hundred minae, whether of the principal or of the profits as he who paid the remaining ninety-nine" (3.9, 1280a28, passage already cited). To tell the truth, I have often noticed that power and wealth have more than one connection with each other. What is in any case entirely clear is that this particular justice has a common denominator in its various forms, which is *equality*, whether numerical or proportional.

The *Politics* too uses this distinction between numerical and proportional equality, a doctrine that Aristotle attributes to his ethical treatises, represented as already existing.[51] Thus, at 5.1, 1301b29, Aristotle distinguishes numerical equality and "equality according to merit." In the *Politics*, in fact, proportional equality is differentiated from numerical equality primarily by the fact that proportional equality concerns *persons*,[52] a point on which the *Nicomachean Ethics* insists much less. Furthermore, the *Politics* defines the merit of each individual *politically*: it is determined by what each one brings to the political community. The *political* problem that is posed both to the political philosopher and to the legislator is that people are habitually in error about their own merit: "Most people are generally bad judges of their own case" (3.9, 1280a14). The *Ethics* is hardly interested in that sort of problem.[53]

---

51. Cf. *Politics* 2.2, 1261a31; 3.9, 1280a18.

52. "Whereas justice implies a relation to persons as well as to things, and a just distribution, as I have already said in the *Ethics*, implies the same ratio between persons and between the things, they agree about the equality of the things, but dispute about the equality of the persons" (*Pol.* 3.9, 1280a16).

53. It is interesting that the description of particular justice is not the same in the *Ethics* and *Politics*, although this form of justice includes the same elements, namely, the distribution of goods and power according to an arithmetic proportion and a distribution according to a geometrical proportion. But the *Nicomachean Ethics* goes on to gather these two operations under the heading of equal sharing, the attribution of advantages proportionally to a factor considered as fundamental for social relations (nobility, wealth, virtue, or something else considered by those in power as excellent) being a form of *equality*. When, in contrast, the *Politics* asserts that "everyone agrees that justice is proportional (κατ' ἀναλογίαν) equality" (5.1, 1301a26), that means that when justice consists of giving each one a numerically equal part, this equality is considered as a (limiting) case of proportionality. This situation can present itself in two cases: either this sort of relation is extended to the entire society, especially in terms of distribution of power, and we then are dealing with a democratic constitution, or it concerns only a limited part of social life. In commercial transactions all constitutions, rare exceptions apart, expect equal exchange.

Another remarkable difference between the *Politics* and the *Ethics* would be that in the *Politics* considerations of numerical equality are nearly completely absent, unless as a manifestation of an incorrect understanding of justice: democrats think that political power, as well as various social advantages, ought to be shared according to numerical equality among the citizens, and in that, they are mistaken. The principal reason for this absence is doubtless that, as I have said above, numerical equality is fundamentally apolitical. Commercial transactions, as it happens, do not belong to the political sphere.

As for legal justice, it is on a more global level and is rightly called "general," or, as Aristotle himself puts it, "total" (ὅλη). According to this form of justice, "one who violates the law is unjust, one who conforms to the law is just" (5.1, 1129b11). Inevitably a question arises: What about when the law is bad? We even run into a contradiction in terms, since at *Politics* 3.11, 1282b11, we read, "Laws that correspond to correct constitutions are necessarily just and those that correspond to deviant constitutions are not just" (passage already cited, cf. 10, 1281a36). It looks like it would be just to obey laws that are not just . . . It seems that the *Nicomachean Ethics* does not envisage the possibility that there would be bad laws because they are in force in a deviant constitution. Thus, even when Aristotle seems to make a distinction between just and unjust laws, it is illusory. That is the case at 3, 1129b23, where after having enumerated a certain number of cases where the law prescribes virtuous behaviors (a passage to which I will return), Aristotle writes: "And similarly, with regard to the other virtues and vices, commanding some acts and forbidding others; the rightly framed law does this rightly, and the hastily conceived one less well."[54] What Aristotle is pointing to here is a technical error by the legislator, who has not taken the time to make a law well adapted to the spirit of the constitution, with the consequence that this law has unwanted perverse effects.

A passage in *Nicomachean Ethics* 5 is even more interesting. It has been particularly discussed, and amended by the editors; it is found right before the passage we have just quoted: "Now the laws in their enactments on all subjects aim at the common advantage either of all or of the best or of those who hold power by some virtue, or something of the sort" (1129b14).

---

54. The word ἀπεσχεδιασμένος is a *hapax legomenon* in Aristotle, and indicates something done in haste, in the heat of the moment.

Some have proposed suppressing "the best," others "by some virtue," but if we keep the text as it is, we see here that Aristotle thinks that cities function for the benefit of those who exercise power, whether their superiority is due to virtue or whatever else. The expression "whether of the best or of those who hold power by some virtue, or something of the sort," obviously recalls the passages in the *Politics* in which Aristotle recognizes a certain legitimacy of the qualities that different groups of citizens put forward in claiming access to power: liberty, virtue, wealth, noble birth.[55]

And the passage in the *Nicomachean Ethics* continues: "So that in one sense we call just those acts that tend to produce and preserve happiness and its components for the political community" (1129b17).

This passage can be interpreted in two ways depending on the sense that one gives to the word "happiness." If this word has its strong sense of virtuous activity of the person, then this passage of the *Nicomachean Ethics* is thinking only of cities with a correct constitution, since they alone can realize the happiness of their citizens. If, on the contrary, Aristotle also means by "happiness" what vicious people think it is, then the passage means that legal prescriptions that go in the direction of satisfying the people in power would be just, which confirms the sense of the lines that precede this passage, as I have separated them above. The "political community" in an oligarchy, for example, could be reduced to a very small number of men. In any case, in the *Nicomachean Ethics* the problem of the relationship between general justice and constitutional rectitude is carefully avoided.

The *Nicomachean Ethics* may, if I dare say so, allow itself something that would be totally impossible in a work like the *Politics*, namely, to analyze the idea of justice and especially its relation to the city without asking the question of the correct or deviant nature of the constitution of that city. As in book 1 of the *Politics*, in *Nicomachean Ethics* 5 the city is the location of human ethical actualization, independent of the constitutional forms that can belong to it.

It is important to note that the reason for the silence of the *Nicomachean Ethics* is not that Aristotle was unaware, when he wrote this treatise, of the difference between correct and deviant constitutions. Thus the passage analyzed above, that says that "there is only one constitution that would be naturally best everywhere" (5.7, 1135a5) really does refer to constitutional excellence. As for the passage already cited that says, "All

---

55. Cf., for example, *Politics* 3.12, 1283a15ff.; 13, 1283a30ff.

men agree that what is just in distribution must be according to merit in some sense, though they do not all specify the same sort of merit, but democrats identify it with the status of freemen, supporters of oligarchy with wealth or with noble birth, and supporters of aristocracy with excellence" (5.6, 1131a25), shows that Aristotle does not ignore in the *Nicomachean Ethics* his theory of the vicious sorts of justice in deviant constitutions. Thus, the first reason that the *Nicomachean Ethics* is not preoccupied with the value of the laws is that, although ethics is a part of politics and that consequently the *Nicomachean Ethics* is a political work, it is not a work *about* politics, or more precisely, about political philosophy. For that reason, the *Nicomachean Ethics* does not have the goal of considering how to establish or conserve an excellent constitution. We will see the second reason a little later; it is much more interesting for our purposes.

This legal justice is simultaneously global and political. That it would be global Aristotle expresses by means of the thesis that, as justice is a virtue, "this justice (legal justice) is not a part of virtue, but complete virtue" (1, 1130a9), or, though this does not come to precisely the same thing, "this form of justice, then, is complete virtue—not absolutely, but in relation to others" (1129b26). I believe that we must understand this expression ὅλη ἀρετή, translated "complete virtue," in the first sense of "complete," in which a whole is a sum of parts. And that is indeed what Aristotle says in the definitely crucial passage at 1, 1129b20, considered above, when he writes that the law commands the performance of acts of courage, temperance, mildness. Thus, the person who is just in the general sense will also be just in the restricted sense, since he will not seek to damage equality between citizens. Justice in the restricted sense is a virtue, and since a just man in the wide sense possesses all the virtues, he also has this one.

But this legal justice is also *political*, and that is even the characteristic that Aristotle points out before noting that it includes all the virtues. Legal justice, in fact, enjoins performing just actions, but, as we have seen, "in a sense we call those acts just that tend to produce and preserve happiness and its components for the political community" (1129b17). The passage at 1129b19 seems to establish a logical order between the two characteristics when it says that legal justice establishes happiness in the city, "but the law enjoins us *also* to perform" virtuous acts. But as a matter of fact, it is indeed the exercise of the various virtues that is the major precondition for happiness, so much so that I understand Aristotle's reasoning goes this way: legal justice ought to establish happiness in the city, and it also happens, one may say *happily*, that it commands the performance of virtuous actions, and since virtue produces happiness. . . . Always, of course, in the case of a city with a correct constitution.

As a result, finally, Aristotle does not make that big a deal of legal justice. John Burnet was certainly right, and a good many commentators have accepted his analysis, when he thought that "in a certain sense we call those acts just" (1129b17), which is introduced by a μὲν, is taken up again at 1130a14, at the beginning of chapter 2, by the "but (δὲ) what we are investigating is the justice that is a particular virtue" (1130a14). That would be a way of signaling that the real investigation begins with the examination of justice as equality and that therefore legal justice is only a general introduction, signified by the words "in a special sense."[56]

One fact shows especially clearly that the "serious" examination begins with the study of justice as equality, namely, that it alone is truly a virtue. It alone, in fact, is situated between two vices opposed to each other (for example, in the case of equal exchange of values, both the greedy person who tries to obtain more than he ought, and the prodigal who lets go of goods for much less than their value, are both unjust), while this schema is inapplicable in the case of legal justice. One cannot, in fact, situate it between a too weak obedience and a too strong obedience to the laws.

Hence the way that I read *Nicomachean Ethics* 5.9, in which Aristotle explains that both vice and virtue seem easy to achieve, since nothing is easier than to "sleep with the wife of one's neighbor, slug somebody, bribe somebody" (5.9, 1137a6), and it is no more difficult to abstain from doing those things. But, Aristotle remarks, the person is not virtuous, *nor vicious*, who wants to be so, because to have a virtue or a vice is the result of "a state of character, which is not easy to get and does not depend on us" (1137a9). In fact, as we know, it is necessary that virtue and vice be inculcated in individuals by the regular practice of virtuous or vicious actions. In a remarkable synoptic volume published in 2002, Richard Kraut[57] argues that legal justice does not simply sanction blind obedience to the laws, but demands that one be conscious of doing so for the greater good of the political community. I believe that that would be asking legal justice to perform a task that it cannot do.

---

56. John Burnet, *The Ethics of Aristotle* (London: Methuen, 1900), 202.

57. Richard Kraut, *Aristotle: Political Philosophy* (Oxford: Oxford University Press, 2002), 19.

So here is how I see the series of theses in *Nicomachean Ethics* 5. There are two approaches to justice, not unrelated to each other, because justice as equality is a part of legal justice. In fact, equality justice is a *virtue*, while *in a certain way* legal justice is all the virtues. General justice as the result of obedience to the laws is a little empty. Nevertheless, it remains that the virtue of justice is acquired by obeying good laws, like all the other virtues. In fact, just as the law commands us to be courageous, to not commit adultery, avoid corruption, and so on, it also proposes that one must assure a fair distribution of goods and honors, that is, of power, among the citizens. That is even the major problem that should face every legislator. When, then, one is just in the narrow sense, one is just in the general sense, and if one allows oneself to be carried along by the movement of justice in the legal sense, that is, take it upon oneself to obey the laws, which enjoin us to perform virtuous actions, one will come to practice justice in the narrow sense. But between legal justice and equality justice there is all the difference that exists between simple virtuous behavior and a true virtue that brings it about that virtuous actions "emanate" naturally from the virtuous person and satisfy him. We have seen that this "true" virtue is difficult to acquire. Legal justice can attain true worth *in time*. By performing correct actions as prescribed by law, and thus just according to legal justice, men, especially if they are young, may hope to become virtuous, that is, along with other virtues, just according to particular justice.

Thus, it is up to politics to complete the treatment of the problem of justice, and, in the *Politics*, Aristotle does that in a way that seems bizarre at first glance. The distinction between legal justice and equality justice seems to be absent here, to such an extent that one is tempted to ask whether Aristotle has abandoned that distinction, or not conceived of it yet, when he wrote the *Politics*. Actually, both concepts of justice are indeed present in the treatise, but in a different way than in the *Nicomachean Ethics*. The *Politics* version can be summarized thus: it is the law that, by setting the modalities for the distribution of wealth and power, defines that which is just. In other words, the two sorts of justice distinguished in the *Nicomachean Ethics* are articulated in one single unity: the just is indeed that which conforms to the law, but the law is above all that which sets how the distribution of goods and of power ought to be made, and to be just is indeed to accept, and practice, correct distribution. But then the worst plundering becomes just, provided that the law authorizes it, as we have seen in the case of the poor who oppress their wealthy fellow citizens (cf. *Pol.* 3.10, 1281a14). The same for power: if the law limits deliberation on common affairs to a tiny number of citizens, that is just. That amounts to saying that the problem of the difference between just laws and unjust laws becomes central. The *Politics* thus incarnates the analyses of the *Nicomachean Ethics* into the real world of the cities.

Does that mean that in the *Politics* particular justice has simply disappeared? Or, for a more moderate version of this thesis, that particular justice can exist only in cities that have a correct constitution? As a matter of fact, Aristotle recognizes the presence of virtuous people in all, or nearly all, cities, no matter their constitutions. When, in the famous chapter 4 of *Politics* 3, he writes that the virtue of the citizen depends on the constitution, but that "the good man is he who has one single excellence which is perfect excellence" (1276b33), there is no reason that that would not apply to particular justice. In a vicious city, therefore, where acts of plunder are called legal justice, for example, there are people who have the virtue of particular justice, and who reject such acts. Similarly, when, at the beginning of his study of sedition, to which I will return in detail, Aristotle declares that "those who would have the most just motives to provoke sedition, and who nevertheless do so the least" (1301a39), are the virtuous people, so such people indeed exist in the cities who are not virtuous.[58]

These virtuous citizens who live in the heart of a perverted city are in danger of often being unhappy, because their legal conception of the just (if, for example, the law endorses plundering the rich) is in conflict with their virtue of justice, which makes it so that they *are disposed* to treat their fellow citizens according to the rules of equality. Aristotle says nothing about the inner conflicts of these virtuous people, but what he indicates several times is that their presence in the heart of cities with deviant constitutions has a great *political* importance for the legislator, in that they are a factor for ameliorating the constitution, as we will see in the next two chapters. These people represent the "pure food" noted in *Politics* 3.11. We also call attention to the fact, as the examples developed in the study of seditions will show, that the cities with a correct constitution include vicious citizens, partisans of a deviation, whether democratic or oligarchic or tyrannical. If everything goes well, a correct constitution will,

---

58. That is also what Aristotle says in a passage already cited, *Politics* 3.13, if you take it literally: "Everyone may have a claim on power, in a certain sense, but not all have an absolute claim" (1283a30). That presupposes that there is someone whose claim is absolutely just.

in the course of time, make *all* the citizens virtuous and happy. This ideal stability, which ought to last forever, or at least a very long time, because it represents a state of *perfection*, does not exist in the world of cities. We will see the causes when we reveal Aristotle's great originality as a thinker of the unstable and the ephemeral. Aristotle, in any case, did not conceive of a city that would completely take control, ideologically speaking, of all its citizens and adapt them completely to its constitution. A homogeneity like that, whether the constitution were correct or deviant, would obviously be a guarantee of durability for the city. But wait! There are always people who remain rebels against the indoctrination of the citizens by the dominant classes, whether these people are rascals impervious to the good, or are witnesses to virtue in a vicious environment.

That allows us to grasp another important difference between correct and deviant constitutions. A deviant constitution, as we have seen and will see again in detail, rests on a mistaken conception of justice. Democrats think that it is just to share power equally among all the citizens without regard to their merit and without regard to what they bring to the city. As for the oligarchs, they think that it is just to distribute everything pro rata according to the wealth of each one, something that often will exclude many people from political power. But each of these conceptions transforms the whole of political and social life when it gains ascendancy in the city. Aristotle demonstrates that especially for tyranny: the villainy of the tyrant *stains* his subjects who become fearful, vicious, and spineless. But one can assume that that is also true in an oligarchy. The overvaluing of wealth and the lure of gain transform the citizens and distance them from political virtue: they will be, for example, ready to go to war against their fellow citizens in order to preserve their privileges, even in appealing to a foreign power to subdue their own people. But it is above all their conception of particular justice that would be affected: oligarchs, like democrats, have a gravely erroneous conception of what ought to be equality in the city.

In correct constitutions, on the contrary, it is *the same virtue*, and notably the same particular justice, which is accepted in all parts of the city, at least among the virtuous citizens. The only difference, from this point of view, between a monarchy, an aristocracy, and a polity, is the number of virtuous people who can be found in the social body. In the case of correct constitutions, then, the analyses of particular justice to be found in the *Nicomachean Ethics* are completely valid, so in this sense none of the laws of the city occasion a conflict with the virtue of particular justice possessed by the virtuous citizens.

CHAPTER 5

On the Positive Use of Deviance

By relying on everything that has been said, we can see the traces of the true nature, and especially the various possible results, of constitutional deviance according to Aristotle. To put the matter briefly, deviation can be a step on the road to evil, but not necessarily. Of course, as we have seen, every dominant class that bases its domination on its own interests has a tendency to solidify more and more the unilateral and oppressive character of the constitution, and its power will end up taking a tyrannical form if the other "parties" do not hold out against the appetites of that dominant class. That is where the salvation or destruction of deviant constitutions comes from.

Everything, both best and worst, comes from the fact that there are almost no "pure" constitutions for a legislator to work on. In fact, we have seen that the ideal situation in which a correct constitution promulgates virtue in the whole body of citizens and, from that fact, makes them all cohere with that model, that of the virtuous man, is not to be found in the world of cities. Not all the citizens share a common ideology, mainly, Aristotle recognizes, because they do not have the same social position: the rich and the poor cannot come to an understanding with each other; each group fears becoming the slave of the other (cf. *Pol.* 4.12, 1296b40). And that is just as true for the deviant constitutions. A pure oligarchy, that is, one whose legislation is constituted entirely on the basis of oligarchical principles, might exist for a short time in a crisis situation (after a military defeat, for example, as was the case for the oligarchy imposed on Athens by victorious Sparta), but that can hardly endure, because one cannot maintain for a long time a regime in which, according to Aristotle's expression, "there are no people" (*Pol.* 3.1, 1275b7).[1] In general, "to organize a constitution, simply and completely, according to either kind of equality [those anticipated by democrats and oligarchs], is not a good thing; the proof is the fact that such forms of government never last" (5.1, 1302a2).

So, the legislation of an oligarchic constitution that is going to endure necessarily carries the marks of the presence within the city of a democratic party opposed to the very principle of the oligarchy. That means that the legislation of the constitution in question includes laws inspired by a democratic perspective, that the oligarchs, as we have seen, accept because they are not strong enough to refuse them. These laws would be all the more numerous and would concern domains all the more strategic to the extent that the democratic party would be stronger. That which is true of the laws is also true of the "parts" of the constitution, that is, the deliberative, executive, and judicial, about which we will speak at length below, and of the magistracies attached to these functions. Thus, an oligarchy may have a tribunal with a democratic orientation, which would temper its oligarchic character. Obviously, there is a critical threshold beyond which the constitution could no longer be called oligarchic. In any case it is a general rule that equality of forces in a constitution brings it into a period of instability:

> Constitutions also change when parts of a city that are believed to be opposed to each other, such as the rich and the people, become equal to each other, and there is little or no middle class. For if either of the parts becomes greatly superior, the remaining one will be unwilling to risk going up against the manifestly stronger one. (*Pol.* 5.4, 1304a38)

We must note once again that this mixture of parties and laws of different colorations can imply constitutions both correct and deviant, also showing that they all belong to the same political space. At *Politics* 6.1, 1317a2, for example, Aristotle speaks of "oligarchical aristocracies and relatively democratic polities," a manner of expression that if one insists on the first distinction applied in *Politics* 3.7, between correct and deviant

---

1. Tricot translates "the people are nothing," but it is more likely that Aristotle means to say that the assembly of the people (one of the senses of the word *dēmos*) has no power, or is nonexistent. That's how the standard English translations read it.

constitutions, would be totally incoherent. In order to be able to speak in these terms, Aristotle had first to make some decisive theoretical progress in his apprehension of the diversity of constitutions, a subject that we will consider when the time comes.

Up until now, in fact, Aristotle has not adopted positions that would be completely original in comparison with those of his predecessors. The idea that some constitutions mix the traits of various "pure" constitutions was just as widespread as the fact that it matched the political reality of the time. Thus, Plato's *Republic* established timocracy, the regime that followed aristocracy, as situated between (ἐν μέσῳ) aristocracy and oligarchy (8, 547c). The idea that such mixed constitutions ought to function better, because they would adapt themselves more easily to a given historical situation, should also have been rather widespread. Cicero and Polybius attribute the excellence of the Roman constitution to the fact that it was a mixture of all the other constitutions, simply recycling an opinion that already existed in Aristotle's day, since

> some say that the best constitution is a combination of all existing forms, and that is why they approve of the Lacedaemonian because they say it is made up of oligarchy, monarchy, and democracy; they claim that the kingship is a monarchy, and the council of elders an oligarchy, and it is democratic by virtue of the Ephors; for the Ephors are selected from the people. (*Pol.* 2.6, 1265b33)

And in fact, until Aristotle's day, most cities were mixtures of oligarchy and democracy, demonstrating the presence in them, already noted, of democratic and oligarchic parties. The history of Greece showed to Aristotle the virtues of constitutional mixture. The reforms of Cleisthenes aimed to mix together the citizens of the various Attic demes. On the surface this mixture appears "technical," but it is in fact highly political, because the old system had favored the "city people," and thus the old aristocratic families. Before Cleisthenes, Solon had constructed a true constitutional mixture:

> As for Solon, some think that he was an excellent legislator, in that he put an end to the exclusiveness of the oligarchy, emancipated the people, and established the ancient Athenian democracy, by harmonizing the various elements of the state. In

their opinion, the council of the Areopagus was an oligarchical element, the elected magistracy, aristocratic, and the courts of law, democratic. (*Pol.* 2.12, 1273b35).

However, we need to make two remarks here. In the first place, the properly political analysis, more precisely constitutional, of this mixture, is the result of a later account (by "some," not identified by Aristotle), and not due to Solon himself. Secondly, the lines that follow this extract show that "some," doubtless not the same as the first ones, did not think that Solon's reforms were useful, and Aristotle himself seems reserved about the Athenian legislator. And otherwise, in general, the *Politics* does not provide a flattering image of Solon.

The *Politics*, especially in its "realist" books and passages, never stops telling us that correct constitutions do not last forever, while a general presumption of Greek thought was that the perfect does not change or changes only with great difficulty. But nothing seems easier than for a correct constitution to change, and this change can happen in two ways. First, kingship and aristocracy can change toward a polity, as has been said several times, that is, toward a correct constitution based on a more widely shared virtue. Secondly, any correct constitution can change into a deviant form, because the original correct constitution contained, according to the image noted above that Aristotle uses in *Politics* 3.11, a share of "impure food." But even in the first case, we have seen that the passage from kingship to a larger regime, as described in *Politics* 3.15, can occur as the consequence of exigencies that are not necessarily ethical. By the same token, kingship, a correct constitution established to enjoy the "beneficence" of the king, can immediately or rapidly be replaced by a plutocratic regime (cf. 1286b14). That is all the more possible, and frequent, because changes often bear on secondary details and for that reason often occur at the beginning more or less unobserved. On this point, Aristotle cites the example of Ambracia, where the financial qualification for becoming a magistrate was so low that it was thought that there would be little difference in suppressing it entirely, something that gave a strongly democratic character to the existing regime, which was supposed to be oligarchic in tendency, and overturned it entirely (*Pol.* 5.3, 1203a23). The same sort of series of events could happen in correct constitutions. Deviance is thus a huge phenomenon, as huge as mixture.

If it is true, as Matthew attributes to Jesus, that every kingdom divided against itself is destined to fall, then in the Aristotelian theoretical construction, cities, whether they have a correct constitution or a deviant constitution, cannot hope to remain in place for a very long time. But at the same time this internal division opens remarkable perspectives to legislators in their attempt to bring into being excellent constitutions. These attempts are based upon what I have above called the most advanced spearhead of the Aristotelian political philosophy, which is a totally new analysis of the relationships between excellence and deviance. There is here, on Aristotle's part, a reconfiguration of the idea that seems, as we have seen, to have been widespread, that mixture benefits constitutions.

This analysis utilizes two results of Aristotle's thought, already noted, first, that the viewpoint of each social class that supports a deviant constitution is partially just without being absolutely just; second, that every constitution is composed of elements at least partially incompatible, because they reflect the incompatible interests of the opposed classes that compose the city. From that, Aristotle will make a *dynamic* theory of constitutions, which will surpass those of his predecessors both in terms of explanatory strength and in terms of practical efficiency.

For there are two ways of mixing opposed traits in the constitution, depending on how one juxtaposes the good or bad viewpoints of the positions of the antagonistic classes that cohabit the city. If a constitution adds the greed for money of the oligarchs to the confiscatory violence of the democrats, it rapidly becomes the worst of all, a tyrannical constitution that will soon become totally lawless. In *Politics* 5.10, Aristotle explains that "tyranny is composed of oligarchy and democracy in their most extreme forms. . . . It is made up of two evil forms of government, and has the perversions and errors of both" (1310b3), and a little later, in a passage that blends, as often in the *Politics*, a strong explanatory structure with a fine appreciation of empirical reality, Aristotle shows exactly why "tyranny has all the vices of both democracy and oligarchy" (1311a8): on the one side, the taste of oligarchs for wealth, which alone can allow the tyrant to lead his unbridled life, distrust of the people, and on the other side, the hatred that the democrats have for the notables to the point that they would execute or exile them.

But there is another sort of possible mixture. If a constitution succeeds in blending the taste for liberty and equality of the democrats, which is, after all, the very foundation of political life, with the idea that each one ought to receive in proportion to what he brings to the city, which would be rather an oligarchic, or even an aristocratic tendency, one would obtain a correct constitution. Aristotle is more precise, saying that the polity, which is one of the correct constitutions, is "a mixture of oligarchy and democracy" (4.8, 1293b33), which he defines as a "mixture of wealth and liberty" (1294a17). Starting from *Politics* book 2, Aristotle has attributed this analysis to Plato, but in a form that one could call "subconscious": "The whole system of government (of Plato's city in the *Laws*) tends to be neither democracy nor oligarchy, but something in a mean between them, which is usually called a polity, and is composed of hoplites" (2.6, 1265b26). Hoplites are heavy infantry, a battle formation that corresponds to an egalitarian regime, but hoplites are not poor people, they are contrasted to the cavalry typical of aristocracy. This is a way of describing a polity as the constitution that gives the preponderance of power to the middle class.

We find in chapter 4.8 a remark that seems bizarre at first sight, but which is very interesting in that it allows us to complete, and even to rectify, our concept of constitutional rectitude. After saying that a polity is the mixture of oligarchy and democracy, Aristotle reports that the term "polity" "is usually applied (εἰώθασι δὲ καλεῖν)" to those forms of mixture that "lean toward democracy," while one calls aristocracies those that lean toward oligarchy. It is difficult to decide who exactly is "usually" accustomed to this use of language, but the use of *politeia* to designate a type of constitution is especially an Aristotelian trait, although one does find, in Demosthenes and Isocrates, for example,[2] this term applied to a popular regime. But it is doubtless impossible to find someone other than Aristotle who maintained the thesis that "a constitution mixing democracy and oligarchy that leans toward democracy is called a polity." In fact, this is expressed in a kind of reciprocal way in a passage already cited, 6.1, 1317a2, when Aristotle speaks of "aristocratic oligarchies and rather democratic polities." We have there a remarkable generalization of the production of rectitude, since aristocracy also can result from a mixture of the good parts of democracy and oligarchy. In that case it would obviously be a mixed aristocracy as we have characterized it above. It is possible to imagine how that would happen. An aristocracy is a constitution that assigns power to a minority for the sake of common advantage. Normally it is defined as a regime that has as its government a minority of virtuous people, but the two descriptions are equivalent, since only virtuous people can govern for the sake of common advantage and not for personal profit.

---

2. Cf., for example, Demosthenes *Olynthian* 5 and *Philippics* 2.21, Isocrates *Panegyric* 125.

We have seen that a sufficient accounting for virtue in the assignment of power would be enough to call a constitution an "aristocracy."

If, then, the mixture gives a preponderant place to liberty, but preventing the minority of the wealthy from being exploited by the poor majority, that would, among other consequences, tend to rely on the elevated number of citizens, even if they are not all involved in the most important political functions. We would thus find ourselves in the presence of a polity of the kind that Aristotle recommends in *Politics* 3.11. Thus, Aristotle calls this polity "democratic," first because it clearly relies on the people. But it is also called "democratic" because it has recourse to procedures and legislation that are more congenial to democracies, for example, when one selects important magistrates by drawing lots. Consequently, it satisfies the "democratic party" present in the city. An analysis of this kind allows us to read between the lines in Aristotle's approach to the diversity of constitutions, as we will examine it below in more detail, when Aristotle characterizes as "a polity with an aristocratic tendency" (ἀριστοκρατικῶς, 4.15, 1300a41) one in which, for example, access to magistracies undergoes certain imitations, thus satisfying the aristocratic party.

If, on the other hand, the accent is put on the rights of the minority without ignoring its civic duties, and that, for example, one makes room for wealth as a qualification to be nominated to some magistracies, the mixture leans toward the aristocratic side by satisfying certain demands of the oligarchical part, and one gets what Aristotle calls an "aristocratic oligarchy." But a regime of this kind can also allow to the members of the people who want it to participate in power to somehow do so, because if they were prevented, one would have the kind of oligarchy that could not mix harmoniously with democracy. But it will be insisted upon, particularly by way of the laws, that this participation should be deserved. The idea that one must above all keep in mind from this analysis is that democratic action on an oligarchy can produce an aristocracy, just as oligarchic action on a democracy can produce a polity. From that one gains an understanding of what it means to say that a polity or an aristocracy inherits the *good* sides of oligarchy and democracy, because when it comes to the bad sides, matters are quite clear. It is necessary that the polity, or the aristocracy, borrow from each deviant constitution what would be, so to speak, recyclable in a correct constitution. But a correct constitution is one that rules in a city for the sake of the common advantage of its citizens, that is, that leads them to happiness by developing virtue in the civic body. One may consider that what I have called the "good sides" of oligarchy and democracy correspond to the correct aspects of the conception of justice of each of these two parties.

Another remark, very important for avoiding impressions that are too simplistic. The Aristotelian doctrine, well attested, that a polity is a mixture of democracy and oligarchy needs to be specified on two points. In the first place, it is a matter of what may be called a minima formula, because a polity may have other elements in its composition, notably aristocratic traits. In the second place, this formula is not reciprocal, because even if every polity is at the least composed of democracy and oligarchy, it is definitely not the case that every constitution composed of democracy and oligarchy is a polity. In fact, we have seen that Aristotle thinks that certain aristocracies result from such a combination. We also see all the polities in question here have obviously moderated the demands belonging to a polity that may be called "absolute," namely, the regime that is blessed with a preponderance of a large number of virtuous people. In any case that is what Aristotle said in the first characterization of correct constitutions in *Politics* 3. Let us cite this text again, but more completely this time:

> When the many administer the city for the common interest, the government is called by the generic name—a polity. And it is reasonable.[3] One man or a few may excel in excellence; but as the number increases it becomes more difficult for them to attain perfection in every kind of excellence, though they may in military excellence, for this is found in the masses. (3.7, 1279a37)

For there to be a polity, it is enough that the multitude govern for the sake of the common advantage, because one cannot demand that this multitude be composed of virtuous people. Thus, we do not find, in the case of the polity, the same duality that opposes pure kingships and aristocracies to their mixed versions.

Here I will allow myself an analysis that can hardly be supported by any explicit statements by Aristotle. It bears on the notion of the "good sides" of oligarchy and democracy; I have claimed that they alone can

---

3. I don't understand why this is "reasonable," because I don't want to relate it to what follows. But I will offer a hypothesis below.

enter into the mixture of a polity. When a democracy accepts into its constitution some legislative measures that can gain for it the acceptance of the oligarchical party, and thus will put it on the road to a polity, it is necessary that it be, as we have seen, the *good* side(s) of oligarchy that it borrows. Because when mixed with democratic liberty, unbridled competition for wealth would surely not contribute to constructing a polity. But in the operation of a mixture of the good sides of the two constitutions, what the oligarchs are after is certainly wealth and the means for being sure that wealth contributes to acquiring power. For it to be politically recyclable, it is necessary that from this demand for the monopolization of power by a minority the constitution that results from the mixture retain in some way the form and not the content. What the oligarchical ideology should in fact *teach* the citizens of the polity is not that the wealth is a good thing (although it is, *to a certain degree*), but that citizenship should be merited. The same goes for the democratic side of the polity. In pleading for their liberty, what the democrats want to do with it is that this liberty be associated with a total equality that would make the citizens equal in every respect. Aristotle thinks, as did Plato before him, that this position is fatal to constitutional correctness. In this case too, the polity ought to go beyond the primary goals of the partisans of democracy.

Democrats, as much as oligarchs in fact, certainly do not make the distinction between the good and bad sides of their respective ideologies. Only the political philosopher and the legislator are able to carry out an analysis of that kind. And in fact, it is the role of the legislator to carry out the screening of good from bad. By setting a very low property qualification for citizenship or certain magistracies, for example, he will impede the oligarchs from giving free rein to their perverse desires. But all that rests on a kind of gamble: that everyone will ultimately benefit from it. That presupposes a fundamental conviction that we will again find operating, notably concerning tyranny, that virtue is contagious, because it agrees with the core nature of human beings. The very practice of the institutions of a polity would thus be enough to convince the two parties, democratic and oligarchic, that this correct constitution satisfies them.

This mixture of democracy and oligarchy can be brought about by law, as is shown, in another domain, by an example given by Aristotle in *Politics* 4.9. In oligarchies, at least some of them, a fine is imposed on the rich for not attending the deliberations of the assembly. As we have seen above, in fact, the wealthier classes often are tempted to abandon the political sphere in order to devote themselves to their private affairs, something that is clearly fatal to an oligarchy. For people who are less well off, on the other hand, there is no kind of incentive to attend, they are not fined if they do not attend, nor are they compensated if they do. A democracy, in contrast, will give compensation to the poor for attending and abstain from penalizing the rich for not attending. "The union of these two modes is a common or middle term between them, and is therefore characteristic of a polity, for it is a combination of both" (4.9, 1294a41). Doubtless two combinations are possible: no pay and no fine for anybody, or fine the rich and pay the poor, the best solution depending on the political, economic, and ethical circumstances of the people under consideration. As will be shown in the next chapter, intermediate solutions exist, like imposing a fine on everyone, but more on the rich. Aristotle says that that's what Charondas of Catania did to get the citizens to participate in juries (*Pol.* 4.13, 1297a23).

Let's see how far we have gone. In the strict sense, if one respects the terminology that Aristotle himself established in *Politics* 3.7, an "aristocratic oligarchy" is a monstrosity, because aristocracy is a correct constitution and oligarchy is a deviant constitution; the same would hold for a "sufficiently democratic polity." In an expression like that, probably "sufficiently" is the strangest word. That's how I translated the comparative form δημοκρατικωτέρας (6.1, 1371a2), which doubtless means that a polity like that leans more than others toward democracy. Now we are immersed in an eminently unstable political world, in which cities are never ruled by "pure" constitutions, where class struggle is the driving force of history, but in which, despite wind and wave, Aristotle maintains his ethical demands while continuing to supply brilliant realist analyses, powerfully based on a very ample historical documentation.

Sometimes Aristotle comes very close to an ethical disconnect. There is a passage at the beginning of *Politics* 5.9, little noticed by interpreters, which clarifies the Aristotelian position very well. At that point in the text we are in the middle of "realist" politics. Studying the causes of sedition, a topic to which we will return in detail, it's a matter of giving to legislators and magistrates the means to make their constitutions last. The problem posed by Aristotle is also "realist": For carrying out a public duty, is it better to have a vicious expert or an ethical incompetent? The response is "realist": for functions that require rare abilities, such as military general, it is better to hire an able bad (πονηρός) man; while for functions that many people are able to perform, such as guardian of the treasury, it is better to prefer the virtuous. Then comes the temptation to hold on to realism while throwing normative politics overboard; "But it may be asked, why do we need virtue if a man is both able and loyal to the constitution?" (5.9, 1309b8). The example of the difference between the general and the treasurer suggests a position like that of Callicles, according to which those who make a show of their virtue in order to have a share of power in the city are in fact people who are unable to do so on the basis of their abilities. But this is precisely the position Aristotle cannot decide to adopt, because politics is above all a matter of virtue. But if the individual in question is intemperate, that is, as Aristotle reminds us, if he does bad things even though he knows what is good, and by that fact, he hurts himself, what is there to assure us that he will not do the same to the city? But a good magistrate is one who works for the common advantage.

The same for the remarkable reversal of the relationship between "correct" and "deviant" in *Politics* 4.3. There Aristotle posits as a reference point that which exists in actuality and massively, everything else, because rare, being nothing but a deviation. A practice like that finds support also in the Aristotelian conception of nature, since that which exists by nature exists "always or for the most part."[4] But one finds in the Greek world of his time that democracies and oligarchies were by far the most numerous. Relying on a comparison with the winds, among which one takes north and south as fundamental, and with harmonies, with two fundamental ones, Dorian and Phrygian, other winds and other harmonies being only derivative forms, Aristotle ends up saying that aristocracy is a deviant form of oligarchy and polity a deviant form of democracy . . . Here the word "deviant" is used in a purely functional sense. But this functional approach has to cohabit with that foundation of "normative" politics which says that a deviation is a deviation from a correct form, and that it is the correct form that allows us to understand that deviation, and not the opposite: "Now we see that governments differ in kind, and that some of them are prior and that others are posterior; those that are faulty or deviant are necessarily posterior to those that are correct" (3.1, 1275a38).

In this respect, "deviant" is somewhat like "prior." "For us," that is, in our immediate experience, the child is obviously prior to the adult, but "per se" or "by nature" the adult is prior to the child in that the adult presents the program that the child ought to actualize. Similarly, habituated

---

4. This is a supporting argument but not conclusive because, although everything that is natural exists for the most part, not everything that exists for the most part is natural.

as we are to see democracies and oligarchies, polities and aristocracies seem to us to be rare specific forms. But democracies and oligarchies are unthinkable apart from polities and aristocracies, of which they are the defective copies.

This idea, which few readers of Aristotle have been and still are ready to accept, that excellence can result from a combination of vices, has immense consequences. We note some of them.

First, it confirms the fragility of correct constitutions, even if some are more fragile than others and undergo in different ways different kinds of aggression. When we will examine Aristotle's analysis of seditions, we will see that, for example, he distinguishes attacks from without from those coming from within the city. Most of the time, in fact, a polity arises from an oligarchy in which democratic reforms have been carried out, or from a democracy that has had to include in its constitution, either by choice or by force, oligarchical elements. The turnaround, sometimes caused by a violent action, but more often by a minor constitutional alteration, can occur in the reverse direction, taking the polity back toward either oligarchy or democracy. This situation gives the political analysis offered by the philosopher considerable weight and offers the philosopher a historical role. The remedies are as numerous as the maladies; their identification and study require the entire knowledge base of the philosopher.

Here too there is a notable difference from Platonism. The Platonic philosopher must make the city conform as much as possible to the cosmic order with the goal of establishing institutions good enough to last a long time, even if Plato in the *Laws* modified his ambitions from those of the *Republic*. It is true that the *Republic* could allow itself to propose measures so extreme that there would be no expectation that they would be put into effect. But it is especially the "many-sidedness" of the Aristotelian analysis that distinguishes it from that of Plato. We see that in the critique that Aristotle provides in *Politics* 5.12 of the constitutional changes in the *Republic*. Plato's constitutions too change from one to another, but in a determinate order: necessarily timocracy follows aristocracy when a certain taste for wealth makes its way into the soul of aristocrats; the cycle of transformations inevitably ends at tyranny, which transforms itself, not less necessarily, into aristocracy. "He (Plato) only says that the cause is that nothing is abiding, but all things change in a certain cycle" (*Pol.* 5.12, 1316a4). Here we find once again the great schism that separates Plato and Aristotle. Aristotle does not want to think about the changes in the human practical world in terms of physical and cosmic change. Certainly, theoretical sciences like astronomy and physics have nothing to say *directly* to the legislator. That does not mean that he has no recourse at all to them.

A second consequence is the emergence of an image of a political philosopher very original at its time, and one that can speak with ready ease to the people of our time. On the one hand, the fundamental and essentially normative difference between correct and deviant constitutions is not obliterated by Aristotle's immersion in realist waters, an immersion that we have so far grasped only partially. The goal of the political philosopher is still that of giving the legislator the means for establishing an excellent constitution, that is, the correct constitution that corresponds to the situation of the people for whom he legislates. But on the other hand, even though he indeed shares in the classical problem inherited from his predecessors, Aristotle profoundly modifies the ideas of constitutional correctness and deviation.

The concept of a "correct constitution" undergoes a remarkable transformation. Let us look at the remarks about aristocracies, beginning with what he says about them in *Politics* 4.7–8. At the beginning of chapter 8, Aristotle feels the need to justify the order of exposition that he has adopted, since he has treated in order democracy, oligarchy, and aristocracy, and he means now to deal with polity and tyranny. So why insert aristocracy and polity between oligarchy and tyranny, although they are not deviant? In fact, the relevant question from an Aristotelian point of view is this: given that aristocracy, like all constitutions, both correct and deviant, has several forms, what allows us to call all these forms "aristocracies"?

We saw above the important step that Aristotle took by putting together in the same category pure and mixed constitutions. The absolute form of aristocracy, obviously unarguable, is that in which people who are completely virtuous govern "and not people who are good from a particular point of view" (4.7, 1293b4). And "the good man and the good citizen are one and the same person" (1293b5). Constitutions like that are, one imagines, fairly scarce. But there are forms that are neither oligarchies nor polities and that one may call—and we must understand that according to Aristotle we have the right to call them—aristocracies. Aristotle provides as a characteristic of these forms that he is thinking about the fact that "magistrates are not chosen only from the wealthy, but also among the better people" (1293b10). And Aristotle generalizes, looking at existing constitutions: where one takes account of wealth, virtue, and the people as at Carthage, and even where only the people and the virtuous are put in power, as at Sparta, one has regimes that one may justly call aristocracies. But we can now go beyond the stage of description and understand why certain mixtures can be justly called aristocracies, and others not.

Because to say that in order for it be an aristocracy it is necessary that virtue be in power, even if it is not the only element in power, is not enough. In a way, in fact, virtue is present in (almost) all constitutions: "Even in regimes where the concern for virtue is not shared, nevertheless there exist some people who are held in high esteem and are thought worthy of respect" (7, 1293b12). Unfortunately, there are usually not many of them, which prevents them from putting together a revolution and taking power (cf. 5.4, 1304a5). But the explanation of why there is sometimes an aristocracy and sometimes not does not come only from a threshold effect. The answer to our question is taken from a remark at *Politics* 4.8, 1293b33ff., a passage that we have discussed above. When a constitution results from a mixture of the good aspects of democracy and oligarchy, that should bring about a polity, as Aristotle reminds us at 1293b33, but we call the resultant constitution a "polity" if the democratic aspect dominates, and "aristocracy" if the oligarchical aspect dominates. As we have already said, the correct mixture of democracy and oligarchy will be called an "aristocracy" if it tends to give power to a small number rather than to the mass of citizens or if it adopts measures that tend to please the oligarchical party more than the democratic party.

But then why not say that it is an oligarchy? If my analyses are correct, we should respond: because the minority government has been purged of its oligarchical vices, or of a significant part of that vice, by its mixture with democracy. Obligated to take account of the aspirations of the people, the oligarchs no longer govern uniquely in terms of their class interest, but, at least in part, for the common advantage. Thus, we have a regime that deserves to be called an aristocracy. Ultimately, we will call "aristocracy" the constitution that gives the most important power to a minority, doubtless to the profit of that minority, but also in view of the common advantage. Aristotle introduces this modification surreptitiously when he notes that aristocracy is not only the government of the best:

> Among the constitutions that give power to a small number of people, but more than one, we call them aristocracy either because the best have power, or because one governs for the greatest good of the city, and for those who are members of it. (3.7, 1279a34)

Finally, we may call "aristocracy" a constitution in which virtue is among the criteria for attributing power, which gives a more important role to a minority than to the multitude, and which functions, at least in part, for the common advantage. We will see, in a later chapter, that Aristotle sometimes enlarges the semantic field of the term "aristocracy" even further by taking the word in its etymological sense as "government by the best" or "the best government."

Consequently, the order of exposition: democracy, oligarchy, aristocracy, polity, tyranny is not chaotic, because aristocracies and polities are surely correct constitutions that correspond to oligarchy and democracy (cf. 4.8, 1293b24: they "are not deviations"), but one may also consider them as moving away from absolute aristocracy, so much so that one may count them as deviations (1293b26). It would certainly be inexact to say that the correctness and deviance are *relative* notions, the same constitution being correct in relation to a second and deviant in relation to a third. For a constitution to be correct, it is necessary and sufficient that it aims at the common advantage and that it puts virtue in power to a significant enough degree that the laws bring about an increase in the virtue and happiness of the citizens. The difference between different correct constitutions thus depends on the number of people who possess the most significant share in power. Thus, the aristocratic constitution would be the one that, in addition to these criteria, gives power, or most power, to a minority, and the polity would be the regime that gives it to the people. But there are degrees of correctness, absolute aristocracy being nearer to the "pure food" according to the image used by Aristotle in *Politics* 3.11, than the Carthaginian constitution, for example. Hence the impression that this one gives of being a deviation. We notice that Aristotle does not say, at 1293b25, that "real" polity and aristocracy are *deviations* of such and such a correct constitution, but that they are "a step away (παρέκβασις) from the most correct constitution." That means that they nevertheless remain within correctness, exactly like the oligarchies and democracies that we have seen have the right to be called aristocracies because they instill in their criteria for power-sharing some bits of virtue.

Finally, constitutional correctness no longer belongs to the sphere of a perfection that would ensure to political regimes a survival if not everlasting, at least very long. We have here a sort of act of mourning for a Greek thinker who otherwise posited as an axiom the eternity and perfection of the universe. Correct constitutions have ceased being stable in themselves; their stability sometimes demands some exertion from the people in power. That is the state of things that Aristotle conveys when he remarks that "oligarchies as well as aristocracies may last, not from any inherent stability in such forms of government, but because the rulers are on good terms both with the disenfranchised and with the governing classes, not maltreating any who are excluded from the government" (5.8, 1308a3).

The Greek position, shared by Aristotle, which links excellence and duration, allows us to understand that a deviant constitution needs all the capacities of its rulers to maintain itself in power, and especially strategies designed to conciliate the enemies of this constitution without losing the support of those who are favorable to it. But if an aristocracy is in the same situation as deviant constitutions, that shows definitively that, contrary to what people like Plato would have hoped, constitutional excellence cannot break away from the historical process. Not even absolute aristocracy is sheltered from the attempts of the less virtuous to grab a share of power, as we saw above (cf. *Pol.* 3.15, 1286b14). The beneficent consequence of this descent of rectitude from heaven to earth is that deviation too loses its absolute character.

From the fact that two deviations added together may add up to an excellence, a deviant constitution is no longer that pathological entity that would not disappear unless one overturns it by force—something that does in fact happen sometimes, for example in the case of extreme tyrannical regimes—but it can also bring perfection. Sometimes it takes very little to bring it about that a well-constituted constitution begins to deviate from type. Thus, in *Politics* 5.8 Aristotle warns against small violations of the laws, "for transgression creeps in unperceived and at last ruins the city, just as the constant recurrence of small expenses eats up a fortune" (5.8, 1307b32). But reciprocally it often takes very little in a deviant constitution to set in motion a kind of rectification process: sometimes that oligarchy will win hearts and minds of a part of the popular mass by a small decrease in property qualification for office. That opens to the legislator an immense field of action.

So, let us recapitulate Aristotle's thought process as I believe I have reconstructed it. The legislator ought to try to establish, or reestablish, an excellent constitution, and that constitution is excellent which is the correct one corresponding to the people who compose the city, the "only constitution that would naturally be everywhere best," as the *Nicomachean Ethics* passage cited above says. But the principle that Aristotle posits at the beginning of his analyses, that a constitution is correct if it governs for the sake of the common advantage, presupposes that the people in power are virtuous. Thus, the temptation, into which Aristotle sometimes seems to fall, of thinking that the only correct constitution is aristocracy, with kingship as the limiting case, but anyway impractical in his day. At the end of the day, that is a Platonic position. A correct popular regime is in fact impossible, because how could there be a multitude of virtuous people? In fact, as *Politics* 3.4 shows, the necessary virtue is also *ethical* virtue, not just the ability to fulfill one's rule in the city. How indeed would one deliberate well and make decisions for the sake of the common advantage if one is cowardly, dishonest, and depraved?

A first step toward the solution of this problem is taken by the analysis of constitutions that are unquestionably correct per se. A constitution in which virtue is *mixed* with other criteria for the attribution of power does not necessarily leave correctness, as Aristotle illustrates by showing that constitutions like that of Carthage can *also* be called aristocracies. Although Aristotle does not propose a long analysis of the topic (he will deal with it in another way when he talks of the conservation of constitutions), doubtless it is a matter primarily of proportionality: if the criterion of virtue is drowned beneath other criteria, to the point that it has negligible weight, one could no longer call this constitution aristocratic.

A second step opens the space for a correct popular constitution. It's the famous chapter 11 of *Politics* 3, which shows that there is a collective virtue of the people, provided that the people are not villainous. But for that virtue to serve as the basis for the establishment and functioning of a correct constitution, of a polity, several preconditions are needed. In the first place, the political power of the people needs to be limited, since the enactment of laws and the higher magistracies need to be beyond them. Next, this alchemy cannot function unless there exists in the heart of the city a certain number of ethically virtuous citizens—"the pure food."

The third and final step is even more difficult. Aristotle recognizes that excellence can be achieved, besides the mixture of pure and impure, from a mixture of two deviations. We need to provide some specifics about this last mixture, thinking about its dominant and so to speak unique form, the mixture of democracy and oligarchy that results, most often, in a polity.

Certainly, the two mixtures can be added together and, most times, the game is played by more than two partners, since often, as we have seen, a democratic or oligarchic city includes a certain number of virtuous citizens who form a kind of aristocratic party. It also contains, often enough, a certain number of people who have citizenship but are unworthy of it, that is, a demagogic and thus tyrannical party. But the mixture of democracy and oligarchy is enough to establish a correct constitution.

Aristotle uses here the term "mixture" (μίξις) in its precise technical sense as it is defined in *Generation and Corruption* 1.10, 327b24: "The compound may be actually other than the constituents from which it has resulted; nevertheless, each of them may still be potentially what it was before they were combined."

Thus, it is not a matter of a fusion (κρᾶσις) in which the components are suppressed. In fact, that is what this passage says:

> This is the kind of mixture: when democracy and oligarchy are well mixed, then it is possible to speak of the same polity as a democracy and as an oligarchy. Clearly those who say this, do so because they feel that the mixture is good. (4.9, 1294b14)

The polity is potentially a democracy and an oligarchy, to such an extent that different people could feel things differently, some having the impression that the constitution is democratic, others that it is oligarchic.

This is very important both for the legislator and for the political philosopher. In fact, adherence of democrats and oligarchs to the new constitution coming from a mixture would be the result of the fact that each one finds, or believes oneself to have found, satisfaction of one's interests. One can then assume that we find ourselves faced by a situation analogous to that of the movement from a village, or federation of villages, to the city. It is in order to improve their daily lives that men formed the first city, but from what I have called a "trick of Nature," the possibility of a "happy life" cannot come about except in a city; it is given to them as a bonus. But there is nothing wrong, if one can put it that way, with trying to improve one's daily life. In the case of the polity, things are a little different, and to tell the truth, unexpected. Because it is indeed because they thought they would satisfy their deviant conception of justice that oligarchs and democrats cling to the polity. The oligarchs think that they will be able to exercise power on the basis of their wealth, the democrats expect to take advantage of their status as freemen to exert power to their own benefit. Thus, it is by wanting to satisfy their vice that these people work for correctness and thus for virtue.

We can make a more general remark though, lacking texts, we are in this case in the territory of pure conjecture. It is certainly the case that Aristotle thinks that ultimately it is indeed virtue that allows us to be happy.

More precisely, men cannot achieve happiness except as citizens of a city with a correct constitution. Furthermore, even the functioning of a correct constitution spreads virtue in the civic body, since by habituating citizens to obey just laws according to the constitution, it implants in them the virtues that will make them happy. It is the very functioning of the polity that makes them virtuous and capable of happiness. We will see a rather comparable process when we read the passage in which Aristotle gives advice to the tyrant for remaining in power. We find there a remarkable optimism. Giving power to the best people so that they will administer the city in accord with their virtue, whether it's a matter of a pure aristocracy or of a mixed correct constitution, causes love for that virtue.

Not All Wolves Are Gray

What has been said above seems to attribute to Aristotle a balanced position: the partisans of democracy and of oligarchy are equally wrong and equally right. Only the partisans of the ultimate deviant constitution, tyranny, are massively wrong. But in fact, Aristotle does not make the balance equal between democracy and oligarchy. When he says that political power, one of the principle objects of his study, "belongs to men who are free and equal" (*Pol.* 1.7, 1255b20), he recognizes that democracy, which, to be precise, rests on freedom and equality, is, in a way, "more political" than oligarchy. Was Aristotle, like us after him and many others, intoxicated by the Athenian democratic ideology? Isn't it rather the case that this democratic ideology is fundamentally more in accord with the reality of the city than is the oligarchic ideology? We should leave this last question to the historians, and pay attention to Aristotle's own declarations.

The major role of the Aristotelian legislator, as we will have occasion to see several times, is to *rectify* deviant constitutions, those of his own city if he is at the same time a magistrate, or those of other cities if he has been called upon to reform them. "Rectify" means to transform into a correct and lasting form. But a democracy is easier to rectify than an oligarchy, and that for several reasons.

Concord is easier to obtain in a democracy:

> Democracy appears to be safer and less liable to revolution than oligarchy. For in oligarchies there is the double danger of the oligarchs falling out among themselves and also with

the people; but in democracies there is only the danger of a quarrel with the oligarchs. No dissension worth mentioning arises among the people themselves. (5.1, 1302a8, passage partially cited earlier)

And concord between citizens is a condition, if not sufficient, at least necessary, for a virtuous functioning of the city.

We have seen that stability is a condition for the diffusion of virtue in the civic body, and we will see below that it also has the result that from that fact stability is one of the signs of constitutional excellence. I think that one may even say that for Aristotle stability is a condition for the effective intervention of the legislator. That is what one gathers from passages in the *Politics* in which it is said that before any reform, the first duty of a constitution is that the people in the city who are partisans of the constitution be stronger than their adversaries:

We have now to consider which and what kind of constitution is advantageous to what kind of people. I may begin by assuming, as a general principle common to all governments, that the portion of the city that desires the permanence of the constitution ought to be stronger than that which desires the reverse. (4.12, 1296b13)

This passage deserves extensive commentary; here are some: "All constitutions" includes both correct and deviant. We readily see that thus we are here in "basic" politics, prior to the intervention of the legislator, which intervention is summarized in the first sentence, since it is a very good idea to describe the goal of the legislator by saying that he needs to point out the "advantageous" constitution for a given people.[5] First stabilize the constitution, then reform it; that is the procedure for the Aristotelian legislator, who is, it seems, reluctant to engage in hasty interventions.

In the first place, Aristotle seems to maintain a kind of symmetry between popular and minority regimes, just as he does for the conceptions of justice. Thus, continuing in *Politics* 4.12, we will not be surprised to find that Aristotle conceives of the life of the city as determined by the

---

5. "Advantageous" translates συμφέρει, which may be an allusion to the "common advantage" (τὸ κοινῇ συμφέρον), but it is not certain.

relationship between forces. What I have characterized above as an opposition between classes, which brings it about that in the heart of every city there cohabit an oligarchical party and a democratic party, he here describes in a broader way in terms of an opposition between quantity and quality:

> Now every city is composed of quality and quantity. By quality I mean freedom, wealth, education, good birth, and by quantity, superiority of numbers. Quality may exist in one of the classes that make up the city, and quantity in the other. For example, the meanly born may be more in number than the well born, or the poor than the rich, yet they may not so much exceed in quantity as they fall short in quality; and therefore, there must be a comparison of quantity and quality. (1296b17)

And, Aristotle continues, when the quantity, the mass of people of modest means, prevails over a qualitative superiority of the elite, "there is naturally (πέφυκεν) a democracy" (1296b26). "But where the rich and notables exceed in quality more than they fall short in quantity, there oligarchy arises" (1296b31). Aristotle does not explain how quality and quantity may be commensurable, but after all there is no need that they really be so; it's enough that one understands that all these qualities can be interpreted in terms of *power*. Mass has power because, as one says, it has weight. But education too, because it makes those who have it more able to speak and thus to convince, is an advantage in the struggle for power. The same goes for the aristocratic virtues like courage. As for wealth . . .

But in fact this parallelism between democracy and oligarchy, and more generally between popular and minority regimes, is entirely theoretical and, in reality, popular regimes are expected to be stronger. This is true to such a degree that Aristotle, with perhaps a touch of irony, notes that a regime that gives power to a large number is able so to speak to indulge in the luxury of also satisfying the criterion according to which oligarchy tries to distribute power:

> The many may urge their claim against the few; for, when taken collectively, and compared with the few, they are stronger and richer and better (3.13, 1283a40). Thus, the many may claim to have a higher authority than the few; for the people, and the council, and the courts consist of many persons, and their

property collectively is greater than the property of one or of a few individuals holding great offices. (3.11, 1282a38)

The oligarchy, in contrast, cannot satisfy the fundamental criterion of democracy, that all the citizens be equal and thus have equal access to power. To continue in the same vein, we may cite this passage:

As to property qualification, no absolute rule can be laid down, but we must see what is the highest qualification sufficiently comprehensive to secure that the number of those who have the rights of citizens exceeds the number of those excluded. (4.13, 1297b2)

Those who have the rights of citizens (literally, those who share in the constitution: τοὺς μετέχοντας τῆς πολιτείας) are those who have access to power. "Those excluded" are here those who could have the right of participation, because beyond the fact that, as we have seen, many inhabitants of the city do not participate in political life at all (slaves, women, foreigners) and are more numerous than the citizens, there are also free autochthonous men who do not have full citizenship. In other words, these are people who would be citizens according to democratic criteria. We have here a kind of unspoken assumption that recognizes the legitimacy of the democratic position: it is in relation to the group of potential citizens, who would be actual citizens in a democracy, that an oligarchy aware of its self-interest ought to set the property qualifications for belonging to the politically functional body. The masses that an oligarchy excludes from full citizenship in a way nevertheless have a share in it.

A particularly striking example of the fact that the shadow of democracy hovers over the political space is the definition of "citizen" at the beginning of *Politics* 3, discussed above. We recall that this definition says that the citizen is "one who participates in a judicial function or a function as a magistrate," that is, in political power (3.1, 1275a22). But in addition to many magistracies that provide for such participation for a limited time, the functions of a member of the assembly of the people and of tribunals give that sort of power in a permanent way. Contrary to the habit that refuses the name "magistrate" to such people, Aristotle proposes calling them "unlimited magistracies," since "it would be ridiculous not to recognize the power of those who are all-powerful" (1275a28). And

Aristotle concludes, "That is pretty much the definition of citizen that is best adapted for all the people who are called citizens" (1275a33).

Then comes a passage too often neglected by the commentators:

> But we must not forget that things of which the underlying principles differ in kind, one of them being first, another second, another third, have, when regarded in this relation, nothing, or hardly anything worth mentioning in common. Now we see that governments differ in kind, and that some of them are prior and that others are posterior; those which are faulty or perverted are necessarily posterior to those which are perfect. . . . The citizen then of necessity differs under each form of constitution. (1275a34)

It may be in the *De Anima* where this doctrine is best explained:

> It is now evident that a single definition can be given of soul only in the same sense as one can be given of figure. For, as in that case there is no figure apart from triangle and those that follow in order, so here there is no soul apart from the forms of soul just enumerated. Even if one proposes a common definition for figure that will fit all figures, this would not express the peculiar nature of any figure. . . . Hence it is absurd in this and similar cases to look for a common definition that will not express the peculiar nature of anything that is and will not apply to the appropriate indivisible species, while at the same time omitting to look for an account that will. The cases of figure and soul are exactly parallel; for the particulars subsumed under the common name in both cases—figures and living beings—constitute a series, each successive term of which potentially contains its predecessor, for example, the square the triangle, the sensory power the self-nutritive. (2.3, 414b19)

We may also find an example in the *Politics* itself:

> The temperance and courage of the man and the woman are different. For a man would be thought a coward if he had no more courage than a courageous woman, and a woman would

be thought loquacious if she imposed no more restraint on her conversation than the good man; and indeed their part in the management of the household is different, for the duty of the one is to acquire, the other to preserve. (3.4, 1277b20)

Let us paraphrase a bit. It is not interesting to define figure as "surface limited by a line," because that definition tells us nothing about the correct definition of a triangle, for example. In the same way, to define courage as "virtue of the audacious" would tell us almost nothing, because that which is courageous for a woman is cowardly for a man. In the case of the citizen, "the subjects which differ specifically, of which one is first, another second" would be constitutions, in this instance correct and deviant constitutions, correct being prior, as we have seen, to deviant. As for the "things contained" in these subjects, that would be the citizens.

Here we are faced by two assertions by Aristotle, which, without being contradictory, tend to obscure each other, so to speak. On the one hand, the fact of participating in power is "close to the definition of 'citizen,' which is best adapted to all the people who are called citizens," and, on the other hand, there is no definition, except empty and useless, of "citizen" that can be applied in all constitutions. Aristotle resolves this difficulty in the following way:

> The definition of a citizen that we have given applies especially to citizenship in a democracy; under other forms of constitution it may hold good, but will not necessarily do so. For in some cities there is no people [no people's assembly, or the assembly has no power, as we noted earlier]. (3.1, 1275b5)

In other words, the democratic definition of citizen is the reference definition; other definitions of citizen, for example the oligarchic definition, are incomplete versions, as the virtues of women are incomplete versions of the virtues of men. How could there be a better way of saying that there is a kind of kinship between democracy and citizenship, that is, politics?

To all that we must add that democracy allows a better functioning of political life, especially by assuring better deliberation: "They will advise better if they all deliberate together, the people with the notables and the notables with the people" (4.14, 1298b20), the same as "a feast in which everyone participates is better than one that is offered by one individual person" (3.15, 1286a29; cf. 3.11, 1281b2). And deliberation is consubstantial with the political life.

All that leads us to the conclusion that oligarchy and democracy are not equally bad in relation to the politically correct state. It would obviously be better if a city would be governed by a moderate oligarchy than by an extreme democracy, which latter would almost inevitably result in a tyranny of the majority, and then simply in a tyranny. "Would be better" means that it would be easier for the legislator to remedy and to orient toward a correct constitutional form. Polity is, certainly, a mixture of democracy and oligarchy, but "a constitution that relies on the middle class more nearly approximates to democracy than to oligarchy, and is the most stable of the constitutions of this kind" (5.1, 1302a14).[6] "The constitution that relies on the middle class" designates the regime described in *Politics* 3.11 in which the majority of the citizens govern for the common advantage thanks to their collective virtue. This is a constitution simultaneously majoritarian and correct, that is, a polity.

There is a text that goes in this direction; it too leaves something unsaid. In *Politics* 4.4, Aristotle reviews the various kinds of democracy, as we shall see in detail below. Why, in his summary of all the kinds in chapter 6, with the important difference that he there gives the *causes* of each of them, doesn't Aristotle present any corresponding kind in chapter 6, to the first kind in chapter 4? Here is the passage:

> Of the forms of democracy first comes that which is said to be based strictly on equality. In such democracy the law says that it is just for the poor to have no more advantage than the rich, and that neither should be masters, but both equal. For if liberty and equality, as is thought by some, are chiefly to be found in democracy, they will be best attained when all persons alike share in the government to the utmost. And since the people are the majority, and the opinion of the majority is decisive, such a constitution must necessarily be a democracy. (4.4, 1291b30)

---

6. Normally the phrase "constitutions of this kind" is understood to designate popular constitutions. But that is not entirely clear, and it can be applied to all the constitutions under discussion in this passage.

There is a noteworthy textual disagreement at 1291b32. Newman chooses the reading of most manuscripts, ὑπάρχειν, which would mean that neither the poor nor rich, taken as two different classes, possesses more than the other. I currently think that that solution seems more interesting than the reading ὑπερέχειν, chosen by Dreizehnter and which I followed in my French translation ("que rien ne mette les gens modestes ou les gens aisés les uns au-dessus des autres").[7] But the remarks that follow here remain valid in either case.

This equality between the poor and the rich, whether it would be only an equality of power, or an equality of both wealth *and* power, gives this democracy a strong appearance of a polity. When Aristotle says that this democracy is the "first," isn't it a recognition on his part of a kind of essential characteristic, beyond the different instantiations, which would explain why this variety does not have a particular corresponding entry in the list in chapter 6? We can even take a further step: if Newman is right (as I now think he is), Aristotle's text posits clearly that equality, the foundation of this democracy, is an equality between classes and not between individuals. For this reason, this democracy is not really a democracy since the people in it share power *on an equal footing* with the wealthy. The criterion of liberty, which "some" make the principle of democracy, can very well, on the other hand, put up with a power, including a tyrannical one, exercised by the people. Therefore, this is a list of democracies whose introductory form, in a way exemplary, is a polity . . .

To become "true" democracies, the other forms will have to violate the basic principle of "democracy" as it is enunciated in this first form, that is, the equality between classes. And that is in fact what happens immediately after this first form of democracy. The two last sentences of the passage that I have quoted show that. If one links equality and liberty, one gets a regime in which "all persons alike (ὁμοίως, 1291b37) share in government to the utmost," which doubtless means that each one in it claims his liberty. But then the equality between classes on which the first form was founded is, in fact, abolished, since the system of *one man one vote* inevitably results in the sovereignty of the majority (cf. κύριον, "decisive," 1291b37), while in a regime based on equality no one group is sovereign (cf. κυρίους, "masters,"

---

[7]. Vettori, followed by many editors, proposed ἄρχειν, "rule," but then what would be the use of the next clause? In the English translation we use Jowett's translation here ("no more advantage than"), suitably ambiguous between the Newman and Dreizehnter texts.

1291b33). That's what the last sentence of the passage quoted says even better; I find its relationship with the preceding sentence (slightly) problematic. I have the impression that after having brought the first, paradigmatic, form of democracy close to polity, Aristotle "redemocratizes" things, by recalling that the basic principle of democracy is popular sovereignty. Nevertheless, it remains that this paradigmatic form of democracy will be that which is least deviant from a polity, since, as we have seen, the correct constitutions are prior to the deviant constitutions. In fact, the polity is characterized by its equilibrium between rich and poor taken as classes; in the polity, neither is sovereign over the other.

A consequence of that would be that, except in exceptional cases of great deviance, it will be easier to get to a polity starting from a democracy, by adding to it some oligarchical characteristics, than to get there by democratizing an oligarchy. This latter transformation is, in any case, a heavy lift, since it is very true that an oligarchy is threatened in its very essence when it accepts democratic measures, while on the other hand, *given its strength and stability*, democracy can accept oligarchic traits. But the more profound reason is given, even if in a somewhat subliminal manner, by the passage cited above. In making room for the demands of the rich (most often by including oligarchic traits in the constitution), a democracy rediscovers its basic orientation, as it is defined in this "premiere" form, that is, equality between classes.

At the same time, we may assume that the relationships between oligarchy and aristocracy, of which it is a deviation, are very different. It would be difficult for oligarchs used to the lure of profit to direct themselves toward the rule of virtue that characterizes aristocracy. A passage in *Politics* 4.7, which we will visit again a little later, explains that a transition of this kind, of oligarchy toward aristocracy, can begin when "one chooses magistrates not only among the wealthy, but also among the best" (1293b10). That seems more difficult to bring about than to add democratic bits into an oligarchy for the following reason: if one realizes that the dominant classes will not give up their monopoly on power and thus move in the direction of tyranny except because of the resistance of the dominated classes, one will see clearly that many oligarchies will accept democratic characteristics only because of the power of the democratic party. It is not likely to happen very often that an oligarchic city would have in its heart an aristocratic party that would be able to do the same thing, for "good birth and excellence are rare, but wealth and numbers are more common. In what city shall we find a hundred persons of good birth and excellence?

Whereas the rich everywhere abound" (5.1, 1302a1). In contrast, we get the impression that Aristotle does not see great difficulty in moving from a democracy, relatively moderate we must repeat, to "a constitution that rests on the middle class." For the people, who by definition rule in a democracy, to become "middle class," whose collective virtue has been defined in *Politics* 3.11, two conditions are essentially needed. In the first place, it is necessary that the law be sovereign, a law, as we have seen, that the masses cannot easily change at will. Nevertheless, it remains, as we will see in the next chapter, that the assembly keeps the possibility of making the law. Secondly, it is necessary that the majority in question not be in dire poverty, because then it would lack the property necessary for political life, that is, leisure. But "it is impossible to have leisure when one does not have sufficient revenue" (4.6, 1292b32).

It is in *Politics* 4.11 that Aristotle develops most explicitly his argument for a constitution giving power to the middle classes. He adds there an approach to polity slightly different from that which he proposes elsewhere, but which will help us understand the relationship of polity to oligarchy and to democracy. Best to quote the passage:

> These considerations will help us to understand why most constitutions are either democratic or oligarchical. The reason is that the middle class is seldom numerous in them, and whichever part, whether the rich or the common people, transgresses the mean and predominates, draws the constitution its way, and thus arises either oligarchy or democracy. There is another reason— the poor and the rich quarrel with one another, and whichever side gets the better, instead of establishing a communal and equal constitution, regards political supremacy as the prize of victory, and the one party sets up a democracy and the other an oligarchy. Further, both the parties that had the supremacy in Greece (i.e., Athens and Sparta) looked only to the interest of their own form of constitution, and established in cities, the one democracies, the other oligarchies; they thought of their own advantage, and of the advantage of the other cities not at all. (4.11, 1296a22)[8]

---

8. Cf. 5.1, 1301b39: "Hence there are two principal forms of government, democracy and oligarchy; for good birth and excellence are rare, but wealth and numbers are more common."

Perhaps a passage like this can give the last word about what Aristotle thinks on the subject of the establishment of a polity, for it is indeed that which he characterizes as the government of the middle class. To be sure, an oligarchy may lean toward a polity by introducing into its constitution democratic-tending laws, particularly when pressed by the democratic party that exists in the city. But here we have an analysis of the polity as a result of a social situation. I said above that the middle class *neutralizes* the extremes. This passage shows what must be understood from that: when it is strong, the middle class prevents both oligarchs and democrats from imposing their point of view, and even from fighting for power. The middle class, then, suppresses or at least suspends the struggle between classes; that is why it assures a remarkable stability for constitutions in which it dominates.

Thus, it seems that there would be something like the seeds of virtue among the people when it has not yet been destroyed by demagogues. On the other hand, we do not see any seed of that kind that would lead oligarchs to become aristocrats. Doubtless Aristotle would not find it an exaggeration to say that polity is a kind of democracy, while in no case would aristocracy be a kind of oligarchy, except etymologically. A discrete victory for Athenian ideology or not, it does seem that Aristotle, just like us, thinks that democracy, because of its frequency in the real world of cities, is in a way the normal form of political life. To return to the comparison that Aristotle makes between constitutions and winds (and harmonies), it is much easier to think of polity as a deviation of democracy than aristocracy as a deviation of oligarchy.

A final remark, to tell the truth, rather weighty. What I have said above could lead one to believe that Aristotle thinks that it is relatively easy to establish a polity: "you only have to" give a certain level of prosperity to the people to transform the popular mass into a middle class and to have a constitution correct and stable. But that amounts more or less to saying that in our society "you only have to" give work, access to culture, and an agreeable standard of living to the young people of neighborhoods called "underprivileged" to discourage them from delinquency and radicalism. Aristotle is certainly not so naïve, and it seems to me very important to hold on to the spirit of the conclusion of his chapter in book 4 (thus of realist politics) on the excellence of government of the middle class: "For these reasons the middle form of government has rarely, if ever, existed, and among a very few only" (4.11, 1296a36). Whether in individual people or in cities, the seeds of virtue rarely grow.

What, After All, Is a Polity?

We have seen that the term πολιτεία normally means "constitution" or "regime," but that Demosthenes and Isocrates used it, to be sure rarely, to designate a popular regime. When Aristotle writes that the constitution that puts the majority in power for the sake of the common advantage carries the common name of all constitutions, namely, πολιτεία, he does not say whether he has coined this sense himself, or if it had been used in certain philosophical or political circles, and if so, which. As for understanding why that is "rational," as I have said, I leave it to one side, for the moment . . . What is unarguably the case is that this usage of πολιτεία in the sense of a *correct* popular regime is Aristotle's doing, and massiveness of this usage in his text is at least as notable as the terminological innovation that he has devoted to it.

Another given that is as important as it is difficult to interpret is that, as we have seen, in the *Nicomachean Ethics* Aristotle calls "timocracy" what he calls "polity" in the *Politics*. One may be tempted to see there a Platonic influence, since timocracy is one of the constitutions reviewed by Plato, and possibly even tempted to offer a hypothesis on the relative chronology of the two treatises. We can add a further argument for those who are crazy about chronology, that the last two books of the *Politics*, which they like to think are old and Platonic, do not speak of "polity." But we can immediately reduce this last remark to nothing, by noticing that neither do they speak of timocracy.

There are two traits that seem to characterize polity in Aristotle's *Politics*: it is a correct constitution, and it is the result of a mixture of oligarchy and democracy. But, as we have seen, this latter trait is not peculiar to polity, since it also characterizes certain aristocracies, for example. The situations of polity and aristocracy are no less different for what we are interested in here. In the case of aristocracy, there is a pure or absolute form, of which the others are nothing but more or less degraded copies. It's that these "second choice" aristocracies are mixtures, including either democratic or oligarchic elements, or both democratic and oligarchic at the same time. Polity, on the other hand, does not have a pure form, but always exists in a mixed state. That is why I said above that only aristocracy and its limiting form, kingship, could have a "pure" form. It's easy to understand why. In the initial list of constitutions, in which they differ from each other by the number of people in power (one could also say by the number of people who enjoy complete citizenship), polity is a correct constitution, that is, based on virtue, which gives power to a large number of men who, therefore, have to be virtuous. But, as the passage already noted says,

> one man or a few may excel in virtue; but as the number increases it becomes more difficult for them to attain perfection in every kind of excellence, though they may in military excellence, for this is found in the masses. (3.7, 1279a39)

But military virtue is not political virtue, and it is not sufficient for making excellent citizens. Even more, it can be a factor in deviation, since a city that has for its principle goal to make war cannot be a happy city. All that is another way to say that a "pure" polity does not exist. Of course, the absolute polity, in which all the members of the popular mass would be perfectly virtuous, is not inconceivable, but it remains a kind of ideal type that Aristotle says clearly is unattainable. Thus, polities are always mixtures having more or less "an acceptable form though distant from that of an excellent organization," as Aristotle says of oligarchies and democracies (5.9, 1309b32).

Let us return to *Politics* 4.11. It is framed by statements whose harmonization poses issues of interpretation. Aristotle begins by declaring that he is going to interest himself in

> the best constitution for most cities, and the best life for most men, neither assuming a standard of excellence that is above ordinary persons, nor an education that is exceptionally favored by nature and circumstances, nor yet an ideal city that is an aspiration only, but having regard to the life in which the majority is able to share, and to the form of government that cities in general can attain. (1295a25)

That constitution indeed seems to be a polity, ending with noting that such a form is very rare. We have seen the reason for that state of affairs above: by opposing the emergence and empowerment of a middle class, both oligarchs and democrats impede the appearance of the *social* conditions for a polity. Such a state of affairs is not, in fact, entirely hopeless for the legislator, because, once again, he has nature on his side. In the same way as if, as Aristotle believes to be the case, virtue is fundamentally in accord with human nature, so that one may hope that it will end up spreading through the citizenry. Likewise, if the constitution dominated by the middle classes is that which suits most cities, then the legislator may hope to establish it, if not all at once, at least step by step. Nevertheless, it remains that constitutional correctness is not an easy thing.

The following sentence, incidentally, tells us a lot about polity. Aristotle says that one must seek the constitutional form that suits most cities,

> for the constitutions that are called aristocracies, that we have been talking about just now, they either lie beyond the possibilities of the greater number of cities, or they approximate what we call polity, and therefore need no separate discussion. (4.11, 1295a31)

The aristocracies that lie beyond the possibilities of most cities are those that are pure or are so close to pure forms that they are difficult to actualize. "The others," in question here, are doubtless those that have been characterized above as mixtures, and they deserve the name of aristocracies because they take virtue into account. According to what we said above, the regime that takes account of virtue in the attribution of power and generally functions for the sake of the common advantage can be called an aristocracy if it has a form more or less minoritarian and a polity if it takes a more enlarged form. Aristotle does not pretend that such aristocracies are easier to establish, all the more because he recognizes that they are near to polities and he says about these, at the end of the chapter, that they are rare. But to say that these mixed forms of aristocracy are so close to polities that one may include them in the same category is to characterize polity by its taking account of virtue.

To summarize then, a polity is a constitution that mixes democracy and oligarchy in such a way that each of these two deviant constitutions remain apparent in it, but which puts a sufficient emphasis on political virtue (the virtue that makes us act for the sake of the common advantage) that one may see in it a form of aristocracy, what one may call "an enlarged aristocracy." Polity seems to us ultimately as the most *political* of constitutions because it mixes all the forms of regimes that are not autocratic. More than all the others, precisely because it does not have a "pure" form, polity embodies the acceding of mixture to excellence. Ultimately it is perhaps for this reason that Aristotle finds it "reasonable" that polity carries the name of all constitutions.

CHAPTER 6

The Legislator

The Legislator and the Magistrate

We have frequently alluded to the actions of the legislator. Now we need to see who or what the legislator is. The legislator, νομοθέτης, literally, "the one who places laws," is, for Aristotle as for the Greeks in general, the highest form of "political man." In fact, in the political realm there cannot be a more eminent function than to make the laws for a city. The importance of the law, both in the common conception of the Greeks, and in Aristotelian political philosophy, cannot be overestimated. Regimes that do without laws are not really *political* regimes. We have seen that already in the case of tyrannies, but that is also true for dominant classes in every deviant constitution, classes for which we have understood that tyrannical ambition was limited only by the resistance of the dominated classes. There is a more sophisticated way of doing without laws, used especially by democracies, which consists of replacing the laws with decrees. Thus, as we have seen, in *Politics* 4.4, 1292a2, Aristotle describes an extreme form of democracy in which "the masses are sovereign and not the law," and explains that "this is the case when decrees rule and not the law." Everything then becomes purely the effect of circumstances, because a decree is made to resolve an immediate problem. The *Nicomachean Ethics* explains very clearly the difference between a law and a decree. We have also seen that, since law is universal, decrees are indispensable both for making the law apply to a concrete reality, and when the circumstances do not lend themselves to a universal legislation (cf. *EN* 5.10, 1137b29). Still in the *Nicomachean Ethics*, not far from the passage already cited about the "everywhere" natural character of the excellent constitution, Aristotle explains that those who think that everything having to do with "political justice" is on the level of the decree are those for whom "justice" is conventional and variable (5.7, 1134b24).

Thus, one of the functions of the magistrate locates him fairly far from the legislator. In this function, the magistrate does not make law; the area of his intervention is located between law and decree. Let us read again:

> The law ought to be supreme over all, and the magistracies should judge of particulars according to the constitution. So that if a democracy is indeed one of the constitutions, it is clear that a system in which everything is regulated by decrees is not properly speaking a democracy, because no decree can be universal. (*Pol.* 4.4, 1292a32; cf. 3.11, 1282b2)

One cannot say it better, that to rule a city by decrees makes it leave the political space, while constitutions, even deviant constitutions like democracy, belong to that space.

In fact, if the area of interventions by a magistrate extends between the universality of the law and the particularity of the concrete situations that make up the daily life of the city, the magistrates would have an important function of dealing with the precise problems that are presented to the city by the promulgation of decrees supposed to translate into reality the spirit of the law as they have received it from the legislator. Then, the place where the magistrate acts is in fact the domain where one may exercise *prudence*, as we have already seen. In the 1960s there was a dispute between interpreters of this central concept of Aristotelian ethics, whether the prudent person deliberates concerning the end of ethical action, or if he deliberates only about the means of achieving that end, which would be handed down from elsewhere. The second became the consensus position, correctly, because it is not the prudent person who defines the nature of the good life, which is the ultimate goal of ethical action. Thus, we find again the problem of the kind of prudence that we should attribute to different actors in political life addressed in *Nicomachean Ethics* 6.7–8. In other words, in dividing up their tasks, the legislator and the magistrate rediscover the distinction between legislative prudence and political prudence, because the legislator has legislative prudence, and the magistrate has prudence that is "practical, that is, deliberative"; that's almost terminological evidence.

As was suggested above and has often been proposed by the commentators,[1] it is indeed necessary that the magistrate has access to the universal so that one may be able to attribute to him a kind of prudence. But this universal is the law that he has received from the legislator, who has enacted it, or given it a new form. It is in fact impossible that the magistrate remain confined in the particular sphere of the decree, applying a law that he does not understand and, notably, it is impossible that he does not grasp why it is good, something that Aristotle in fact seems to say sometimes, for example when he describes magistrates, as we have seen, as "people who work like handworkers (χειροτέχναι)" (1141b29). But in fact, this expression only reflects the subordinate position of the magistrate in relation to the legislator. *Workman* of the law, the magistrate *makes it work*, but obviously we will not find any passage in which Aristotle says that he does not understand the law.

Why, given that state of affairs, aren't the roles of legislator and magistrate better distinguished in the *Politics*? This relative lack of distinction results from several factors, of which the least important is that legislators may be found to be magistrates in their city. It is also shown in Aristotle's terminology. To designate magistrates in the political and not judicial sense, he uses the masculine plural present participle of the verb ἄρχειν, "to rule": οἱ ἄρχοντες. But there is a third word, which I have translated "political man" (ὁ πολιτικός). It's this "political man" who appears, ever since the first chapter of the *Politics*, as the bearer of political power, alongside the master of slaves, *pater familias*, and king (cf. 1.1, 1252a7, 12). What then designates this "good legislator, the true political man (τὸν ἀγαθὸν νομοθέτην καὶ τὸν ὡς ἀληθῶς πολιτικόν)" of the beginning of book 4 of the *Politics* (4.1, 1288b27)? This expression is made more difficult to understand if one gives καί a coordinating sense, as translators often do ("the legislator *and* the true statesman").

Thus, it is necessary to assume that there is a greater interpenetration between the position of legislator and that of magistrate than their titles alone would let us suppose. And, in a general way, we will have to reconfigure the shape of the legislator. I called attention above to the fact that the legislator was one of the greatest objects of the Greek imagination. The Greek Seven Sages, a controversial list since antiquity, were almost all legislators. But Aristotle's legislator was rather different from the old

---

1. See, for example, the long notes by Richard Bodéüs to this passage in his French translation of the *Nicomachean Ethics*.

legislators. Of course, he has lost his semi-divine status, and Aristotle's political reflections have placed him squarely in the world contemporary with his author, in which there are almost no new cities to be founded, at any rate among the Greeks. We will see that the essential work of the Aristotelian legislator consists of intervention in existing constitutions, to transform them more or less fundamentally by modifying their laws to lead these constitutions toward a condition of excellence. That is why there is need for the theoretical instruction of the philosopher.

But the magistrate does not have only one function, which one may call "everyday," that of applying the law. He is actually the source of the law, and that can be seen, as is often true, even better in borderline cases. In the first chapter of *Politics* 3, we saw that Aristotle proposed to define the member of a democratic assembly as an "unlimited magistrate," because the real power resides in the hands of the members of this assembly. But the ultimate form of this power is to make laws. The same goes for minority regimes: to be a magistrate in such a government is to participate in the sovereign power of making or modifying the laws, at least in important *political* magistracies, and not in magistracies that are purely technical, with limited objectives. This important distinction will be clarified in the next chapter. Consequently, in an oligarchy, for example, those who are qualified to participate in the government can also be considered as "unlimited magistrates." In any case, in both popular and minority governments it is the body of *real* citizens who hold power, and particularly power in regard to the laws. If a magistrate is *functionally* distinct from his fellow citizens, nevertheless he derives his power from the citizen body. If, then, it is difficult to distinguish the magistrate from the legislator, it is even more difficult to distinguish him from the citizen.

The distinction between legislator and magistrate is thus more situational than essential. The person who is exclusively or principally devoted to the establishment of a constitution, or more often, to the reform of an existing constitution, would more often be called "legislator," while to be called a "magistrate" would more likely mean that he is in charge of making function the current constitution of the city. In his pure form, the legislator does not take part in the political life of the city in which he lends his assistance. Thus, Plato's Academy, lacking the ability to put philosophers directly in power, imagined a kind of body of traveling legislators charged, for cities who asked for it, to propose measures that would aid them to govern better. That project should not have seemed too unrealistic to the Greeks who saw this sort of practice in effect in other domains. Thus, the existence of itinerant physicians who offered their services from city to city is well attested. So, the legislator has, in relation to the magistrate, even when one imagines him as able to modify the legislation of his own city, a special quality of distancing himself from the situation of the city in which or for which he intervenes. This distance is a guarantee of his objectivity.

As for the "political man," he is doubtless the significant figure of the gray area between legislation and politics, being a citizen of the city, but who creates for himself enough distance from daily political life to be able to give advice and useful recommendations to his city. A look at a Greek dictionary will show that the use of the adjective πολιτικός as a noun is, if not exclusively, at least predominantly done by philosophers reflecting on political life: Plato, Xenophon, Aristotle. They all give the πολιτικός a rather positive image, far from that which we today call a "politician." The *Politics*, as a treatise written by a political philosopher, is addressed primarily to the "pure" legislator, or ultimately to the "political man," according to the role assigned to him by Aristotle, and such as we have described above.

The first chapter of *Politics* 4, the beginning of that which many consider to be the "realist" version of Aristotle's *Politics*, is one of the best documents that we have for giving an idea of the tasks that he assigns to the legislator, and consequently, what the Aristotelian legislator is. This passage is very difficult, and I am not confident enough that the interpretation that I proposed a number of years ago is correct in all its details, but in general, I have kept the same reading.[2] This chapter sketches the outlines of a *science of constitutions*, which is, from the first line of the chapter, aligned with other sciences and with arts such as gymnastics. I still think that the object of this science is "the excellent constitution" (or "the best constitution"), that this expression is expressed or understood in the three or four cases examined one after the other, after an initial comparison with gymnastic science.

It is noteworthy that Aristotle compares constitutional science to gymnastics, adding at the end of his introduction naval construction, medicine, and tailoring. These are sciences, or rather arts (τέχναι), which do not aim at pure knowledge and which have to take account of very

---

2. Pierre Pellegrin, "La *Politique* d'Aristote: Unité et fractures. Élogue de la lecture sommaire," *Revue philosophique de la France et de l'Étranger* 1085 (1987), 2: 129–159.

different situations. It's this last characteristic that is underlined for gymnastics. We must note that here Aristotle abandons the distinction that he recalled in his study of slavery, between action and production.

Here is the passage that particularly interests us:

> It is obvious that constitution too is the subject of a single science, which has to consider what constitution is best and of what sort it must be, to be most in accordance with our aspirations, if there were no external impediment, and also what kind of constitution is adapted to particular cities. For the best is often unattainable, and therefore the true legislator and statesman ought to be acquainted, not only with that which is best absolutely, but also with that which is best relatively to circumstances. We should be able further to say how a city may be constituted "best" under any given conditions; both how it is originally formed and, when formed, how it may be longest preserved. I mean, for example, if it happens that a city neither has the best constitution nor is provided with the conditions necessary for the best, nor being the best under the circumstances, but of an inferior type. We ought, moreover, to know the "best" form of constitution that is best suited to cities in general; for political writers, although they have excellent ideas, are often unpractical. We should consider, not only what form of constitution is best, but also what is possible and what is easily attainable by all cities. There are some who would have none but the most perfect; for this many natural advantages are required. Others, again, speak of a more attainable form, and, although they reject the constitution under which they are living, they extol some one in particular, for example the Lacedaemonian. (4.1, 1288b21–1289a1)

To start with, Aristotle is not talking about the legislator, but about the "science" that considers the best constitution, saying that "it is the same science that considers the best constitution in accordance with our wishes," and the other forms. But the other forms of what? I think we must understand "the other forms of excellent constitution," which is confirmed by the parallelism that Aristotle established between the science of constitutions and gymnastics in the passage that immediately precedes the one quoted just now. There it was said that it is the same gymnastics that is concerned with the exercise adapted to the body of the athlete as well as that which concerns the body of any random person. There has been a dispute among commentators about whether the two lists, that where gymnastics is inserted into the account, and that where it's a matter of the science of constitutions, are exactly parallel or not.[3] Rather than decide this question, since both camps have good arguments, I will draw the conclusion that, just as Aristotle posited that for gymnastics there is a unique objective—"what is the most beneficial exercise for which body" (1288b13)—which may be decided in several ways depending on who is consulting the trainer, there is also a single objective for the constitutional science here under consideration. In any case, according to Aristotelian epistemology a single science corresponds to a single object. This single object is the excellent constitution, which may take several forms.

Doubtless this science properly belongs to the political philosopher, but sooner or later it reaches the legislator. But, as we are in the practical domain, knowledge must translate into action. The knowledge that the legislator acquires from these various versions of constitutional excellence is destined to nothing other than guidance of his action in actualizing that excellence. Because that is indeed the basis of his intervention.

Thus, we must get a good grasp of what is at issue in the various cases that Aristotle enumerates, and especially, for the moment, in the first three cases. First, the legislator may have to consider the excellent constitution, "which would in the highest degree conform to our wishes if nothing external impedes" (1288b22). It is noteworthy that Aristotle does not bring to the foreground of his "wishes" a determinate constitutional form, saying for example that the excellent constitution according to our wishes would be an aristocracy or a polity. I think that the "wishes" that the legislator hopes to see fulfilled when he wants to organize the absolutely excellent city are the more or less "trans-constitutional" characteristics, and that the favorable conditions are those which are studied in *Politics* book 7, and in a more indirect way, in book 8. These conditions are what Aristotle calls, a little farther on, "a lot of equipment (χορηγίας)" (1288b39). Those concern, among other things, the optimal size of the

---

3. Peter L. Phillips Simpson argues for a strict parallelism, in *A Philosophical Commentary on the Politics of Aristotle* (Chapel Hill: University of North Carolina Press, 1998), 285, against Nicholas Smith and Robert Mayhew, in "Aristotle on What the Political Scientist Needs to Know," in *Aristotelian Political Philosophy*, ed. C. Boudouris (Athens: Kardaminsky, 1995), 189–198.

territory, neither too large nor too small, with access to the sea but also with a significant quantity of agricultural land, the size of the population, large enough, but not too large—Aristotle, like Rousseau, thinks that the whole body of citizens should be able to assemble in a single place and consist of people who pretty much know each other—and not too diverse, ethnically speaking, the clear separation of commercial activities from properly political occupations of citizens who ought to lead a life of leisure. Among these favorable conditions there is also the fact that the city regulates matrimonial unions and is concerned with the education of children, the subject of *Politics* book 8.

It is difficult to determine exactly what Aristotle is thinking of in the first case, that of "the most valuable constitution." Is he talking about a city that the legislator ought to *found* in the way that the city in Plato's *Laws* is founded, in favorable external circumstances? I argued, in the article to which I have referred, that the two last books of the *Politics* are concerned with the situation of the legislator who has the task of founding a city. And there are, indeed, passages in book 7 that indubitably relate to the situation in which the legislator has to establish a city that did not exist previously. Thus chapters 5 and 6, suggesting choosing for the city a location situated in such and such a way—the importance that Greek physicians and philosophers placed on climates, winds, waters, and their effects on human character has been noted above—lead us to think that Aristotle has indeed in mind the foundation of a city *ex nihilo*. Even if, as I have said, this circumstance is rare, it could occur in his time, notably if the city to be founded is the colony of a city that already exists. But to stop there is to adopt a very impoverished reading of books 7 and 8. In the first place, a certain number of the characteristics of the "city of our wishes" that seem at first sight to concern only the foundation of a city can, in fact, be applied to a city that has already been founded. Thus, for the military characteristics of the geographical configuration of the city's territory, Aristotle notes that the philosopher, that is, in this case, the one who is writing the *Politics*, should "refer on some points to experts in strategy" (7.5, 1326b39). One may certainly read this recommendation as pointing in two directions: if one has to choose a location for an original foundation of a city, the advice of experts in strategy would be welcome, but, if the city has already been founded, these experts may palliate the defects of the location of the city by technical means, for example fortifications. That would be one of the ways that "art completes nature" (cf. *Phys.* 2.8, 199a15).

The question of the status and function of book 7 of the *Politics* is so important that we will have a chapter almost entirely devoted to it. I will show, notably, that *Politics* 7 and 8, which many have considered to have been written early in Aristotle's career, and influenced by Platonism, do not at all define the "ideal" constitution that, according to him, would be adapted to the city "according to our wishes." The problem posed by book 7 that interests us here is very well expressed by Aristotle himself in 7.4: "As the weaver or shipbuilder or any other artisan must have the material proper for his work, . . . so the statesman or legislator must also have the materials suited to him" (1325b40).

For, as Aristotle wrote a few lines earlier, "The best constitution cannot be realized without the appropriate equipment" (1325b37). I will show, in the chapter dealing with *Politics* 7 and 8, that they are not concerned, or not mainly concerned, with the constitutional form that ought to be adopted for the city in which the legislator intervenes, but that these books are preliminary to constitutional science, and that they include recommendations that can be applied to every city no matter its constitutional form. An aristocracy, just as much as a polity, has in fact an interest to have a population that is not too ethnically disparate, and so on. But the conditions "according to our wishes" in no way constitute *sine qua non* conditions, whose absence should dissuade the legislator from intervening to establish an excellent constitution. In fact, even in the situation, habitual for him, where he needs to correct the existing legislation, and not found a new city, the legislator has every interest in knowing the correct size of a city, how it would be convenient that it be physically divided into a political zone and a commercial zone, and so on.

For a city to be completely "according to our wishes," it is also and above all necessary that the legislator who founds it, or reforms it if it exists already, has available the appropriate human material, that is, that the citizens who make it up, or will make it up, have a sufficient degree of virtue, in particular political virtue, to establish a correct constitution that will assure the happiness of its citizens. Nevertheless, it remains that this passage at the beginning of *Politics* 4 seems to consider that this excellent constitution "according to our wishes" is, one may say, even more excellent than the others, which means that it is not absurd to imagine that Aristotle has in mind a "pure" excellent constitution. But in that case, he is talking about an aristocracy or a kingship, for the reasons that we have offered above.

But what interests us the most are the cases that follow. We can immediately say this: they are not about a constitution established, or reestablished, "according to our wishes," which means that the action of the legislator must take account of conditions that are not under his control, perhaps even that he would rather have done without. In other words, in performing his function, the legislator is under *constraints*.

For the second case, Aristotle explains this situation with two expressions: the legislator should consider "which constitution [understand: best constitution] is adapted to which cities [or which people]" (4.1, 1288b24), and this second constitution is "the best in the given conditions" (b26). The legislator, in this second case, thus finds a constitution that, "in the given conditions," functions badly and of which he needs to make an excellent constitution. The third case, that of the excellent constitution "in a given form," is hardly clearer than the second. "In a given form" translates ἐξ ὑποθέσεως, that is, "from a presupposition" or, etymologically, "from a hypothesis." These two cases must differ from each other, because otherwise, why would Aristotle say "thirdly"?

It still seems to me that the one case refers to a city in which the constitutional form must be changed because it is not adapted to the people it intends to run, the other to a constitution whose functioning must be adjusted without calling into question its general orientation. On the other hand, I am not as sure as I once was of the reference of each of them. I argued, in the second case, that the legislator ought to change the form of the constitution, for example to move from a minority regime to a popular regime, and in the third case, to preserve the form: if, for example, the city has a popular regime, the legislator who wants to improve its functioning ought to do so by conserving the form of the regime but changing some of its legislative arrangements. But it is not impossible that the opposite is true. "In the given conditions" would then mean rather that the legislator ought to establish an excellent constitution while conserving the general form of the constitution in effect, while establishing an excellent constitution "from a presupposition" could rather refer to the situation in which the legislator posits in advance that a new constitutional form ought to be established, and it would be this form that would constitute the *hypothesis* that must be posited in advance. This latter reading would be confirmed by what Aristotle says at 1288b33: the constitution in a given form would be "a worse constitution" than the constitution in given circumstances. If the constitution must change its form and not only reorganize its legislative details while conserving its fundamental orientation, the constitution in fact is worse at fulfilling its function, and the task of the legislator is shown to be more difficult. Thus, the list of cases presented in this passage goes from better to worse.

But ultimately it does not matter very much. In these two cases the legislator works on a constitution that exists and already functions, but functions badly, and the legislator has, if one may say so, in his portfolio of duties, that of changing the constitutional orientation, or changing the functioning while conserving the orientation. So then, the constitution "according to our wishes" would perhaps be a pure excellent constitution, while in contrast it is clear that in the two following cases the legislator finds himself in the world of constitutional mixture.

The last type of constitution that the legislator needs to consider is "that which is most easily and most commonly available to all cities." It seems to me that here too it is a matter of the best constitution, and once again this expression has a distributive sense, as can be seen, implicitly, in the critique that follows. This critique is aimed at least at Plato:

> There are some who would have none but the most perfect; for this many natural advantages are required. Others, again, speak of a more attainable form, and, although they reject the constitution under which they are living, they extol some one in particular, for example the Lacedaemonian. (1288b39–1289a1)

While the Aristotelian legislator will consider what will be in each case the easiest to bring into effect, the Platonists, and possibly others, want to impose a single form, Lacedaemonian or something else, on all cities.

Thus, the end of the passage that we are examining develops three ideas, all important. First, according to Aristotle, his predecessors did not try to translate their reforming or revolutionary projects into reality. Is this criticism justified in the case of Plato, for example? It's not certain, if one realizes that the *Republic* is anything but a work of social reformation, and the *Laws* makes a good deal of room for what is realizable. But it is not convenient to deal with that subject in this place. The second idea is that in "abolishing existing constitutions" these reformers considered only the circumstance in which one makes a clean slate of the past. Thus, they forgo the principle activity of the Aristotelian legislator, that of *remediating already existing constitutions*. Immediately after the passage cited above, Aristotle writes:

> Any change of constitution that has to be introduced should be one that men, starting from their existing constitutions, will be both willing and able to adopt, since there is quite as much trouble in the reformation of an old constitution as in the establishment of a new one, just as to unlearn is as hard as to learn. And therefore, in addition to the qualifications of the statesman already mentioned, he should be able to find remedies for the defects of existing constitutions, as has been said before. (1289a1)

The expression "the qualifications already mentioned" doubtless refers to the fact that the statesman, here the legislator, the one that our text calls "the truly political man," is able to decide which constitutional form is appropriate for which city. What our passage says is that in addition to that theoretical qualification, the legislator ought also to be able to work with existing constitutions *to reform them*. In fact, it is one thing to say that a particular city ought to have an aristocratic constitution of a certain sort, whether it is a democracy or already aristocratic, but of a form inappropriate for the situation of the city, and quite another thing to translate these analyses into reality without having the convenient precondition of a clean slate. Indeed, it is illusory to try to evade the difficulties in founding a city from square one. For a very interesting example, Phaleas of Chalcedon fell into this illusion. Aristotle tells us that he saw in the inequality of inheritances the origin of all civic evils. He therefore envisaged equalization of fortunes. "He thought that in a new colony the equalization might be accomplished without difficulty, not so easily when a state was already established" (2.7, 1266b1). A few lines farther on, in a particularly brilliant analysis to which I have already alluded, Aristotle attacks the very root of this naïve egalitarianism, showing that since desire is limitless, human perversity is not restrained by the satisfaction of needs: "One does not become a tyrant not to suffer from cold" (1267a14). Aristotle is decidedly not fascinated by the purity of origins. We will see that again, several times, notably concerning his lack of reverence for ancient legislation, and we have seen his distrust of the state of infancy.

The third idea of this passage is absolutely fundamental in Aristotle's political thought, and we have already encountered it. It is the understanding that excellence is plural. It would be absurd to want to impose the same constitutional form on every city under the pretext that it would be "ideal."

Thus, it would be exceptional that the legislator would have to initiate changes of a revolutionary or abrupt kind. His intervention therefore approaches political action. Of course, the legislator can come from within the city, while in the archaic Greek tradition, as in Platonic practice, it is most often people come from without who provide laws for a new city or new laws for a city, as we have seen. The Aristotelian legislator, in contrast, far from being a *deus ex machina*, is a witness, even a participant, in the functioning of the city. That agrees with what we noted as the proximity of legislator and magistrate that I have characterized as "essential." Because of the fact that what one may call Aristotle's "trivialization" of the figure of the legislator, the functions, and thus the status, of the governor and of the legislator are so close to each other that in the passage we have been considering Aristotle twice identifies them by speaking of the "good legislator, that is, the true statesman" (4.1, 1288b27), a passage already cited and that we cannot avoid comparing to what Plato says in the *Statesman*,[4] and when he says that the "statesman" (πολιτικός) comes to the aid of existing constitutions (4.1, 1289a6). At the beginning of *Politics* 2.12, Aristotle enumerates all the possible forms of the legislator: some have engaged in political activity and others have not taken part at all; some have legislated for their own city and some for other cities; some have only made laws, and others also a constitution, "like Lycurgus and Solon, for these simultaneously established laws and a constitution" (1273b33). But if we understand clearly what it means to propose laws without designing a constitution, on the other hand it would be difficult to imagine a legislator conceiving of a constitution without making laws, or at least without sketching the outlines of intervention for those who would make them. Aristotle once again is thus far from the idea, notably Platonic, that would establish an excellent constitution by a strong and sudden foundational act, which is thought to establish it forever, or at least for a very long time, with the relationship between classes at least stabilized if not quieted.[5] As we have seen, and will see again in more

---

4. "The statesman, that is, the good legislator" (309d).

5. I have insisted several times on the idea that Plato meant to found an excellent city once and for all, and for the long term. Plato's position is in fact more nuanced. Thus, in *Laws* 6, 769ff., the Athenian shows that the original legislator will have to be aware that his legislation will need to be made more precise and ameliorated over time. Nevertheless, the Athenian does not envisage a profound deterioration of the original constitution: his successors will have to work within the "outlines" (770b) traced by the original legislator. We must notice that this, in the words of the Athenian, leads to making the guardians of the laws into legislators. That coincides with what we said above about the relationship between legislator and magistrate in Aristotle.

detail when we discuss sedition, Aristotle shows us constitutions in perpetual change. If then the legislator, as his name indicates, is indeed the creator of a legislative system, that is, of a constitution, of a city, it is in a way a continuous creation.

The legislator needs to apply his legislative prudence in taking account of three principle elements: first, the means that he will have to bring to the work; second, the situations in which he will have to intervene; and finally, the theoretical tools he must have in order to be able to use these means in these situations. Because, doubtless, the first moment of the intervention of a legislator who has been called to rescue a city that is doing badly, or who arises from the heart of the civic body itself, is an evaluative work; we may call it an "audit." It's this kind of analysis that Aristotle himself provides when, in *Politics* 2, he examines the various constitutions, real or imagined by theoreticians, before judging the constitutions of Sparta and Crete:

> Two things have to be considered: first, whether any particular law is good or bad, for establishing the best constitution; second, whether there is anything that goes contrary to the foundation and form of the constitution proposed by the various legislators. (2.9, 1269a31)

There are two ways of understanding the last part of this sentence: we must examine either if there is something in the Spartan or Cretan constitution that is contrary to the fundamental orientation of that constitution, or if something in the facts is opposed to that constitution. In the first case, which seems to me to best translate Aristotle's thought, it's a matter of seeing if the legislative arrangements in a city are in contradiction with the nature of its constitution or with the form that it has taken; in the second, it is necessary to evaluate the degree of adaptation of the constitution to its environment, which would be, for a city, its economic resources, geographic location, relationship of forces to those of its neighbors, or the ethical status of its people. The two evaluations are, in any case, the concerns of the legislator.

Thus, we rediscover the importance of the political documentation gathered in the Lyceum. A passage in the *Rhetoric* shows this, saying that "books of travel are useful aids to legislation, since from these we may learn the laws of different peoples" (1.4, 1360a33).

What Are the Means That the Legislator Must Put into Operation?

The legislator has only two ways of improving a constitution, either by changing its form, or by improving its functioning while keeping its form. Either he will impose these changes by force by taking the lead in a seditious movement, and will establish a new system of laws, or he will achieve his goals by a progressive modification of the laws, by convincing the citizens of the city in question to confirm the modifying steps. Obviously, there are mixed solutions, for example when sedition is greeted almost unanimously favorably, or when the legislator turns to some sort of blackmail of the citizens, who might be his fellow citizens, to get them to accept his propositions. To carry out effectively the first sort of enterprise, it is better to have military training than political. That is nevertheless a possibility for which the teaching of Aristotle the philosopher should prepare the legislator. A particularly important example, already noticed, of these rapid constitutional changes that, without actually resorting to warlike processes, nevertheless look like a kind of coup d'état, is giving citizenship to groups that did not yet have it, often following an extraordinary event. Thus Cleisthenes, after expelling the tyrants from Athens, naturalized "many foreigners, slaves, and metics," which brought about a major change of the constitutional equilibrium of the city (*Pol.* 3.2, 1275b36). We have seen other noteworthy cases of this practice. But it is incontestably by acting on the constitution with the consent of the citizen body, or a large part of the civic body, or even at its demand, that the legislator most often successfully carries out his function. In any case, is not consent one of the foundations of political life?

Thus, it can happen that the legislator ought to dictate a new constitution, either because the people to whom he means to give these institutions have never been assembled in a city, or because the city must change its constitution. The first case, more or less Platonic, perhaps happened more frequently in the past, but would hardly happen for an Aristotelian legislator, as we have said several times. But in the vast majority of cases it would be by acting on the laws that compose the constitution that the legislator would be able to reform it. *Minimal* reform when, while conserving the constitution in place, he would change several laws that were injurious in their original form, or a more profound reform when the legislative changes bring about a revision in the constitution itself. The constitution can therefore change form in two ways, either that the legislator in concert with the citizens decides to move to a new form because the old one was no longer appropriate, or that this change, not having been expressly desired, is nevertheless entailed by a legislative reform more or less large. How, for example, can one preserve an oligarchy when the essentials of the legislation are drawn from the democratic side? A well-trained and adept legislator ought to be able to avoid this last case.

Thus, there is here a kind of reversal. We saw, in fact, that the laws depend on the constitution, and in particular that they get from it their just or unjust character. Aristotle's constitutional analyses, especially in the books of the *Politics* thought to be "realist," show us also that the modification of the laws, whether great or small, desired or not, has repercussions, sometimes marginal, sometimes decisive, on the constitution itself. Let us speak a bit about the laws.

The Laws

The ancient Greeks were, if one may say so, affected by *nomolatry*. We have already seen that when the law is suspended, or when men, either individually or as a group, place themselves above the law, we leave the realm of politics. Aristotle shows this on two different points concerning the Cretan constitution, which is characterized by a magistracy, that of the Cosmi, which gave very extensive powers to ten citizens elected from members of dominant families for a term of one year. Aristotle compares this institution to that which corresponded to it at Sparta, that of the five ephors. In the midst of these two magistracies were chosen "elders" or *gerontes*, who belonged to a college of people named for life and assigned to decision-making in important matters, notably in trials. The fundamental vice of these two magistracies is that of choosing people to whom one is giving power "at random" (οἱ τύχοντες) (2.10, 1272a30), in an ethical sense, and not social, since, while the Spartan ephors were chosen from among all the citizens, the Cretan Cosmi were chosen from members of families of notables (cf. 1272a34). But in both cases, it's a matter of people who show no particular excellence or special ability. At last the Spartan magistracy has the effect of making the people less hostile to the constitution, because they have the sense of being represented in the government, since the ephors are not necessarily notables. To hand over the government to these people "not according to written laws, but according to their individual judgment, that is dangerous" (2.10, 1272a38). But the way that the Cretans had for getting rid of Cosmi, especially when they feared their judgments, either by expelling them from office, or even temporarily suspending this magistracy, is a remedy worse than the disease, because that tramples on the law. Aristotle repeats twice that for this reason the Cretan constitution is more nearly an arbitrary regime than a constitution. "Arbitrary regime" is a translation of the term *dynasteia* (δυναστεία), and it is a form of government related to oligarchy as tyranny is to kingship (cf. 4.5, 1292b10), and thus one in which the leaders are above the law. What aggravates this case is that oligarchy is already a deviant constitution, whereas kingship is a correct constitution. The city leaves political space when it is governed by an "extreme democracy" (cf., e.g., 4.6, 1293a32). In short, "there where the laws do not govern, there is no *politeia*" (4.4, 1292a32), *politeia* meaning here, of course, "constitution," but also, more generally, "political life, life in a city."

The central role of the law in Aristotle's ethics has already been noted, but we must provide a better understanding of the mechanism before giving an analysis of the role of law in Aristotle's political philosophy. The relevant and crucial passage for this is at the end of the *Nicomachean Ethics*. Remember what we have already seen. Just as ethologists have shown that certain animals naturally have in themselves certain abilities, but they need to be in a way activated by external intervention, most often by that of their parents, who "teach" their young how to perform this or that action, in the same way Aristotle thinks that no matter how natural virtue may be, it does not arise spontaneously unless human beings, especially young people, adopt morally correct conduct:

> For to live temperately and hardily is not pleasant to most people, especially when they are young. For this reason, their nurture and occupations should be fixed by law, for they will not be painful when they have become customary. (10.9, 1179b32, already cited)

Only regular obedience, forced if necessary—for "most people obey constraint sooner than reason, and punishment sooner than good sense" (1180a4)—to good laws results in good habits that end by implanting virtues in the individual.

The text in which Aristotle pushes the farthest the intermingling between ethics and politics is perhaps the short chapter that ends *Politics*

3. This chapter relies on the reaffirmation of two fundamental theses. The first is the distinction between the three correct constitutions according to the number of people in power; Aristotle takes advantage of the occasion to assert again that the leadership of the city ought to be assigned to virtuous people who will exercise their function for the sake of the common advantage, here described as that which permits "living the most desirable life" (3.18, 1288a37). The second is that, *in a city with a correct constitution*, the excellence of the good man and that of the citizen are the same. Then the conclusion:

> Clearly then in the same manner, and by the same means through which a man becomes truly good, he will frame a city that is to be ruled by an aristocracy or by a king, and the same education and the same habits will be found to make a good man and a man fit to be a statesman or a king. (1288a39)

It should be noted that Aristotle, while he indeed speaks of "three correct constitutions" (1288a32), thus including the polity, when he envisages, a few lines farther along, the establishment of an excellent city, he seems to consider only kingship and aristocracy. Doubtless Aristotle does not want to reexamine the problem of virtue in a large number of people and is satisfied with the constitutions indubitably founded on virtue, that is, the correct constitutions that, as we saw above, can present themselves in a pure form. In any case this apparent reduction of correct constitutions to kingship and aristocracy poses an interpretive problem to which I will return in a later chapter. But perhaps there is no other place in the *Politics* where Aristotle asserts so clearly that it is the same education that makes a "good man" and, not only an excellent citizen, but also an excellent "statesman," that is, at least an excellent magistrate, and at most an excellent legislator.

This poses a political problem of greatest importance, the most important perhaps for the legislator, and it has been seen as such by all political philosophers—that of the education of children. In the Platonic city, even in that of the *Laws*, the collectivist structure of the society allows the legislator to have direct control of the education of the citizens, but in the Aristotelian approach, it is difficult to reconcile political educational imperatives with the autonomy of paternal power. For Aristotle, in fact, education remains a familial matter. Without dealing with the problem for its own sake here, we can provide a couple of suggestions. First, the

Aristotelian excellent city will in fact be heavily involved in the education of children, even though they are not taken away from their families. Second, the real solution, according to Aristotle, would be that the father of the family "acquire the ability to be a legislator" (*EN* 10.10, 1180a32). In other words, it is necessary at least that he be virtuous, that is, that he has been educated by good laws. One also sees, in reading a passage like this, no matter how offbeat and metaphorical it may be, how far the Aristotelian legislator has been removed from the figure of the hero founder of a city to bring him closer to the virtuous governor. To act as a legislator, for a father, is not a matter of handing down laws to his child, but one of teaching him how to conform his behavior to the laws of the city. We understand from that why *education* (which is then the education that one has received) counts, alongside liberty, wealth, nobility, and so forth, among the qualifications in the name of which one has the right to demand a share in political power (cf. 4.12, 1296b18).

This ethical function of the law has a crucial consequence for the legislator, which comes from the fact that the laws, in order to accomplish this function of forming character, *need time*. Consequently, if the laws change too often, this fundamental function of legislation can never be effective. That is the root of Aristotle's fundamentally conservative politics, for which he has often been blamed, but it is an optical illusion of conservatism. In an article that continues to be famous, in which he opposed the analyses of Jacqueline de Romilly, Jacques Brunschwig definitively demonstrated that for Aristotle the advantages of changing the law largely outweigh those of keeping it the same.[6] This question is so important that we must say a bit more about it, still following Brunschwig. He is right to notice that the aporia posited by Aristotle—Should it be easy to change the law or not?—is for him a true aporia, and is resolved by the treatment that Aristotle gives to it. We must emphasize that none of the six arguments put forward by Aristotle, three for change and three against, are refuted, but all are considered acceptable. We note to begin with the fact that the context in which Aristotle writes is itself divided, since most of the cities present a strong reticence to touching their laws, while the "progressive" ideology, that is, that which encourages changes in the name of progress, was reinforced during the previous generation.

---

6. Brunschwig, "Du mouvement et de l'immobilité de la loi." This article responds to Jacqueline de Romilly, *La loi dans la pensée grecque* (Paris: Les Belles Lettres, 1971).

It is in any case remarkable that the discussion of changes in the laws be introduced by Aristotle when he is looking at a law suggested by Hippodamus of Miletus, according to which anyone who "found something advantageous for the city" (2.8, 1268a6) should be rewarded monetarily. This is, Aristotle says a little later, a "dangerous" proposal, because it would encourage slanderous accusations and constitutional upheavals. Hippodamus was in fact a "revolutionary," to the point of planning cities according to principles of rational urbanism.

Brunschwig thinks that the proposal of Hippodamus is placed at a too-great degree of generality in that "it can encourage innovation in any domain whatever: whether you have discovered a silver mine, invented a way of making triremes go faster, uncovered a conspiracy against the city, imagined an interesting judicial disposition,"[7] you will be compensated. Possibly Brunschwig has been a bit hasty on this point, because Aristotle's examples show that he is thinking only of "discoveries" in the political sphere, since "slanderous accusations" doubtless refers to the revelation of supposed conspiracies against the city. But basically, Brunschwig is right: the arguments of the partisans of change, who infer from the fact that innovation is good in all forms of science and technology and who think that primitive man lived in a savage state that we would not accept, show very well that they do not take account of the specific characteristics of the political domain. Brunschwig shows that they come to the point of bringing together everything to the very general question of knowing whether change is or is not preferable to immobility. In the same way Aristotle blames Plato for maintaining that the cause of constitutional changes is that everything changes in some way.

The arguments of the adversaries of change, as they apply to the laws, are all taken up by Aristotle, as we have said; these arguments place the debate at its true level. First, it is better to tolerate a slightly harmful law than to give citizens the idea that one may change the laws at every turn and thus undermine the authority of the magistrates. Second, and this continues what was said above, it takes a long time for a law to have an effect, which means that the analogy with technical improvement is not valid. Finally, it is not within the competence of any random person to decide which law to change and how to change it, when we think of the consequences that that would have on the constitution (cf. 2.8, 1269a26). Possibly there is here, on Aristotle's part, a veiled criticism of Hippodamus,

---

7. Brunschwig, "Du mouvement et de l'immobilité de la loi," 537 (trans. A. Preus).

of whom he says was the first legislator who had not engaged in political life. Short of having been able to read the "realist" books of the *Politics*, Hippodamus would have done well to have rubbed shoulders with "real" politics. But the arguments of the partisans of change, which Aristotle also accepts, show in fact that to change the law is a practice that is neither reprehensible nor something to be limited to exceptional cases. Thus the statement "everyone desires the good, not just what is handed down from one's ancestors" (1269a3), which, when it concerns legislation, goes against the official ideology of many cities, including democratic cities like Athens, posits in a way the framework of Aristotle's analysis. And when he writes that "most old constitutions are less well constructed than the more recent ones" (2.10, 1271b23), here too Aristotle assuredly does not join the side of the originalists and reactionaries.

Finally, the law has two major characteristics, universality and stability; in a way these two cancel themselves out. In fact, law avoids the traps of particularity. So, when even the best of men cannot free himself from the passion and desire that obviously derive from the sphere of individuality, the law is "reason without desire" (4.16, 1287a32). This is why, if one recognizes as citizens people who, as individuals, are not sufficiently virtuous, and thus when they are given a share of power in the city, it is necessary to delimit them as much as possible by the law, in forbidding them, obviously, from changing or even simply discussing the law, and even restricting as much as possible the range of their deliberation. Thus "most legislators take pains to prevent the judges from holding any deliberation together" (2.8, 1268b9). Here we must remember that, in the case of the popular government advocated by Aristotle in *Politics* 3.11, the people do not discuss the laws. But, as we have seen, the universal character of law makes it difficult to apply in concrete cases, and this opens up the space for political action in the strict sense, that of the government that translates the laws into decrees. In the strict sense, the law does not govern. At the same time, the law is a pole of stability in the flux of the changing and contradictory human opinions. This stability permits *order*: "the law is a certain order" (7.4, 1326a30), and even, Aristotle clarifies, a harmonious order. But this stability is not inviolable in that change is ultimately always justifiable when it results in something better, which is in any case fortunate for the legislator who otherwise would lose any possibility of acting. And above all, this stability of the law is based on an essential variability, since the laws depend on constitutions, which are in turn diverse and variable.

In order to obtain the constitutional effect that he hopes to realize, the legislator thus resorts above all to legislative changes, one may even say to a new legislative dosage. Since constitutions are systems of laws, to act upon the laws necessarily has an effect on the constitution. We have also seen that minimal changes can have large effects. Those effects would be destabilizing when the change introduces one or more laws that are contrary to the spirit of a constitution, and that triggers the fall of the constitution; they are conservative when they constitute a legislative rectification that can restore an equilibrium that it had lost. J. Brunschwig is therefore right: fundamentally, Aristotle is not a conservative. Quite the contrary, one can even say that the very basis of the activity of the Aristotelian legislator is legislative change, with the rider that too much change kills change by annihilating its beneficial effects.

The Situations in Which the Legislator Intervenes

From a general point of view, the good legislator sets himself the goal of giving a city an excellent constitution and of furnishing it with the means of conserving it. This excellent constitution, by its very functioning, will develop the virtue of the citizens, thus making them able to lead a "happy life." But, as we have seen, this activity only rarely takes the form of a new beginning or revolution. To be sure, the legislator can have in mind profound changes, since sometimes his diagnostic is that it is necessary to change the form of the constitution. In that case it is a question of a revolution in the primary sense of that word, since the city is overturned and replaced by another, to such a point that the new city, even if composed of the same citizens as the old one, is not accountable for the decisions of its predecessor. But paradoxically the modalities of that intervention, as revolutionary as it might be, usually have a frankly conservative aspect. It's a matter of adjusting the legislative equilibrium of the constitution to lead it to reforming itself. We can see clearly by reading the *Politics* that one of the major abilities that the Aristotelian legislator ought to demonstrate is that of saving constitutions by giving them the means to resist the forces that tend to destroy them. The legislator must "give it time," and doubtless preserve rather than overturn. We will see that, for that, he needs to have an objective knowledge of the nature and mechanisms of seditions and revolutions.

Let us look at an example. The Carthaginian constitution, Aristotle says, is reputed to be "superior in many ways to others" (2.11, 1272b25). It aims at aristocracy, that is, it gives power to the most virtuous. So it is the magistracy of the kings, since in Carthage they don't always belong to the same lineage, nor to a random lineage, nor even to the oldest, but they are chosen because they are most eminent in virtue. But the seed of deviation was introduced into the constitution because the "mass of people" thought that the magistrates could not exercise their tasks correctly unless they had leisure to do so, something that is not contrary to Aristotelian ideology. But unhappily these people also thought that only material ease could provide sufficient leisure, and they thus introduced the oligarchical measure to put the two main magistracies, those of king and chief general, up for sale, thus reserving them for rich people. That, Aristotle says, is a "mistake of the legislator" (1273a31), who ought rather to have guaranteed by legislative means that the best people would have leisure rather than that those who have the leisure because of their fortune would also find themselves in power. But Carthage was able to find the antidote to the oligarchical poison with which it had inoculated itself: "Although they have an oligarchical constitution, the Carthaginians avoid in the best way its inconveniences by increasing wealth, by constantly sending out part of its population to client cities" (1273b18).

We should doubtless understand that poor Carthaginians are sent out into the colonies where they become wealthy, and thus become favorable to the constitution. This measure impedes the emergence of an excessively closed oligarchy, which would inevitably follow from the circumstance of the rich being very few in number. And Aristotle continues: "Thus, they correct their constitution and make it more stable. But that happens randomly, while it should be the legislator who ensures that there are no revolts" (1273b21).

"Randomly" translates the word τύχη, usually translated "luck." In fact, neither translation works perfectly here. It seems that Aristotle wants to say that the solution put into operation depends on a situation that one finds in this particular case—the fact that Carthage dominates other cities—and not from a rational analysis by a legislator who could have found another way to give leisure to virtuous people, thus reinforcing the aristocratic character of the constitution. One of the results of this way of proceeding is that the solution brought to the problem does not amend the constitution, which keeps an oligarchic orientation. One may thus presume that, if he had to deal with the Carthaginian constitution, the measures that would have been taken by the Aristotelian legislator would have tried to give leisure to the virtuous people to give them the opportunity to exercise power. Obviously, this is a difficult task, because by remunerating magistrates, for example, one introduces a democratic modality in that people of modest means would do everything they could to become magistrates. It's that the task of the legislator is all the more delicate as his science is not a theoretical discipline, but practical. As many analyses have shown, those of Pierre Aubenque about "prudence" for example, the decisions of people like legislators have to be taken in a contingent world, unstable and thus unpredictable. That is why intuition, the grasping of the opportune moment, and firmness of character are the indispensable components of practical excellence, that, as we have seen, of a Pericles, which is not the same as that of an Anaxagoras. Furthermore, the conditions that must be taken into account in such an action are indefinitely many. As has been said, historical documentation is also of the highest importance.

In his legislative alchemy, which aims to rectify the constitution or, at least, to prevent it from becoming worse, the legislator is thus never sure of achieving his goal, for many reasons of which the least is not the difficulty of evaluating the various components of the situation. For example: in the city of Thurii, which we know had democratic institutions because it was in fact an Italian colony of Athens, a law imposed a delay of five years before one could return to the office of general. This is a crucial point, as we have also seen in Athens, because with democratic institutions that presupposed an alternation of terms in office, one could not really have clout in the city except by taking on a "technical" magistracy, especially if, as is the case of the function of general, it offers a specific power. The law of Thurii is thus a typical example of a measure taken by a wise legislator to prevent popular institutions from being threatened by "Caesarism." But young people talented in warfare, having attracted the admiration of soldiers and the favor of the people, wanted to repeal the law and display their distrust of the existing institutions. The magistrates were opposed, but they ended by making the following calculation: it was better to concede the repeal of the law and thus avoid a dangerous conflict. "But when, subsequently they wanted to prevent other changes, they could not do it, and the entire constitutional order changed into a dynasty of those who introduced these innovations" (5.7, 1307b6ff.). That is what a good legislator ought to be able to avoid in the city.

Functional Excellence

Thus, in practice the legislator is conservative, because he ought to try to conserve *as much as possible* the constitution that he is trying to reform. This position that the legislator is led to take produces a kind of particular version of the grand division that extends throughout Aristotle's political philosophy, and the entire *Politics*, between the normative and realist approaches, in that up against the ethical norm of constitutional excellence there is established *a norm that can be called "functional."* Thus, speaking of the Cretan constitution, Aristotle remarks that "a sign that this constitution is well organized is that its common people remain in their place in the constitutional order, and the city has never known sedition, which is worth mentioning, nor tyrant" (2.11, 1272b30).

In a general way, as for the beginning of his final study of the diversity of constitutions, possibly the most fascinating part of Aristotle's political thought, to which we will of course return at length, Aristotle distinguishes three major components of every constitution, and notes that "when these parts do well, necessarily the constitution does well" (4.14, 1297b39).

According to an ethical norm, a constitution is excellent when, in the conditions that are those of the city that it organizes, it brings to power people who govern for the common advantage by leading the citizens to virtue and happiness. We have seen that that ought to be done by assigning magistracies to virtuous people, whether it is a matter of individual virtue or collective virtue. The happiness of the citizens is thus a sign of the excellence of the constitution, and Aristotle, simultaneously fierce and sarcastic, critiques Plato, who claims to make the whole city happy while all its members are unhappy (*Pol.* 2.5, 1264b15ff.). We have seen in that case one of the criticisms that Aristotle aims at the totalitarian primacy of the collective over the individual. This criticism goes very far, since the position of Aristotle is that "happiness is the same for each person taken individually and for the city" (*Pol.* 7.2, 1324a5), and goes all the farther since he presents this position as based on general agreement: "But this is also obvious: everyone, in fact, agrees in saying that it is the same" (1324a5).

Everything that has been said above about the diversity of constitutional excellence remains valid, but all these excellences are not of the same worth, and to paraphrase Orwell again, some are more excellent than others. Aristotle certainly has always established a difference between the inhabitants of a city and its citizens, and one of the primary tasks of the legislator is to prevent, as much as possible, the accession of unworthy people to citizenship and above all to important responsibilities in the city—the unworthy being, above all, people incapable of political virtue (women, slaves, manual laborers, merchants). But Aristotle also recommends increasing the body of citizens as much as possible, within the limits imposed by the fact that a city, as we have seen, should not grow beyond a rather restricted size, to avoid losing its character as a city. This recommendation of developing the citizen body is derived from both normative and realist politics. From normative politics because, as we said earlier, the polity is an end point in the history of correct constitutions. From normative politics also because the functioning of a correct constitution has the effect of developing virtue in the civic body, which will tend to enlarge the number of its members. "It is necessary to enlarge the body of citizens" thus means that it is necessary to spread virtue in the city. From realist politics because, as the passage about the Cretan constitution cited above says, and as we have seen on the subject of the sovereignty of the masses advocated in *Politics* 3.11, a constitution is more stable if the people approve of it.

Let us reemphasize this point: Aristotle believes that constitutional kingship is an excellent constitution, but outdated. Also, the enlarged form of excellent constitution, aristocracy, is "more to be desired" (3.15, 1286b5) than a kingship. Even if one considers deviant constitutions, the virtuous tendency of democracy that, when it is associated with the virtuous tendency of oligarchy, gives rise to a polity, does so by integrating more men into the civic body. There is thus a movement of amelioration of constitutions of which the end is a "polity." This movement can very well be interrupted or even reversed by various events, for that's how history happens, and the role of the legislator in the search for ethical excellence in the constitution has three parts. First, he needs to prevent imbalance in the constitution, that one party gain too much importance; this is sometimes difficulty when, for example, an unexpected event brings about this tendency. Thus, at Athens, contrary to what Solon had intended, the people took too much power, which led to a demagogic regime; this followed naval supremacy, which followed victories in sea battles in the Persian War, for the navy is essentially popular: "The people became proud and chose the side of bad demagogues" (2.12, 1274a13). Secondly, the legislator needs to facilitate the transition toward larger correct forms, mainly by modifying the laws, for example in weakening the oligarchical character of some of them. Finally, he needs to try to get beyond the opposition between rich and poor by favoring the appearance of a middle class that would neutralize the two extremes. On this last point also normative and realist considerations coincide since the preponderance, or at least the importance, of a middle class makes the constitution more stable (this aspect is treated especially in *Politics* 4.12), and at the same time it reinforces the ethical excellence that this middle class spreads in the civic body, as we said above, and as is explained in *Politics* 3.11. Let us look at these two aspects in a more detail.

The development of a middle class has indeed an ethical effect. We have seen that Aristotle envisages that one of the possible solutions for the problem, that it is necessary for the citizens of an excellent city to be virtuous, was to consider the collective virtue of the people, not rather than, but together with, the individual virtue of virtuous people. But these people are in fact a middle class composed of people who are neither rich nor poor. The poor, in fact, oppressed by need, live a mean life incompatible with the leisured life of a true citizen. The mobs that Aristotle says are like savage beasts (3.11, 1281b19) are most often impoverished mobs. As for the rich, they are most often little inclined to virtue. But there are also very realist considerations that encourage Aristotle to anticipate favoring access to power for the middle class.

Then the functional norm is at work. That's what appears in *Politics* 4.12, 1296b35ff., for example, where Aristotle explains the reason for the preponderant role that the legislator ought to give to the middle class: it is because "there is no danger that the wealthy will ever form an alliance with the poor against the middle class" (1296b40). That means that the hegemony of the middle class, if put in power, will never be questioned by anybody, because there is no class sufficiently strong to do it, only an alliance between the wealthy and the poor could do it, but such an alliance is impossible and therefore the constitution is stable. The functional norm, in fact, considers that a constitution is all the better to the extent that it proves to be able to endure. It's when one takes this point of view that one can discern the presences of organic structures at work in Aristotelian political analysis. The constitutions that survive are healthy constitutions: that's a point of view that I have already called "Darwinian."[8]

---

8. See my essay "Naturalité, excellence, diversité. Politique et biologie chez Aristote," in *Aristoteles' "Politik." Akten des XI. Symposium Aristotelicum*, ed. Günther Patzig (Göttingen: Vandenhoech & Ruprecht, 1990), 124–151. Turned around the other way, "the animal is constituted like a city with good laws" (*MA* 10, 703a29).

Two conditions for this good health are provided in two very interesting passages of the *Politics*. Let us first look at the text to which we have alluded above, 5.3, 1302b33, where Aristotle writes:

> Changes in constitutions also spring from a disproportionate increase in any part of the city. For as a body is made up of many members, and every member ought to grow in proportion so that symmetry may be preserved, but it loses its nature if the foot is four cubits (5') long and the rest of the body two spans (16"); and, should the abnormal increase be one of quality as well as of quantity, it may even take the form of another animal; even so a city has many parts . . .

A passage like this deserves extensive commentary; we can say at least this: something like that cannot happen in the animal world, since Aristotle is strictly fixist and conceives animal species as everlasting, but it can happen in the political world, since constitutions change quantitatively by increase or decrease of certain of their parts, and that can bring about also a mutation from one form to another. A disproportionate increase of this sort occurs, as the passage that follows explains, either as the effect of the functioning of the constitution itself, or as the consequence of an exterior event (a war, for example: 1304a3), that is, as the result of an illness or injury.

The second passage is found at 6.6, 1320b33:

> For as healthy bodies and ships well provided with sailors may undergo many mishaps and survive them, whereas sickly bodies and rotten ill-manned ships are ruined by the least mistake, so do the worst forms of constitution require the greatest care.

Every biologist knows that a living organism has more chance to survive if it is able to undergo larger changes in its metabolism and can overcome more significant challenges from its environment. So, we are right in the middle of Darwinian politics: those organisms survive, and survive better and longer, that perform better and have greater resilience than others.

To make constitutions endure one does not have to avoid all change because, as we have seen, in the case of deviant constitutions, but even for correct constitutions too, political life proceeds on the basis of a struggle between classes whose demands have equivalent bases, and is menaced by enemies both internal and external. If one of the major tasks of the legislator is to protect cities from every kind of sedition, one of the most important lessons that he has to get from the philosopher precisely concerns seditions, whose nature and causes he must know in order to be able to anticipate controlling them. Thus, we cannot stint in providing a serious examination of the Aristotelian idea of "sedition" (στάσις), but for the moment we can limit ourselves to this: the task of the legislator is to prevent seditions, or if that is impossible, to combat them, or if that is impossible, to steer them in the right direction and limit their negative effects. That does not prevent there being, sometimes, desirable seditions.

But what is most interesting for us, and which sends us back to the fundamental question of the relationship between normative and realist in Aristotle's politics, is to see what relationship exists between these two norms, ethical and functional, according to which a constitution is excellent. Let us look at the main aspects of that relationship.

What we have already said leads us to understand that, far from being indifferent to the permanence of the constitution, the politics of ethical excellence establishes a kind of binary relationship between virtue and endurance. Virtue needs time to establish itself in the civic body, because it is the effect of the functioning of good laws that does not happen except over time. And, reciprocally, if Aristotle's analyses on virtue as the main factor of happiness are correct, virtue ought to be a guarantee of long-lastingness, because who would want to change a situation that makes him happy? We have already seen that the fragility of virtue, which we can hardly ignore when we think about human history, is a very difficult problem for Aristotle, and in any case, for all the Greeks.

In *Politics* 5, Aristotle deals with seditions, their nature and causes, and consequently the means of preventing them. The normative aspect of Aristotle's political philosophy seems to be here, if not nullified, at least assigned to a lower subsidiary role. The distinction between correct and deviant constitutions has not been abandoned (thus at 5.9, 1309b19, Aristotle speaks of deviations), but it is, if one may say so, recovered at an unexpected level. When he studies the causes and progression of seditions in *Politics* 5, Aristotle not only deals successively with all the constitutions, correct and deviant, without making any noteworthy difference between them, but in fact he applies the same analyses and concepts to them all to explain their decay and ruin. We are thus right in the middle of objective political philosophy, nearest to modern social science. In fact, I still believe the paradoxical thesis that I presented in the article cited above, that it is in book 5, the apex of realist political thought, even cynical and Machiavellian, that Aristotle establishes most effectively the distinction between correct and deviant constitutions. To show that, I will use the same example as in the essay, that of tyranny.

Faithful to his program, Aristotle in fact analyzes the causes of seditions that can lead a tyranny to fall and proposes remedies. Tyranny is a regime with diverse forms and, historically, some tyrants have been able to be enlightened despots. But in Aristotle's day, before they were replaced by absolute monarchs as we know, tyrants had a bad reputation and were almost unanimously considered harmful to their city. Tyranny remained, in Aristotle's day, a question sufficiently crucial that he needed to give it a brilliant and effective analysis. As we have seen already, although tyranny is included in the list of constitutions—deviant, but a constitution no less—it marks the threshold where a group of human beings leave politics. Because, in general, tyranny is not the first constitution established after the prepolitical condition (that of an association of villages, or a tribe), but it follows a constitution that, by its excesses, has already begun to abolish the *political* relationships between its citizens. A failure for a city and, consequently, a failure for the legislator, tyranny runs contrary to all political values: the tyrant rules his subjects in a *despotic* way, that is, he treats them like slaves, he fears virtue because virtuous citizens are dangerous to his power; he governs exclusively, or at least as much as possible, for his own benefit and the benefit of his clan. Thus, the effects of the functioning of a tyranny are the opposite of those of the functioning of a virtuous city, namely, that, if it lasts long enough, tyranny *degrades* the subjects of the tyrant, and indeed the tyrant himself.

Although tyranny is presented as the deviant counterpart of kingship, and thus can proceed from a kingship that has degenerated, in fact tyranny can issue from any regime, even though it is more likely to result directly from democracy or extreme oligarchy, because the essence of tyranny is that it is a mixture of the worst aspects of democracy and oligarchy. Conversely, tyranny can be changed into any regime whatever. Thus:

> But in point of fact a tyranny often changes into a tyranny, as that at Sicyon changed from the tyranny of Myron into that of Cleisthenes; into oligarchy, as the tyranny of Antileon did at Chalcis; into democracy, as that of Gelo's family did at Syracuse; into aristocracy, as at Carthage, and the tyranny of Charilaus in Lacedaemon. (5.12, 1316a29)

As always in Aristotle, it's that there are several kinds of tyrannies that are more or less distinct from that which we could consider as the "pure" variety. Thus in *Politics* 4.10 two sorts of tyrannies are distinguished that correspond to two sorts of kingship that were differentiated "in an earlier discussion" (1295a4)—which indeed seems to be found in 3.14–17, a new proof, even if incidental, that the normative and realist chunks that constitute the *Politics* are not without connection to each other, and that Aristotle intends that they be taken together—before he adds "the most typical form," which I called the "pure" variety. This plasticity of the concept, which is actualized in different situations that are "more or less tense" as Aristotle says in a different context,[9] seems sufficient to explain undeniable textual differences. Thus at 4.10, 1295a15, Aristotle says that the two kinds of tyranny correspond to the two kinds of kingship examined in book 3, exercised according to law and with the consent of the subjects, while at 3.14, 1285a27, he explicitly recognizes that tyrants govern people who do not consent.

It is easy to understand that tyranny runs many dangers and that a tyrant must take great, sometimes extraordinary, precautions to remain in power. That is why Aristotle devotes most of the long chapter 11 of *Politics* 5 to advice to tyrants on how to keep their power. But he makes a noteworthy division into two parts, because, Aristotle says, "tyrannies are preserved in two quite opposite ways" (5.11, 1313a34). The "traditional" way (1313a35), that is, the one that has been handed down from earlier tyrannies and even from barbarian monarchs,[10] consists of always becoming more and more tyrannical. On this occasion Aristotle demonstrates with extraordinary brilliance the tools of the tyrant: he needs to fight against everything that weaves among the citizens threads of virtuous friendship and mutual confidence, prevent all intellectual culture, keep everybody under observation—notably by penetrating family units, and for that end, the tyrant relies on women, who take power in the home, and slaves, who see in this the chance for a more relaxed discipline exercised toward them. But it is also necessary to overwhelm the people with taxes in order, by forcing the people to constant labor, to take away

---

9. Cf. 4.3, 1290a27, where we find these terms that are used about harmonies, and that Aristotle uses particularly in *Politics* 3.

10. Cf. 1313a36: "Many of these dispositions have been instituted, they say, by Periander of Corinth, but also many have been borrowed from the sort of power that is exercised among the Persians."

every means of conspiring against him or forming a militia. "Tyranny loves vice" (5.11, 1314a1)[11] and thus produces subjects who have at least these three characteristics: they are stingy, they mistrust each other, and they are incapable of the least initiative.

There we have a remarkable example of a constitution, if we're going to accept the idea that tyranny *is* a constitution, in which those in power, or rather he who is in power, increases tension. One may imagine, thinking about Aristotle's many assertions in very different domains, that this tension cannot continue to increase indefinitely, and that doubtless this first set of measures prescribed by Aristotle for saving a tyranny will end in failure. In any case, as he says in *Politics* 6, "the worse a constitution is, the more vigilance it takes to save it" (6.6, 1320b32). Is that one of the reasons why he needs another approach? It can't be the only reason. Nevertheless, in this part of *Politics* 5 Aristotle does indeed propose several bits of advice to tyrants to save their regime by increasing harshness.

The second way of saving tyrannies, "pretty much the opposite of the first" (5.11, 1314a31), ought, according to Aristotle, to occur to the mind of the tyrant if only he thinks about how tyrannies fall. Since that happens when they become more tyrannical, one must conclude that for tyranny "safety lies in becoming more kingly" (1314a35). There follow several pages that have hardly any equivalent in later political literature, in that they mix a cold analysis to the point of cynicism that leads to an ethical condemnation of tyranny, and at the same time advice whose Machiavellianism, as we will see, results in the triumph of virtue. The only thing, the text tells us, that the tyrant cannot give up is his power, which is characterized by Aristotle as the ability to govern just as well "with and without the consent of his subjects, for to give that up is to give up being a tyrant" (1314a36). But for the rest, it is necessary that the subjects have the impression that the actions of the tyrant are not motivated in the ways habitual for tyrants. Two examples: it is necessary to persuade his subjects that his excessive expenses are done for the benefit of all, for example to embellish the city; when he wants to rape a boy or girl, he needs to proclaim that his intentions are serious, and that he is motivated by love, transforming the dangerous resentment of the young person's parents into pride. As we will see when we look at Aristotle's analysis of seditions, the sexual conduct of the tyrant is a subject of extreme political importance.

---

11. The text is corrupt, but the meaning is clear.

But the cardinal political advice that Aristotle gives to the tyrant, and in which we recognize the basis of his analysis of the sociopolitical reality of the city, is to bring it about somehow that in the struggle between the two classes, those of modest means and those who are well-off, each believes that the tyrant helps them against the other. In at least one of the two cases, when the tyrant addresses prosperous people, he's going to be lying, because tyranny always keeps something of the situation that brought it into being, namely, that the tyrant, coming from the people, justifies his power by pretending to defend the people against the wealthy. It is interesting to note that from this angle, kingship and tyranny arise from opposite sources:

> Kingship was in fact established to serve the better classes against the people, and a king is chosen among the notables because of his superiority in virtue, or in the actions to which virtue has inspired him, or the superiority of his ancestry in these domains; the tyrant, in contrast, comes from the people and the many in opposition to the notables, so that the people not suffer by their actions. (5.10, 1310b9)[12]

But the virtuous government by the king purifies its power from this unilateral origin that may be called "oligarchical." Thus, Aristotle writes a little later:

> The idea of a king is to be a protector of the rich against unjust treatment, of the people against insult and oppression. Whereas the tyrant, as has often been repeated, has no regard to any public interest, except as conducive to his private ends. (5.10, 1310b40)

To be perceived as a king or as a head of a family rather than as a tyrant (1315b1) thus provides a more stable power. For us it is crucial to understand the perspective from which Aristotle gives this sort of advice to the tyrant. And we rediscover the separation between the normative

---

12. Perhaps this does not work for all tyrannies, and indeed the next sentence clarifies that "almost all tyrants have been demagogues who gained the confidence of the people by working against the notables."

and realist dimensions. Unquestionably the good legislator is the one who proves to be able to give the most effective advice for the conservation of constitutions, and the best philosopher is the one who will furnish him the most precise analyses on which the legislator will base his advice. From this point of view, this chapter of Aristotle's work is a flowering example of political science both in the Aristotelian and the modern sense. But the last lines of *Politics* 5.11 are a game-changer in that they restore the primacy of ethics over Machiavellianism, which is in any case undeniable, in the Aristotelian analysis. If in fact the tyrant "plays king," no matter how hypocritical this imitation might be, it will have two effects. Aristotle says so in a sentence in which we must weigh each word:

> These actions necessarily make the power of the tyrant not only better and more desirable by the fact that he will rule better people whose spirits are not crushed, and who do not hate and fear him, and they make his rule more durable; the more that the tyrant will be thus in his character, well disposed toward virtue, being half-honest, he will not be bad but half-bad. (5.11, 1315b4)[13]

In the same vein, we have seen other examples given by Aristotle of vice working on behalf of virtue, for example deception for the sake of the good. One example, proposed in a chapter of *Politics* 4 already cited, provides a useful completion of this example of the tyrant. Aristotle advises the magistrates, or the legislator, of oligarchies to require the wealthy to possess heavy armament and to engage in military training (4.13, 1297a29). The primary motivation is, obviously, so they would be ready to defend the oligarchy against the claims of the party of the people. Thus, it is a matter of reinforcing an arbitrary power and consolidating a deviant constitution. But can one not hope, although Aristotle does not say so in this passage, that this would make the wealthy less bad, for example, by developing in them manly qualities like courage? Thus, bad reasons will make the constitution tend toward aristocracy, which strongly approves of warlike virtue.

---

13. We should note that Aristotle recommends also to oligarchs and to democrats to dissemble by acting as if they love the people, in the first case, and the well-off, in the second; cf. 5.9, 1310a2ff.

Here we are again confronted with Aristotle's irrepressible ethical optimism. By dint of imitating virtue, one improves oneself, because, basically, it is in and by virtue that we actualize our nature. But the means for that amelioration is notable, since it is because the tyrant, for example, engages in relationships with people who are no longer slaves, or who are slaves to a lesser degree, that he is pushed toward virtue.

CHAPTER 7

The Theoretical Tools of the Legislator

Having considered the means that the legislator can put in place to establish as much as possible an excellent constitution, and the situations in which he may intervene, we must study, as we said, the theoretical tools that the legislator will borrow from the political philosopher. It is not too surprising that we find a list of the theoretical tasks of the legislator in the introduction to the realist part of the *Politics*, that is, at the beginning of book 4. Once chapter 1 has settled the goal of the legislator, that is, to establish an excellent constitution, the short chapter 2 shows itself to be of great methodological importance. First, because, at the same time as it proposes to study deviant constitutions, it reaffirms a "strong" ethical perspective, with, perhaps, a bit of irony against Plato, who is not named, but accused of claiming that all constitutions are sometimes correct and sometimes vicious. Aristotle reaffirms that all deviant constitutions are bad, and oligarchy, for example, cannot be called "better" than tyranny, but only "less bad." Then he gives a list of studies to be undertaken. These studies will provide the legislator with a certain store of elements of *knowledge*, which I am calling "theoretical tools." These elements of knowledge are three, and may be divided into two great sets. The first turns on the notion of *diversity*, and the second on that of *sedition*. In fact, the legislator needs first to know "how many kinds of constitution there are" (4.2, 1289b12), and once having grasped this constitutional diversity, he should be able to determine which constitution is suitable for which city, both absolutely and relatively: which is the best for the city in question, which is next best, and so on. Aristotle says: which is "aristocratic" at 1289b16, a word that here should be taken in its etymological sense.[1] Next, the legislator needs to know how to establish excellent constitutions, and the answer to this question may be found in the study of the means employed by the legislator, studied above. Finally, he will have to "ascertain the modes of corruption and safety of constitutions" (1289b23).

The Diversity of Constitutions

I wonder why Aristotle's study of the diversity of constitutions has not attracted more attention of commentators. Have they been too stunned by an intellectual construction that is indeed stunning? Aristotle stresses the problem of diversity of constitutions continually and insistently, almost to the point of obsession. He approaches this question in several ways and from several directions. These approaches are very different, but they complement each other more than they conflict with each other, and they represent, I believe, the stages of a doctrine that, as it develops, furnishes the legislator with more or less sophisticated means in such a way that the later stages neither negate nor render useless the earlier ones. Although the question of constitutional diversity is at issue throughout the *Politics*, with the exception of book 1, one may grasp this development by going through book 4.[2]

In *Politics* 4.2, Aristotle recalls the "canonical" list of various constitutions that he had adopted "in our first study," probably referring to 3.7. Additional proof, as if that were needed, that Aristotle did not think

---

1. As I have indicated above, Aristotle, doubtless relying on this etymological sense, comes to call "aristocratic" a fairly large number of regimes that he thinks are good. Here is a passage on this issue, noted earlier and taken up again here: "There are some cities that differ from oligarchies and also differ from what is called polity; these may be called aristocracies, seeing that in these constitutions magistrates are chosen not only from among the wealthy, but also among the best. Such a constitution differs from the other two and is called aristocratic. . . . Where the constitution takes account of wealth, virtue, and the people, as at Carthage, it is aristocratic, and even those that take account of only two of these elements, virtue and the people, like the Lacedaemonians, one has a combination of democracy and virtue" (*Pol.* 4.7, 1293b7). This passage has been partially cited above.

2. For the question of the diversity of constitutions I follow very closely an essay that I published in a festschrift for Enrico Berti, "Parties de la cite, parties de la constitution," in *Aristotle: Metaphysics and Practical Philosophy. Essays in Honour of Enrico Berti*, ed. C. Natali (Louvain-la-Neuve: Peeters, 2011), 177–200.

that the normative and realist sides of his political work were separate entities. Constitutional diversity, a fact of life for the Greeks, as I said earlier, was an important theme of ancient political speculation, and I have cited Herodotus and Plato for examples. In manipulating a bit the lists he had received from the tradition,[3] Aristotle derived from them a list of six constitutions, three correct (kingship, aristocracy, and polity, the last added by Aristotle) and three deviant (tyranny, oligarchy, and democracy), a list that he will make more precise by distinguishing several sorts of each of these constitutions, but that he never gives up. We have seen that the *Nicomachean Ethics* is aware of this division, but that the terminology that we find there is slightly different than that of the *Politics*, since the polity is called "timocracy," a term doubtless borrowed from Plato.

In a justly famous passage of *Politics* 4.4, to which I have already alluded, Aristotle, after having said that this list of six constitutions is insufficient, proposes a method for determining the number of constitutions, which he compares to a method permitting grasping the diversity of animal species. It is noteworthy that there is no trace of this method elsewhere, not in Aristotle, notably not even in his very extensive zoological corpus, nor in any other ancient author. But, and this is no less important, this method shares the "spirit" of Aristotle's biological research, which is a moriological,[4] in that it means to reconstruct living things on the basis of a schema that would be the most unique possible. It is a matter, in the *Politics* passage, concerning animals, to determine the different kinds of each of their "necessary parts," specifically digestive, sensory, and motive parts, the number of animal species then being equal to those of the combinations of these parts. And Aristotle concludes: "It's the same for the constitutions about which we have been talking. For cities too are composed not of one single part but of several, as we have often said" (4.4, 1290b37).

This almost inexhaustible text, which condenses the two different approaches to constitutional diversity that we will find in book 4, sets in motion a combinational method that is developed over the last three chapters, and an approach to diversity of constitutions as dependent on the diversity of *the parts of the city*. More precisely, we will see that book 4 moves from an approach that we can call sociological, which relies on

---

3. On this point, see the work, already cited, by Bordes, *Politeia dans la pensée grecque jusqu'à Aristote*.
4. "Moriology" is a study concerning "parts" (*moria*). I introduced this term in 1982 apropos Aristotle's zoology in *La Classification des animaux chez Aristote*.

the diversity of the *parts of the city*, to a purely formal approach, which rests on a combination of *the parts of the constitution*.

Thus, we will interest ourselves first in the parts of the city. At the beginning of *Politics* 4.3, Aristotle writes:

> The reason why there are many forms of constitution is that every city contains many parts. In the first place we see that all cities are made up of families, and in the multitude of citizens there must be some rich and some poor, and some in the middle condition. (1289b27)

This is not a matter of the same division carried out in two steps, but of two divisions with different logical structures, each one being complete in itself. The first divides the city into prepolitical *societies*, and Aristotle doubtless could have cited others besides the family (e.g., religious associations, phratries, etc.), but the family is the one that is everywhere present. The second is social. Each of these divisions applies also to the other, since there are wealthy, poor, and middle-class families, and rich, poor, and middle-class persons do belong to families. It is above all the second division that is going to interest Aristotle most. Thus, he says at 4.11, 1295b1: "There are three parts within any city: the people who are well-off, the people who have very little, and the people between them."[5] The first division of the city into social groups like the family, on the other hand, is of no use in the examination of the diversity of constitutions, except in a very indirect way, as, for example, when one says that kingship is something like a family.

But one must first be clear about the very idea of a *part* of the city, which Aristotle does by way of a distinction that is typical of him. A little after the comparison between animals and constitutions, we read:

> In the *Republic*, Socrates says that a city is made up of four sorts of people who are absolutely necessary; these are a weaver, a farmer, a shoemaker, and a builder; afterward, finding that these are not enough, he adds a smith, and again a herdsman, to look after the necessary animals; then a merchant, and then a retail trader. All these together form the complement of the

---

5. If one takes account of their respective contexts, this passage is in fact compatible with 6.3, 1318a30: "The city is composed of two parts, rich and poor."

first city, as if the city were established merely to supply the necessities of life, rather than for the sake of the good, or stood equally in need of shoemakers and of farmers. . . . It is necessary to accept as parts of cities, before those that contribute to necessary utility, the military part, and that which hands down justice juridically, and the deliberative. (4.4, 1291a11)

This distinction between the conditions necessary for the existence of the city and the parts, properly speaking, of the city carries the trademark of a specifically *political* thinker. A city cannot exist without slaves, artisans, marriages, and so forth (cf. 3.9, 1280b3, already cited), nor without "food, a territorial expanse, or other things of this sort" (7.8, 1328a27). On the other hand, it is those who have access to political power who form the parts of the city, properly speaking, that is, groups by means of which the citizens exercise their power. When a tyranny reduces the citizens to the status of slaves, that means that they are no longer "parts" of the city, properly speaking, but they become merely necessary conditions. Here we have a reaffirmation of the fact that the city exists at its proper level as a supreme society under which all other relationships are arranged, and it does not exist simply "to live."[6]

We may make two remarks at this point. First, this sort of analysis of the Platonic position is unfair to Plato in that it suggests that Plato puts all the functions of the city on the same level. But most of the *Statesman* is devoted to the distinction between "the royal art," which alone deserves the name of "political,"[7] and the auxiliary arts, which the Stranger of

---

6. Several interesting passages could be cited here. Thus at 4.3, 1289b40: "Besides differences in accord with wealth, there are differences in accord with birth, with virtue, and with whatever else that we characterized as part of the city in our treatise on aristocracy. We distinguished there the number of parts necessary for each city. Of these parts, sometimes all, sometimes a smaller or larger number, have a share in the political power." It is difficult to decide to which "treatise on aristocracy" Aristotle here alludes, but I think, as does Newman, that it could be a reference to 3.12, 1283a14ff. Note that "political power" here translates *politeia*. *Politics* 6.8, the last chapter of that book, is devoted entirely to this distinction between indispensable parts and political parts in a city.

7. Cf. 305e: "The science that controls all of these, and the laws, and cares for every aspect of things in the city, weaving everything together in the most correct way—this, embracing its capacity with the appellation of belonging to the whole, we would it seems, most appropriately call political (πολιτικήν)."

the dialogue calls "sciences of the servant" (διάκονος). Among all these arts, some are more worthy than others: at 305b, Plato seems to say that the "power" (δύναμις, which also means "function") of the judges is the highest form of these auxiliary arts, above even the function of priests and of warfare. But all these functions remain in the antechamber of politics. The great work of politics, which it alone can accomplish, is to select the individuals worthy of being citizens of the well-governed city, by eliminating those who are unworthy (309a), and to mix well their characteristics, which are often opposed to each other, and notably to *weave* together the energy of courage and the moderation of temperance. We can see the affinities that exist between this Platonic hierarchy *of sciences* and Aristotle's *political* analysis. But we also grasp the profound difference that separates the Platonic opposition between a supreme science whose goal is to *establish* a perfect city by furnishing it with its citizens and the auxiliary sciences, on the one hand, and on the other hand, the Aristotelian distinction between that which is properly political and that which is not. For Aristotle, the political power may well be bad, because in bad hands, but it nevertheless remains the political power.

Furthermore, a second remark, this distinction between the political and the necessary, which we will find again in another form farther on, should not have seemed as surprising as we might think among the Greeks of Aristotle's time. In a brilliant book, cited above, Paulin Ismard[8] shows very convincingly, by taking many examples in numerous cities over a rather long period of time, but keeping, like all of us, classical Athens principally in view, that the functions that we would call technical or technocratic were carefully kept out of the political arena. These functions, for example those concerning public order, fiscal administration, currency control, but also the maintenance of the archives of the city, particularly a catalog of the laws, an absolutely crucial activity, were not only indispensable to the city, but conferring on those who did these things real power over the citizenry. Often, and possibly even usually, these tasks, which could not be carried out by citizens because they would have called into question their civic status, were left to public slaves. Ismard's book shows that many public slaves acquired an important social position, in any case very different from that of other slaves, even though they were surely reminded from time to time of their servile condition. Ultimately it is Plato who, by distinguishing less carefully than Aristotle the duties

---

8. Ismard, *La démocratie contre les experts. Les esclaves publics en Grèce ancienne*.

that belong to political power (*archē*) from those that belong to administration (*hyperēsia*), finds himself, if one may say so, in violation of the fundamental rules of the self-consciousness of the city.

But it would be too easy to oppose a sociological point of view, which makes shoemakers and sailors necessary parts of the city, with a political point of view, which recognizes as a part of the city only an individual or group that shares in political power. In fact, political power is usually monopolized, or conferred, according to sociological criteria. Thus, the multiplicity of viewpoints according to which power can be distributed, the list of which can become rather motley. We quote again this passage:

> Besides differences in accord with wealth, there are differences in accord with birth, with virtue and with whatever else that we characterized as part of the city in our treatise on aristocracy. We distinguished there the number of parts necessary for each city. (4.3, 1289b40)

We should note that in this passage the word "necessary" does not have the same meaning as it had in the passage cited just before, since this word is not opposed to "political," but there is here a difference in usage that is not surprising in Aristotle. In fact, it is Aristotle himself who explicitly formulates the politicization of sociological differences:

> Clearly in the political sphere it is reasonable to claim power . . . on the basis of what the city is made of. . . . It is thus reasonable that the well-born, the free, and the wealthy, dispute over honors. (3.12, 1283a10–16)

Hence a first sort of approach to the plurality of constitutions: one must see which social group, or possibly which individual, governs the city, and then one will know what its constitution is, for "the constitution is the government (πολίτευμα)" (3.6, 1278b11).[9] "It is therefore necessary that there be as many constitutions as there are organizations of magistracies according to the superiority and variety of the parts of the city" (4.3, 1290a11).

But by this procedure one hardly advances farther than the original division into six constitutions: when a minority of virtuous people is in

---

9. Cf. 3.7, 1279a25: "Constitution and government mean the same thing."

power, one has an aristocracy; when it's a minority of wealthy people, it's an oligarchy, and so on. But this method of division includes within itself the principle of its own development:

> That there are several constitutions, and why, has already been explained. We now should say that there are several kinds of democracies and oligarchies: that obviously results from what we have said. For there are several kinds of common people and several kinds of what we call notables. (4.4, 1291b14)[10]

From this last division, Aristotle distinguishes several sorts of democracies from 4.4, 1291b31, to the end of the chapter, and several sorts of oligarchies in chapter 5.

Before seeing more concretely the constitutional taxonomy developed by Aristotle, we must note this remarkable textual fact, that at 4.6, that is to say in the same book, Aristotle again gives lists of different kinds of democracies and different kinds of oligarchies, leaving a distinct impression of déjà-vu. We will see that we should not conclude from that that we are faced with two independent texts placed end-to-end by an editor, who would have been, in this case, really silly. Before proposing an explanation of this parallelism, it will be useful to consider an example in some detail. One may take the case of the two lists of democracies:[11]

> I.1: The "first democracy," based primarily on equality, in which rich and poor "all share basically in the same way political power" (4.4, 1291b36). This species of democracy does not have an equivalent in the second list. Nevertheless, it is indeed a species on its own, since at 1291b32 Aristotle explains, "thus it is a species of democracy," before going on to the next. I have already given a long citation of this passage. In fact, this species is outside the list because it does not take account of something that marked the theoretical advance of this new examination of the diversity of constitutions, namely, that it

---

10. I am not too sure what to make of the repetition of this formula, already used at 1290b21. Newman (vol. 4, 162) concludes that the passage included between the two formulas is an addition. That guess is at least hazardous.

11. I use the following symbolism: I.1 means the first species on list I, II.1 means the first species on list II, and so on.

is necessary to distinguish several kinds of people. In fact, it gives a "basic" description of what democracy is,[12] and we have seen that this description makes us think readily of a polity. The four subsequent species, in contrast, take clear account of this distinction, and each has a species that corresponds to it in the list in chapter 6. We should note, besides, that the order of exposition of the two lists is the same.

I.2: Access to magistracies is determined by a property qualification, but it is low.

II.1: The farmers and the moderately well-off of the people are sovereign. The citizens do not have the leisure to go often to assemblies, this is why they favor the rule of law. This constitution and that of I.2 are theoretically oligarchical, because participation in power depends on a property qualification, but they are in fact democratic because the property qualification is low.

I.3: Everyone indisputably a citizen participates in power but under the rule of law.

II.2: All those of unquestioned birth—one immediately understands that that means "indisputably a citizen" in chapter 4—can participate in power under the rule of law. But among them there are only some who participate in power, those who have the leisure. "That is why in a democracy of that kind the laws govern, because the citizens do not have enough income" (1292b37).

I.4: All the citizens govern under the rule of law.

II.3: All the citizens govern, with the clarification that the citizens are freemen, under the rule of law, but not all participate

---

12. That is a reason for not suppressing one of the appearances of the word "principally" (μάλιστα) in the text, which it in fact repeats: "For if liberty and equality, as is thought by some, are principally to be found in a democracy, it will be principally if everyone shares principally in the same way in political power" (1291b34).

in power for the reason, as in the preceding case, that some lack leisure because of their poverty.

I.5: The same characteristics as in the preceding cases, except that it is the mass and not the law that governs.

II.4: This is the last form that appears when cities have become larger and richer. The mass is sovereign and not the law, because the less prosperous people, who are paid to attend assemblies, have the leisure to be involved in politics, in contrast to the wealthy, who no longer are involved in anything other than their private interests.

Thus, we see that the difference between the two lists is that the second proposes *causes* for which the different species of democracy are what they are. We thus have a more advanced version of the method, which consists of thinking about the diversity of constitutions via the diversity of the parts of the city seen according to their social and political characteristics. In the article that inspired these lines I noted that this moriological logic was pursued yet a bit farther in a very original analysis that Aristotle presents in book 4.12, a passage that I used above from another point of view: "Every city is composed of a quality and a quantity. By 'quality' I mean freedom, wealth, education, illustrious birth, and by 'quantity' I mean the numerical predominance" (1296b17).

He goes on to explain that when the quantity and quality do not belong to the same part of the city and that when, for example, "people of modest means are more numerous than the wealthy, without however their quantitative superiority overwhelming their qualitative inferiority" (1296b22), there is an oligarchy, and there is a democracy if the numerical superiority overbalances the qualitative inferiority. Aristotle seems to suggest that one could construct a taxonomy by playing with the variation of these two factors, quality and quantity. But he does not do that, nor does he explain, as we have seen, how he means to make realities of this sort commensurable.

With these two parallel lists in book 4, the second being etiological, Aristotle affords the legislator an approach that is extremely precise, and thus extremely efficacious, to constitutional diversity. But it's a matter of a refined form of the general description that he had previously proposed, the one that distinguishes three correct forms and three corresponding deviant forms of constitutions. Even if, for reasons that were given previously, at this point of his exposition Aristotle is interested only in deviant constitutions, and among those, chiefly in democracy and oligarchy, the distinction between correct and deviant constitutions clearly remains in the background of this new method of division. That appears clearly in the very order of exposition of the sorts of constitutions. If we take, this time, the example of oligarchy, we see, in 4.6, that Aristotle offers a scale of forms of oligarchy from the least oligarchical to more "strict,"[13] to finish at an extreme form. We have here not only an implicit value judgment, because it's a matter of a list that goes from better toward worse, but also a message passed along to the legislator, who needs to take account of the possibility of deterioration. There is, in fact, as was shown above, a sense of the history of deviant constitutions that pushes them toward more and more deviant, and finally extreme, forms. This course of history does not translate into a necessary series of events, because many factors are opposed to such a necessity, both exterior events, and the resistance of the dominated, as we have seen.

If we recall that up to and including *Politics* 4.13, Aristotle examines all the other constitutions (with the exception of kingship, the various species of which were studied in 3.14–17),[14] and that this book 3 includes remarkable praise for the domination of the "middle class" in chapter 11, we see that the legislator does not lack weapons when facing the massive reality of constitutional diversity. In fact, knowing what sort of democracy or oligarchy that one is dealing with is a necessary prerequisite for any attempt at reformation. Nevertheless, this is not Aristotle's last word on the question of the diversity of constitutions.

In 4.14, Aristotle accomplishes a theoretical leap of incredible daring. He thinks it is enough to say that he is adopting a new point of view, which is really a euphemism: "Let us speak anew about each of them separately in order, taking the starting point that is convenient" (1297b35). The old method that Aristotle is setting apart here is that

---

13. Cf. 1293a26: "When this power is intensified by a further diminution of their numbers and the increase of their property"; "is intensified" translates ἐπιτείνωσι, literally, "is tightened." We have encountered this image, and we will see it again below.

14. At 4.2, 1289a34, Aristotle doubtless refers back to book 3: "We have determined previously how aristocracy and kingship differ from each other, and in what cases one should favor kingship." Similarly, at 4.10, 1295a4: "We have defined kingship in a previous discussion."

which consists of approaching constitutional diversity by taking account of the plurality of the parts of the city; what is new here is an entirely combinatory approach to constitutional diversity. Thus, we have moved, as we said before, from grasping the diversity of the parts of the city to grasping the diversity of the parts of the constitution. Why does Aristotle, in the very midst of this *Politics* book 4, go from one method to another? One may think that in his work of forging the theoretical tools that the philosopher ought to furnish to the legislator, Aristotle is of the opinion that the second method is more effective than the first. This new approach fills the last three chapters of book 4. It is quite astonishing that many readers of the *Politics* have been unwilling to grasp the theoretical audacity of these chapters. Most readers wonder about the reason for this strange construction, and suggest answers no less strange to this question; I will give at least one example below. In the reading that I propose, the reason is clear enough, since we will see that this new kind of approach to constitutional diversity gives the legislator a flexibility both remarkable and unequaled in his evaluation of the constitution that he has to amend and in the legislative changes that he needs to introduce to bring this about. From the beginning of this part of book 4, Aristotle in any case announces his practical goal: concerning the parts that this method will allow us to distinguish in each constitution, "the good legislator must consider what is advantageous for each constitution. When these parts do well, necessarily the constitution does well" (4.14, 1297b37, partially cited earlier). "Each constitution," that is, the correct constitutions, but also, and doubtless above all, the deviant constitutions. The reference to correctness has disappeared.

Starting at *Politics* 4.14, then, Aristotle proposes a completely political analysis of constitutional diversity, without any sociological content. This construction is based on a purely functional definition of "constitution." Here is the entire passage that we have just mentioned:

> Every constitution has three parts for which the good legislator must consider what is advantageous for each constitution. When these parts do well, necessarily the constitution does well, and constitutions differ from each other according to the specific differences of each of these parts. Of these three parts, one deliberates on common matters, the second concerns the magistracies (namely, which one needs to have, over what they need to be sovereign, and in what way one needs to choose

these officials), the third is that which renders justice. (1297b37)

A constitution, we have seen, is the political organization of a city, but it is also the system of laws of that city, and it is in a way the soul of that city: all these definitions are correct. But here they are superseded by this new approach that makes of a constitution an organism in which three systems function and interact, the legislative, executive, and judiciary, to use modern (and somewhat inadequate) terminology.

Let us look at some aspects of the analysis of the deliberative part, the first considered by Aristotle (chapter 14). In every constitution, the deliberative part concerns itself with questions like war and peace, alliances, laws, important punishments such as execution, exile, or confiscation of goods, appointment of magistrates, auditing accounts. Turning his back to any empirical procedure, which would start from the consideration of actual constitutions, Aristotle gives himself the means to construct a priori all possible forms of the deliberative part by positing a list that he represents as exhaustive:

It is necessary either that all these decisions be assigned to all the citizens, or all of the decisions to some people (for example, to one person or several), or some to some individuals, other decisions to others, or some to everyone and others to specific individuals. (1298a7)

Possibly the inanity, even silliness, of the critiques aimed at this procedure by modern interpreters will help to gain an understanding of its nature. One example: it has been asked how the Athenian practice of having the same people deliberate and judge can fit into Aristotle's schema. So that would be missing from the "exact description"[15] that we expect from him. But demanding of him that he describe groups of people is to understand nothing of Aristotle's position, since he means to define the *functions* characterized apart from any sociological or historical reference. One must be blind not to see that in these three chapters Aristotle does everything except "describe." To deliberate and decide can very well be *described*, in a particular constitution that actually exists, as being two roles of the same people, but nevertheless they remain two politically

---

15. Richard Robinson, *Aristotle's Politics Books III and IV* (Oxford: Clarendon Press, 1962), 116.

different *functions*, and their difference, Aristotle says several times, is essential for legislation.

Let us look at what may be called the first "case" in the table concerning the deliberative part: "everyone decides everything." This possibility is "characteristic of popular regimes"; Aristotle uses the word *dēmotikos* (δημοτικός, 1298a10), a term more appropriate than the word "democratic," because in this combinatory analysis, there is no longer a place for a distinction between correct and deviant constitutions, and this form of deliberation applies just as well to democracies as to polities.[16] This popular form has several "modes" (τρόποι), depending on how we understand the word "all." The meaning of this word can in fact vary along two axes: either all the citizens gathered together decide everything, or everyone takes turns in the role of deciding everything; in the same way, everyone may decide certain matters, other matters being decided by people chosen by everyone, either by election or by drawing lots. Several modalities can be distinguished according to the role that one assigns to these elected or random magistrates. Obviously, one can, like the chemists filling out the Mendeleyev table of "real" elements one by one as their discoveries proceeded, find that such and such a combination describing a particular regime that actually exists, and Aristotle does not omit noting that. Thus, the mode in which the assembled citizens decide everything, leaving to the magistrates only the role of putting those decisions into effect, "is precisely the actual mode of administration of extreme democracy" (4.14, 1298a31), which was operative in the Athens of his time.

The entire architecture of the traditional distinction between constitutions, which Aristotle had developed and refined in the preceding chapters of book 4, is short-circuited by a system that allows (re)constructing the constitutional world in a much more precise way. That can be seen, among other things, in the way that Aristotle uses and subverts the habitual ways of speaking. Starting at 1298a33, after the popular modes, he turns to the oligarchical modes. This word needs to be understood here in its etymological sense of "minority regimes," since Aristotle calls some of these modes "aristocratic," and some are called polities, while traditionally the polity is a popular regime (cf. 1298b10). The principle here is: "some decide everything." Let us return to the distinction, noted above, between deliberating and deciding. In some minority regimes ("oligarchies"), the

---

16. Nevertheless, Aristotle uses the adjective "democratic" in the transition sentence at 1298a34, but he carefully avoids saying that he has given a list of kinds of democracy.

whole people can very well deliberate about important matters, "on war, peace, and auditing accounts" (1298b6), but it would be a restricted panel of magistrates who decide. If these magistrates are elected or chosen by lot from a list of elected citizens, the constitution leans toward aristocracy; if some of the magistrates are chosen by lot from among the citizens, the constitution has a popular bent and tends toward polity. That is how, where Aristotle is in his analysis, aristocracy and polity become kinds of oligarchies . . .

But one of the most remarkable examples of this surpassing of the traditional account is to be found at the very end of book 4 (16, 1301a10–15). Recapitulating "all the possible modes under which courts can exist," Aristotle gives three: in the first, the judges are chosen from among all the citizens, and judge everything, corresponding to popular regimes; in the second, certain ones judge everything, which is characteristic of minority regimes. For the third mode, the text is not clear. It has been interpreted in at least two ways: (i) certain judges are chosen, either by election or by lot, from among all the citizens, others are chosen from among a limited list; (ii) certain trials are judged by everyone, others by certain individuals. In fact, the text is elliptical, as is often the case in Aristotle, and one must understand: "among all the courts, certain courts judge certain cases with judges taken from everyone, other courts judge other cases with judges selected from a limited list."[17] But Aristotle says that this last sort of arrangement results in "aristocratic and political" constitutions, the word "political" being justly understood by the commentators as signifying "characteristic of a polity." In the other direction, courts in which certain individuals judge everything are all oligarchical (1301a12). This cannot be properly integrated with the previous construction.

Aristotle writes at 4.14, 1298b11, that "thus the deliberative part is divided in this way in relation to the constitutions." It would be completely erroneous to understand that the division of constitutions makes intelligible the divisions of the deliberative part. On the contrary, it's the variations of the deliberative part as they are restored by the combinatory method of chapter 14 that allow us to understand why there are several species of constitutions. Then the diversity of constitutions is really *thought*, and the

---

17. The form in which "everyone judges" is divided thus: (i) everyone judges everything and all are elected; (ii) everyone judges everything and all are selected by lot; (iii) everyone judges everything, and some are elected and others chosen by lot; (iv) everyone judges only certain cases.

new combinatory method reduces the method prior to *Politics* 4.14–16 to a procedure that is, if not descriptive, at least empirical.

But obviously the legislator does not construct the table of all possible forms of constitutions just for the pleasure of an intellectual exercise. He needs to use it for improving constitutions, as Aristotle says at the beginning of chapter 14: "The good legislator needs to consider what is advantageous for each constitution" (1297b37). Thus, at the end of chapter 14 (from 1298b13 on), Aristotle returns to what is "advantageous" (συμφέρει, 1298b13) for the two major constitutions, democracy and oligarchy. To do that he repeats one of his recipes, which is to bring into participation in power in the city the most people possible by mixing wealthy and poor, "they will advise better if they all deliberate together, the people with the notables and the notables with the people" (1298b20, passage cited above). It is interesting to remark that concerning a measure that oligarchies often impose for their own safety, namely, to put a fine on the wealthy who refuse to participate in the deliberations of the courts, Aristotle recommends to democracies that they apply this rule in the case of the assembly, because democracies have an interest in including the wealthy in the political system. In the one case, it is necessary to enroll people who are members of the dominant party, in the other, those who are in the dominated party, in both cases, as it turns out, the wealthy . . . Aristotle also goes so far as to advise democracies to also impose a fine on the poor who do not want to participate in deliberations, while in his day popular regimes tended to remunerate the poor to attract them to attendance in the assembly.

But even when he rediscovers the political content that his combinatory method had emptied out, Aristotle is not in the place where he was before his "discovery" of this combinatory method. If it's for the sake of improving deliberation in the city, the legislator can now determine the exact point where he needs to modify the laws. Another possibility that the prior analysis of the diversity of constitutions did not provide: Aristotle prescribes the improvement of functioning of the *deliberative* part of extreme democracies by having them adopt a measure used by some oligarchies in their *judicial* part: "It is advantageous for a democracy . . . so that its deliberative body function better, to do as is done for the courts in oligarchies" (1298b13), namely, to impose a fine on those whom one wants to attend and who refuse to do so.

Chapter 15, dealing with magistracies, is for us even more important than the previous chapter. But the very idea of a magistracy needs to be clarified before Aristotle can proceed to the same sort of table construction that he had elaborated for the deliberative function. In fact, not every function is a magistracy, since priests, heralds, and ambassadors are not magistrates, even if some of them are elected. A magistracy is a function that has "the power of deliberating, deciding, and giving commands, especially the last" (4.15, 1299a26). That is, magistracies do not belong to the economic sphere, they do not make technical decisions, but they are *political* functions, and more precisely functions that exercise political power. We have seen that concerning the definition of "citizen" as holder of an "unlimited magistracy," and concerning the distinction between necessary and per se parts of the city. Then a serious difficulty is encountered, because magistracies cannot be defined in the abstract, as we could define in general the different ways of deliberating. Because two magistracies, even if it is determined that they are concerned with the same matters, will differ specifically if they are included in different constitutions. For example, it is not the same thing to be a member of the assembly in a city where that assembly is all-powerful and in a city where the assembly has almost no powers. There is a large difference between power functions and honor functions. It is so true that the constitution defines the form, the field, and the mode of exercise of a magistracy, that one might well ask how Aristotle can possibly succeed in applying to magistracies the purely formal approach that prevailed for deliberation. Don't we have, in the case of magistracies, the revenge of content over form?

Aristotle resolves this difficulty with a reversal as sudden as it is efficacious: "Enough of these matters. We must try to examine from the beginning appointments to magistracies" (4.15, 1300a8). So, we need to consider not the magistracies themselves as elements of diverse constitutions, but the manner of appointment (καταστάσεις) to magistracies. We're not going to try to give a detailed interpretation of this passage here; that would be very difficult, since the text is one of those that editors have corrected the most. We may consider the appointment to magistracies from three points of view: who appoints, who is appointed, and according to what modalities. The first two are divided in the same way (by/among all, by/among certain, certain by/among all, and others by/among certain), while the third is divided thus: by election, by lot, some by election, others by lot. This gives at least a dozen combinations, and a table could be constructed. As for chapter 16, it is devoted to the judicial part.

Thus the "old" distinction between constitutions is actually torn to pieces. We can see that at 4.15, 1300a41–b1, where Aristotle constructs a mode of appointment to magistracies that corresponds to a "polity with an aristocratic tendency," which must be distinguished from a "democratic polity." We have already seen that these monsters could also help Aristotle indicate the unstable state of constitutions already challenged by a death instinct, as when he speaks, in a passage cited above, of "oligarchical aristocracies and rather democratic polities" (*Pol.* 6.1, 1317a2). But here it is not yet a matter of the demise of constitutions, a question that is posed later in the *Politics*.

There is a task that Aristotle recognizes not only as possible, but in the case of the legislator, necessary, that of constructing all the possible constitutional forms by a coordination of the three tables. Thus, the legislator finds himself provided with a theoretical tool of unequaled precision. Let us quote again near the beginning of *Politics* book 6:

> Moreover, we ought to consider the various combinations of these modes themselves; for such combinations make the constitutions overlap each other, so that some aristocracies have an oligarchical character, and some polities incline to democracies. When I speak of the combinations that remain to be considered, and thus far have not been considered by us, I mean such as these: when the deliberative part of the government and the election of magistrates is constituted oligarchically, and the law courts aristocratically, or when the courts and the deliberative part of the city are oligarchical, and the election of magistrates aristocratic, or when in any other way not all the parts of the constitution put together share the orientation of the constitution. (1316b39–1317a10)

In fact, the demand for internal consistency in constitutions is a powerful means of safeguard for them.

I will satisfy myself by citing a final point about the understanding of the diversity of constitutions by this combinatorial method, a point that I have already mentioned in my article but on which I have since made hardly any progress. It is not at all surprising that in the list of the components of a constitution, as so to speak in any list given by Aristotle, one of the members dominates the others. That is the case with the deliberative part, which is called "sovereign" (4.14, 1299a2; 6.1, 1316b32). Doubtless one must understand "sovereign" as meaning "politically sovereign," in the sense that it is the deliberative body, the assembly of the people for example, which exerts real power in the city. The deliberative body is in fact the location par excellence of political power. But this preeminence of one part over the others reappears in another form. For when it is a matter of distinguishing between constitutions, it is the part that concerns magistracies that is the most important, because "a constitution is an organization of the magistracies in the city, the way in which they are shared, and what element is sovereign" (4.1, 1289a15; cf. 3.6, 1278b8; 4.3, 1290a7).

Furthermore, as we have seen, in the distinction that Aristotle makes between deliberation and decision, it is indeed decision that serves to characterize a regime, since if a minority decides, one is in an oligarchical regime, even if everyone deliberates. There is research to be done about the gap that Aristotle places between a properly political primacy and a primacy that one may call functional between cases of different constitutions.

Finally, we must note that no matter how revolutionary it may be, this method of understanding the diversity of constitutions in no way eliminates the procedures that Aristotle earlier put in operation. These methods do not offer the same precision or the same breadth as the method of 4.14–16, in terms of the pure grasp of differences, and from this strict point of view, the earlier methods are so outclassed that they have become useless. And perhaps it is for this reason that Aristotle did not earlier introduce his method of determining the differences by the method of combining quantity and quality, a method in question above. But what the method used in these earlier chapters of book 4 on democracy and oligarchy reveals, and what the combinational method cannot grasp, are the causes that bring it about that the varieties of these different constitutions are as they are. The legislator thus will make use of both methods according to the needs of the moment.

To Save the Constitutions

We have seen that Aristotle joins a positive approach to political change with a fundamental conservatism, if only because time is a necessary factor in improvement. Thus, we have shown that he would prefer to accommodate slightly defective legislative dispositions than to recommend changing them, which is never risk-free (cf. 2.8, 1269a14). For installing magistrates into an environment of permanent change takes away their authority (1269a18). The attributes of the legislator include preventing changes to the constitution and using changes and directing them when they are inevitable. In order to do that, he must get *knowledge of* the nature, varieties, and process of political change. Hence the second important theoretical tool that the philosopher puts at the disposal of the legislator: a theory of *stasis*, a word that means both "sedition" and "dissension." On this point too, we will see Aristotle going against the grain of ancient thought, with, among other consequences, a surmounting of the opposition between change and conservation.

The very word *stasis* presents us with several questions. Nicole Loraux, in a clear allusion to Freud, calls one of the sections of her work *The Divided City: On Memory and Forgetting in Ancient Athens*[18] "Stasis: A *Gegensinn*." Ten years earlier, in a very subtle article, she tried to see how the *Cratylus* dealt with the problem she poses here.[19] In 1910 Freud published a note, "The Antithetical Meanings of Primal Words," inspired by an 1884 work by Karl Abel, with the same name in German.[20] The gist of Abel's argument, generally taken to be fantasy by later linguists, rests on what he takes to be an accepted fact, that certain words in ancient Egyptian had opposite senses. Abel furnishes, among other things, several examples from other languages, including some from Latin, frequently cited: *sacer*, meaning both "holy" and "damned"; *altus*, meaning both "high" and "deep." Freud uses this theory for the interpretation of dreams. For him, dreams do not have the logical means of expressing negation, and thus borrow devious means for the purpose. Thus, an object may signify its opposite. But if a language as "archaic" as ancient Egyptian does that also, as a "scholar" like Abel has established, that proves the equally archaic character of dreams. Not Freud's greatest moment.

The word *stasis* could have been used by both Abel and Freud, since its semantic spectrum seems to be stretched between two extreme opposites. This is even true within the Aristotelian Corpus. On the one

---

18. Nicole Loraux, *La Cité divisée. L'oubli dans la mémoire d'Athènes* (Paris: Payot et Rivages, 1997); English translation by Corinne Pache and Jeff Fort, *The Divided City: On Memory and Forgetting in Ancient Athens* (Brooklyn: Zone Books, 2002). The section title is on 104 in the English version.

19. Nicole Loraux, "Cratyle à l'épreuve de *stasis*," *Revue de Philosophie Ancienne* 5, no. 1 (1987): 49–69.

20. Sigmund Freud, "Über der Gegensinn der Urworte. Referat über die gleichnamige Broschüre von Karl Abel 1884," in *SE* 11, 155–161. Abel's essay was published in *Sprachwissenschaftliche Abhandlungen* in 1884, 313–367. In the 1924 edition of his collected works Freud suppressed the subtitle.

side, *stasis*, which comes from the verb ἵστημι, marks the fact of standing straight, at a position, and means both stop and immobility, but also, on the other side, sedition and discord, the sense that it has very much more often in Aristotle. To resolve this question Nicole Loraux deploys all her linguistic ingenuity to be able to write: "Civil war is *stasis* inasmuch as the clash between two equal halves of the city erects (just like a *stēlē*) conflict in the *meson*."[21] Fortified with this obscure clarity Nicole Loraux ridicules Pierre Chantraine who, in his *Dictionnaire étymologique de la langue grecque*, writes for *stasis*: "stability, place, act of establishing, from whence sedition." She is quite wrong, and here's why.

In fact, the enigma of *stasis* is a mystery in plain sight, to quote someone who is hardly ever named anymore, for good reason.[22] The verb ἵστημι actually means, as a transitive verb, "to make to stand erect, to fix, to immobilize," and as an intransitive verb, "to stand up, to remain immobile."[23] One finds parallel senses of the noun *stasis*: "the fact of being immobile," "the act of standing up," and the result of these actions, notably "faction," which is a group of people who have stood up for or against a cause. Somewhat like the word *physis* understood as "growth" also designates the "nature" as a result of this growth, *stasis* as the movement of standing up leads to *stasis* as the situation for which one has stood up. What is particularly important for our reading of Aristotle's political texts is that in *stasis* it is not the movement that is revealed in a dominant way, but the word carries the affirmation of a *position*. That can have either of two aspects, either a position marking the end of a movement,[24] or a position taken in opposition to a given state. One therefore understands that in Aristotle the term *stasis* comes, often enough, to mean the "party" or "faction." So Chantraine was not wrong.

I am going to try to show that *stasis*, far from being a subsidiary concept that Aristotle has to clarify a bit because he needs to deal with the overthrow of constitutions, is in fact a cardinal idea of Aristotelian political philosophy, notably one that permits delimiting the political sphere. I claim that there is here, if not a hermeneutic revolution in our

---

21. Loraux, *The Divided City: On Memory and Forgetting in Ancient Athens*, 106.

22. Allusion to the rightist Maurice Barrès (1862–1923), who wrote a book entitled *Le Mystère en pleine lumière*, published in 1926 (trans. note).

23. The verb takes this sense fairly frequently in its middle form, ἵσταμαι.

24. Cf., for example, *Physics* 5.4, 228b6: εἴ τις κίνησις στάσει διαλαμβάνεται, "if a motion is interrupted by a *stasis*."

reading of Aristotle's political philosophy, at least a new orientation and, as we will see, one that is full of consequences. Among other things, it has an effect on the very definition of political space. But, as the definition of the space proper to politics is Aristotle's most characteristic act, one that distinguishes him from all other ancient thinkers, it is not so surprising that his conception of *stasis* differs profoundly from those of others.

Let's begin with the others. There is an opposition that is largely, or nearly unanimously, accepted by the Greeks between *stasis* and *polemos*, "sedition," and "war." According to that common position, *stasis* is an internal matter, while *polemos* is directed outward. Aristotle keeps the distinction, but does not draw the same consequences as others. We find it in numerous texts, but we can cite Plato, especially a passage in *Republic* 5, 470b–c, as very representative: the sort of conflict that is "proper" and "familial" (τὸ μὲν οἰκεῖον καὶ συγγενές) is *stasis*, while when the conflict concerns another, a stranger (τὸ δὲ ἀλλότριον καὶ ὀθνεῖον), it's *polemos*. Thus, war is, as Jean-Pierre Vernant says, absorbed into the civic sphere, because it is an essentially political act, from the fact that it opposes the city assembled as a whole to that which is external to it, whether that be other cities or barbarian tribes. With this difference, noted among others by Vernant in his preface to *Problèmes de la guerre en Grèce ancienne*,[25] that one did not make war in the same way against other Greeks as against barbarians. In fighting against Greeks there were rules of warfare, which one could disregard when fighting against barbarians. Starting from this distinction, Plato proposes a different version that reveals an underlying organicism in which the political organism in which one part is fighting against other parts is described as a sick organism. It is a fact that Plato describes political sedition as a sickness of the social body. From this perspective, there are actually several distinct levels of organicism. Greeks and barbarians do not really form one organism, so that fights between them cannot be considered as maladies. Between Greek cities things are more complex, and we will not go into that here.[26] Within a given city, in contrast, the organic metaphor is applied completely, and it is made stronger, "more tense" Aristotle would say, by the fact that Plato does not establish a specific difference between city and family.

---

25. Jean-Paul Vernant, ed., *Problèmes de la guerre en Grèce anciennes* (Paris, La Haye: Mouton, 1968).

26. I will just mention the passage in *Republic* 5, 471a, where Plato repeats that among Greeks it is *stasis* and not war, and that one must wage the conflict "as with people with whom one must reconcile" and thus avoid the sort of violence and destruction that would make reconciliation impossible.

We have seen that Nicole Loraux—and this is one of the most brilliant aspects of her *City Divided*—notes the alignment of Vernant and those who share his point of view whom she calls, as we know, "the anthropologists," on the very ideology of the Greek city. A critique like that makes of Loraux a kind of parricide, which must have been difficult for her, given her great debt to Vernant. By referring to the "egalitarian *polis* of consensus,"[27] Vernant therefore would have believed Plato, who goes on to explain that the Greeks and barbarians are strangers to each other, while the Greeks are "close and related" to each other. Thus, there is *polemos* with the barbarians and *stasis* between Greeks. Similarly, Aeschylus said that there ought not be *polemos* among "birds of the same plumage" (*Eum.* 866). But since the Greeks are *natural friends*, the *stasis* that arises among them is contrary to nature, it is an illness. It is a more serious illness when it occurs in the heart of the city, and even more serious in the midst of a family. We see therefore that the distinction between *polemos* and *stasis* serves *the* great mystification of Greek ideology, to which Plato has given the most sublime form, that which makes of the city a big family, while the city is precisely *not* a family and the set of Greek cities and peoples does not constitute a society of friends. That allows Plato to go very far in describing political discord as a revolt against one's parents, and the attempts to change the constitution as parricidal and fratricidal enterprises, especially when they resort to violence. Everyone knows, even Plato who is its most talented defender, that it is a mystification, and in any case when he tells the members of the republic that they are born of the earth and are thus brothers and sisters, Socrates recognizes that it is a lie (*Rep.* 3, 414b–c).

Aristotle rejects this Oedipal politics. And in Aristotle's critique of this Platonic position we rediscover the very foundation of Aristotle's position, expressed ever since the very first chapter of the *Politics*, which posits a specific difference between the powers of the magistrate, the father, the husband, and the master of slaves.

Aristotle's *Stasis*

To grasp well what *stasis* is for Aristotle, we must first resist two temptations that are, in a sense, the inverse of each other. First, that of making *stasis* a catchall idea, including all sorts of conflict. As often in Aristotle,

---

27. Loraux, *La Cité divisée. L'oubli dans la mémoire d'Athènes*, 28.

the fact that a term has taken on a "technical" sense does not prevent its use in other contexts, including those in the neighborhood of obviously technical uses. In fact, even if Aristotle has demonstrably distinguished a mostly "technical" and precise sense of the word *stasis*, a nontechnical sense nevertheless appears in several passages in the *Politics*, often because Aristotle is not speaking his own language or is not expressing himself in his own name. Thus, in the critique of Plato in *Politics* 2, for example at 2.6, 1265b12, when Aristotle writes that "poverty brings about *stasis* and delinquency," *stasis* can be translated here as "sedition," but he is not referring to political sedition in the precise sense of the term. At 4.11, 1296a8, the word doubtless has the sense of "faction." This sense seems to be recognized in the *Constitution of Athens* 11.2, where the word *stasis* without any doubt means "faction," in the expression, "the two *staseis* (στάσεις ἀμφοτέρας) had changed their opinion," the same at 15.1; at 13.4 it is a question of αἱ στάσεις τρεῖς, "the three parties." But one must handle the *Constitution of Athens* with care, and we have seen that from sedition to faction is not a great distance, provided that one avoid the error of seeing the word *stasis* essentially designating a movement. The bridges between the technical and nontechnical senses of *stasis* are not entirely collapsed.

Even in *Politics* 5, which is devoted to the analysis of seditions and, precisely, distinguishes its technical sense, the word can take a sense a bit out of line with its technical sense. Thus at 5.4, 1303b28, the word *stasis* refers to disagreements between "the chiefs and the powerful" without necessarily having in view a sedition. In any case it is not a matter of a complete sedition, because these people wanted to take power in the city without changing it; they didn't want to change the constitution or even reform its functioning in order to correct what they perceived as an injustice. Similarly, the verb στασιάζω means "to have disagreements," for example among the oligarchs at 5.6, 1305b16 and 18. At 5.6, 1306a38, it is said that at Heraclea and Thebes there were two similar affairs leading to condemnations for adultery "justly but in a partisan manner (στασι-αστικῶς)." Steven Skultety makes a big deal out of this στασιαστικῶς.[28] I concede to him that it means that the verdict went outside its normal juridical sphere, and I grant even more gladly that this shows that there is a difference between judgments and *staseis*. In fact one may understand

---

28. Steven Skultety, "Delimiting Aristotle's Conception of *Stasis* in the *Politics*," *Phronesis* 54 (2009): 346–370.

things in two ways: either this judgment, which is just because adultery is a crime punishable by law, is rendered στασιατικῶς because it serves to satisfy a faction of the oligarchs who want thus to humiliate one another (*stasis* then has the sense of "faction"), and that may be seen particularly in the disproportionate punishment that was applied, the pillory; or στασιαστικῶς means that the judgment was "seditious" in that it provoked a sedition, thus *stasis* in its technical sense. The Greek seems to me to favor the first reading, and the context the second.

We can call attention to a particularly interesting instance at 5.4, 1304a11ff., where Aristotle reports that concerning an inheritance, there was a *stasis* in connection with the two parties, that of Mnaseas and that of Euthycrates. Despite Aubonnet's interpretation, it was not a dissention between them, but a sedition that came about in relation to them. For once Aubonnet did not follow Newman, and he was wrong . . . This quarrel was somewhat special because it happened in Phocis, the province that includes Delphi. As it happened, it provoked a sacred war between cities.[29] But Aristotle adds immediately that "a marriage-quarrel was *also* the cause of a change in the constitution of Epidamnus" (1304a13): here there is a *stasis* in the proper sense of the word without the word being present, *stasis* and constitutional change being closely tied, as we will see. In the first case, we find the term *stasis* in its technical sense, but it takes an unusual turn in that it provokes a war and not a change in constitution; in the second case, we have a real *stasis*, but without the term being present in the text.

Next, the second temptation to be resisted is that of making *stasis* an insurrectional and violent form of political change, as Marcus Wheeler claimed in a rather odd article, where he tries notably to show that Aristotelian *stasis* is not Marxist class struggle.[30] Passages like that at 4.11, 1296a27, could lead us to that error: "*staseis* and fights arise between the people and the well-off." At the same time, when Skultety posits as his *definition* of *stasis* that it uses "the instruments of force or deceit,"[31] he

---

29. Possibly the Third Sacred War, 355–346. We don't know how it came about that a quarrel between families degenerated into a war that involved most of the Greek cities, and ended with the victory of Philip II of Macedon.

30. Marcus Wheeler, "Aristotle's Analysis of the Nature of Political Struggle," *American Journal of Philology* 72, no. 2 (1951): 145–161.

31. Skultety, "Delimiting Aristotle's Conception of *Stasis* in the *Politics*," 348.

cites no passage that says this, and it would be hard to do. To be sure, at 5.4, 1304b7, Aristotle says that "constitutions are changed by force or by deception," or a mixture of the two, but that is not a part of a definition, and I agree with Newman in thinking that this passage is not meant to say that these are the only ways of making this change happen. And that can be seen very well in an example offered in the same chapter: in Athens, "the reputation gained by the Council of the Areopagus during the Persian Wars" (1304a20) seemed to "tighten" the constitution in an oligarchic way, while the victory at Salamis strengthened the democracy, both Aristotelian examples of *stasis* (cf. the passage cited above, 2.12, 1274a13). But there was neither force nor deception in these cases. Nothing indicates then that *stasis* would necessarily be violent, even if no one can deny that violence sometimes, doubtless even often, accompanies *stasis*.

Let us try, then, to specify the "technical" sense of the word *stasis*, that is its proper and not metaphorical meaning. To delimit the *range*, the *field of application*, of *stasis* will help a lot. In Aristotle true *stasis* is confined to the city, and therefore there is no *stasis* between relatives or between friends. But more precisely, *stasis* seems to concern exclusively, at least when the word is used in its "technical" Aristotelian sense, the *constitutional* sphere. That means, notably that when the word *stasis* is used to describe a quarrel between rich and poor for access to wealth or honors, for example, that quarrel is not a *stasis* in the full sense unless it leads to an attempt to change the constitution or, at least, to take control of the constitution, as we will see below. The question of the relationships between *stasis* and constitutional change is more difficult than it appears at first glance. A fairly common position is to say that the category "change of constitution" is broader than that of *stasis*, because there are changes of constitution that can come about without *stasis*. Obviously, we can accept this distinction, which we will discuss again below, on the condition that we do not do it in the way that people like Wheeler do, who conceive, implicitly or not, of *stasis* as a violent factional enterprise and thus think that changes without *stasis* are peaceful changes. To see that more clearly, we can say something about the beginning of the first two chapters of *Politics* 5.

From the outset, in the first chapter, after a sentence that says that the subjects previously announced have been dealt with, a sentence that in fact belongs to the end of book 4, Aristotle announces the plan of his study. He says that it will be necessary to consider (i) the number and nature of the causes of constitutional change, (ii) what leads each sort of constitution to be destroyed, (iii) from which to which constitutions are the most frequent changes, (iv) what is the safeguard of constitutions both in general and of each sort individually, (v) how each constitution may best be preserved. As the arrangement of the text reveals, the distinction between "in general" and "individually" applies in the same way to the destruction and the preservation of constitutions.

At 5.1, 1301a25, where some editors mark the beginning of the second paragraph of the chapter, Aristotle returns to his often-expressed thesis, and reminds us that it has already been presented, according to which many constitutional forms are as they are because they embody a unilateral concept of justice.[32] Then comes *stasis*. Some citizens, because they do not benefit from the organization of powers set by the current constitution, "engage in sedition" (στασιάζουσιν, 1301a39). We may draw at least two implications from that. First, that a constitution based on a completely correct conception of justice would have no reason to change, since everyone would benefit from it. We will see once again, shortly, that things are more complex than that, and in fact, even correct constitutions need to worry about sedition. Second, another implication, there are just *staseis*; at 1301a39, Aristotle says that virtuous citizens could have very just reasons to provoke a *stasis*, even though they don't have the habit of doing that. At this point in the text, *stasis* is the only cause of constitutional change to be accounted for. And "the principles and sources" of every *stasis* are also provided; the differences of approach that concern justice.[33]

Aristotle shows that *stasis* is deployed in the constitutional domain, even when the constitution itself does not change. That's what *Politics* 5.1, 1301b6, says; it is generally badly translated. After having explained that seditions arise from the fact that a group of citizens think themselves deprived of advantages to which they think they have a right, Aristotle says: "That is why constitutional changes *also* (καί) (i.e., like *staseis*) occur in two ways." A translation like that, which seems quite natural from a grammatical point of view, allows one to take it that Aristotle claims that the division into two sorts of change that come from seditions is deduced from a division into two sorts of seditions themselves.[34] But nothing that comes before can support such a reading. It would be better to understand

---

32. Cf. 1301a36: "They all have something of the just in them, but speaking absolutely they are mistaken." We have already encountered this subtle and precious analysis.

33. I think that that is the significance of αὗται at 1301b5.

34. Among the many interpreters who understand this sentence in this way, we may cite Newman: "Hence the changes also [as well as the *staseis* that lead to them] come into being in two ways" (i.e., arise either from a *stasis* that seeks a complete change of constitution or from a *stasis* that does not) (4, 286).

Aristotle's reasoning this way: seditions occur because of the dissatisfaction of groups of citizens; changes that follow these seditions take two forms: one changes the constitution, the other preserves it; thus, it is the same for seditions. Thus, it is necessary to translate: "That is why the changes 'resulting from *stasis*' also occur, and they occur in two ways."

But beyond this hermeneutic hairsplitting, the important point that emerges from this passage is that the effect of *stasis* can be characterized by way of several dichotomies: the factional party can change the constitution, or control it as it is.[35] But the change can be generic, when, for example, an oligarchy becomes a democracy, or specific, and Aristotle then says that the constitution at the beginning and that which results from the *stasis* differ according to "the more and the less" (1301b13), which conforms to his description of specific difference in biology. As he says several times, there are several species of democracies and of oligarchies. This specific modification can itself take two forms: in tightening or loosening existent institutions, that is, by hardening or relaxing their democratic or oligarchical character;[36] by changing their parts by establishing or suppressing a magistracy, like Lysander who, at Sparta, tried to suppress the monarchy (1301b19).[37] The threat of change brought about by seditions is thus very great, and Aristotle cannot better express the fact that, for him, *stasis* operates in the constitutional domain. Nevertheless, it remains that, if it is true that *stasis* originates in a consciousness of a bad application of justice in a given constitution, it should be, in most cases, rather difficult to show that a real sedition does not entail a change in the constitution. We should also note that the passage that we have been considering also confirms that there are good *staseis*, since Aristotle gives as examples of changes brought about by *stasis* the passage from democracy to oligarchy and the reverse, but also from polity to democracy (5.4, 1304a28), as well as the passage from these two forms to aristocracy and to polity. Thus, there are *staseis* that rectify constitutions.

---

35. The last case is rarer than the first, but does occur. See, for example, 5.4, 1304a33: at Chalkis the people "made themselves master of the constitution."

36. The image of tension and relaxation is applied several times to constitutions by Aristotle. As is shown by the passages 4.3, 1290a27, and 5.4, 1304a21, it is rather the minority and authoritarian regimes that correspond to the "tension" and to popular regimes that apply the "relaxation." But here the comparison takes a more general value.

37. The fact that Aristotle considers this a *stasis* shows clearly that for him a *stasis* is not necessarily a revolutionary major event.

Politics 5.2 poses a new problem: "In considering how *staseis* and changes arise in constitutions, we must first of all ascertain their beginnings and causes from a general point of view." At this point in Aristotle's analysis, *staseis* and constitutional changes are so closely tied together that when, at 1302a18-22, he gives the list of "beginnings and causes" in question, which he says are "three in number, and we have now to give an outline of each," the sentence that follows shows that for Aristotle it is a matter of the beginnings and causes of *staseis*; but when, in the immediately following sentence, Aristotle says that "therefore it is necessary to posit a general cause" (1302a23), the structure of the text shows that it is the cause of change that is in question.

Let us now see how *stasis* occurs, and, prior to that, what is the very structure of *stasis* according to Aristotle. To do that it is appropriate to situate precisely, *chronologically and logically*, the different levels that explain *stasis*. The first level reveals the condition of possibility of *stasis*, namely, that the organization of the laws that define what is just and what is unjust do not have the universal, or even strongly majority, support of the citizens, because they have divergent conceptions of justice, and one party of the citizens, often a substantial part, feels wounded. That allows us to make two very important remarks.

The first starts with a doubt. Aristotle, at 5.1, 1301b40, confirms what has been said above, that there is no room for *stasis* in a virtuous city. But is that so sure, so simple? This doesn't seem that difficult to admit in the case of a virtuous city in which the citizens unanimously, or mostly, admit that this virtue is itself in their interest. And in principle such a city could exist, since an aristocracy considers only virtuous men as citizens—with the various relaxations of that rule noted above—and who, besides, will fulfill ultimately other conditions, like that of having been born from citizens of that city. But such a situation is not as tenable as it had been in ancient times, if it ever was. Aristotle confirms that indirectly when he remarks immediately after this assertion that there are very few virtuous people,[38] which means that an aristocracy will no longer be the regime that reserves civic rights to virtuous men alone, but the regime that puts virtuous men in a position to govern a mass of *citizens* who are not virtuous, or even simply to participate in the government of that

---

38. Aristotle clarifies that what is even more rare are people who are both virtuous and well born: "one cannot find one hundred anywhere" (1302a1, passage already cited), but aristocracy tends to value noble birth.

mass. According to the examples that we saw in a previous chapter, and in this one, most of the constitutions that Aristotle calls "aristocracies" are mixed aristocracies, and are very far from the restricted club of virtuous men. A mixed aristocracy of this kind runs the risk of being subject to strong internal tensions and is very difficult to establish, and if it is once established, it will be menaced by sedition.

This situation, of a city governed by virtuous people but not all the citizens of which are virtuous, was considered, as we have seen, in *Politics* 3.4. Our analysis of this chapter showed us that the absolutely virtuous citizens, that is, those who possessed both ethical and political virtue, are able to command excellently and also to obey excellently. The citizens who do not have ethical virtue are able to have an "instrumental" political excellence, comparable to the excellence of a good sailor. All of this functions adequately as long as the nonvirtuous citizens, or at least most of them, have the excellence that leads them to work to keep the constitution in place. But what we now understand is that when the nonvirtuous citizens do not want to defend the constitution, it will be in danger, no matter how correct it may be. That allows us to take a further step, one that Aristotle did not make in an explicit way, in our understanding of *stasis*.

Aristotle has explained to us that what makes *stasis* possible is that the groups of citizens composing the city do not have the same conception of justice. But he also insisted on the point that none of these groups have an *entirely correct* conception of justice, what he calls "justice in the absolute sense." But here we are confronted by an entirely different kind of case, because the virtuous citizens who govern the city have indeed a correct conception of justice. Thus, it seems that he does not need to limit the frame of *stasis* to situations in which two unilateral conceptions of justice confront each other. In fact, that is what Aristotle says, for example at 5.7, 1307a5, when he explains that aristocracies and polities find themselves destroyed when they mix their components badly. Aristotle specifies: in the case of polities, it is when they mix their oligarchical and democratic components badly, but in the case of aristocracies, it is when they mix "these two components and virtue" (1307a9) badly, that is, that these aristocracies do not manage to bring it about that the virtuous governors on the one hand, and a part of the citizens who are not ethically virtuous on the other, live together harmoniously, this part being large enough to menace the existing constitution. Similarly, at 5.7, 1307a23: aristocracies are transformed into democracies because the poor feel aggrieved. I believe that we can make examples like this "speak" in order to construct a doctrine that Aristotle himself has not formally thematized.

We have here, as often in Aristotle, almost trifling remarks—for it seems completely trifling to note that aristocracies are overthrown when the popular masses are discontented—that lead us toward important realizations. If all constitutions, correct as well as deviant, are indeed threatened by sedition, if virtue is not sufficient to maintain a constitution in place, why try so hard to establish excellent constitutions? We find ourselves, *mutatis mutandis*, before the problem that obsessed ancient ethics, namely, that of *akrasia*. Why are there so many bad people when virtue would make them happy? How can someone respond to that question when he does not have resort to the doctrine of original sin? Similarly, in politics: why do correct constitutions need to defend themselves, since they guarantee the happiness of their citizens? And they do indeed need to. That is *also* why the legislator needs to be an expert in the preservation of constitutions.

But, an observation that is the reciprocal of the one developed just now: a constitution has no reason to change if all the citizens, or a great majority of them, think that their interests are served by this constitution, and that would be true whether the constitution is correct or deviant. Up to this point, Aristotle seemed to be trying to get us to think that all the efforts of the legislator for establishing a correct constitution would be in some manner repaid by the fact that this constitution, as a consequence of its *ethical effects*, would be stable. We have just seen that that is not true, and that the struggle of the legislator to maintain a correct constitution will not be less difficult than the struggle he had to establish it. But the legislator is faced by another dilemma. In fact, a deviant constitution that has acquired the support of most of the citizens, a demagogical democracy that rules in a city in which the wealthy class has been reduced to almost nothing, for example, is not in danger. Must then the legislator *also* become an expert in sedition and the overturning of constitutions, since it would indeed be necessary to overturn constitutions that are vicious but solidly installed, in order to open the way to virtue?

The second remark is brief, but no less important. In the affirmation at 5.1, 1302a2, according to which a constitution that is "entirely" based on one of the two conceptions of justice named (democratic or oligarchic) will not last long, we rediscover the fundamental thesis of Aristotle's realist politics, according to which it is necessary to mix the contrary interests of the antagonistic classes in the city, a thesis of which we are reminded at 1302a7. But that presupposes that there are classes with opposed interests. Aristotle does not envisage the case, in fact very unlikely, of a city composed entirely of wealthy people or of people of modest means. Thus, for Aristotle the class struggle is perhaps a phenomenon sometimes regrettable, but it is not a pathological phenomenon in that it is the normal basis of city life. Aristotle has no intention of eradicating this phenomenon, as if it were a chronic disease. He fights for a society in which the interests of various classes are taken into account, not for a classless society. As the passage cited above says, the nobles, the wealthy, and the others have the right to demand a share of power, because one cannot make a city out of poor people alone (cf. 3.12, 1283a16).

We can even go farther by relying on one of the results of our research. We have seen that the resistance of the dominated to the hegemonic goals of the dominant classes was one of the elements, possibly the most decisive element, that allowed cities to escape a tyrannical destiny, or to put it in a more striking way, it is this resistance that guarantees the existence of political space that otherwise would dissolve into a tyranny. Thus, it would be disastrous for the legislator to put in place procedures that would eradicate or go beyond the class struggle. Nevertheless, here too, it seems that this struggle of the dominated has no place to exist in correct constitutions, since the common advantage rules the relationships between citizens.

Decidedly, then, the situation of the legislator is quite difficult and his task quite arduous. He needs to promote virtue by rectifying the constitution with which he is concerned, but he needs to continue his work once the constitution is rectified, because the danger of subversion of the good by the bad persists. He needs to know how to make regimes last, notably by quieting the objections of those who are opposed to their constitution, but he must not purge the civic body of all its potentialities of revolt, even when the constitution is correct, because, when vice returns to power, it will be good that the ability of the dominated classes to resist has not been too stifled.

At a second level of exposition of the structure of *stasis*, Aristotle presents the causes, or starting points, of seditions and changes; there are three causes, but the third is also the cause of the first two.

The first cause, in the order of exposition adopted by Aristotle, is the state of mind (πῶς ἔχοντες) that leads some citizens to engage in sedition. At 5.2, 1302a22, Aristotle provides the "main universal cause" of the fact that citizens have a mental disposition that pushes them to *stasis*, namely, as we have seen, that the existing constitution violates their conception of justice.

The second cause (starting point) consists in "for the sake of what" they engage in sedition, or the final cause of the *stasis*. This cause is that the citizens want to get profit and honors, and avoid loss and dishonor, for themselves and their friends. We note that Aristotle does not say that they are always wrong. On the contrary, concerning the state of mind that encourages demanding more for oneself, or less for others, Aristotle says explicitly that "these aspirations are sometimes just, sometimes unjust" (5.2, 13021a28). Aristotle does not describe *stasis* as a political maneuver, violent or not, to acquire power or wealth, but as the result of a feeling of frustration. Even when he gives examples of people seizing power by "taking the lead," because they feared being mistreated (5.3, 1302b21), the same goals are at work. *Stasis* is thus not an initiative of ambitious people, but a reaction of unsatisfied citizens. That's an important point on which many have made mistakes. Kostas Kalimtzis, for example, goes so far as to say that it is because they believe that wealth or power is the sovereign good that some undertake a *stasis*.[39] That is far from being always true. Once again, the goal of *stasis* is to establish, or reestablish, an equilibrium that the seditious believe to have been broken to their disadvantage.

The state of mind urging *stasis* and the sought-for goals themselves have several possible causes and starting points, which themselves constitute the third cause, which is subdivided into several particular causes. This causal relation between causes is not understood by Newman, among others, when he writes that, with this third cause, "now we study the causes of revolutions in more detail" (4.295). The "seven or more" particular causes that make up the third cause are responsible for the fact that people who engage in *stasis* have such a state of mind and from the fact that they set themselves the goals that we have seen. These seven causes are: profit, honor, insolence, fear, excess, contempt, disproportionate increase.

There are two "brute facts" of which we should make short work. First, profit and honor are constituents of the second cause, and they reappear in the third cause but, says Aristotle, "not in the same way (οὐχ ὡσαύτως)" (5.2, 1302a38). Second, with one of those short and oracular

---

39. Kostas Kalimtzis, *Aristotle on Political Enmity and Disease: An Inquiry into Stasis* (Albany: State University of New York Press, 2000), 108: "What is sought for as an end in *stasis* are apparent goods, 'honor' and 'gain.'"

sentences, full of meaning, that are not lacking in Aristotle, he adds at 5.3, 1302b3: "Moreover causes of another sort (ἄλλον τρόπον) are intrigues, negligence, small details, dissimilarity."

Concerning the first of these "brute facts," Aristotle himself explains the difference between the two appearances of "profit" and "honor":

> Two of them [causes and starting points of *staseis*] are the same as those which we have mentioned, but not in the same way. Profit and honor excite people against one another not because they want to acquire something for themselves, as we said before, but because they see others, either justly or unjustly, monopolizing them. (1302a37)

That means that in the second cause, that is, as goals of *stasis*, profit and honor are advantages that one seeks for oneself, and thus a final cause of *stasis*; in the third cause, in contrast, it is the spectacle of happiness and, doubtless, of unhappiness, of others that provokes the state of mind that leads to *stasis*. Profit and honor are thus motive causes of *stasis*, but nonimmediate motive causes. We can draw two important lessons from that.

In the first place, the particular causes that make up the third cause are not causes of *stasis*, but of a disposition that causes *stasis*. To say, like Ronald Weed, that the causes making up the third cause are triggers of "desires, emotions, and actions" that provoke *stasis* is not exact.[40] The causes composing the third cause prepare the terrain for the appearance of a mental disposition propitious for *stasis*. Skultety insists[41] on the fact that these causes can be located well upstream, temporally, from *stasis*, and that is true, because there are often old grievances that reappear on the occasion of a *stasis*. On the other hand, we see that *stasis* presupposes personal involvement of the agents and the engagement of their own interests. But in the case of the profit and honor that reappear in the third cause, that is, the profit and honor that one sees assigned or denied to others, this is not (yet) the case. This third cause provokes a state of mind that provokes *stasis*. In the second cause, in contrast, the desire for profit

---

40. Ronald Weed, *Aristotle on Stasis: A Moral Psychology of Political Conflict* (Berlin: Logos Verlag, 2007), 118.

41. Steven Skultety, "Delimiting Aristotle's Conception of *Stasis* in the *Politics*," *Phronesis* 54 (2009): 346–370.

and honor or the frustration of being deprived of them are *direct* causes, and more precisely *direct final* causes, of *stasis*.

Concerning the second fact, the "other sort" has been interpreted in different ways, no one being sure. It is certainly false to say, like Vettori,[42] that the causes enumerated at 5.3, 1302b3, are of "another sort" because they imply neither quarrels nor armed action. But Newman, who considers them as only *possible* causes is also wrong, because the seven others may also be possible causes. Perhaps one should understand, as Newman actually does, that it's a matter of more indirect causes, that is, ones that less directly provoke the state of mind that pushes toward sedition. But why would political intrigues, which are part of the list belonging to the "other sort" have an effect less direct than the contempt that make citizens who believe that they are its object acquire a seditious mind-set? Aristotle has not tried very hard to make these matters clear; this fact itself has a significance that we need to bring out.

At 5.2, 1302a34, then, begins a long enumeration of causes, which I have gathered under the heading "third cause." There are first the seven listed above, then, "of another sort," four other causes. Then, in chapter 3, we find a set of short analyses of causes, most of them taking up again the causes enumerated in the two preceding lists, some of them possibly included in those lists, others, finally, seeming to be really new causes. Thus, the absence of ethnic community (5.3, 1303a25) is perhaps a particular case of the "lack of homogeneity" (1302b5), but the territorial separation of territories of the city (1303a7) was not previously listed. I think that Aristotle does not give a complete list here, and that he recognizes this as he writes that the causes and starting points "in a sense are found to be seven, in another sense more numerous" (5.2, 1302a36). This is remarkable too: what is well defined is the mode of action of the different sorts of causes on each other. Thus, the causes of the third list provoke those of lists 1 and 2, which bring about *stasis*. But Aristotle leaves relatively open the question both of the number of causes in the third list, and of the way in which they differ in their mode of action. It does not seem to be excluded that one might propose additional causes. His theory thus unites a determinate *form* with an indeterminate and open *matter*, two characteristics that Aristotle ordinarily attributes to form and matter. I also think that this explains his negligence when he presents the causes

---

42. In his magnificent commented edition of 1576.

in list 3, something that has as a result that we are not able to understand completely what he means by "of another sort."

So, here's how it goes. Suppose there is a city the constitution of which has laws that combine two antagonistic conceptions of justice, as a rule one oligarchical and the other democratic, or worse yet, imposes just one of these conceptions. Some citizens have lived or have seen others live in situations that they resent as miserable: they see people who do not receive what is owed them, they are submitted to humiliations at the hands of those in power or near power (sexual attacks on their children, to be whipped by Euripides because someone told him that he had bad breath, etc.), or other things, sometimes benign, but often repeated, and sometimes long ago. These citizens then acquire a disposition of mind that makes them resent the current distribution of wealth and honors in the constitution as unacceptable. From that moment, they intend to redistribute wealth and honors. But they think that the solution cannot be anything else but modification or control of the constitution. That is what makes them have recourse to *stasis*.

There is here an important point that sheds light on one of the criticisms that Aristotle aims at Plato at *Politics* 5.12, 1316a39ff. According to Aristotle, in fact, the people who establish an oligarchy do not do it because they are greedy and speculators, as Plato believes, but because they are persuaded that they have been unjustly treated in view of the treatment that they thought they deserved because of their larger fortune. He does not at all doubt that they are often also greedy, but for there to be a *stasis*, there has to be consideration of this eminently political notion, (in)justice. The counterexamples that show that greed is not enough are interesting: there are oligarchies where the rulers are not businessmen, and non-oligarchies where they are. Aristotle asserts this very clearly:

> It is absurd to suppose that the city changes into oligarchy merely because the members of the ruling class are lovers and makers of money, and not because the very rich think it unfair that the very poor should have an equal share in the government with themselves. Moreover, in many oligarchies there are laws against making money in trade. But at Carthage, which is a democracy, there is no such prohibition. (5.12, 1316a39)

Kostas Kalimtzis must have missed this passage.

We must note that at *Politics* 5.3, a difference slips into *stasis* on the one side and constitutional change on the other, while up to here the two proceeded together. Intrigues, for example, can change the constitution "without *stasis*" (5.3, 1303a14). It arises from an examination of the causes at 5.3, 1303a13–b, that in fact they can provoke constitutional change but not necessarily *stasis*. One may say that these causes are accidental—for instance, at 5.6, 1306b6: constitutional change that happens "fortuitously," ἀπὸ συμπτώματος—in that they do not involve any political project, for, without any choice on the part of political actors, the imperceptible and progressive diminution of the property qualification *brings it about* that at some moment the city has left oligarchy. This change is produced *automatically*, in the etymological sense of the word. This is not so much a cause that provokes a change in mind-set that will lead to *stasis*, as objective givens that make impossible the functioning of the constitution as it presently is and thus provoke a change of that constitution or at least changes in that constitution.

So, for there to be a *stasis*, there has to be a conflict or an opposition, which could have had a private origin, an adultery for example, but has been *politicized*. If a citizen of the popular party sees his wife seduced by an oligarch who has overwhelmed her with gifts, or his son raped by the tyrant, there will not be a *stasis* unless, far from engaging in a personal vendetta, the citizen analyzes this offense as ultimately caused by the bad practice of justice in the current constitution, and this bad practice as being the result of the defects of this constitution. It is also necessary that the victim succeeds in gathering around him a "party" that shares his analysis. One may doubtless even go farther and think that the initiators of *stasis* could perfectly well remain in the purely private sphere of their personal disputes, and that the *stasis* be found to be the unintended effect of their frustrations. Thus, at 5.4, 1303b19–26, there was *stasis* at Syracuse when the groups to which belonged young people opposed to each other in an amorous matter—one person took the wife of another who had seduced his boyfriend—found themselves "dragged into this quarrel" (1303b25). The people who were immediately involved in this affair doubtless did not see farther than their personal thirst for vengeance.

In fact, it is remarkable that the seven causes that lead to the adoption of a state of mind leading to *stasis* can appear in the political sphere just as well as in the private. In the first case, *stasis* never leaves the political sphere, while in the second it's a matter of *politicizing* a personal emotion. In the situations described in *Politics* 5.10 concerning seditions in monarchies, especially in tyrannies, most of the primary actors seem not to have had the intention of leaving the private sphere. They took action in order to get revenge; most of those who revolt do so out of pure anger and not at all to take power.[43] Aristotle takes the example of Harmodius and Aristogeiton, who, he claims, revolted for personal reasons, but whose action took a political turn, because it made a large enough group of people have the feeling of having been injured by the fact of the nature of the constitution, or by who was in control. We should note that the example of Harmodius and Aristogeiton was very strong, because it goes against the democratic myth of the tyrannicide, in an example considered paradigmatic. To say that that Harmodius and Aristogeiton revolted against Peisistratus because somebody mistreated the sister of one of them, the other because somebody mistreated his beloved, had to be experienced as insulting the Athenians.

Thereby *stasis* turns out to be a key concept in Aristotelian political philosophy. We can see that better in contrast with Plato.

Aristotle versus Plato, Again.

Aristotle's idea of *stasis* did not prevail any more than his idea of the political. Plato had an analysis much closer to the dominant Greek approach. The basis of the opposition between Plato and Aristotle on the analysis of *stasis* is ultimately, as often, the radical difference between their approaches to power, and that sends us back once more to the first chapter of the *Politics*. Thus, we have seen several times that for Aristotle the split between the political and the nonpolitical, what concerns the family for example, is fundamental. But actually, Aristotelian *stasis* is one of the means of mediating between the political and nonpolitical. And not just any "nonpolitical," but the most intimate part of the life of the citizens, which doubtless explains the very large presence of sexual affairs in triggering seditions. Even if the ancients did not have the same relationship as we do with sex, in fact, for them too it represented the intimate par excellence. By theorizing the ways in which one goes from intimate individual psychological events to a political act, Aristotle gives us a flexible and applicable model for explaining historical changes that

---

43. Cf. 5.10, 1311a35: "When people are angry, they nearly all revolt in order to take revenge and not out of ambition," even less to change the constitution. That is why Kalimtzis seems to me to be wrong in thinking that there is in *stasis* a *logos* guiding the rebels, although a "*logos* tied to private ends" (125). It is often, perhaps very often, but not always, true.

occur in the cities. It is not in fact, or not only, the institutional logic that makes constitutions change, but something absolutely individual, human passion.

Let's return to Plato, and to Nicole Loraux. Loraux is right when she shows, although she does not express it in these terms, that the Platonic description of *stasis* is clearly ideological, in the Marxist sense of the word. Plato says that to attack the institutions of the perfect city, and he conceives of that attack as often violent, would be parricide and fratricide. Doubtless the Platonic theory of constitutional change, which puts this change into an unalterable and necessary cycle that Aristotle critiques with a kind of irritation at the blindness of his teacher to reality, in *Politics* 5.12, also tends to show that individual aspirations to change are destined to fail. In Aristotle, on the contrary, no ideology. Each person has his own political nature, ultimately but not only determined by the class to which he belongs. If he belongs to the prosperous nobility, he will have an aristocratic nature; if to the wealthy bourgeoisie, an oligarchic nature; if to the proletariat, a democratic nature. Consequently, class struggle is a natural phenomenon. It's a matter of a "realist" analysis that coexists with an axiological analysis of virtue: those citizens who have an oligarchical or democratic nature are not ethically virtuous and thus are not perfect citizens, as we saw when we analyzed *Politics* 3.4. And, by naturalizing class struggle, Aristotle also normalizes *stasis*. It would be true to say that *stasis* is an illness, as almost all Greeks except Aristotle said, if passion itself were an illness. Possibly illness is a passion, but passion is not an illness.

The absolute originality of Aristotle's position should not be underestimated, not only in the context of antiquity, but for many centuries. Only when we come to certain Marxist-leaning analyses will we find a weakened echo of it. Certainly, Aristotle shares with other Greek philosophers a reverence for the unchangeable, but his approach to the human world, and more particularly the world of cities, makes a great deal of room for change. Far from believing that a city cannot be excellent until it has torn itself away from history, Aristotle sees in the class struggle, the latent state of revolt and sedition that accompanies it, and the ideological dissonance that corresponds to it, the normal condition of political communities. Therefore, the political philosopher must learn to think history, and the legislator he instructs must definitely be the man of opportunities and dosages.

So, in fact, for Aristotle the essence of the art of the legislator is knowing how to temper the mixtures, particularly the mixture between oligarchy and democracy. We have taken a long look at that. But *stasis* is one of the ways to change these constitutional mixtures, whether it preserves the type of the current constitution, or leads to changing it. I believe that there is in Aristotle a clear invitation to the legislator to use *stasis*. Thus, when he gives advice to the tyrant on how to avoid *stasis*, Aristotle distinguishes between bad advice—make the constitution more and more tyrannical—and good—make the tyrant more like a king—we have analyzed this extraordinary text above. But this invitation to subvert tyranny by making it more similar to kingship is precisely a *stasis*, even if it is a controlled and peaceful *stasis*, and even if it is done by the tyrant himself who, anticipating matters, acts in place of his rebellious subjects.

In this perspective, and given the solidarity that unifies laws and the constitution, we see that *stasis* is simply a more complete form of the legislative change that, ultimately, Aristotle advocates. Paradoxically, if one wants to try to avoid *stasis*, the best way to prevent its appearance would be by anticipating what it would demand, a better mixture of constitutional components. At the same time, it would be recognizing its natural character.[44] At the point to which I have arrived in my consideration of Aristotle's political philosophy, I tend to think that what he advocates against troubles in the cities is a kind of vaccination, which would inoculate an attenuate form of sedition in relation to existing laws, to avoid the feverish and uncontrollable forms of sedition. To continue the medical metaphor: given the cohabitation of social groups with divergent interests and among whom struggle is the *normal* state of the city—another characteristic and fundamental trait of Aristotle's political philosophy, as I have said—*stasis* exists there *naturally*, as an endemic condition. The end rejoining the beginning, I thus find again what I said at the start: *stasis* is more a state than a modification.

---

44. Even before he studies *stasis* in its own right, Aristotle posits that *stasis* and the safety of constitutions that he proposes studying later are natural phenomena: "we will endeavor to ascertain the modes of ruin and preservation of constitutions generally and of each sort, and to what causes they are to be attributed *most naturally* (μάλιστα . . . πέφυκεν)" (4.2, 1289b23).

CHAPTER 8

Political Matter

A consensus is easily, too easily, established among the commentators of Aristotle's *Politics* who think that in book 7, to which they generally attach book 8, the last of the work as it has come down to us, Aristotle gives his conception of the excellent constitution, some even daring to say "ideal." Whence several inferences that many have not been able to avoid: if the ideal city is at stake, this looks a bit Platonic, and thus these books would have been written early in Aristotle's career, since Werner Jaeger's representation is the one most often in favor among "chronologists." There is also a widespread tendency to move books 7 and 8 toward the beginning of the *Politics*, usually after book 3, in any case before the "realist" books 4 through 6, or at least books 5 and 6. In fact, if you look carefully, you find that the majority of commentators have adopted that solution, including those who, as editors and translators, conserve the traditional order of the texts transmitted by the manuscripts out of the reverence that one should feel for the manuscript tradition.

Even before challenging the bases of this reasoning, we can see a fundamental weakness. If book 7 of the *Politics* tells us, at the beginning, what the excellent constitution is, what use are books 4 through 6 (or 3 through 6, if you put 7 after 2), which try, with many difficulties, to define the excellent constitution? One may well wonder, particularly, what are Aristotle's subtle considerations on constitutional mixtures leading to excellence doing here? To these criticisms, those who hold to the Platonizing reading of the two final books of the *Politics* could respond that the "realist" books would have as their goal to direct a given people, whether they are already organized into a city or not, toward the ideal constitution described in book 7. These "realist" books, which would then be about a kind of political *tactics*, would recall Aristotle's frequently expressed desire to propose achievable projects and would bear witness to the reformism that we have recognized in his work. Some have a slightly different thesis, but which, in my opinion, comes to the same thing as the one just presented, namely, that the "realist" books propose solutions adapted to cities that are not, or not yet, mature enough for a perfect constitution. A position like that can find textual support, particularly in the famous first chapter of *Politics* 4. Richard Kraut chooses this approach and proposes a seductive justification, that one cannot appreciate the more or less good, the more or less bad, if one does not know what is perfect.[1]

These readings can find some support in the text, right from the first line of book 7, which addresses "those who want to do appropriate study into the excellent constitution," while situating this study following an exposition of the difference between power over freemen and power over slaves, that one can refer to books 1 and perhaps 3 of the *Politics*.[2] As for "the previous examination of the various constitutions" (7.4, 1325b34) to which Aristotle refers, one is tempted to see in it an allusion to book 2.[3] Given the close relationship that books 7 and 8 make between ethics and politics, it would be difficult to deny that these books are firmly located on the "normative" side of the *Politics*. In no other text does Aristotle insist so much on the relationship between virtue and happiness to life in a city with an excellent constitution, as in book 7. Finally, the argument most highly prized by the partisans of the placing of book 7 after book 3, because it seems to be based on philological rigor, is that the initial sentence of book 7 ("someone who wants to do appropriate study into the excellent constitution," 7.1.1323a14) and the last sentence of book 3, doubtless unfinished ("it is thus necessary for someone who wants to do appropriate study [into the excellent constitution]" 3.18, 1288b5) seem to connect to each other.

We saw all that in our summary presentation of the positions of Werner Jaeger, and we know too how his positions were both more nuanced and more solid than people sometimes say.

---

1. Kraut, *Aristotle: Political Philosophy*, 194.

2. Cf. 7.3, 1325a28: "There is as great a difference between rule over freemen and rule over slaves as there is between slavery by nature and freedom by nature, about which I have said enough at the beginning of this treatise."

3. As for example Newman, *The Politics of Aristotle*, vol. 3, 340.

Now I must explain why *I don't believe one word* of all that, first by calling attention to some blindingly obvious evidence. In fact, the legislator who would have only the last two books of the *Politics* at his disposal, even if one added the first three, would doubtless be stymied in any attempt to establish an excellent constitution. To be sure, he could be quite clear about the very basis of what Aristotle sometimes calls "political science,"[4] and by the same token about what he has to achieve, namely, what is proper to politics, and also what is the correct form of constitutions. *Politics* book 7 figures, as I noted above, among the Aristotelian texts that assert most strongly the relationship between virtue and happiness in making the virtuous city the necessary setting for the happy life. It is also book 7 that best elucidates the difference between citizens and noncitizen inhabitants of a city, a difference that, in the case of the excellent city to be established, becomes the difference between those who deserve to be citizens and those who do not deserve citizenship.

The general rule that the good legislator observes is that power should be given to the virtuous. Thus book 7 reminds us that artisans should not be citizens, but adds that neither should peasants, the first because they are "base" and sunk in sordid calculations, the second because they lack leisure. Book 7 puts special emphasis on the necessity of leisure for the virtuous life of the citizen. But book 7 gives us, ultimately, much less information, and much less precise information, than book 3, which clarified the difference between ethical virtue and political virtue, and confronts the different virtues with *political* virtue, which is the virtue according to which should be determined the distribution of power. We should also note that books 7 and 8 do not refer to the "common advantage," which is the criterion of constitutional correctness in the previous books. Even the *realist* advice that Aristotle gives the legislator in book 7.9 (because book 7 is not a text that restricts itself to generalities or remains in the "ideal" sphere) to choose the same men to deliberate and to fight in the army, but at different ages, is a repetition of a measure already anticipated in the famous chapter 3.4, which provides a very important additional specification, that young people ought *to learn* to rule by obeying.

This lack of novelty in books 7 and 8 in relation to books 1 to 3, concerning the fundamental requirements for the allocation of power, is largely compensated by the large number of analyses that are found only in book 7. This is even more true of book 8, which deals principally with

---

4. Cf. *Politics* 2.3, 1253b19.

education and music. All, or nearly all, of these analyses are aimed at the excellent city: what topography and what size it should have, what would be the most desirable ethnic makeup, how it should relate to its access to the sea and its naval forces, how to arrange the agora, and so on, as we have already seen.

But the greatest difficulty for the legislator is that in the last two books of the *Politics* there is no advice about the main point, namely, the *constitutional form* that he must give the happy city. But the essential task of the legislator is precisely to decide if and to what point a city should have an aristocratic constitution, or a popular constitution, and to determine the means of getting there—usually, as we have seen, step by step, by dosage and mixture. The politically crucial question of who should participate in magistracies is answered in book 7.9 in a very interesting way for anyone who wants to understand the goal of the two last books of the *Politics*. So, let us look at the passage from 7.9, 1328b24 to 1329a2.

Aristotle begins by noting that the question that he posed in the form "should everyone participate in the functions or only certain ones," does not receive the same answer in all the constitutions, and he cites the cases of democracy and oligarchy. Then he answers the question:

> But since we are examining the excellent constitution, that under which the city will be perfectly happy, and as we have said before, happiness is impossible without virtue, it is clear that in the city that is best governed and that has men who are absolutely just, and not merely in the context of a particular constitution, the citizens must not lead the life of either an artisan or a merchant, for such a life is base and contrary to virtue; those who are destined to become citizens will not be peasants either, because leisure is necessary both for the development of virtue and for political activities. (7.9, 1328b33)

Thus we see that Aristotle here, without forgetting his doctrine of constitutional diversity and of the dependence of laws on the constitution, gives an answer that will be frustrating for the legislator, because at the level of generality in this part of the discussion, Aristotle simply answers that the excellent constitution will give power to the virtuous people, something that, as we have amply seen, applies to *all* correct constitutions. And all that to arrive at the conclusion that one must exclude artisans and peasants from citizenship. In other words, one should not look to the last two books of the *Politics* for an answer to the question, which sort of regime to establish in order to make the city happy. Furthermore, when he says that he is not putting this "in the context of a particular constitution,"[5] Aristotle even refuses explicitly to consider the question.

An impressive number of commentators have pulled themselves out of that embarrassing situation (which is especially embarrassing for the legislator), by arguing that book 7 in fact argues for a particular form of constitution, or rather two forms, kingship and aristocracy. One of their arguments, which also reinforces in their eyes the reordering of the books of the *Politics*, is that the end of book 3 declares that kingship and aristocracy are the two excellent forms of constitution and that this position is in a way transferred to book 7, the first sentence of which, as we saw, takes up the last sentence of book 3. Here is the short final chapter of book 3, which we will have to comment on; it is a text that we have partially analyzed earlier:

> We maintain that there are three correct forms of constitution, and necessarily the best is that in which the administration is in the hands of the best. That is the case when it happens that one individual, a whole lineage (γένος), or all or most (πλῆθος) of a group of people surpass the others in virtue, these being able to obey, and those to govern, for the sake of the most desirable life. We showed in the first part of our inquiry that the excellence of the good man is the same as that of a citizen of an excellent city. Clearly then in the same manner, and by the same means through which a man becomes truly good, he can establish a city governed aristocratically or royally, and the same education and the same habits that make a man virtuous will be pretty much those which make a man a statesman or a king.
>
> After having dealt with these points concerning the constitution, we must now try to deal with that which is excellent: how it exists naturally and how it is established. It is thus necessary for someone who wants to carry out an appropriate study . . . (3.18, 1288a32)

---

5. There is no reason why the expression μὴ πρὸς τὴν ὑπόθεσιν (1328b39) would refer only to deviant constitutions. Newman is certainly right to understand: "not merely just relatively to the principle which may happen to be taken as the groundwork of the State." Possibly I have slightly over-translated this expression that elsewhere I have translated "in a particular perspective" (4.7, 1293b3). In my favor, cf. 2.9, 1269a32.

It's a bizarre chapter; it does not fit well with what precedes it; it can very well be incomplete in the form in which the manuscripts have transmitted it to us, but I am not going to take the easy way and contest its authenticity. The reading of this chapter adopted by Newman, the others on this point being only his epigones, posits that Aristotle establishes a hierarchy between correct constitutions, kingship and aristocracy being the best of the best, if we may put it that way. That provides a supplementary argument, doctrinal this time, to make book 7 follow book 3. It would be a matter, here, of an aristocracy in its purest form, "the government of the best absolutely according to virtue and not people who are good from a particular perspective" (*Pol.* 4.7, 1293b3, passage just cited in a note), and not the mixed forms of aristocracy that are listed following this passage. We would then be in the perspective opened by Richard Kraut: book 7 would give us a summary of the *standard* of which the "realist" books would consider the deviations due to the constraints of various concrete situations.

One might well conclude, in view of everything that precedes, that that is not my reading of the last chapter of *Politics* 3. Read literally, this passage seems in fact to mean that Aristotle is asking himself which of the three correct constitutions is best. Then one should understand the sentence at 1288a34 ("That is the case . . .") as referring to kingship, in which an individual or a lineage is excellent, and to aristocracy, in which a *plurality* of people is virtuous. That is how we should translate πλῆθος at 1288a35, although this Greek word normally refers to an *important* plurality. But it seems much more natural to read the sentence at 1288a34 as a list of cases corresponding to the three correct constitutions (a virtuous man is appropriate for a kingship, a "entire lineage"[6] an aristocracy, a "large number" a polity). The first line of the passage ("We maintain that there are three correct forms of constitution") must allude to the distinction between constitutions in 3.7, forcing us to read in that list here. Thus, the word πλῆθος recovers its "normal" sense in its application to the polity. It is definitely the case that for Aristotle kingship and aristocracy, when they correspond to the ethical condition of the city to which they are

---

6. Perhaps we should not give the word γένος in this place the sense of "lineage," because an excellent lineage is more appropriate for a kingship than an aristocracy; instead, translate it as "group," Aristotle meaning to indicate a group smaller than designated by the word πλῆθος.

applied, are constitutions that are in a way *immediately* excellent.⁷ But we have seen that, since *Politics* 3, and precisely 3.11, Aristotle performs a remarkable theoretical leap in his analysis of the idea of excellence in order to be able to distribute the status of ethical excellence among a multitude of citizens. Thus, I continue to understand that, when it is a matter of constitutions, in this case correct constitutions, the expression "the best of them" as it appears in this passage does not mean the "best" in the absolute sense, but the best in a given situation, and that is exactly what the second sentence shows. As no one escapes unharmed in this kind of hermeneutic conflict, I am obliged to recognize that "he can establish a city governed aristocratically or royally" at 3.18, 1288a40, seems to go in the direction of Newman's reading.

My answer would be that here too "aristocratically" would have the etymological sense of "which gives power to the best when there are several of them," and is applied to aristocracy in the strict sense, and to polity,⁸ in contrast to kingship, where one single man is excellent. I have also tried to show that Aristotle does not hesitate to call "aristocracy" a certain number of minority regimes because their government is sufficiently good. Going in the direction of this reading is the fact that at 1288b2, he speaks of the "statesman and king," where one would have expected "an aristocrat and a king." Perhaps this is, for Aristotle, a way of indicating, especially by the etymological connection between "polity" and "political man" (statesman), that the aristocracy in question is large enough to approach a polity, and in any case to need "professional" politicians.⁹ Earlier, I analyzed *Politics* 5.7, 1307a10, in which Aristotle explains that aristocracy

---

7. We must keep in mind *Republic* 4, 445d, where Plato says that it is a kingship when one man is in power, and an aristocracy when there are several, but that these two constitutions belong to a single species (ἓν εἶδος).

8. That is what I argued above for *Politics* 4.2, 1289b15, "and if there is a (constitution) which would be ruled best and well constituted but adapted to the majority of cities," ἀριστοκρατική, here translated "ruled best," since it cannot here be a reference to aristocracy in the strict sense.

9. Paulin Ismard has shown, better than others, that the Greek cities, and especially the Athenian democracy, practiced the deliberate exclusion of expert knowledge from the political arena. Positions requiring technical expertise were often entrusted to public slaves. Ismard notes that the very ideas of "political class" or "political professional" have no ancient Greek equivalent. Ismard, *La démocratie contre les experts. Les esclaves publics en Grèce ancienne*, 142–143.

and polity differ only in terms of the proportion of the mixture between democracy and oligarchy. In opposition, once again, to Plato, Aristotle thus reaffirms here that neither the acquisition of ethical virtue, nor the ability to govern well, depends on a technical apprenticeship, but comes from a habit acquired through education. As for the pseudo-philological argument about the identity of the end of book 3 and the beginning of book 7, it is very weak, since it is hardly surprising that Aristotle affirms repeatedly, even in the same terms, that the subject of his work is the excellent constitution. Everything considered, I believe that my reading is the worst, except all the others.

I repeat, and stand by it, then, that in the last chapter of *Politics* 3, Aristotle indeed talks about *three* excellent constitutions, and that book 7, wherever it is meant to be situated, *does not introduce* the question of the excellent constitution, because that question is present on every page, so to speak, of the *Politics*. Finally, it is just simply false to pretend that book 7 recommends a specific form of constitution, namely, aristocracy. But then of what use are the last two books of the *Politics*? I have already summarized an answer to that question in the chapter on the legislator, but here we may add more detail.

Politics 7 opens up two large sets of problems. On the one hand there is the question of the relationship between virtue and happiness for the individual and especially for the city. This question, as we saw in the previous chapter, is an eminently *political* question, and we are not surprised to see Aristotle asserting:

> Since we say that the virtue of the citizen and ruler is the same as that for a good man, and that the same person must first be a subject and then a ruler, the legislator has to see that they become good men, and by what means this may be accomplished, and what is the end of the best life. (7.14, 1333a11)

Since the end of the best life is happiness, the legislator leads the citizens to happiness by developing virtue among them, since virtue is, if not the sole condition, then at least the main condition for happiness. To do that he must respect the basic maxim of Aristotle's political philosophy, to give power only to virtuous people.

This text, we notice, strongly resonates with *Politics* 3.4, and with the return to the topic in 3.5. All the same, there is this difference that book 7 seems to regard the virtue of virtuous people as exclusively ethical virtue, while book 3, and the subsequent "realist books," define the contours of a "political virtue," which would be specifically that of the rulers, even if we remain largely dissatisfied on the details of this political virtue.[10] But as we already know, this process of inculcating virtue primarily concerns the young people. Thus book 7 opens the question of the education of children, starting if we may say so from the womb, since Aristotle begins with considerations, inspired by the medicine of his day, on the circumstances of impregnation (age of the partners, frequency of childbearing, time of year for giving birth). We know that for Aristotle the education of children, although the responsibility of families, ought to be closely supervised by the city. Book 8 continues this examination of educational issues, the last three chapters dedicated to musical education. For Aristotle, as for his contemporaries, music has an extremely strong effect on the soul, and it is far from regularly mollifying manners.

On the other hand, book 7 examines a certain number of conditions and attributes that are necessary or at least useful for an excellent city. The legislator can and must take account of these things. Thus, in chapter 11, Aristotle intervenes in the well-known dispute between those who appreciate the efficacy of fortifications, and those who fear that they engender a false sense of security and make the citizens cowardly; he ultimately recommends surrounding the city with ramparts. Many of Aristotle's analyses seem to refer to a city that is to be *founded*. In chapter 4, for example, Aristotle recommends setting the number of citizens in the city in a way that will make it large enough so that it can be autonomous, but small enough that the city does not lose the possibility of deliberation, that is, that it does not lose its *political* character. It is well known that Aristotle's criterion is that all the citizens should know each other (cf. 7.4, 1326b16). Thus, one has the impression that the legislator has the choice of setting as he likes the number of citizens, but we have seen that in the great majority of cases he needs to reform cities rather than to establish them. In fact, one may surely imagine that a legislator called upon to improve a city that is functioning badly diagnoses, among unhealthy factors, a shortfall or excess of population. He could then prescribe an increase in

---

10. Here too, as was the case concerning the alternation of obedience and command, book 7 takes up again the questions opened in book 3, but in a less developed way. If it were necessary to overturn the traditional order of the books, this would lead us to put books 7 and 8 even before book 3, something that few chronological interpreters are ready to do . . .

the number of citizens, as have done, Aristotle reminds us, some cities in some circumstances, for example by granting citizenship to children born to a citizen and a slave, as we have seen, or he could recommend a reduction of population by sending some of them to colonies of the city, as the Carthaginians did. There is also a *political* way of increasing or diminishing the number of citizens, by introducing new requirements for obtaining civic rights. When, in contrast, Aristotle recommends constructing the city sloping toward the east (7.11, 1330a38), it is difficult to resist the idea that he is thinking about founding or refounding a city.

A passage in chapter 6 about access to the sea is very instructive. Aristotle first notes that for a city having access to the sea, and therefore a port, is dangerous in that it opens the city up to traffic and favors the development of a commercial class. But we know that such a class cannot be "politicized," and is a danger "to good legislation" (7.6, 1327a14). And yet, Aristotle writes,

> Apart from these inconveniences, it would be undoubtedly better, both with a view to safety and to the provision of necessities, that the city and territory should be connected with the sea. . . . Nowadays we often see in countries and cities dockyards and harbors very conveniently placed outside the city, but not too far off; and they are kept in dependence by walls and similar fortifications. Cities thus situated manifestly reap the benefit of intercourse with their ports; and any harm that is likely to accrue may easily be guarded against by laws, which will pronounce and determine who may hold communication with one another, and who may not. (7.6, 1327a18)

"These inconveniences" would be the influx for foreigners, the development of a commercial class, and overpopulation, to be prevented by law. In other words, Aristotle's text indicates the most profitable conditions, even if the legislator would not adopt them if they are out of reach (after all, even if "many countries and cities" can have a port near but distinct from the city, this is not always possible), or if their adoption would entail too great detriment. Here we are not looking at the foundation of a city. I am therefore in agreement, in an offbeat way, with Richard Kraut, when he says that knowledge of the ideal city is useful to the person who wants, or needs, to deploy his actions in a world of vicious or half-vicious cities: it is good to know the best location for a city or the best ethnic composition of its members, even if the conditions that the legislator finds in the city that he intends to lead to happiness do not permit the complete realization of the best results.

And suddenly we understand the function of *Politics* 7, at least of the part that deals with the conditions of the excellent city. Right from the first lines of chapter 4, where begins what I have described as the second set of problems dealt with by book 7, Aristotle clearly presents things:

> The excellent constitution cannot exist without adequate means. Therefore, we must presuppose (προϋποτεθεῖσθαι) many conditions according to our wishes, without any of them being impossible. I mean, for example, conditions regarding the number of citizens and the size of the territory. (4, 1325b37)

Here's my thesis: *Politics* book 7, along with book 8, which continues the subject of education, are largely *nonpolitical* parts of the *Politics*. They are included in Aristotle's political studies and are indeed addressed to the legislator to help him achieve the overall goal of Aristotle's politics, which is to bring about the happiness of the citizens by making them virtuous, which is done by establishing good laws, always supposing the establishment of a correct constitution. This establishment is the major task of the legislator. For this establishment, *Politics* 7 considers the necessary, or at least desirable, conditions.

We have seen in detail how the political is based on the prepolitical, that is, the city on the family and the various groups and associations. The problem dealt with in book 7 is almost the same, in that it concerns the *prepolitical*, but in the logical rather than chronological sense. That is marked by the "we must presuppose (προϋποτεθεῖσθαι)" at 1325b38. The crucial passage on this point is perhaps the beginning of chapter 8 of book 7:

> As in other natural compounds the conditions without which the composite whole would not exist are not necessarily organic parts of it, so in a city or in any other combination forming a unity not every necessary condition is a part, for example food, land, or anything else of this sort. (Necessarily there is something common and the same in a community, in which all share equally or unequally.) But when there are two things of which one exists for the sake of the other, they have nothing

in common except that the one receives what the other produces. Such, for example, is the relation in which workmen and tools stand to their work; the house and the builder have nothing in common, but the art of the builder is for the sake of the house. And so, cities require property, but property, even though living beings are included in it, is no part of the city. (1328a21)

Aristotle's general thesis is easily understood. If the citizens do not live somewhere or do not find something to eat, there obviously will be no city. Nevertheless, the territory or the system of producing food are not "parts" properly so-called of the city, that is, they do not belong to its essence, or to put it another way, they are not *political* parts of the city. That also applies to the inhabitants of the city. Slaves are necessary but not proper to the city. The same goes for all those who are not citizens: women, children, foreigners, and, as we have seen, workmen, farmers, and many others. These *instrumental* parts of the city doubtless need to be known by the legislator.

With this distinction between necessary parts and essential parts of the city we find ourselves faced by the application to the city of an explanatory structure that Aristotle uses very often; we saw one version of it at work in the political character of man. I will return to this a little later. It is important to notice that this essential thesis of Aristotelian political thought is not limited to book 7. Thus, we have shown that Aristotle opposed it, perhaps a bit unjustly, to Plato's analyses in *Politics* 4.4 when he was criticizing the "first city" of the *Republic*. In fact, this thesis is present right from the start of the *Politics* (accepting the traditional order of the books) in the distinction between different kinds of power, where I claimed to see the very foundation of Aristotelian politics. Productive and commercial activities, whether they involve servile hand labor or not, do not stem from political power, but from that, notably, of the head of a family. To say that a city cannot live without agriculture does not make it an agricultural community; to say that a city needs to trade with neighboring cities and peoples does not give you license to say that it is a commercial entity, just as the city is not a military entity even though it must necessarily have armed forces. Ignorance of this principle gives rise to deviations, duly analyzed in the "realist" passages, giving us an alternative approach to deviation. The canonical definition of a deviant constitution is that it functions for the benefit of some and not for the "common advantage." Consequently, one may say that the deviation of any constitution leads it ultimately *out of the political*, since it no longer seeks to make the citizens happy by developing their virtue. If, in fact, the city functions exclusively or principally for the benefit of the farmers, the tradesmen, or the soldiers, it cannot have a correct constitution. But *Politics* book 7 establishes more solidly than any other Aristotelian text that virtue is simultaneously the principle means and the intermediate end of politics, the ultimate end being happiness.

In *Politics* 7 Aristotle also describes this distinction between the essential and the necessary in terms of an opposition between means and end. Aligning politics with other arts, he sees three possibilities of deviation. The end may be correctly posited, but the means not adequate; the end may be bad, but the means good (doubtless we need to understand that as signifying that they could be used to achieve a good end); the end and the means may be equally bad. Aristotle cites the example of medicine: to grasp the end consists of discerning "what a body ought to be in order to be healthy" (7.13, 1331b35), the means being the different interventions used by physicians to cure it. He also mentions the example of ethics. Having declared that he has defined "happiness," namely, "an actualization and perfect use of virtue, not hypothetically but absolutely" (1332a9), "in the *Ethics*" (a8) (perhaps it's not a matter of a reference to a precise passage), he takes the example of just actions. It's worth quoting the passage: "Just vengeances and punishments do indeed spring from a good principle, but they are good only because we cannot do without them—it would be better that neither individuals nor cities should need anything of the sort" (1332a12).

We understand what Aristotle means. A punishment may be just or unjust but, even when it is just, it is not a part of the essence of the virtue (excellence) of justice. A proof of that is that to punish, or to exact vengeance, even when it is justified, does not make the virtuous man happier, and it would be better if he could dispense with it.[11] It seems to me that one may apply that to politics in a more general way than it seems at first sight.

---

11. There is an interesting disagreement between editors at 1332a17: the manuscripts record that actions like punishments "assume a certain evil." But since Sepulveda that is often corrected from αἵρεσις to ἀναίρεσις, understanding "are the rejection of a certain evil." But I prefer to understand that punishments and vengeances, even when they contribute to a good, are a "necessary evil." In his book, already cited, Paulin Ismard shows very well how the Greek cities kept the execution of punishment (imprisonment, death penalty) at the margins of the political, in any case in the hands of people who were not citizens. The last person to talk with Socrates in the *Phaedo* was thus a slave charged with bringing him the hemlock.

Contrary to some of the philosophical schools that came before and after him, the Cynics and the Stoics for example, Aristotle always maintained that one cannot be happy without a minimum of the goods called "external." No one can be called happy when he experiences great physical or moral suffering, or is mired in poverty. But it is not health that will make him happy, because if health, which is the harmonious functioning of bodily processes, were the essence or part of the essence of happiness, which, as we recall, is "an actualization and perfect use of virtue," then a man would be essentially an animal. Equally, if a man finds his happiness in external goods, he puts the means in the place of the end. Aristotle nevertheless seems to take a fairly large step in the direction of Stoicism when he writes, "A good man may make the best even of poverty or disease, and the other ills of life; but he can only attain happiness under the opposite conditions" (7.13, 1332a19). What does it mean to "make the best" (χρήσατο . . . καλῶς) of poverty or disease? Doubtless we must understand that in enduring illness I make virtuous use of my suffering in that I manifest courage, which is a virtue. And in fact, this is an example of virtuous conduct in the primary sense, which presupposes deliberation and choice, because although I did not choose to be ill, I have indeed chosen the worthy conduct that I adopt when faced by the illness. It is likely that Aristotle thinks that courageous behavior in the face of illness, although it does not eliminate the suffering caused by the illness, should be a source of satisfaction for the courageous man. Otherwise it wouldn't be a *virtuous* use of the illness.

It's the same for geographical, human, and so on, givens that the legislator finds at his disposal. Things vary, according to a distinction already presented, by whether the legislator is *founding* or *reforming* a city, the first of these situations having become rather rare in the time of Aristotle. This last point demands some comment. Aristotle, who died just after Alexander the Great, lived in an epoch during which many cities were founded by Alexander. But there is an important nuance: these cities were established in barbarian lands, that is, as we have seen, among people whom Aristotle considered incapable of political life. It thus remains that the Aristotelian legislator, in the actual state of affairs—since Aristotle means to propose actualizable political solutions—finds himself massively confronted by already existing cities that need to be reformed.[12] That is

---

12. In fact, even before Alexander founded many cities, in Aristotle's time or just before, a number of cities were founded by the union of several villages (*synoikismos*). But this rarely happened on virgin soil.

obviously what the entire machinery of the "realist" books presupposes. When Aristotle indicates that it is necessary to temper the oligarchic character of a constitution by democratic measures, or the reverse, one can hardly conceive that it would be possible to do that before the existence of a city that functions badly. It would, however, be a mistake to think that, in these conditions, the analyses of the last two books of the *Politics* would be of little interest for the Aristotelian legislator, on the ground that they concern only a marginal aspect of his activity. When, in a passage cited above, Aristotle recommends that we "presuppose many conditions according to our wishes, without any of them being impossible," he provides us, in outline, the way in which the legislator not only will read, but will utilize, *Politics* 7. In this book, and to a lesser degree in book 8, it is a matter of describing "ideal" conditions." But it is necessary to be careful that they do not become "too ideal," to the point of becoming impossible to achieve.

Here then is my conception of the relation that the legislator can and ought to have with the part of *Politics* 7 concerning the conditions for the excellent constitution. First, he must understand what Aristotle means when he calls these geographic and other conditions "necessary." To say that territory is necessary for the city means that without territory there will not be a city. Put this way: if one wants a city to exist, then it is necessary that there will be a territory; this is the formulation that Aristotle uses to characterize "hypothetical necessity," with the most notable examples found in his biology. In a very interesting essay dedicated to the role of the material cause in Aristotle's biological explanation, already mentioned,[13] Robert Bolton shows, in a totally convincing way, that the material necessity that combines with finality so that, for example, a function is carried out, is not necessary in the sense in which things could not be otherwise. Thus, if blood has to be cooled so that a particular animal may live, it is necessary that this animal have lungs; but the existence of lungs is not necessary in the sense that life would be impossible if they did not exist. Aristotle never asserts that the pulmonary system is the only possible or the best possible for any animal.[14] In fact, nature could have

---

13. Bolton, "The Material Cause: Matter and Explanation in Aristotle's Natural Science."
14. In biology, "always bring about the best possible" means that nature brings it about that the situation permits the animal species concerned to survive forever. The best for small fish, since they are eaten in great numbers by other animals, is to be sufficiently prolific to escape extinction (cf. *GA* 3.4, 755a31). But nature could have made them faster, less visible, and so forth.

found a different procedure, which is in fact what she does for example with the gills of fish. It happens that, in a given set of circumstances, the lungs *do the job* so that the cooling of the blood has the material conditions for it to be carried out.

Sometimes the means "chosen" by nature are ultimately not remarkably successful. Thus, an example that I have made great use of elsewhere, when Aristotle writes about deer that the "large size of their horns and their multiple ramifications cause more harm than good" (*PA* 3.2, 663a10), he doesn't say that they don't use their horns: since the males have to be able to compete, the horns serve the purpose, but they fulfill their role in a way that is so imperfect (they are impeded by their horns), that nature has been forced to give them another means of dealing with their enemies, namely, the speed that allows them to escape their predators.[15] Doubtless we are meant to understand that the horns are used above all in combat between stags during the mating season. All that does not prevent the stag from being a *perfect* animal, in the sense in which the advantages of its physical constitution are sufficient to counterbalance the disadvantages of this same constitution, and the difficulties which this animal encounters in its life in its environment, thus permitting its species to survive forever.

If then Nature had written the equivalent of *Politics* 7, but addressing the demiurge that was going to fabricate the various species of animals, she would, in the chapter on horns, explain that the best horns are short but solid, hollow on the inside in order not to be too heavy. And in fact, one finds in the *Parts of Animals* a description of "perfect" horns, which corresponds to the description of the "perfect" geographic situation for a city:

> In other animals (than the deer) the horns are hollow for a certain distance, and the end alone is solid, this being the part of use in a blow. At the same time, to prevent even the hollow part that grows out of the skin from being weak, the solid part fitted into it comes up from the bones. For this

---

15. In fact, the continuation of the *Parts of Animals* passage occasions an additional distinction. At 664a6, Aristotle writes of does that "they lack horns because they would be useless—they are useless to the stags too, but the strength of the stags makes them less burdensome." Although the stags use their horns, Aristotle does not any less think that they are "not useful," which doubtless means that they are more burdensome than useful, which is what the text said a little earlier.

arrangement is not only that which makes the horns of the greatest service in fighting, but that which causes them to be as little of an impediment as possible in the other actions of life. (3.2, 663b14)

Which does not prevent our demiurge from giving to the stag, despite its imperfect horns, a kind of perfection, as shown by the everlastingness of the species of deer. An obviously absurd hypothesis, since as we know, there was no demiurge that put the Aristotelian world in order, since this order, including the species of deer, always existed and will always continue to exist. Neither the universe nor deer have a history.

The city, on the other hand, does have a history, as we have seen, which makes of the legislator a kind of political demiurge, and he knows that the best would be for the city to have a territory sloping toward the east, that the city would be best off to have a city wall. Clearly there are situations where things can be arranged for the best: in the case of the foundation of a city the legislator can choose, to a certain degree at least, the location of the city, and in the case of many of the advantageous conditions surveyed in book 7, the legislator is not without resources. Thus, city walls may be built if the city lacks them.[16] Finally, as nature does in the case of living things, the legislator can take measures to compensate certain disadvantages. If, for example, easy access to the sea, which is obviously an advantage for a city, proves to be perilous for the constitution because this access opens the city to many politically undesirable people, the legislator can take legislative measures to reduce the power to harm of these people, for example by refusing them citizenship or by regulating the relationships between the citizens and other inhabitants of the city. That's what chapter 6, cited above, says.

Politics 7 and 8, in their analyses of the best conditions that can obtain for a city, thus do not only address the person who wants to found a city, but every legislator, and ultimately the distinction between cities founded

---

16. The way that Aristotle deals with the question of fortifications in *Politics* 7.11 shows us how much he was a man of his time, caring about efficacy. He takes seriously the idea, notably held by the Spartans, that by giving a false sense of security, city walls soften the warrior spirit of the citizens. But the progress of military technology had rendered that position obsolete, and in any case, one can act as if one did not have city walls when one has them (when meeting the enemy in open country, for example), but one cannot act as if one had them when one does not . . .

and cities *refounded* is not crucial for Aristotle. The reaffirmation of the ethical destination of the city at the same time as the political foundation of ethics, as found in book 7, is obviously useful for every legislator, no matter what the situation of the city in which he is interested is. As for the necessary conditions for an excellent city, we have seen that taking them into account is far from limited to the foundation of a city. That allows us to better define the difference, on this point, between Plato and Aristotle, and thus do justice to the characterization, fairly widespread among the commentators, that the two last books of the *Politics* are "Platonic" texts.

We need to compare our text to the *Laws* rather than to the *Republic*. In the *Republic*, Socrates and his interlocutors do not have the goal of establishing the city the outlines of which they sketch. At best, that would be the work of subsequent legislators who would have benefited from a Platonic education; in any case the major topic of the dialogue is justice in the human soul. The *Laws*, on the contrary, can be considered as a real work of political philosophy, one that presents important aspects of Platonic conceptions of the constitution and of legislation. It certainly is not a matter of a constitutional project like that of Jean-Jacques Rousseau for the island of Corsica, but a sort of fable (at 6.752a, the Athenian in fact speaks of a fable, μῦθος): after a long introduction in the first three books, terminating with a pseudo-historical examination of the establishment of various constitutions in the Greek world, since the flood, the primitive and patriarchal societies, until the excesses of contemporary Athenian democracy, Clinias declares that he sees a (happy) omen[17] in that Crete is preparing to found a colony and that Cnossos has charged him with providing good legislation for that colony.

It is quite remarkable that the end of book 3 of the *Laws*, and books 4 and following, propose a program that looks like it could have come from Aristotle's *Politics* if that were limited to the books called "old" in the reading of the chronologist interpreters whom I have critiqued above. In fact, it's a matter of first considering what there is good in the various constitutions that exist or have existed, which corresponds to the project of *Politics* 2. Next, it would be necessary to propose a "rational" (τῷ λόγῳ, 3, 702d) model, "as if we were founding this city from the beginning." Plato deals, at the beginning of book 4, with the geographic situation of the city, its access to the sea, with analyses often echoed in Aristotle's *Politics*

---

17. He uses the term οἰωνός (702c), the name of a large bird of the sort from which oracles were derived, cf. *Iliad* 13.243.

7. Thus, concerning the character both beneficial and dangerous of easy access to the sea, useful for trade, but developing the taste for wealth and the easy life. Similarly, for naval power, whose absence, Plato remarks, had put Attica at the mercy of Minos (706a–b), but whose development is dangerous for the virtue of the citizens. Plato goes so far as to say that the real victory over the barbarians was not Salamis, because naval victories only elevate the craft of ship captains and other people of little virtue, but Marathon and Plataea, victories of the true warrior virtue of hoplites. More than one Athenian may have been a bit annoyed with a passage like that, but it is not without echo in *Politics* 7.6, which insists on the political danger coming from the development of a navy because it necessarily produces an increase of the number of sailors, all people inapt for virtue. Aristotle had probably carefully read this before writing *Politics* 7, at least if Plato had not read this book before writing the *Laws*, if it is true that Aristotle wrote *Politics* 7 at the beginning of his career, and it seems accepted that the *Laws* was Plato's last dialogue.

The Order of the Books of the *Politics* Is Anti-Platonic

In fact, *Politics* 7 is profoundly Platonic, but we will see that that does not make it an early work in Aristotle's career. At the end of *Laws* 4, the Athenian explains that the exposition of laws destined to regulate the excellent city need to be preceded by a "prelude" (προοίμια). This prelude ends, according to the Athenian's explicit statement, a little after the middle of book 5 (734e). In a very different form from that of the Aristotelian text, given the differences between the Platonic and Aristotelian ways of writing, this prelude presents noteworthy basic convergence with what constitutes the prelude of *Politics* 7, the three first chapters. In both cases we learn that among the various kinds of goods, it is not wealth, physical attributes, and so on, that are most to be desired, but the goods of the soul, and Plato, just like Aristotle, asks about the kind of life that would be most choice-worthy. To that we must add all the "ethical" passages of *Politics* 7, which support relationships of virtue, happiness, and life in a city, to the excellent constitution, passages that correspond to some in the *Laws*.

Then there is the presentation of the measures to take in order to obtain an excellent constitution. Here too there are numerous parallels between the *Laws* and *Politics* 7, but what is most important is the logic of these presentations. For it is a logic that we can call "preconditional":

before all, the people who will compose the city need to be selected according to certain qualities, or, at least negatively, they must not be hardened criminals, nor poor people easily manipulated by demagogues. Next, given that in the "myth" of the *Laws* the location of the future excellent city has already been determined and that it has a sufficient number of positive characteristics, *it is logical*, still according to the same procedure, that the interlocutors of the *Laws* turn to the problem of the division of land and the related problem of the number of proprietors of landholdings, then come to the examination of measures and laws that concern the patrimony of the citizens. The same logic organizes the exposition of *Politics* 7. With, all the same, a difference that precisely makes all the difference. Let us quote again, but more at length, this passage:

> So much for introduction. In what has preceded I have discussed the various constitutions; the starting point for what remains is the conditions for a city of our wishes; for an excellent constitution cannot exist without adequate means. And therefore, we must presuppose many conditions according to our wishes, without any of them being impossible. I mean, for example, the conditions regarding the number of citizens and the size of the territory. Similarly, in fact, there is need for various artisans, like weaver or boat-builder, disposing of appropriate material for their work—for the better prepared the material, the finer the results of the art. It is the same for the statesman and legislator who need to have available suitable materials. (7.4, 1325b33)

I call attention to just two points in this crucial text. First, Aristotle does not situate the study that he begins with book 7 and which focuses on, as he says in the first line of the book, the excellent constitution, at the beginning of his project of the determination of this excellent constitution. There are, to begin with, "preliminary remarks," which relate to the best kind of life for the individual and the city, and which correspond to what the *Laws* calls a "prelude." And above all, there is "the prior examination of various constitutions," that is, according to the chronologist interpreters, *Politics* 2 and 3, and according to me and others, books 2 through 6. But the prior examination of constitutions consists of a study of the excellent constitution. Book 2 asserts this, from the first line, by explaining that the study of constitutions that have existed either in reality or in the mind of legislators or political philosophers, is a precondition for such a research. Book 3, after having given a *political* definition of the city and the citizen, considers the excellence of the one and the excellence of the other, particularly by positing the distinction between correct and deviant constitutions. As for the "realist" books, I have already deployed considerable effort to show that they all contribute, even when they study seditions and come down to taking a Machiavellian turn, to defining the excellent constitution and the means to establish and preserve it. And they do it at the cost of a remarkable extension of the range of excellence.

Next, Aristotle introduces an important and fundamental distinction in his political philosophy, between the study that he undertakes in *Politics* 7 and those carried out elsewhere on the excellent constitution. He characterizes this distinction by a comparison with the work of the artisan:[18] just as the artisan must have appropriate material carefully elaborated so that he can make a good product, so *Politics* 7 should furnish the material for Aristotle's major work in political philosophy, the study of the means for realizing the excellent constitution. This opposition between matter and form is anything but accidental and marginal in Aristotle. The matter of a physical entity, and notably of this kind of physical entity that is a living being, does not belong to the essence or definition of this entity except in an incomplete and derivative way, for one cannot say that a man *is* the sum of his bones, viscera, and flesh. We may translate this opposition, as it applies to the excellent constitution, thus: the legislator must *put into a political form* the material furnished by *Politics* 7, which is not, properly speaking, a political book.

Plato, in contrast, puts all the measures that he recommends on the same level, whether it is the manner of dividing up the territory or the way of organizing the courts or the Council. For this last case, for example, Plato recommends procedures that find more than one echo in Aristotle's *Politics*. The Athenian prescribes fining the wealthy (the first and second classes) if they do not want to participate in the assembly, and exempting the poor (the two remaining classes) from this fine. Also, he demands a combination of the distribution advantages according to

---

18. Aristotle says, "various artisans, like the weaver and the boat-builder" (1325b41); the weaver is also provided as an example in the passage in the *Laws* that follows the end of the "prelude" (not to mention the *Statesman*), but that of the boat-builder is more suitable to Aristotle's account. Is the mention of the weaver another indication of Plato's influence on Aristotle?

arithmetic equality in some cases, and according to geometrical equality in the more important cases. The text is so close to Aristotelian doctrine, and so contrary to the Aristotelian spirit, that it is worth citing:

> The most genuine equality, and the best, is not so obvious [as arithmetic equality, just examined]. It needs the wisdom and judgment of Zeus, and only in a limited number of ways does it help the human race; but when cities or even individuals do find it profitable, they find it very profitable indeed. The general method I mean is to grant much to the great and less to the less great, adjusting what you give to take account of the real nature of each—specifically, to confer high recognition on great virtue, but when you come to the poorly educated in this respect, to treat them as they deserve. (6, 757b)

When we recall that a little earlier the Athenian defined the excellent city as a mixture of monarchy and democracy (756e), we get the impression that we are swimming in Aristotelian waters. But it would be better to say, in Aristotelian terms, that this city is "a mixture of oligarchy (or aristocracy) and democracy," because it is election, a procedure proper to minority constitutions, that intervenes in the nomination of almost all the magistrates in the *Laws*. The designation to military functions, on the other hand, seems to be very democratic, because anyone may oppose any nomination. Nevertheless . . . What is missing in the *Laws* but strongly thematized in Aristotle is a distinction between political functions and simply technical functions. In the project of establishing a city presented by the Athenian, magistracies are presented one after the other without the establishment of any difference in *level* between them, even if they are presented as having more or less honor. This distinction is, in contrast, at the basis of the Aristotelian analysis. To be sure, the royal art is architectonic for the other arts. There is, in addition, an ethical goal, which certainly distinguishes Plato from Xenophon, for whom a good citizen is the one who enriches his city.[19] It nevertheless remains that all the arts belong to the same space. Once again, Plato sees a difference in degree where Aristotle posits a difference in kind.

We showed that in our analysis of *Politics* 4.15, where Aristotle distinguishes political magistracies, that is, the *real* magistracies, by "the power

---

19. Cf. Louis-André Dorion, *L'Autre Socrate. Études sur les écrits socratiques de Xénophon* (Paris: Les Belles Lettres, 2013), 161–162.

of deliberating, deciding, giving orders, especially the latter" (1299a26). The division of inhabitants of the city into "proper parts" and "necessary parts," which we have already encountered several times, is isomorphic with this distinction. We quote:

> Even if it is right to judge the city by its size, this should not be done by the number of each and every class, for cities are bound to include a large number of slaves, metics, and foreigners; the test should be the number of those who are proper parts of the city; it is the superiority in the number of these that indicates a great city; a city with many artisans but few hoplites cannot be great. A great city and a populous city are not the same thing. (7.4, 1326a16)

As for the beginning of chapter 8 of book 7, Aristotle puts himself at a notable level of generality, justifying at the same time previous resort to biological models. We quote it again:

> As in other natural compounds the conditions without which the composite whole would not exist are not necessarily organic parts of it, so in a city or in any other combination forming a unity not every necessary condition is a part. (1328a21)[20]

Sometimes Aristotle seems to borrow a Platonic trope. Thus, we read in this same *Politics* 7.8:

> First, there must be food; secondly, arts, for life requires many instruments; thirdly there must be arms, for the members of a community have need of them, and in their own hands, too, in order to maintain authority both against disobedient subjects and against external assailants; fourthly, there must be a certain amount of revenue, both for internal needs, and

---

20. Cf. the last words of 7.9: "Thus we have said that without which a city cannot be constituted, and how many parts there are in a city. In fact, farmers, artisans, and the entire class of working men necessarily belong to cities; on the other hand, the military class and those who deliberate are parts of the city, and each of these is distinct from the other, either always or temporarily" (1328a34). Perhaps these lines were interpolated, as Newman thought, but they express an Aristotelian doctrine: that without which there is no city is different from the parts of the city.

for the purposes of war; fifthly, or rather first, there must be a care for religion, which is commonly called worship; sixthly, and most necessary of all, there must be a power of deciding what is for the public interest, and what is just in men's dealings with one another. These are the services that every city may be said to need. (1328b5)

As in Plato, there is thus a difference between the parts, but as Aristotle also posits a difference in kind between material parts and political parts of the city, whoever does more can also do less, and if there is a difference of kind, a fortiori, there is a difference of importance . . .

This opposition between, on the one hand, an absence of a distinction between the indispensable functions and political parts in the *Laws* and, on the other hand, the Aristotelian position, is an additional example of the contrast between Plato's reductionism and Aristotle's distinctions that we find right from the first chapter of the *Politics*, and that I have often talked about. Every magistracy, in fact, whether it is concerned with handing down a death penalty, or supervises irrigation canals, possesses a certain power. But not all of them pertain to a *political* power, that is, in relation to the constitution that it is a matter of making function or defending.

One may thus summarize the foregoing by saying that two characteristics of the project of Plato's *Laws* distinguish it strongly from that of the *Politics*. In the first place, Plato locates himself uniquely in the perspective of founding a city (even if the legislator of the *Laws* finds that the locale of his city is imposed on him), while, as we have seen, this situation is not very frequent in Aristotle's case. Thus, one example among many others, but very interesting because it goes even farther than a simple assertion that the excellent city needs to be founded *de novo*, at *Laws* 4, 709d, the Athenian asks, addressing the legislator, "What conditions in the city are we going to give you that will enable you to run it properly on your own from now on?" To which the Athenian answers immediately that it is necessary to give the city a virtuous tyrant so that it will get "as quickly and efficiently as possible a political system that will enable it to live a life of supreme happiness" (710b). Doubtless one may suspect behind this the idea that if, by some unlucky chance one may say, the legislator has to work on an already existent city, he would need the means of imposing a constitutional clean slate in order that he could, so to speak, "go back to zero."[21] By a remarkable paradox, it is Aristotle (whose legislator works more often in an already-existing city) more than Plato (whose legislator is the founder of the city) who proposes, particularly in *Politics* book 1, an analysis of the birth of cities by the change in level of the dynamic of needs. As for Plato, he is in the grip of a kind of Parmenidean vertigo when it is a matter of creating a city from a previous state without a city, and he ends by resorting to the aid of an already existent city, namely, Cnossos (*Laws* 6, 752dff.). The city of the *Laws* is thus, ultimately, a city that has "neither father nor mother, except for the city that founded it" (*Laws* 7, 754a).

We are here at the antipode of Aristotelian reformism and its keystone, the idea of *amelioration*. On this point too, when the Platonic and Aristotelian texts reveal resemblances, sometimes striking, they hide real discrepancies. In fact, Plato too is aware that his city must improve its legislation. But he conceives of this process of amelioration as due to the fact that the original legislator did not have enough time to legislate concerning all the areas that he should have dealt with. Also, like a painter's picture, retouched with the help of his students to complete his work (cf. *Laws* 6, 769a, the successors of the legislator will need to "complete," συμπληροῦν; *Laws* 6, 770b8, passage already cited). I hope that I have shown how far such an analysis is from that of Aristotle.

Next, and above all, Plato does not define the political space as that of a certain kind of power, and in that respect, he is not a political thinker in as clearly marked a way as is Aristotle. We find once again the fundamental character of the differentiation of powers that Aristotle presents right from the first lines of the *Politics*.

Let us return to a problem that I have until now considered as unsolvable, that of the order of the books of the *Politics*. What the preceding considerations seem, to me at least, to suggest, if not establish, is that the

---

21. A passage that confirms this is at 5, 737b: first of all, one must deal with the problem of land distribution "if people have longstanding complaints against each other, anyone with any sense at all will not proceed (προϊέναι) to organize them, if he can help it. But in the present case, God has given us a group of people to found a new city, in which so far there is no mutual malice." To translate προϊέναι as "go farther in the reforms," as most translators do, is at least imprecise. "Proceed" is definitely better. In any case, the city founded in the *Laws* is not completely founded *de novo*, since this "city of the Magnesians" does not choose its location. This strongly recalls the situation of Phaleas of Chalcedon as reported by Aristotle (*Pol.* 2.7).

traditional order handed down in the manuscript tradition is properly Aristotelian, while the order 1–3, 7–8, 4–6, so often adopted in the past and continuing to have many supporters, is a Platonic order.

A Platonic Aristotle in fact would aim first at establishing an excellent constitution *ex nihilo*. To do that, and because no matter how Platonic he be, he would still remain Aristotle, he would begin by presenting an introduction on the city and the family, then gather a group of constitutions that have claimed to be excellent, and finally define the city, the citizen, and constitutional correctness. Next, after that which the *Laws* calls a "prelude" (book 7, chapters 1–3), books 7 and 8 sketch an excellent constitution according to what I have called the "logic of the precondition": one must first set the territory, the population, and so on, then give laws. Next would come the "realist" books, thanks to which, as Aristotle says at the beginning of book 4, the legislator should be able "to give his assistance to existing constitutions" (4.1, 1289a6). Thus, most interpreters give a Platonizing reading of *Politics* 4.1: the legislator should know how to establish an "ideal" constitution when provided with an extensive set of preconditions and, if that is not possible, he will be contented with a less good constitution, or even a constitution acceptable for most cities. That also would bring the project of the *Politics* closer to that of the *Laws*, since in the *Laws* Plato also reveals a movement of degradation in comparison with the ideal constitution of the *Republic* in a city of a second, and then third, rank (*Laws* 5, 739aff.).

But the traditional order of the manuscripts, in contrast, obeys an Aristotelian logic. After having, from the very first lines, affirmed the specificity of political power, the *Politics* illustrates, in book 1, this specificity by analyzing a nonpolitical instance of power, that of the family. I have, notably, maintained, following Malcolm Schofield, that the long study of slavery also tends to characterize political power. Then, after a book that serves in place of a doxography, Aristotle posits, in book 3, the *political* definitions of the city and the citizen, and immediately interests himself in constitutional excellence by examining the various constitutions in light of the distinction between correct and deviant constitutions. Then he dives into hard-core politics in the "realist" books. In this long *political* analysis of power in all its forms, Aristotle never loses sight of the goal of the entire *Politics*, the establishment of an excellent constitution. Finally comes book 7, completed by book 8. In Aristotelian terms, books 7 and 8 are prior *for us* to the realist books in that before making a city one must provide its "matter," for without land, without inhabitants, and so on, there will be no city. It is this priority for us that marks passages like that which we cited above, "*first* a city has to have a source of food" (8.8, 1328b5). But they are per se posterior to the realist books, because it is the political that gives them their meaning. In the same way, in naval construction, the acquisition and preparation of construction materials is a precondition, but posterior in terms of essence. The constructor must first determine the *form* of the boat that he wants to construct before thinking about the material and the properties of that material. For "prepolitical" is meaningless except in relation to "political." Plato, who says that one must first organize land distribution in order to establish a constitution, remains in anteriority for us alone. For Aristotle, the distribution of land, for example, would depend on the orientation of the existing constitution.

I hope to have shown that book 7 is, if not apolitical, at least nonpolitical, as much in its analyses of the relationship between ethics and politics as in its recommendations concerning the best constitution. Pretty much everything that book 7 recommends is applicable to every correct constitution. To be sure, there are differences, because, for example, a certain topography would be more suitable for an aristocracy, and another for a more popular regime. Thus, an aristocracy would accommodate itself more easily to a territory with steep hills where the aristocrats could reside, and a polity with plains where the infantry could maneuver more easily. But everything depends in the last resort on the constitution: by making the acropolis a civic sanctuary, the Athenian democracy prevented its aristocratic use. But everything considered, every constitution would benefit by establishing itself in a place accessible to the sea, which includes fortifications, and so forth. No correct constitution, as we have known ever since book 3, will give political rights to artisans and shopkeepers, for reasons that have already been given. These conditions obviously cannot be part of happiness, because even wealth and health contribute at best the means to happiness. And as they are not political, the fact that these conditions may not be ideal, or even some of them might be missing, does not prevent attaining political excellence.

The Prologue to Book 7

The first three chapters of *Politics* 7 doubtless deserve a textual explication in the true sense of the term. I will content myself here with a few remarks that will be useful for our purposes.

The very first sentences of the first chapter, the central reasoning of which is not, according to Newman, completely expressible in English, are crucial. To begin with, they situate the topic in politics: the question of the best kind of life, which will constitute the recurrent subject of the prologue, is posed for the benefit of "the person who wants to carry out research appropriate to the excellent constitution." And, in fact, the reasoning that follows is at best curious, at worst vicious. One may formalize it thus: (i) Those who live under an excellent constitution are most successful. (ii) If one knows the best way of life (the life of those who succeed), and (iii) if one has established that the best way of life is the same for the individual and for the city, then (iv) one will know what the excellent constitution is. One would have then a kind of construction the inverse of that of Plato's *Republic*, which goes to the city in order to understand justice in the individual soul; here, understanding individual happiness allows us to understand the happiness of the city.

Then, at 7.1, 1323a21, comes a passage that is also quite astonishing. The problem of the best way of life, Aristotle writes, has already been sufficiently described in the "exoteric discourses." In other words, if it is true as Aristotle has just stated, that, if one determines the best way of life, one will have made an enormous step in our search for the excellent constitution, then the answer to our political question can already be found in the exoteric treatises. I note that the identification of the λόγοι ἐξωτερικοί remains an open question among Aristotelian scholars, and I mean to leave it open. The sense of this expression in our passage is somewhere between two extremes: either Aristotle means to say that he has already dealt with these questions in his ethical writings, or he refers to treatises written by someone else, with, between these two extremes, some uncertainty about his own works to which he may be alluding (the ethical treatises as we know them, the *Protreptic*, etc.).

In fact, what one would find in the exoteric discourses according to our passage of the *Politics*, and which, according to Aristotle, no one would disagree with, is that there are three kinds of goods—external, bodily, and psychic—and to be "blessed" (μακάριος) is to have all three. But this common doctrine leaves a great deal of room for discussion about the appropriate dosage of each of these kinds of goods. Most people, in fact, are content with very little of the psychic good, that is, virtue (but Aristotle does not say that these people totally dispense with being virtuous), while they desire as much as possible of external and bodily goods. Aristotle then undertakes a "demonstration" of his thesis, namely, that happiness is produced by virtue "provided with sufficient means to be able to take part in actions conforming to virtue" (1323b41), and that in two ways. The first is empirical: it is obvious that the accumulation of external goods does not make people happy. Thus, even those who place the sovereign good in pleasure recognize that it is "a harmonious character and intelligence" (1323b4) that allows them to achieve their end. Maybe philosophers see that, but others . . . ? Then, after the demonstration "by the facts," Aristotle proposes a second approach, "logical," which consists, to summarize, in maintaining that only virtue can be practiced to an extreme, precisely because there is no excess of excellence, while for external goods there is a limit beyond which they become harmful. Thus, virtue can be sought without moderation.

From these considerations, weak from an argumentative perspective, and in fact not very convincing, Aristotle draws the conclusion that "each one receives as much happiness as he has virtue and prudence, and acts in accordance with them" (1323b21), that happiness, both ours and that of the gods, is far from the satisfaction that external goods may chance to bring us, and furthermore that this is just as true for cities as it is for individuals. Thus, Aristotle provides, without further ado, the answer to one of the fundamental questions posed at the beginning of the chapter. Plato hardly gave himself (or would not give himself, if, once again, *Politics* 7 is earlier than the *Republic*, which is even less likely than for the *Laws*) more trouble asserting the isomorphism between the individual soul and the city.

It is quite surprising to see Aristotle, at the beginning of 7.2, posing again the question[22] of the identity of the happiness of the individual and the happiness of the city, and even more surprising to see how he decides the question: "But this too is obvious: everyone in fact agrees in saying that they are the same" (1324a7).[23] Why? Because those who think that wealth makes happiness also think that the wealthy city is happy, the partisans of tyrannical domination would like a dominant city, and the partisans of virtue a virtuous city.

---

22. Cf. "this remains to present" (1324a7).

23. Newman tries to save Aristotle from the accusation of repeating himself by saying that in chapter 1 he claimed that the *virtues* are the same for the individual and the city, and now he goes on to the problem of *happiness*. But in chapter 1 he said, as we have seen, "each one receives as much happiness as he has of virtue."

One cannot avoid thinking that Aristotle wrote all that as a kind of introduction to the two questions that are really close to his heart: should one prefer for oneself a contemplative life or an active life, that is, political? Which constitution is better, the one where everyone shares in power, or that in which only a majority participate (cf. 7.2, 1324a17)? This latter question shunts to one side, we notice, any aristocratic prejudice on Aristotle's part, if it is true that aristocracy is a regime in which only a small number of virtuous people participate.

The question of the opposition between the contemplative or theoretical life, and the political life, which has instigated an extraordinary amount of activity among all interpreters, from antiquity until today, is dealt with especially at the end of the *Nicomachean Ethics*. We have two good reasons for not taking up this matter in detail here: one is that it would require an entire book; the other is given by Aristotle himself:

> Since the excellence of the city is the object of theoretical political thought, and not the question of what is desirable for the individual, and we are engaged in a political discussion, the first question (what sort of life to choose) has a secondary interest for us, the latter will be the main subject of our inquiry. (1324a19)

"Secondary" (πάρεργον), that is, involved as a means and not as an end. Without getting into the logic of the doctrine, we must nevertheless recall some aspects and results of *Nicomachean Ethics* 10.6–9.

Until chapter 6, happiness was given as "an activity of the soul according to perfect virtue" (*EN* 1.13, 1102a5), and book 10 continues to support that definition, but with an alteration of stance. In fact, we see that when Aristotle declares that "if happiness is an activity according to virtue, it is reasonable to think that it is according to the highest virtue" (10.7, 1177a12), this supreme virtue is no longer the ethical-political virtue that has been at issue in the earlier books of the *Ethics*. And besides, Aristotle declares unambiguously that the political life cannot be happy "except in a secondary degree" (10.8, 1178a9). To understand his position, one must accept a slight, and legitimate, slippage that he introduces from "highest virtue" to "virtue of that which is highest (or perfect) in us." But that which is the best in a human being is his intellect, which cannot be perfect except in contemplation. Then one has what Aristotle calls "complete happiness" (ἡ τελεία εὐδαιμονία, 10.7, 1177a17). That supreme happiness is acquired in contemplation is not a new teaching when it appears in *Nicomachean Ethics* 10, because right from book 1 Aristotle makes the contemplative life one of the three lives that are chosen by some along with the life of pleasure and the political life (1.5, 1095b18), the examination of the contemplative life being left to "later" (1096a5).

It is interesting to note that these two happinesses, that which the practical life provides and that which accompanies the theoretical life, are not distinguished by a difference in kind, but in degree. That is what *Nicomachean Ethics* 10.7 shows, but the difference in degree is what the biological treatises characterize as a difference in species (or form). Thus, one of the characteristics of happiness is to be stable and not transitory, but theoretical happiness is more stable than practical happiness, thus theoretical happiness is superior to practical happiness. *Politics* book 7 expresses this in a remarkable way:

> It is manifest that these are the two modes of life principally chosen by the men most ambitious of excelling in virtue, both in past times and at the present day—I mean the political life and the philosophical life. (7.2, 1324a30)

Thus, these two lives are two species of the genus "life led in pursuit of virtue."

We must also recall that the many references to contemplation as a divine activity, particularly of the god who contemplates himself, or of the god in us, ought not lead us to adopt a mystical view of contemplative activity in Aristotle. In fact, very few commentators today still stumble into that sort of error. Aristotelian contemplation is an intellectual activity, and more precisely a *theoretical* activity, which is perhaps after all the least bad translation of θεωρητικός, often translated "contemplative"; when this adjective has been applied to the sciences I have transliterated it "theoretical." And if the noun θεωρία often has a sense as vague as "study," it is not inappropriate to translate it sometimes as "theory." Thus, at *Politics* 7.2, 1324a19, a passage quoted above, the expression πολιτικὴ διανοία καὶ θεωρία means "political thought and theory," which I have translated as a hendiadys by "theoretical political thought." We note that this very expression, *theoria politikē* is, from an epistemological perspective a bit monstrous, or at least shaky, since it seems to ignore the divide between theory and practice.

But starting at *Politics* 7.2, 1324a35, Aristotle returns to the topic in which he is interested, and gives the question of the opposition between theory and practice its *accessory* function. What concerns him here are the relations between the choice of life of individuals and the constitutional form of the city in which these individuals are citizens. Aristotle develops on this subject an example from which, I have no doubt, not all the substantiating marrow has been extracted. Constitutions of the "despotic, that is, tyrannical, form" claim to be the only ones to be happy (1324b2). A city of that kind would endeavor to dominate its neighbors, whether other cities, or tribes. But it is not only a matter of violent domination, as is generally thought,[24] and then, at the first, Aristotle unifies "despotic" and "tyrannical," but a little later rectifies this somewhat when he says that in such cities "the function of a statesman is to know how to dominate despotically neighboring peoples, with or without their consent" (7.2, 1324b24). In fact, as we have seen, some are tyrants with the consent of their subjects. That could doubtless apply to people dominated by a city.

This correction is very important, in that Aristotle does not mean to say that these cities always oppress their neighbors, but rather that sometimes these neighbors consent to be treated like slaves, and it is to that, that the term "despotic" refers. Taking account of what we have said above about slavery, one may doubtless understand that such a city does not consider its neighbors, including those who live in cities, as other citizens. That may be just, if a population is naturally inapt for a political life. But, Aristotle says, injustice is always possible in despotic relationships: "one may also dominate in an unjust way" (1324b28), which presupposes that one may dominate in a just way. The despotic city is most often also a violent city, but it could also have with its neighbors, relationships of the paternalistic kind as sometimes happened between modern European countries and their colonies, relations in which, however, violence is never very far off.

Thus, we have perhaps in *Politics* 7.2 one of the rare passages in which Aristotle sketches his conception of the relationships between cities. In 3.9, as we saw, he speaks of military alliances or commercial zones involving several cities, but it is in order to say that these agglomerations of cities are not themselves cities, and therefore do not have an ethical perspective. Here Aristotle asserts that a virtuous city ought to have nondespotic relationships with its neighbors. And the text reveals that the alternatives are between "despotic" and "political" (cf. 1324a37). We

---

24. See for example Peter L. Phillips Simpson, *A Philosophical Commentary on the Politics of Aristotle* (Chapel Hill: University of North Carolina Press, 1998), 204.

must insist on that, for there is here a totally astonishing fact that commentators have not recognized for what it is. Thus, Newman comments on this "political" by saying: "if power is exercised as it ought on free and equal men." But, short of inattention on the part of Aristotle, the political would here escape the boundaries of the city and would be exported, so to speak, to neighboring cities. There is no sure way of interpreting what it would mean to treat another city "politically." I tend to think that it's a matter of the magistrates of one city recognizing the political dignity shared by other cities.

One may go a little farther. When Aristotle writes, "and surely there may be a city happy in isolation, which we will assume to be well governed (for it is quite possible[25] that a city thus isolated might be well administered and have good laws)" (7.2, 1324b41), we understand that this would be a rare situation, just as the cases of foundations of new cities are rare. That means that one must take account of the relations with neighboring cities for the happiness of a city. Without that making Aristotle a partisan of *political* structures including several cities, which he surely is not, we see nevertheless that the virtuous city will tend to *recognize* other cities as political entities, that is, as human societies destined for happiness.[26]

The doctrine concerning the differences between the active life and the theoretical life, which Aristotle here calls the political and philosophical lives, is not very different in these first two chapters of *Politics* 7 and the presentation in the *Nicomachean Ethics*. The only new thing, and it is more suggested than explicitly stated, is that cities, whether one may say that they are also happy or unhappy, are capable of choosing a contemplative or active life. This is brought out at 1324a34 in the form of a kind of theorem: "Assuredly the wise are bound to necessarily arrange their affairs in the direction of the better goal—and this applies to the city collectively as well as to the individual human being."

Therefore, it seems that one ought to have bodies politic or constitutions (since Aristotle uses here the term *politeia*) that will be oriented by

---

25. Or: "if after all it is possible."

26. At *Politics* 2.6, 1265a18, there is a somewhat enigmatic passage that says, "It is said (in Plato's *Laws*) that the legislator ought to have his eye directed to two points—the people and the country. But neighboring countries also must not be forgotten by him, because the city for which he legislates is to have a political and not an isolated life." This βίος πολιτικός seems to designate a kind of political life in which the partners are cities, not individual people.

the choice of a philosophical life or a political life, like that of the choice of a warrior life, accompanied by the virtues that attach to it, that is to say primarily courage, which leads the city toward despotism in regard to its neighbors. Hence, in chapter 3, the discussion of the opposition between theoretical and active is carried out at the level of the city. Aristotle conducts this discussion according to his usual method, by showing that both parties are both right and wrong.

Those who think that one must abstain from acting, and here that clearly means abstaining from political life, conceptualize the action in question as an *exercise of power*. Thus, they have an anarchist conception, in the proper and historical sense of the word, of social life, in that the exercise of power is not only unjust for those on whom it is exercised (Aristotle does not raise that point here) but is also injurious for those who exercise it. Thus, to command a slave is to take part in a servile power relation. In that respect, Aristotle says, they are right. But they are wrong on two points. First, in believing that all power is essentially despotic—and Aristotle here clearly alludes to political power, "power over free and equal men," which in no way degrades the person who exercises it. That is why I suggested above translating *archē politikē* as "political authority" rather than "political power," without committing myself to a complete break with traditional usage. Second, it is false to say that one is happy when one does not act, because happiness is action, and good actions produce good results. It seems that Aristotle here pulls the sense of "action" (πρᾶξις) toward the sense of "activity" (ἐνέργεια). In any case, to justify the value of an action on the ground that it provides the happiness that follows the good that this action produces, that is, virtue and virtuous actions, is to remain within the practical conception of the happy life.

At the same time, those who think that the best life is active also think that action is the exercise of a power. Their argument can be called "naturalist": "one who has the ability to govern ought not leave it to his neighbor" (7.3, 1325a36), because, as the preceding line says, this "ability to govern" should thus be understood as a *natural* ability to govern. They are right, provided that they also take account of the fact that *political power is exercised on free and equal men*.

It is not until the end of the chapter that we really understand what Aristotle is thinking about when he talks about the city that chooses between a practical and a contemplative life. Aristotle's conclusion is just as badly established and enmeshed in its details as the arguments that lead up to it, but it is relatively clear: he intends to show that there are activities that reconcile theory and practice, and that this is just as true for individuals as for cities. To support that, he offers two arguments: "Not that a life of action must necessarily have relation to others, as some think, nor are those thoughts only to be regarded as practical that are pursued for the sake of practical results" (7.3, 1325b16).[27] Newman is right to raise the difficulty of reconciling these two assertions with other passages in Aristotle. Let's concentrate on trying to *understand* what Aristotle is saying.

There are actions that are means for achieving an end, but there are also actions that are ends in themselves, and the same goes for thoughts. In other words, there are things that one does with no other purpose than to do them, and thoughts that one thinks for their own sake. Such a position is formally in disagreement with the passage in the *De Anima* cited by Newman, which says that "practical thoughts have an end, for they all are for the sake of something other than themselves" (1.3, 407a23). The only way to escape this contradiction is to suppose that Aristotle has, in the *Politics*, in a way "enlarged" the semantic field of the word "praxis." That is in fact what Newman anticipates by relying on Zeller, who cites a passage in the *Nicomachean Ethics* that talks about the praxis of God, which, due to his unique nature, is pure pleasure (7.14, 1154b23). Thus, we find the second argument established. As for the first, it is illustrated by an example for the sake of which this argument is, in fact, proposed: that the active life would not necessarily be in relation with others, one sees in the fact that some cities live without external relationships, and that one cannot say that they are therefore inactive. Similarly, for individuals, the best example being God and the universe, "which do not perform external actions in addition to those that relate to themselves" (7.3, 1325b29).

What Aristotle means is anything but clear. Generally, one understands that a city that relies on nothing but itself is autarkic, self-sufficient, withdrawn into itself, protected by a natural environment that isolates it from other peoples, for example an island. There is a fallacy here, because if it is true that contemplative activity does not put the person who practices it into a relationship with other people (for example, God does not act on anything), that does not imply that every activity that does not establish relationships with others would be of a contemplative variety. But, says Aristotle, such a city is not "inactive" (cf. ἀπρακτεῖν, 7.3, 1325b24), and he gives as proof (cf. the γάρ at 1325b25) the fact that these cities, being

---

27. Or: "thoughts derived from practice for the sake of certain results."

composed of several parts, will have common relationships (Aristotle says "communities," κοινωνίαι, 125b26) between these parts. Newman thinks that these communities are the governors and the governed. But it can also include the nonpolitical parts of the city. Thus, we have cities that act on themselves in a sort of contemplative solitude, like God, whose sole activity is thinking himself. But every city that functions well is supposed to take itself as a reference point, which is, as we have seen, what Aristotle calls "autarky." Thus, these cities, "which rest only on themselves," are not isolated exceptions, but display the status to which every city ought to aspire. The city, in the proper sense, thus resembles God on an important point: it is autonomous and active.

In short, when we read closely the first three chapters of *Politics* 7 we are not tempted to chalk them up to Aristotle's credit as father of logic . . . On the other hand, I think we can see well enough what he is getting at. There is a point that I have left to one side, or rather have saved it for last, for dessert so to speak. At 7.3, 1325b21, we read: "Even with actions done in relation to external objects we predicate action in the full sense chiefly of master craftsmen who direct the action by their thoughts."

"Even with actions done in relation to external objects" means: also, a fortiori, in the case of actions that are not done in relation to external objects. From that derives the idea that the person who can act without relation to anything external is in an architectonic position. But what, at the level of the individual and no longer of the city, is the individual who produces "autonomous speculations," which can at the same time be considered as *actions* "in an absolutely proper sense" and, though they *entirely concern action*, do not have "practical results"? That would certainly not be the legislator. My thesis, which I believe at the moment has not (yet) been shared by anyone, is that it is the political philosopher from whom the legislator gets his inspiration. And in fact, "the thoughts and contemplations that are independent and take themselves as objects (τὰς αὐτοτελεῖς καὶ αὐτῶν ἕνεκεν θεωρίας καὶ διανοήσεις, 1325b20)" of which Aristotle speaks apply very well to himself when he proposes, in the *Politics*, analyses that are carried out for their own sake, but which will find practical consequences in the action of the legislator. That is what was said, at least in part, already in *Politics* 3.8, 1279b13, in talking of "the person who behaves like a philosopher, that is, does not consider only the practical side of things."

Once again, it is in comparison with Plato that we can appreciate Aristotle's position. That the essential activity of the philosopher would be, for Plato, the contemplation of realities that are unchangeable, intelligible, and more real than their empirical copies, is understandable. But this "philosophical life" diverts the Platonic philosopher so little from the political life that he claims to be the only one who should govern the city. To install *cohabitation* in the philosopher of the theoretical and practical lives, the *Republic* recommends constraint. It is necessary to force the dazzled dialectician to go back down into the cave to busy himself with liberating the chained imbeciles who are likely to thank him by making him drink the hemlock . . . The clear separation that Aristotle makes between the role of the philosopher and the role of the governor allows escaping the obligation to go to such extremes and, by the way, avoid the unhappiness of the governor that flows from that.[28]

The philosopher, when he speculates about the excellent city, does not expect practical results. He has, in fact, clean hands, not because he does not have hands,[29] but because his analyses are *taken in hand*, to continue the metaphor, by the legislator.

---

28. Cf. Aristotle's allusion at *Politics* 7.2, 1324a38: to govern one's fellow citizens "politically" and not despotically is certainly not unjust but "is a great impediment to the well-being of the governor."

29. "Kantianism has clean hands because it has no hands." Charles Péguy, *Oeuvres en prose complètes*, tome 3 (Paris: Gallimard, 1992), 331–332.

Conclusion

Let us return, then, to Michel Foucault and *The Archaeology of Knowledge*. Foucault, reflecting on his previous books, asks himself about the epistemological status of cultural formations like medicine per se, grammar per se, political economy per se, ensembles of discourse that cannot be reduced to a collection of books, nor considered as sciences. Then he makes a distinction that particularly interests us, one that separates *scientific domains* from *archaeological territories*. Thus, an example provided by Foucault, *D'Alembert's Dream* and what it

> says about the development of species may well express certain of the concepts or certain of the scientific hypotheses of the period; it may even anticipate a future truth; it does not belong to the domain of scientificity of Natural History, but it does belong to its archaeological territory, if at least one can discover in operation in it the same rules of formation as in Linnaeus, Buffon, Daubendon, or Jussieu.[1]

To *D'Alembert's Dream*, Foucault adds Charles Bonnet's *Palingénésie philosophique* and Benoît de Maillet, *Telliamed*, which in contrast to Diderot's work definitely had pretentions that we may call scientific, but that we would consider less "advanced" on the road of science than the works of Linnaeus or Jussieu. According to Foucault, then, all these works, which are more or less distant from "scientificness," are rooted in the discursive practices that are identical or at least analogical, which means that we can refer them to the same archaeological territory.

---

1. Foucault, *L'archéologie du savoir*, 239; in the English translation *The Archaeology of Knowledge*, 188. Denis Diderot, *Le Rêve de d'Alembert* (1769).

Foucault is heir to the tradition of August Comte, though it is hard to say whether he accepts that heritage, and to what degree. To make Linnaeus and Diderot belong to the same category, Foucault begins by introducing the idea of "knowledge" (*savoir*):

> To analyze positivities is to show in accordance with which rules a discursive practice may form groups of objects, enunciations, concepts, or theoretical choices. The elements thus formed do not constitute a science . . . ; but neither are they items of knowledge piled up one on top of another, derived from heterogeneous experiments, traditions, or discoveries, and linked only by the identity of the subject that possesses them. They are on the basis of which coherent (or incoherent) propositions are built up, more or less exact descriptions developed, verifications carried out, theories deployed . . .
>
> This group of elements, formed in a regular manner by a discursive practice, and which are indispensable to the constitution of a science, although they are not necessarily destined to give rise to one, can be called *knowledge*.[2]

But Foucault then offers simply a series of *stages*, though he does not use this word, stages that are not very distant cousins of the "states" of Auguste Comte.

Every discursive formation must cross several "thresholds," and will cross them all if it ends by producing a completely developed science. When it individualizes itself, it crosses the "threshold of positivity"; when it proposes "norms of verification and coherence," and applies them to knowledge, there is a "threshold of epistemologization"; when that "epistemological figure" satisfies certain formal criteria, it crosses a "threshold of scientificness"; when this scientific discourse defines its foundations, its elements, and its structures, it passes the "threshold of formalization." To be sure, Foucault challenges the image of a group of fields of knowledge marching in step toward science. And, more importantly for our subject, he asserts that the self-development of discursive formations does not necessarily end in science:

> To the question posed above—Is archaeology concerned only with sciences? Is it always an analysis of scientific discourse?—

---

2. Foucault, *L'archéologie du savoir*, 237–238; *The Archaeology of Knowledge*, 181–182.

we can now give a reply, in each case in the negative. What archaeology tries to describe is not the specific structure of science, but the very different domain of *knowledge*. . . . The orientation towards the episteme has been the only one to be explored so far. The reason for this is that, because of a gradient that no doubt characterizes our cultures, discursive formations are constantly becoming epistemologized.[3]

He gives three examples of archaeological analyses bearing on discursive formations that were not destined to end up as sciences (sexuality, painting, political knowledge), which he hardly develops, doubtless saving them for the opportunity to deal with them more completely later, which he seems not to have done. Obviously, these "extra-scientific" examples interest us the most if we want to bring Aristotle's *Politics* into the Foucauldian schema.

Before trying to see whether the *Politics* crosses any, and how many of these thresholds, let us ask ourselves whether there is an archaeological basis to which one may refer the *Politics*. At first glance that does not seem too difficult, because, even if Aristotle was the first to reflect on what politics really is, the simultaneously rational and reformative approach to social life was one of the components of Greek philosophical investigation since its beginnings.[4] But I have tried to show that in this confrontation between identity and difference, Aristotle's originality was so crushing that the resemblances between him and his contemporaries limited themselves into a range of more or less empty generalities. Of course, Aristotle, like all the others, talked about the city, he thought that the good citizen was a virtuous man, and so forth. Nevertheless, there is a certain way of talking about life in the city that belongs only to Aristotle.

Like all the ancients, Aristotle tried to find a *natural* condition both before and after the denaturalizations that this nature has undergone—one might well take this as an example of Hegelian *Aufhebung*. The archaeological territory to which one may refer the Greek way of thinking social reality is characterized fundamentally, perhaps even essentially, by its reference to the idea of a universal harmony. That is because he is a part of the *cosmos*, that is, a rational order, harmonious and beautiful, that the

---

3. Foucault, *L'archéologie du savior*, 255; *The Archaeology of Knowledge*, 195.
4. Gerard Naddaf makes the study of the origin of the *polis* one of the chapters of the "Study of Nature." He develops this point especially in the case of Anaximander in *The Greek Concept of Nature*, 92ff.

Greek man feels at home in the world, as the nineteenth-century philosophers, especially German, have repeated in their critique of Judeo-Christian "alienation." But Aristotle fractured that beautiful "universal entity" that the philosophers who came after him tried to reconstitute. The first fracture is cosmological, distinguishing between super- and sublunary. It is extended, at the epistemological level, in the difference between theoretical and practical sciences, to which we must once again return. Aristotle defines a region of "human things"[5] in which political thought is deployed. Aristotle thus does not *abandon* the project of finding in the world of cities the rigor and regularity that ancient thinkers had attributed to the cosmos, since the break between super- and sublunary disqualified that project. As a direct consequence, far from recommending to magistrates to adjust to a second-order constitutional correctness, he was able to provide an achievable excellence as a *goal*. All interpreters—and they are many—who have regarded Aristotle as a partisan of the "second best choice" have tried to refer his theory to an archaeological basis that I think he was one of the few to escape in antiquity, namely, the exclusive congruence of perfection and immutability.

But Aristotle did not think of the study of human affairs as a simply empirical procedure. To that end he introduced a special class of disciplines that possibly he and surely the tradition have called "practical sciences." In fact, there is only one practical science, political science, because ethics, which is the other practical science that is ordinarily attributed to Aristotle, is nothing but political research carried on according to a certain point of view. None of the objectives of ethics take on its true dimensions until one envisages them from the political angle. That's how it is for ethical virtues, whose developed forms are the virtues of the good citizen. The courage or the moderation of women, children, slaves, and other noncitizens are nothing but truncated, often feeble, sometimes ridiculous, versions of citizen virtues. The other tie between ethical and political virtues[6] is that these virtues are acquired by the regular practice

---

5. To designate what one finds in the "region of human things," Aristotle uses the terms τὰ ἀνθρώπεια or τὰ ἀνθρώπινα. Interpreters of Aristotle, including me, have made a big (too big?) deal of the expression "philosophy of human things" (περὶ τὰ ἀνθρώπεια φιλοσοφία) found at *Nicomachean Ethics* 10.9, 1181b15.

6. It's not the same for the intellectual virtues, which, as I have remarked, are learned. I do not intend to deal with the relationship between the intellectual virtues and politics, although it is a very interesting topic.

of good actions. But as Aristotle thinks that it is unlikely that an individual would find in himself the desire and ability to become virtuous—because virtue from the start seems difficult and harsh—he is led to posit that the performance of virtuous actions can come only from obedience to the laws, if possible since childhood.

Ethical science was not born with Aristotle, since he did not assign it a special domain. Nevertheless, ethics is a point of view that possesses its own coherence and its own requirements. It is not simply the shadow cast by politics. Even if the famous chapter, *Politics* 3.4, ultimately argues for the presence of perfect ethical virtue and political virtue in the same man, it also immediately reminds us that there exists an *ethical ideal* that is independent of the actual political regime in a city. There is an important point there, which has not been part of my treatment, but it does deserve at least a few remarks.

We noted above the difference of tonality that distinguishes the two Aristotelian *Ethics*, the *Eudemian* insisting, more than its *Nicomachean* sister, on the excellence and happiness of the individual. Thus, it is not surprising that it is in the *Eudemian Ethics* that Aristotle establishes the clearest distinction between individual excellence and excellence in relation to the city. We may recall the example of the chapter on courage (3.1)—Catherine Dalimier's analysis was cited above—where Aristotle asserts clearly that "civic courage" (1230a21), which causes Hector, for example, to face danger from Achilles "out of shame," lacks the essential characteristic that would make it "true courage" (ἡ δ' ἀληθὴς ἀνδρεία, 1230a21), that is, that it has been *chosen* "for the sake of a certain end, and that end is the noble" (1230a28). This is a particularly striking example since courage seems to be essentially a political virtue.

A political thinker, Aristotle thus does not put ethics into competition with politics but clearly defines an individual perspective for excellence, and consequently happiness, which as we have seen contributes to saving his philosophy from any sort of totalitarianism. There is an ethical accomplishment of individuals, notably an individual ethical virtue, which does not come automatically from obedience to good laws. Aristotle's *Ethics* is, from that point of view, a real treatise on human happiness, relying on the complex and precise definitions not only of virtue but also of friendship and pleasure that appear in it. Even if he prefers the image of the philosopher engaged in the improvement of his city to that of the thinker who has retired from the world, and even if he deploys, with more or less success, a lot of effort to erase the difference between contemplative and practical happiness, Aristotle does not banish from the philosophical stage the character, incarnated by Socrates, and destined for prosperous future, of the sage who does not engage in the active political life of his city.

In the relationships that Aristotle establishes between ethics and politics, both benefit. First ethics, which if alone cannot hope to realize in individuals that have become virtuous the happiness that it offers as the goal of human life. Without recourse to law, ethical virtue can concern only a very restricted number of excellent individuals. It is noteworthy that the ethical treatises are so little prescriptive, realizing that in a way ethics does not have hands. We have seen that the legislator needs to be an attentive reader of the ethical treatises if he wants to get political profit from them. But we have also noted that the good legislator does not need to acquire an extraordinary ethical erudition in order to do a good job. What politics borrows particularly from ethics is nevertheless no less than the criterion for the "happy life," that is, the very foundation of normative politics. As a famous passage of the *Politics*, quoted several times in this work, says, "Political society exists for the sake of noble actions, and not of living together" (3.9, 1281a4). But we have to look in the ethics for the definition of "noble actions." Hence the most striking "exterior" aspect of the *Politics* for people today, which I have described by calling this work "split." But obviously we are the ones who make this judgment. Aristotle does not seem to have had any difficulty in making the normative and realist sides of his political research work together. I have already noted that Aristotle never abandons his demand for "moral beauty" and virtue, even when he allows himself to advise a tyrant.

Aristotle's ethics was doubtless anything but surprising for his contemporaries, since he takes up the principle themes of what may be called "ancient morals," notably on the relationships between nature, virtue, and happiness. Nevertheless, it remains that this shape of the relationship between politics and ethics, with the first including the second, keeps its own pertinence shared by no other ancient morals. At the same time, I hope to have shown in the preceding pages that Aristotle accomplishes three strong "gestures" by which he shapes the contours of a political philosophy that has no equivalent in the thought of the ancients. The first of these gestures is the one that installs the very field of politics. From that there follows, across the complexities of constitutional science, the essentials, at least in volume, of the Aristotelian political enterprise. The two other gestures, which perhaps one may think of as forming just one, redefine from top to bottom the notion of excellence. Purity, simplicity, and immutability lose their pretention of necessarily accompanying excellence. To arrive at this result, Aristotle proposes, in a second gesture, a new conception of constitutional rectitude and, a third gesture, an entirely original approach to *stasis*.

The preponderance of the political over the other approaches to social facts can be found in the very heart of human nature. One of the theoretical bases of Aristotelianism, I have noted, is that of thinking of reality in relation to its most developed state. It is in being faithful to this fundamental requirement that Aristotle refuses to explain the life of a city as a response to its needs, the first being survival. The city defines the decisive level of the existence of human beings, because Nature has given them a political tendency that prevents them from achieving their blossoming until they become citizens of a good city. Even if the great majority of human beings, for various reasons that we have examined, cannot achieve this political state, even if this exclusion applies to the feminine half of humanity, it nevertheless remains that "man is naturally a political animal." It is only in a city that one can achieve the "happy life," even if one must surpass multiple obstacles to arrive there. All the relationships that human beings weave between each other need to be situated, appreciated, and utilized, in relation to the city. In any case, this inscription of the political in the deepest part of human nature forms the basis for a kind of naturalistic optimism, which seems to have given Aristotle the conviction that happiness remains accessible to citizens.

Aristotle was the only person in antiquity to propose a *specific* definition of politics, while the life in a city was felt by most ancient Greeks as properly belonging to them. That is why, no matter how important it may be, the specificity of the Aristotelian approach does not really deracinate Aristotle from the archaeological substratum from which, I have claimed, he has on the whole freed himself. Right from the first lines of the *Politics*, Aristotle explains that the relationship between citizens is not reducible to the other relations that structure the social body, those between husbands and wives, between parents and children, between masters and slaves, between king and subjects. Obviously, we need to make an effort, as the Greeks did not need to do, to remind ourselves that the term "political" applied to someone or something means *of the city* (*polis*). But for Aristotle, but not, or not as completely, for other Greek thinkers, the city was characterized by certain traits and marks a certain level of reality. The city, which Aristotle defines, without justifying this more or less etymological definition, as "a determinate multiplicity of citizens" (*Pol.* 3.1, 1274b41), is differentiated from other forms of human associations, above all by a certain sort of power, which I have said was "oxymoronic." While the very notion of "power" seems to imply a hierarchical relation between those who exercise it and those who submit to it, "political power is applied to men who are free and equal" (*Pol.* 1.7, 1255b20). These men are the citizens. More precisely, political *archē*—a word perhaps better translated in some cases by political "authority" than political "power," because it is a matter of a relationship of subordination, but it is both temporary and accepted by the people it includes—rests on the alternation in power under the sovereignty of the law. The exceptions to these rules are only apparent. Thus, in certain correct constitutions, that is, those that produce virtue and happiness, the same people are continued in power. But in fact, that is because the mass of citizens has not yet acquired the ethical qualification necessary for the correct exercise of power. The first danger, existential, which weighs on the political, is thus to see itself aligned with other relations of subordination. A wife should not be treated like a slave, even in the case of a "soft" slavery, nor a slave like a wife, no more than a city ought to be governed like a family, nor a family like a city. When Aristotle writes that the father of a family ought "to acquire the ability to be a legislator' (*EN* 10.9, 1180a32, passage already cited), that should not be taken literally, because the father of a family is not as such a legislator for his city.

This typology of the forms of power finds an echo in our era in that which, among others, Georges Balandier has called "political anthropology," but it is in profound contradiction with the Greek approach to power.

In thus defining the city as a necessary condition for the excellence of "human things," Aristotle probably did no more, here again, than reformulate in philosophical terms an assumption largely shared among the ancient Greeks, at least those of the era called "classical." If the fact of living in a city, that is, being subject to a political authority, was, in the mind of the Greeks, at least those who poked themselves to think a little, the most obvious mark of their superiority over the barbarians, it is not so surprising that they were inclined to give to the city a form of perfection. But if the city is a necessary condition for human perfection, philosophers like Plato and Aristotle have strongly indicated that it was not a sufficient condition. History shows very well that the fact of living among equals under the authority of laws common to all is far from being, among citizens, an assurance of virtue and happiness. In order to play its ethical role, the city has to fulfill conditions in addition to the formal conditions of its existence as a society of equals ruled by laws. For it is not any random legislation that makes people virtuous and happy. That's where political philosophy gets going.

For the city to be productive of virtue, in fact, it is necessary that its laws be good. But the laws of a city depend on its constitution and not its constitution on its laws.[7] And let us recall one more time: "Laws that correspond to correct constitutions are necessarily just, and those that correspond to deviant constitutions are not just" (*Pol.* 3.11, 1282b11). The study of constitutions constitutes Aristotelian political philosophy, particularly the study of what makes constitutions "correct," that is, excellent. That is what the philosopher provides to the legislator.

Thence the second "gesture" that consists in reconfiguring the notion of excellence when it is applied to the world of the cities. Aristotle's project is not primarily the establishment of a "perfect" constitution on a new foundation. And even in that which concerns cities already established that should be reformed, we have seen that the Aristotelian legislator does not expect revolutionary transformations, or he expects them only rarely. In an unstable political world torn between the demands of antagonistic groups, it's a matter of reinforcing the side of virtue. The work of the legislator is thus found to be first an audit of the constitution, which he needs to lead toward correctness, then a task of dosage. We have analyzed two remarkable examples. First, there is the idea that virtue has an effect even when it is submerged in a matrix of vice. To give power, or at least some power, to virtuous people, will have an ethical effect. That is why it is not only a regime that reserves power to people who are entirely virtuous alone that would deserve the title "aristocracy," even if that would deserve it the most. Constitutions like those of Crete or Carthage have good reason to be called aristocratic. But there is, obviously, a breaking point, when virtue is so diluted in the ethical condition of the civic body that it cannot any longer play its role as catalyst. Having understood the extent of virtue of a given city at a given moment, the legislator must therefore, primarily by means of the laws, bring it about that the leavening of virtue can develop.

---

7. There is a criticism, indirect but real, of the distrust of real relationships between the constitution and laws by Plato in *Politics* 2: "In the *Laws* there is hardly anything but laws; not much is said about the constitution. This, which he had intended to make more of the ordinary type, he gradually brings round to the other form," that is, that of the *Republic* (2.6, 1265a1).

The second example of the political chemistry (or perhaps, political alchemy) in which the legislator needs to be expert, and on which I have written at length, rests on the idea that a combination of the good aspects of deviant constitutions leads toward excellence. Here too it is a matter of careful measurement, because a law that reinforces one side too much or weakens another too much can sink a constitution into deviation for a long time. One must count on the immune responses of constitutions for them to be able to resist internal and external attacks.

Possibly I slightly exaggerated the novelty of that doctrine, because the idea that a constitution has an interest in mixing different aspects of different kinds of regimes seems to have been fairly widespread. Even before the analysis of Polybius according to which the Roman constitution was the best possible because it mixed elements of all the correct constitutions, all that Aristotle says, in *Politics* 2, about the Spartan and Cretan constitutions as mixtures of oligarchic and democratic elements could have been approved by Herodotus and Xenophon. What seems to me to be new in Aristotle is the idea that the combination of *vices* could produce excellence. In fact, what else than that is the polity? It's a *democracy* that has included in its constitution arrangements that take account of the demands of the oligarchic party. But these demands are not struck with the coin of virtue—what the oligarchs want is that their criterion for access to power, wealth, should be taken account of. Thus, we are in a different place than that of the *Republic* in which Plato shows that timocracy borrows from both aristocracy and oligarchy. For him, in fact, aristocracy, a correct constitution, *improves* timocracy, which would otherwise be worse. Glaucon, with Socrates's approval, expresses the matter well: "You are talking about a constitution composed of a complete mixture of bad and good" (8.548c).[8] For Aristotle, in contrast, neither democracy nor oligarchy, whose mixture is a polity, is a correct constitution.

The fact that constitutional transformations belong to the region of human things, and thus belong to the "philosophy of human things," that is, politics, plants Aristotelian speculation firmly in history. If, in fact, history were a science for Aristotle, something that he neither affirms nor denies, it would surely be a practical science. Aristotle knows that *anything can happen* in the world of cities, which means, for him, that nothing is

---

8. The same for the passage already cited from the *Laws* (6.756e), where the Stranger describes the constitution of the excellent city as a mixture of monarchy and democracy.

firmly established, which makes both better and worse possible. Thus, the way that Aristotle takes account of the instability of the political world constitutions is his third "gesture."

In fact, not only does Aristotle accept the existence of radical instability, but he thinks that it is the *normal* condition of the human world. I have tried to show this in my interpretation of the Aristotelian theory of *stasis*. Let us remember how much this word is itself charged with ambiguity, since it indicates also a state of immobility, which Greek thought made a kind of ideal, to which, in fact, Aristotle generally clings in his physics and epistemology. It seems to me that Aristotle is not on the side of those who think of conflict as an exception, one may say a "parenthesis," in human history. *Stasis* is no longer an illness in the social body, but an ever-present *dynamis* that accompanies a city throughout its history. The idea that the resistance of the dominated maintains political life against the hegemonic temptations of the dominant goes in the same direction: if civil peace is indeed a harmonization of divergent interests, Aristotle thinks of it as based on a relationship between forces. Just as deviant constitutions maintain themselves as long as they are able, a correct constitution that wants to endure must also find force. One might almost say that for Aristotle political life is confrontation continued by other means. That does not mean that he is unaware of the bad consequences of conflicts, or that he does not want to avoid them. But realism obliges; if there is conflict, it is best to use it for good purposes.

The most positive and most unexpected effect of seditions is that they permit an extension and reinforcement *of politics*. I have tried to show that that is produced by a *politicization* of emotions and individual ventures.[9] If the response to an outrage does not take the form of private revenge, but if its ultimate cause is identified as stemming from the position of the author of the outrage in the power relations defined by the constitution of his city, then the theft, the rape, the murder that an individual has undergone, or that he has seen done to the detriment of one of his close associates, becomes a political affair. That is a great victory for the city which, as we have seen, must fight against everything

---

9. In a work published in 2015, Giorgio Agamben develops this idea that *stasis* politicizes the "unpolitical." His only error is that he attributes that idea to all the Greek thinkers, not seeing that it's about a position that belongs to Aristotle, a philosopher that he inexplicably neglects. Cf. Giorgio Agamben, *La Guerre civile. Pour une théorie politique de la* stasis (Paris: Éditions Points, 2015).

that is apolitical, and especially against things that stem from pre-political communities such as the family. Nothing is more destructive of political ties than private violence, while political violence can reinforce that tie: all politicians know that a "good war" reinforces national cohesion. *Stasis* is therefore a kind of recognition of a situation of antagonism that can be resolved politically.

These three "gestures" uproot Aristotelian political philosophy from the soil from which it was born much more than they implant it further. We can see this clearly in the confrontation between Plato and Aristotle. Plato too recognizes the instability of human affairs, particularly the life of cities. But Plato intends to put an end to that, to the extent that he can, by bringing together the political and cosmic orders by imposing on the city an appropriate constitution. Aristotle, in contrast, seems to make this instability the very material of political life. The goal of the legislator would thus be to make use of it, rather than purge it from the city. Christianity's assimilation of Greek philosophy reinforced for many centuries the tendency to look beyond the concrete for the meaning of the existence, both individual and collective, of human beings. Among many others I have noted that Aristotle's political philosophy has not had the sensational success of other parts of his work—metaphysics, biology, poetics, among others—due to the fact that in relying on the classical city, it had an evanescent foundation. We can now see, with the help of Michel Foucault, that this political philosophy is, we may say, soil-less, in that one cannot, either at all or very little, refer it to the archaeological foundation on which other ancient discourses on human society depend.

Now let us confront the *Politics* with the second part of the Foucauldian analysis recalled above, that which asserts that discursive formations advance by "thresholds." Aristotle, like all the other post-Parmenidean Greek thinkers, conceived of the object of science as immutable. That necessarily creates tension, to put it mildly, between that demand and the science of human action. That tension is even greater than that which Aristotle had to confront when he claimed to conciliate the epistemological model of immutability and the study of the concrete, particularly living beings. Aristotle uses at least two methods for resolving this difficulty. The first depends strictly from his cosmological response to the Parmenidean challenge, and brings us back once again to the image of Aristotelian political philosophy as a "deracinated," "soil-less" thought.

In an epoch-making study, Friedrich Solmsen showed that Aristotle was the first, and perhaps the only, *cosmologist* in antiquity.[10] By positing an everlasting universe, fundamentally identical with itself and globally perfect, Aristotle evades the "mortal" question of the origin of things and of the world. Thus, animal species are everlasting, permitting the Aristotelian zoologist to formulate about them universal propositions, always valid ("all animals with lungs have red blood"). There too Aristotle is found to be "soil-less." One could fear all the more that the social "instinct" that Aristotle attributes to human beings imposes animal naturalism on them, since, great connoisseur of the living world that he was, he might have recourse to the same explanatory schemas for the various properties of animals as for certain social characteristics of human beings. But we have seen that Aristotle does not succumb to that temptation, if it tempted him at all, of aligning politics with biology. Even though he compares cities to living organisms, he never considers them to *be* living organisms.

Of course, human beings have not appeared more suddenly in the world than the other animal species. Thus, there have not only always been human beings, but there always will be human societies. But human societies, in contrast to animal societies (including those that Aristotle calls "political"), have a history full of ups and downs, because it is marked by human freedom. So, the city, which is the *natural* frame of the *natural* blossoming of mankind, not only demands special conditions to be able to appear—since the barbarians are naturally inept for political life—but it is the result of a historical process. From that point of view, Eduard Meyer was wrong.[11]

But for the human world to be integrated into an everlasting universe, it is necessary that it too participate in everlastingness. As I have noted, Aristotle seems to think that humanity—and it is impossible to say if it is a matter of all humanity taken together or of all human populations successively—is constantly brought down to a primitive condition by periodic cataclysms. In what sense they are periodic, that is, if they are so in the strong sense that they return after equal periods of time or a duration determined in advance, or if it is simply a matter of events that

---

10. Friedrich Solmsen, *Aristotle's System of the Physical World* (Ithaca: Cornell University Press, 1960).

11. See p. 89 earlier.

occur from time to time, we have no way of knowing. But what we do know is that this indefinite repetition of human history is not an identical reproduction, as the Stoics for example believed. The periods between cataclysms do not resemble each other in all respects. But they should nevertheless resemble each other a bit. Anyway, in the political domain, "almost everything has been discovered, even if in some cases the systems have not been recorded, and if in other cases they are known but have not been applied" (*Pol.* 2.5, 1264a3).

It is equally impossible to say what Aristotle thought about this relationship between resemblance and lack of resemblance among periods of human history. But it does seem, when one reads the first book of the *Politics*, that the Greeks, or at least many of them, ended up reaching the level of the *polis*. Possibly that gives us some elements for the solution of the problem raised earlier about Aristotle's historical blindness. We asked ourselves then how it could be possible that he did not understand that the time of cities was coming to an end, which would have to prevent him from considering the life of the city as the perfect form of human life. This changes somewhat if one conceives human history as marked by perpetual new beginnings. Isn't it then possible to think of the establishment of the great empires as a kind of accident of human history, which, in any case, should be corrected by the next cataclysm? All that remains extremely conjectural . . .

But this combination of the everlasting and the unexpected in the region of human things is not Aristotle's only response to the Parmenidean epistemological demand. Aristotle proceeds to an "epistemologization," to take up Foucault again, of the study of the polychromatic diversity of political reality, by means of a formalization that is so *extraordinary* that it has generally not been noticed. Thus, he puts aside, in the last three chapters of *Politics* 4, the historical-empirical approach to constitutional diversity that starts from the study of the parts of the city to turn to a modeling based on taking account of the parts of the constitution. So, the reduction proposed since book 3 of the question of the city to that of the constitution is completed. We have here a scientific procedure in the modern sense, but without any response in antiquity. Thus, here too there is no archaeological enrooting at all on Aristotle's part.

I have indicated, as something remaining to be investigated, that this formalization crosses into an additional step. In fact, Aristotle varies the structure that he has just constructed by moving its principal element. Because it's a matter of a structure that is not single-leveled, but hierarchical: from the *political* point of view, that is, from the point of view of power, it is the deliberative part of the constitution that orders the others; but from a *constitutional* point of view, that is from the point of view of a particular constitution in an array of a group of possible constitutions, it's the part concerning magistracies that sets the tone. It seems to me, although it would require more profound study, that the political point of view ought to dominate over the constitutional point of view. If one transposes that into the domain of living beings, one may say that the functional point of view dominates over the taxonomical point of view, as in the era of Cuvier—and Michel Foucault has shown this too very well in *The Order of Things*—biology took over from natural history. And from this point of view the famous passage in *Politics* 4.4 comparing constitutions to animals also proposes a comparative anatomy based on the idea of function and not a taxonomy based on the resemblance or lack of resemblance of characteristics.

On this point too, in fact, we can offer a parallel between Aristotelian politics and biology. Foucault has shown, as I have just noted, how after natural history, but breaking with it, a true *biology* was born, to which the name of Georges Cuvier is particularly attached. But when we read the brief but striking description that Foucault gives, in *The Order of Things*, of this change in paradigm—and simultaneously of archaeological territory—we see that Aristotle, and he alone, has been, prior to Cuvier, a true biologist and that he was placed as a cornerstone of the work of Cuvier, who was in any case an enthusiast of Aristotle if there ever was one. The same goes for politics. It was necessary to wait for the difficult and dangerous reconquest of its autonomy by the "region of human affairs" in order to rediscover, in very different conditions, an Aristotelian inspiration. It is difficult to determine exactly when that reversal occurred, but we can say that it was completed with Machiavelli.

It was necessary to wait, and wait a long time, for the truly *biological* approach to living things initiated by Aristotle, and pretty much abandoned after him, to be reactivated. If, in fact, Galen and maybe some others were able to maintain a vitalist perspective of the Aristotelian type, ancient medicine was massively "materialist" and mechanist, explaining illnesses by bad mixtures of the material components of the body, often the "humors." Biology arises, or rearises, against the alliance of mechanistic reductionism, from Descartes to molecular biology, with natural history. The same for politics. It is certain, as I have noted several times, that Aristotle was more or less deactivated by the fact that he rested his political philosophy on the city, at the moment when the city was exiting the historical stage. But there is another reason, possibly more profound, that made Aristotle inaudible in politics, and that would be his unprecedented ambition, for a long time without descendant, to make the science of human affairs cross the "epistemological threshold" described by Foucault, while conserving its precarious and unstable character. He does that in the first place by reducing the question of the city to that of the constitution, and then by the study of the diversity of constitutions, and finally by an ultimate grade of that diversity by means of a kind of comparative anatomy of politics that takes the form of an extremely formalized combinatorial analysis.

To conclude, let us dream a little. I have, several times in this book and elsewhere, laid out a parallelism, as just now, between Aristotle's politics and biology. In an old essay,[12] I set in opposition two concepts of the diversity of constitutions, each of which relied on its own approach to the excellence of these constitutions. If one thinks that a constitution is excellent when it assures the happiness of the citizens after having led them to virtue, then constitutional diversity can be thought in a form that I called "Lamarckian" because by the very functioning of a primitive correct constitution (a kingship, for example), one moves on to more and more perfect forms, up to a polity in which all the citizens are ethically virtuous and thus happy. But the dominant model in the *Politics*, especially in the "realist" sections, is more nearly "Darwinian," in that the passage from one constitutional form to another can go in all directions, that all the combinations are tried, that the various forms are in competition with each other and that history determines the selection of the best adapted constitutions in the given circumstances.

I recalled above how, in a few brilliant pages, Michel Foucault described the transition with Cuvier from natural history to a true *biology*. Foucault did not mention Aristotle, whom he did not know very well, and thus could not notice how his biological project was more or less cloned by Cuvier. Aristotle was a real biologist, and as such, he produced a structure that was more or less reactivated in the work of Cuvier, who shared with him the demands of a true biology, which is the study of *organisms* in which organs coexist functionally, are subject to an internal hierarchy, itself founded on a hierarchy of functions (respiration depends on circulation), all the time conforming to a plan of organization, itself hierarchical, which includes each one in a more vast complex, which forms the basis

---

12. Pellegrin, "Naturalité, excellence, diversité. Politique et biologie chez Aristote."

for a comparative anatomy. Cuvier knew, as did Aristotle, how to discern the profound identities beneath the apparent diversity of the organs that appear in various species, but fulfilling identical or analogous functions.

For natural history before Cuvier, in contrast, the Same and the Other belong to the same space, and any random characteristic can serve as the key for classifying animals. And Foucault was absolutely right in thinking that Lamarck relied on the same archaeology as that of natural history, while Darwin was obviously a descendant of Cuvier. However, Cuvier also had in common with Aristotle some less glorious sides of his zoology, since like the Stagirite he was absolutely fixist, a sin more difficult to pardon in him than in Aristotle. That is why Jules Barthélemy-Saint Hilaire was right, in the long preface to his French translation of the *History of Animals* published in 1883, to claim that Aristotle's zoology and Cuvier's could be classified in the same family. This family is that of pre-Darwin and pre-Mendel systems of biology. But they are all *biological* systems. As a consequence of his novel approach to living beings, Cuvier eventually supported vitalist positions that, in his inimitable style, Foucault described thus:

> ... life becomes a fundamental force, and one that is opposed to being in the same way as movement to immobility, as time to space, as the secret wish to the visible expression. Life is the root of all existence, and the non-living, nature in its inert form, is merely spent life; mere being is the non-being of life.[13]

This vitalism that considers the living being as more complete than the nonliving is shared by Aristotle: "The soul is better than the body, the ensouled better than the inanimate because of its soul, being better than non-being, living than non-living" (*GA* 2.1, 731b28).

How should we analyze this theoretical convergence? Could we say that Aristotle was a "precursor" of Cuvier? Did Aristotle produce a model that is in a way "transhistorical"? We see that its main power comes from the fact that Aristotle and Cuvier deployed it on the same field, that of the study of animals.

We have noted that Aristotle did not push the analogy between zoology and politics to the point of making of the city an *ousia*. That does

---

13. Michel Foucault, *Les mots et les choses* (Paris: Gallimard, 1966), 291; English translation, *The Order of Things* (New York: Pantheon Books, 1970), 303.

not prevent constitutions from in fact having characteristics of *organisms*: when Cuvier writes that "all the organs of one and the same animal form a single system of which the parts hold together, act, and react upon each other; and there can be no modifications in any of them that will not bring about analogous modifications in them all,"[14] it is easy to see, if one has paid attention to everything that has been said in this book, that that applies precisely to a constitution according to Aristotle. But taking account that, as I have just said, the world of cities, and its conceptual image in the space of constitutions, is not confined by the constraints of fixist biology; it is absolutely, as I have said, a Darwinian model that the Aristotelian science of constitutions offers us.

We have seen that this model where, in the war of all against all, the stronger wins, but where it is very difficult to determine which character is advantageous and which is not—for that one needs all the science of the legislator informed by philosophy—was ultimately profoundly alien to the Greek world that produced it. When political philosophy eventually came down again from the heavens to earth, that model could at last play its role as a model.

Aristotle explicitly proposed in *Politics* 4.4 (discussed above) the establishment of a parallel between animal diversity and constitutional diversity. A priori reconstitution, à la Mendeleyev, of animal diversity by the combination of the various forms of vital organs is entirely at the same level as the project of comparative anatomy initiated by Aristotle. He waited until the last three chapters of *Politics* 4 to apply completely to constitutions this project without precedent, and hardly without successor, in history. So what can we dream of? Perhaps of this: Cuvier, if he had read, or read more carefully, Aristotle's *Politics*, would have been able to find in Aristotle's constitutional science a model applicable to the animal kingdom, traveling in the opposite direction the road laid down by Aristotle, and would have introduced into the animal world variability, which Aristotle had made one of the characteristics of the world of cities.

---

14. *Rapport historique sur l'état des sciences naturelles*, 330, cited by Foucault, *Les mots et les choses*, 277. (English trans. p. 289)

Bibliography

Aristotle's Texts and Translations

Aubonnet, Jean. *Aristote, La Politique*, 5 vols. Paris: Belles Lettres, 1960–1989. Critical text and French translation in the Collection des Universités de France.

Barnes, Jonathan, ed. *The Complete Works of Aristotle*. Princeton: Princeton University Press, 1984.

Beare, J. I. *Aristotle: On Sense and the Sensible*. In *The Works of Aristotle*, vol. 3, edited by W. D. Ross. Oxford: Clarendon Press, 1931.

Bekker, Immanuel. The text of the *Politics* is in vol. 2, 1252–1342, 1831, whence the standard references to Aristotle's text.

Bodéüs, Richard. *Aristote: Éthique à Nicomaque*. Paris: GF-Flammarion, 2004.

Brunschwig, Jacques. *Aristote. Topiques*, tome 1, livres 1–4: Text établi et traduit. Paris: Les Belles Lettres, 1967; tome 2: livres 5–8, 1990.

Bywater, J., ed. *Aristoteles: Ethica Nicomachea*. Oxford: Oxford Classical Texts, 1894.

Dalimier, Catherine, trans. *Aristote, Éthique à Eudème*. Paris: GF-Flammarion, 2013.

Dreizehnter, Alois. *Aristoteles' Politica*. Munich: Wilhelm Fink, 1970. This is the best text currently available.

Dreizehnter, Alois. *Untersuchungen zur Textgeschichte der aristotelischen Politik*. Leiden: Brill, 1962.

Jowett, Benjamin. *The Politics of Aristotle*. Oxford: Clarendon Press, 1885.

Lord, Carnes. *Aristotle, The Politics*. Translated with an introduction, notes, and glossary. Chicago: University of Chicago Press, 1984.

Newman, William Lambert. *The Politics of Aristotle*, 4 vols. Oxford: Clarendon Press, 1887–1902. Critical text with very useful philological, historical, and philosophical commentary.

Ogle, William. *Aristotle: The Parts of Animals*. London: K. Paul, French and Co., 1882.

Pellegrin, Pierre. *Aristote: Les Parties des animaux*. Paris: GF-Flammarion, 2011.

Pellegrin, Pierre. *Aristote, Les Politiques*. French translation and introduction by Pierre Pellegrin. Paris: GF-Flammarion, 1990; new edition 2015.

Platt, Arthur. *Aristotle: On the Generation of Animals*. Oxford: Clarendon Press, 1910.
Rackham, Harris. *Aristotle Politics*. Cambridge, MA: Loeb, 1932. Noncritical Greek text, but indicating some conjectures of other editors, with English translation.
Rackham, Harris, trans. *Aristotle, Athenian Constitution, Eudemian Ethics, Virtues and Vices*. Cambridge, MA: Loeb, 1935.
Reeve, C. D. C. *Aristotle, Politics*. Indianapolis: Hackett, 1998; new edition 2017.
Ross, G. R. T., ed. *Aristotle: De Sensu and de Memoria: Text and Translation with Introduction and Commentary*. Cambridge: Cambridge University Press, 1906.
Ross, W. D., ed. *Aristotelis Politica*. Oxford: Oxford Classical Texts, Clarendon, 1957.
Ross, W. D., ed. *The Works of Aristotle*. Oxford: Clarendon Press, 1908–1952.
Ross, W. D., J. O. Urmson, and J. L. Ackrill, trans. *Aristotle: The Nicomachean Ethics*. Oxford: Oxford University Press, 1980.
Schütrumpf, Eckart. *Aristoteles Politik*. 4 vols. Berlin: Akademie Verlag, 1991–1996. German translation and rich commentary.
Solomon, J., trans. *Aristotle: Eudemian Ethics*. In *The Complete Works of Aristotle*, Revised Oxford Translation, vol. 2, edited by Jonathan Barnes. Princeton: Princeton University Press, 1984.
Thurot, Charles. *Études sur Aristote. Politique, dialectique, rhétorique*. Paris: Durand, 1860. Especially the first 104 pages, "Observations critiques sur la Politique," which suggest many corrections, some of them excessive, but mostly interesting, of the text.
Tricot, Jules. *Aristote, La Politique*. Nouvelle traduction avec introduction, notes et index. Paris: Vrin, 1962.
Vettori, Pietro. *Petri Victorii commentarii in VIII libros Aristotelis de optimo statu civitatis*. Florence: Iunta, 1576.

Other Ancient Texts

Diodorus Siculus. *Library of History*. Translated by C. H. Oldfather. Cambridge, MA: Loeb Classical Library, Harvard University Press, 1933.
Diogenes Laertius. *Lives of Eminent Philosophers*. Translated by R. D. Hicks. Cambridge, MA: Loeb Classical Library, Harvard University Press, 1925.
Hippolytus. *Refutation of All Heresies*. Translated by J. H. MacMahon. In *Ante-Nicene Fathers*, vol. 5, edited by Alexander Roberts, James Donaldson, and A. Cleveland Coxe. Buffalo, NY: Christian Literature Publishing Co., 1886; revised and edited for New Advent by Kevin Knight and available online at www.newadvent.org/fathers/0501.htm.
Plato. *The Laws*. Translated by Trevor J. Saunders. London: Penguin Books, 2004.
Plato. *Plato Complete Works*. Edited by John M. Cooper. Indianapolis: Hackett, 1997.
Plato. *Statesman*. Translated by C. J. Rowe. Oxford: Oxford University Press, 1995.

Plato. *Statesman. Philebus. Ion*. Translated by Harold North Fowler and W. R. M. Lamb. Cambridge, MA: Loeb Classical Library, Harvard University Press, 1925.
(Pseudo)-Plutarch. *Placita Philosophorum (Opinions of the Philosophers)*. Edited by G. N. Bernardakis. Leipzig: Teubner, 1893.
Stobaeus. *The Greek Anthology*. Edited by W. R. Paton. Cambridge, MA: Loeb, 1857–1921.
Xenophon. *Memorabilia*. Edited by J. Henderson et al. Cambridge, MA: Loeb, 2013.

Books, Articles, and Essays

Abel, Karl. "Über der Gegensinn der Urworte." *Sprachwissenshaftliche Abhandlungen*, 313–367. Leipzig: W. Friedrich, 1884; reprint, Norderstedt: Hansebooks, 2016.
Agamben, Giorgio. *La Guerre civile. Pour une théorie politique de la* stasis. Paris: Éditions Points, 2015.
Aubenque, Pierre, ed. *Aristote politique. Études sur la "Politique" d'Aristote*. Paris: PUF, 1993.
Aubenque, Pierre. "Politique et éthique chez Aristote." *Ktèma. Civilisations de l'Orient, de la Grèce et de Rome* 5 (1980): 211–221.
Aubenque, Pierre. *La Prudence chez Aristote*. Paris: PUF, 1963.
Baldry, Harold Caparne. "Zeno's Ideal State." *Journal of Hellenic Studies* 79 (1959): 3–15.
Benveniste, Émile. *Vocabulaire des institution indo-européenes*, 2 vols. Paris: Éditions de Minuit, 1969.
Betbeder, Philippe. "Éthique et politique selon Aristote." *Revue des Sciences Philosophiques et Théologiques* 54 (1970): 453–488.
Bodéüs, Richard. *Le Philosophe et la cité. Recherches sur les rapports entre morale et politique dans la pensée d'Aristote*. Paris: Les Belles Lettres, 1982; English translation by Jan Edward Garrett, *The Political Dimensions of Aristotle's "Ethics."* Albany: State University of New York Press, 1993.
Bodéüs, Richard. *Politique et Philosophie chez Aristote. Recueil d'études*. Namur: Societé des Études Classiques, 1991.
Bolton, Robert. 1997. "The Material Cause: Matter and Explanation in Aristotle's Natural Science." In *Aristotelische Biologie. Intentionem, Methoden, Ergebnisse*, edited by W. Kullmann and S. Föllinger, 97–124. Stuttgart: Franz Steiner.
Bonitz, H. *Index Aristotelicus*, 2nd. ed. Graz: Akademische Druck- U. Verlagsantalt, 1955; photo-reproduced from vol. 5 of *Aristoteles Werke*. Berlin: Königliche Preussischen Akademie der Wissenschaften, 1870.
Bordes, Jacqueline. *Politeia dans la pensée grecque jusqu'à Aristote*. Paris: Les Belles Lettres, 1982.

Bourriot, Félix. *Kalos kagathos: d'un terme de propogande de sophistes à une notion sociale et philosophique*, 2 vols. Hildesheim: Georg Olms, 1975.
Brunschwig, Jacques. "L'esclavage chez Aristote." *Cahiers philosophiques* (September 1979): 20–30.
Brunschwig, Jacques. "Du mouvement et de l'immobilité de la loi." *Revue Internationale de Philosophie* 133–134 (1980): 512–540.
Burnet, John. *The Ethics of Aristotle*. London: Methuen, 1900.
Canguilhem, Georges. "Le vivant et son milieu." In *La Connaissance de la vie*. Paris: Vrin, 1967; English translation by John Savage, "The Living and Its Milieu." *Grey Room* (Spring 2001): 7–31.
Chantraine, Pierre. *Dictionnaire étymologique de la langue grecque*. Paris: Klincksieck, 1968.
Cohn-Haft, Louis. "Divorce in Classical Athens." *Journal of Hellenic Studies* 115 (1995): 1–14.
Connell, Sophia M. *Aristotle on Female Animals: A Study of the "Generation of Animals."* Cambridge: Cambridge University Press, 2016.
Cooper, John. "Political Animals and Civic Friendship." In *Aristoteles "Politik." Akten des XI. Symposium Aristotelicum*, edited by Günther Patzig, 220–240. Göttingen: Vandenhoech & Ruprecht, 1990.
Crubellier, Michel, and Pierre Pellegrin. *Aristote. Le philosophe et les savoirs*. Paris: Seuil, 2017.
Dalimier, Catherine. "Les enjeux de la reformulation syllogistique chez les commentateurs grecs du *De Caelo* d'Aristote." In *Le Commentaire entre tradition et innovation*, edited by M.-O. Goulet, 377–386. Paris: Vrin, 2000.
Defourny, Maurice. *Aristotle. Études sur la "Politique."* Paris: Beauchesne, 1932.
Demongeot, Marcel. *Le meilleur régime politique selon saint Thomas*. Paris: André Blot, 1928.
Demongeot, Marcel. *La Théorie du Régime Mixte chez saint Thomas d'Aquin*. Marseille: F. Carbonel, 1927.
Demont, Paul. "Note sur les premiers emplois de èthikos (ἠθικός) chez Aristote. Le sentiment d'amitié et les transactions de gré à gré." *Ktema. Civilisations de l'Orient, de la Grèce et de Rome* 5 (1998): 81–90.
Deslauriers, Marguerite. "Aristotle on the Virtues of Slaves and Women." *Oxford Studies in Ancient Philosophy* 25 (2003): 213–223.
Dillon, John, and Tania Gergel. *The Greek Sophists*. London: Penguin, 2003.
Dorion, Louis-André. *L'Autre Socrate. Études sure les écrits socratiques de Xénophon*. Paris: Les Belles Lettres, 2013.
Finley, Moses. *Democracy Ancient and Modern*. Ann Arbor: University of Michigan, 1973; revised second edition New Brunswick: Rutgers, 1985; French translation *Démocratie antique et démocratie modern*. Paris: Payot, 1976.
Foucault, Michel. *L'archéologie du savoir*. Paris: Gallimard, 1969; English translation by A. M. Sheridan Smith, *The Archaeology of Knowledge*. New York: Routledge, 2002.

Foucault, Michel. *Les mots et les choses*. Paris: Gallimard, 1966; English translation *The Order of Things*. New York: Pantheon Books, 2002.
Frede, Dorothea. "The Endoxon Mystique: What Endoxa Are and What They Are Not," 2012. Available online at ancphil.lsa.umich.edu/-/downloads/osap/43-Frede.pdf.
Freud, Sigmund. "Über der Gegensinn der Urworte. Referat über die gleichnamige Broschüre von Karl Abel 1884." In *The Complete Psychological Works of Sigmund Freud (The Standard Edition)*, vol. 11, 155–161, originally published in *Jahrbuch für psychoanalytische Forschungen*, vol. 2, 179–184, 1910; "The Antithetical Meaning of Primal Words." In *Collected Papers*, vol. 4, 184–191. London: Hogarth Press, 1957.
Gauthier, René Antoine, and Jean-Yves Jolif. *Aristote. L'éthique à Nicomaque*, tome 1: 1958; tome 2: 1959. Second edition, Louvain: Publications universitaires, 1970; reprinted 2002.
Gernet, Louis. *Anthropologie de la Grèce antique*. Collection of articles published by J.-P. Vernant. Paris: Maspéro, 1968.
Glotz, Gustave. *La solidarité de la famille dans le droit criminal en Grèce*. Paris: Albert Fontemoing, 1904.
Goldschmidt, Victor. "La théorie aristotélicienne de l'esclavage et sa méthode." In *Zetesis. Album Amicorum (Mélanges E. De Strycker)*, 147–163. Antwerp: De Nederlansch Boekhandel, 1973.
Gouguenheim, Sylvain. *Aristote au Mont Saint-Michel*. Paris: Seuil, 2008.
Goulet, Richard, ed. *Dictionnaire des philosophes antiques*. Paris: CNRS, 1989–2018.
Guthrie, William K. C. *A History of Greek Philosophy, Vol. II*. Cambridge: Cambridge University Press, 1965.
Guthrie, William K. C. *In the Beginning: Some Greek Views on the Origin of Life and the Early State of Man*. London: Methuen & Co., 1957.
Hansen, Mogens H. *Polis and City-State: An Ancient Concept and Its Modern Equivalent*. Copenhagen: Munksgaard, 1998.
Ismard, Paulin. *La démocratie contre les experts. Les esclaves publics en Grèce ancienne*. Paris: Seuil, 2015; English translation *Democracy's Slaves: A Political History of Ancient Greece*. Cambridge, MA: Harvard University Press, 2017.
Jaeger, Werner. *Aristotle: Fundamentals of the History of His Development*. Oxford: Oxford University Press, 1948.
Jaeger, Werner. *Paideia: The Ideals of Greek Culture*. Oxford: Oxford University Press, 1945.
Kalimtzis, Kostas. *Aristotle on Political Enmity and Disease: An Inquiry into Stasis*. Albany: State University of New York Press, 2000.
Kamp, Andreas. *Die politische Philosophie des Aristoteles und ihre metaphysichen Grundlagen. Wesenstheorie und Polisordnung*. Munich: Verlag Karl Alber, 1985.
Keyt, David. *Aristotle Politics Books V and VI*. Oxford: Clarendon Press, 1995.

Keyt, David. "Three Basic Theorems in Aristotle's *Politics*." In *A Companion to Aristotle's "Politics,"* edited by David Keyt and Fred D. Miller, 118–141. Oxford: Blackwell, 1991.
Kraut, Richard. *Aristotle: Political Philosophy*. Oxford: Oxford University Press, 2002.
Kraut, Richard. "How to Justify Ethical Propositions: Aristotle's Method." In *The Blackwell Guide to Aristotle's Nicomachean Ethics*, edited by Richard Kraut, 76–95. Oxford: Blackwell, 2006.
Kullmann, Wolfgang. *Aristoteles und die moderne Wissenschaft*. Stuttgart: Franz Steiner, 1998.
Kullmann, Wolfgang. "Der Mensch als politisches Lebewesen bei Aristoteles." *Hermes* 108, no. 4 (1980): 419–443; English translation, "Man as a Political Animal in Aristotle." In *A Companion to Aristotle's Politics*, edited by David Keyt and Fred D. Miller, 94–117. Oxford: Blackwell, 1991.
Labarrière, Jean-Louis. "De la Phronèsis animale." In *Biologie, logique et métaphysique chez Aristote*, edited by Daniel Devereux and Pierre Pellegrin, 405–428. Paris: CNRS, 1990.
Léandri, Antoine. "L'aporie de la souveraineté." In *Aristote politique. Études sur la "Politique" d'Aristote*, edited by Pierre Aubenque, 315–339. Paris: PUF, 1993.
Lennox, James. *Aristotle's Philosophy of Biology: Studies in the Origins of Life Science*. Cambridge: Cambridge University Press, 2001.
Lonis, Raoul. *La cité dans le monde grec*. Paris: Nathan, 1994.
Loraux, Nicole. *La Cité divisée. L'oubli dans la mémoire d'Athènes*. Paris: Payot et Rivages, 1997; new edition 2005; English translation by Corinne Pach and Jeff Fort, *The Divided City: On Memory and Forgetting in Ancient Athens*. Brooklyn: Zone Books, 2002.
Loraux, Nicole. "Cratyle à l'épreuve de *stasis*." *Revue de Philosophie Ancienne* 5, no. 1 (1987): 49–69.
Loraux, Nicole. *Né de la terre. Mythe et politique à Athènes*. Paris: Seuil, 1996.
Meillassoux, Claude. *The Anthropology of Slavery*. Chicago: University of Chicago Press, 1991.
Memel-Fotê, Harris. *L'esclavage dans les sociétés lignagères de la forêt ivoirienne (XVIIe–XXe siècles)*. Abidjan: Éditions CERAP, IRD, 2007.
Meyer, Eduard. *Geschichte des Altertums*, 5th ed. Darmstadt: Wissenschaftliche Buchgesellschaft, 1953; first edition published 1884–1902.
Miers, Suzanne, and Igor Kopytoff, eds. *Slavery in Africa: Historical and Anthropological Perspectives*. Madison: University of Wisconsin Press, 1979.
Mossé, Claude. *Au nom de la loi. Justice et politique à Athènes à l'âge classique*. Paris: Payot et Rivages, 2010.
Mossé, Claude. *Politique et société en Grèce ancienne. Le 'modèle' athénien*. Paris: Flammarion, 1995.
Mugler, Charles. "L'isonomie des atomistes." *Revue de Philologie* (1956): 231–250.
Mugler, Charles. "Sur quelques particularités de l'atomisme ancien." *Revue de Philologie* (1953): 141–174.

Naddaf, Gerard. *The Greek Concept of Nature*. Albany: State University of New York Press, 2005.
Nuyens, François. *L'Évolution de la psychologie d'Aristote*. Louvain: Éditions de l'Institut Supérieur de Philosophie, 1973.
Patzig, Günther, ed. *Aristoteles "Politik." Akten des XI. Symposium Aristotelicum*. Göttingen: Vandenhoech & Ruprecht, 1990.
Peguy, Charles. *Oeuvres en prose complètes*, tome 3. Paris: Gallimard, 1992.
Pellegrin, Pierre. "Aristote arabe, Aristote latin. Aristote de droite, Aristote de gauche." *Revue philosophique de la France et de l'Étranger* (Janvier–Mars 2009): 79–89.
Pellegrin, Pierre. *La Classification des animaux chez Aristote*. Paris: Les Belles Lettres, 1982; English translation by Anthony Preus, *Aristotle's Classification of Animals*. Berkeley: University of California Press, 1987.
Pellegrin, Pierre. "Médecine hippocratique et philosophie." In D. Gourevitch, M. Grmek, and P. Pellegrin, *Hippocrate. De l'Art medical*, 14–40. Paris: Livre de Poche, 1994.
Pellegrin, Pierre. "Naturalité, excellence, diversité. Politique et biologie chez Aristote." In *Aristoteles' "Politik." Akten des XI. Symposium Aristotelicum*, edited by Günther Patzig, 124–151. Göttingen: Vandenhoech & Ruprecht, 1990.
Pellegrin, Pierre. "Parties de la cite, parties de la constitution." In *Aristotle: Metaphysics and Practical Philosophy. Essays in Honour of Enrico Berti*, edited by C. Natali, 177–200. Louvain-la-Neuve: Peeters, 2011.
Pellegrin, Pierre. "La *Politique* d'Aristote: Unité et fractures. Éloge de la lecture sommaire." *Revue philosophique de la France et de l'Étranger* 2 (1987): 129–159.
Polanyi, Karl. "Aristotle Discovers the Economy." In *Trade and Market in the Early Empires: Economics in History and Theory*, edited by Karl Polanyi, 64–94. New York: Free Press, 1957.
Rashed, Marwan. *Aristote de la génération et la corruption*. Paris: Les Belles Lettres, 2005.
Riedel, Manfred. "Metaphysik und Politik bei Aristoteles." *Philosophisches Jahrbuch* 77 (1970): 1–14.
Robinson, Richard. *Aristotle's Politics Books III and IV*. Oxford: Clarendon Press, 1962.
Romilly, Jacqueline de. *La loi dans la pensée grecque*. Paris: Les Belles Lettres, 1971.
Saunders, Trevor J. *Aristotle Politics Books I and II*. Oxford: Clarendon Press, 1995.
Schofield, Malcolm. "Ideology and Philosophy in Aristotle's Theory of Slavery." In *Aristoteles' "Politik." Akten des XI. Symposium Aristotelicum*, edited by Günther Patzig, 1–27. Göttingen: Vandenhoech & Ruprecht, 1990.
Simpson, Peter L. Phillips. *A Philosophical Commentary on the Politics of Aristotle*. Chapel Hill: University of North Carolina Press, 1998.
Skultety, Steven. "Delimiting Aristotle's Conception of *Stasis* in the *Politics*." *Phronesis* 54 (2009): 346–370.

Smith, Nicholas. "Aristotle's Theory of Natural Slavery." In *A Companion to Aristotle's "Politics,"* edited by David Keyt and Fred D. Miller, 142–155. Oxford: Blackwell, 1991.

Smith, Nicholas, and Robert Mayhew. "Aristotle on What the Political Scientist Needs to Know." In *Aristotelian Political Philosophy*, edited by C. Boudouris, 189–198. Athens: Kardaminsky, 1995.

Solmsen, Friedrich. *Aristotle's System of the Physical World.* Ithaca: Cornell University Press, 1960.

Staszak, Jean-François. *La géographie avant la géographie. Le climat chez Aristote et Hippocrate.* Paris: L'Harmattan, 1995.

Vatin, Claude. *Citoyens et non-citoyens dans le monde grec.* Paris: SEDES, 1984.

Vernant, Jean-Pierre. *Mythe et pensée chez les Grecs.* Paris: Maspéro, 1962; English translation, *Myth and Thought among the Greeks.* New York: Routledge, 1983.

Vernant, Jean-Pierre, ed. *Problèmes de la guerre en Grèce ancienne.* Paris, La Haye: Mouton, 1968; second edition Paris: Seuil, 1999.

Vidal-Naquet, Pierre. "Esclavage et gynécocratie dans la tradition, le mythe, l'utopie." In *Le Chasseur noir*, 267–288. Paris: Maspéro, 1981; English translation, "Slavery and the Rule of Women in Tradition, Myth and Utopia." In *Myth, Religion and Society*, edited by R. L. Gordon, 187–200. Cambridge: Cambridge University Press, 1981.

von Arnim, H. *Die drei aristotelischen Ethiken.* Vienna: Hölder-Pichler-Tempsky, 1924.

Weed, Ronald. *Aristotle on Stasis: A Moral Psychology of Political Conflict.* Berlin: Logos Verlag, 2007.

Wheeler, Marcus. "Aristotle's Analysis of the Nature of Political Struggle." *American Journal of Philology* 72, no. 2 (1951): 145–161.

Wilson, Edward O. *On Human Nature.* Cambridge, MA: Harvard University Press, 1978.

Wilson, Edward O. *Sociobiology.* Cambridge, MA: Harvard University Press, 1975.

Index

Abel, Karl, 324, 403, 405
Agamben, Giorgio, 393n9, 403
akrasia, ἀκρασία, ἀκρατής, 31, 35, 335
Alcidamas of Elea, 117n20
Alcmaeon of Croton, 5
Alexander of Aphrodisias, 59
  Commentary on De Caelo, 59
Alexander of Macedon, 18f, 53f, 358
analogy, (κατ') ἀναλογίαν, 115f, 120, 166f, 202, 212, 226, 288, 399
Anaxagoras, 23, 81, 292
Anaximander, 5, 385
Andronicus of Rhodes, 224
Annas, Julia, 144n53, 154
(anthropos), ἄνθρωπος, 92
aporia, ἀπορία, 199, 201, 287
arche, ἄρχειν, (οἱ) ἄρχοντες, 177, 260, 271, 311, 378, 390
Athens, 9ff, 18, 53, 157, 160, 174, 176, 179, 184, 202f, 210, 235, 262, 283, 289, 292, 294, 310, 318, 324f, 328, 330
Aubenque, Pierre, 23, 37n24, 44, 58n47, 203n35, 292, 403, 406
Aubonnet, Jean, 122n29, 329, 401
autarky; αὐτάρκεια, αὐτάρκης, 96ff, 106f, 110, 181, 380

Bachelard, Gaston, 1, 2, 3

Balandier, Georges, 390
Baldry, Harold Caparne, 14, 403
Barrès, Maurice, 325
Benveniste, Émile, 145, 153, 403
Berti, Enrico, 306n2, 407
Betbeder, Philippe, 37n24, 44, 403
Bodéüs, Richard, 35, 42, 48, 58ff, 91, 150, 199, 223, 271, 401, 403
Bolton, Robert, 85, 359, 403
Bonitz, H., 191n22, 201, 403
Bordes, Jacqueline, 182, 307, 403
Bourriot, Felix, 47, 404
Burnet, John, 43n32, 230, 404
Brunschwig, Jacques, 21, 49, 63n53, 123n30, 126, 287f, 290, 401, 404
Bywater, J., 43n32, 401

Canguilhem, Georges, 20, 99, 404
Carthage, 207, 248, 251, 291, 298, 306, 340, 354, 391
Chantraine, Pierre, 325, 404
Chares of Paros, 112
Charondas of Catania, 244
(chrēmata), χρήματα, 108
Cleisthenes, 237, 283, 298
Cohn-Haft, Louis, 196n29, 404
Connell, Sophia M., 164f, 168, 404
Cooper, John, 144, 146f, 152, 161, 402, 404

INDEX

Crete, Cretan, 176, 282, 284f, 293f, 391f
Crubellier, Michel, 39n27, 160n71, 404
Cuvier, Georges, 397ff

Dalimier, Catherine, 46ff, 59, 159, 387, 401, 404
Darwin, Charles; Darwinian, 295f, 398ff
Defourny, Maurice, 89, 404
Deslauriers, Marguerite, 164ff, 168, 404
Demetrius of Phaleron, 10
(*dēmokratikōteras*), δημοκρατικωτέρας, 244
(*dēmotikos*), δημοτικός, 318
Democritus, 6, 19–20
Demongeot, Marcel, 54n42, 404
Demont, Paul, 37n23, 404
Demosthenes, 19, 240, 264
  Olynthian 5, *Philippics* 2.21, 240n2
Descartes, 19, 163, 397
dianoia, διάνοια, 21, 202
diaporematic, διαπορεῖν, διαποροῦντας, 189, 191, 193, 197
Diderot, Denis, 383f
dikē, δίκαιον, 160, 211, 216, 225
Diodorus Siculus, 69ff, 83, 402
Diogenes of Sinope, 15, 70
Diogenes Laertius, 15, 70, 402
Dorion, Louis-André, 366n19, 404
Dreizehnter, Alois, 128, 260, 401
(*dynamis*), δύναμις, 310

Empedocles, 142, 170
Epicurus, 6, 101
ethnos, ἔθνος, ethnic, 11, 96, 180, 182, 339, 348, 354
ethos, ἔθος, 33, 37
ēthos, (*ēthikos*), ἦθος, ἠθικός, 37
(*eleutheria*), ἐλευθερία, 216
(*eu zēn*), εὖ ζῆν, 28
eudaimonia, εὐδαιμονία, 28, 77, 374

eunoia, εὔνοια, 148
Euripides, 69, 142n51, 340
exoteric, *exoterikoi*, 51, 372

Finley, Moses, 10n13, 404
Foucault, Michel, 2, 383–385, 394, 396–400, 404, 405
Freud, Sigmund; Freudian, 40, 55, 154, 160, 163, 324, 405

Gauthier, A., 148f, 152, 183n14, 223n47, 405
genus, γένος, 20, 30, 115f, 223, 349f, 375
Gernet, Louis, 8, 405
Glotz, Gustave, 145, 405
(gnostikē), (μόνον) γνωστικήν, 24
Goldschmidt, Victor, 119, 405
Gorgias, 179f
Gouguenheim, Sylvain, 9n12, 405
Guthrie, William K. C., 12, 69ff, 83, 405

Hansen, Mogens H., 97n1, 405
Hegel, Hegelian, 53, 95, 385
Herodotus, 132, 182, 307, 392
Hesiod, 17
hexis, ἕξις, 29f, 41f, 136
Hippocrates, Hippocratic, 6, 7, 49, 69, 132f
Hippodamus of Miletus, 288f
Homer, 5, 145, 206
(*homoiōs*), ὁμοίως, 190, 260
(*homologia*), ὁμολογία, 152
homonoia, 152, 156
(*hyparchein*), ὑπάρχειν, 260

isonomia, ἰσονομία, 5f, 184
Ismard, Paulin, 125, 310, 351, 357n11, 405
Isocrates, 53, 182, 240, 264

Jaeger, Werner, 47n36, 50ff, 346, 405

Jolif, J.-Y., 148f, 152, 183n14, 223n47, 405

Kalimtzis, Kostas, 337, 340, 342, 405
kalokagathia, kalokagathos, 46f
Kamp, Andreas, 55f, 405
Kant and Kantian, 18, 19, 28, 161, 381n29
Keyt, David, 80, 91, 118n23, 405f, 408
(*koinonia*), κοινωνία (πολιτική), κοινωνεῖν, 75; (τέλειος), 76, 86, 106, 151, 177, 380
Kopytoff, Igor, 126f, 146, 406
Kraut, Richard, 63n53, 230, 346, 350, 354, 406
Kullmann, Wolfgang, 55n43, 80, 85f, 93, 403, 406
(kyrion), κύριον, κυρίους, κυρίως, κυριωτάτη, 76, 179, 201, 216, 260

Labarrière, Jean-Louis, 87, 406
Lamarck, 68, 399
Larissa, 13, 179f
Léandri, Antoine, 203n35, 406
Lennox, James, 56, 406
Linnaeus, 383f
logos, λόγος, 21, 36, 87, 128, 190, 342n43, 372
Lonis, Raoul, 182, 406
Loraux, Nicole, 12, 103, 324f, 327, 343, 406
Lysias, 12

Machiavelli, Machiavellian, 49, 218, 298, 300, 302, 365
Maillet, Benoît, 393
(*malista*), μάλιστα, 313, 344
(*mallon*) μᾶλλον, 24, 81
Marx, Karl; Marxism, 9, 55, 118, 126, 160, 211, 329, 343
Mayhew, Robert, 275n3, 408
Mayr, Ernst, 20

Meillassoux, Claude, 127n35, 406
Memel-Foté, Harris, 117n19, 126, 406
merit, (κατ') ἀξίαν, 212
(*meson*), (τὸ) μέσον, 39
  (οἱ) μέσοι, 219
  (ἐν) μέσῳ, 237
Meyer, Eduard, 89, 399, 406
Miers, Suzanne, 126f, 146, 406
Miller, Fred D., 80, 91n29, 118n23, 406, 408
moria, 307
Mossé, Claude, 11, 173, 406
Mugler, Charles, 6, 406

Naddaf, Gerard, 17, 385n4, 407
Natali, Carlo, 62, 306n2, 407
Newman, William Lambert, 50, 62, 86, 132, 178, 191, 194, 210, 216, 260, 309, 312, 329ff, 337, 339, 346, 349f, 367, 372f, 377, 379f, 401
nomos, νόμος, 33, 225
(*nomothetēs*), νομοθέτης, 269, 271
Nuyens, François, 129n39, 407

Ousia, Οὐσία, 55, 93, 399

Parmenides, 71, 102, 110
Péguy, Charles, 381n29, 407
Pericles, 11–12, 23, 184n16, 292
perioikoi, 176
Phaleas of Chalcedon, 103, 280, 369n21
Philip II of Macedon, 18, 53, 329n29
philia, φιλία, φιλικός, φιλότης, 106, 141ff, 155ff
(*philos*), φίλος, φιλῷ, φίλων, 149
(*philosophia*), φιλοσοφία, 386
(*philosophōs*), φιλόσοφως, 21
(*phronēsis*), φρόνησις, 29, 87, 137, 192
(*physika*), (τὰ) φυσικά, 142
(*phōnē*), φωνή, 82

Plato, 7, 10, 13, 15, 17ff, 23ff, 36f, 49,
  52–53, 70, 73, 88n20, 96, 98, 100,
  103ff, 113, 115, 129, 132, 140,
  142, 162f, 173, 178f, 182, 184n16,
  206, 220n45, 222, 240, 243, 246,
  250, 264, 273, 279, 281, 288, 293,
  305, 307, 309f, 326ff, 340, 342f,
  351n 7, 352, 362f, 365f, 368ff,
  373, 377, 380f, 390, 391n7, 392,
  394, 396, 402f
  Lysis, 143
  Cratylus, 324
  Republic, 8, 10, 14f, 19, 24, 45, 70,
    96f, 100f, 104f, 113, 140, 172,
    179, 182, 222, 237, 246, 279, 308,
    326n26, 351n7, 356, 362, 370,
    372f, 381, 391n7, 392
  Phaedo, 18, 357n11
  Statesman, 24f, 81n11, 101n7,
    113n16, 182, 281, 309, 365n18,
    402, 403
  Laws, 25, 37, 129, 220n45, 240, 276,
    279, 281, 362ff, 373, 377, 391f
Platt, A., 98a3, 402
(plēthos), πλῆθος, 172, 184, 218, 349,
  350
Polanyi, Karl, 105f, 110, 407
polemos, 326f
polis, πόλις, 4, 14f, 17f, 28, 48, 75f,
  91, 97, 103, 151, 171f, 179, 327,
  385, 389, 396
(*politēs, politis, politai*): πολίτης,
  πολίτις, πολίται, 12, 172
politeia, πολιτεία, 46, 178f, 184,
  207, 240, 264, 285, 309, 377
  περὶ τῆς ἀρίστης πολιτείας, 191
  τοὺς μετέχοντας τῆς πολιτείας,
  256
(*politeuma*), πολίτευμα, 311
(*politikē*), πολιτική, 75, 309
  πολιτικὴ διανοία καὶ θεωρία, 375
  πολιτικὴ φίλια, 143, 157

ἰσονομίας πολιτικῆς, 184
  πολιτικῆς ἀκροατῆς, 35
(*politikos*), (ὁ) πολιτικός, 113, 271,
  273, 281
  βίος πολιτικός, 377
  τὸν ἀγαθὸν νομοθέτην καὶ τὸν
  ὡς ἀληθῶς πολιτικόν, 271
(*politikōs*), πολιτικῶς, 179
(*praxis, praktikē*), πρᾶξις 378,
  πρακτική, 21, 199
(*pros hēmas*), πρὸς ἡμᾶς, 39
(*psēphismata*), ψηφίσματα, 27
(Pseudo-) Plutarch, 5n6, 403

quickness of mind, ἀγχίνοια, 27

Rashed, Marwan, 67, 407
Riedel, Manfred, 55f, 407
Robinson, Richard, 317n15, 407
Ross, W. D., 27n12, 43, 128n37, 401f
Rowe, C. J., 24, 25, 402

Saunders, Trevor, 25, 91, 402, 407
Scaïno da Salo, Antoine, 50n39
Schofield, Malcolm, 117ff, 138, 370, 407
(*scholē*), σχολή, 131
Schütrumpf, Eckart, 55n 43, 402
(*semeion*), σημεῖον, 82
Sepulveda, 357n11
Sextus Empiricus, 220
Simplicius, 59
Simpson, Peter L. Phillips, 275n3,
  376, 407
Skultety, Steven, 328f, 338, 407
Smith, Nicholas, 118n23, 275n3, 408
Socrates, 6, 18, 19, 24, 29, 46, 65, 97,
  179, 191, 194n25, 201, 308, 327,
  357n11, 362, 388, 392
Solmsen, Friedrich, 395, 408
Solon, 27, 108, 202, 238, 281, 294
(*sophizesthai*), σοφίζεσθαι, 178
(*sōtēria*), σωτηρία, 120, 138

Sparta, Lacedaimonian, Laconian, 42f, 109, 176, 205ff, 221, 235, 237, 248, 262, 274, 279, 282, 284, 332, 361, 392
stasis, στάσις, 63, 187, 297, 324f, 328ff, 389, 393f, 403, 406ff
στασιάζω, στασιάζουσιν, 328, 331
στασιατικῶς, 328, 329
Staszak, Jean-François, 132f, 408
synoikismos, 358n12
(syzēn), (τὸ) συζῆν, 149
(sympherei, sympheron), συμφέρει, συμφέρον, 183, 254, 320

(technē), τέχνη, 108, 273
(teleios), τέλειος, 76, 109, 151
Thales, 109, 112
theoria, θεωρεῖν, θεωρία, θεωρητικός, 20, 375
ἡ τοῦ θεοῦ θεωρία, 47
τὰς αὐτοτελεῖς καὶ αὑτῶν ἕνεκεν θεωρίας καὶ διανοήσεις, 380

Thucydides, 10–11, 184n16, 194n25
Tricot, J., 148n59, 216, 236n1, 402

Urmson, J. O., 43n31, 402

Vatin, Claude, 11–12, 408
Vernant, Jean-Pierre, 4ff, 8ff, 102f, 142, 173, 326f, 405, 408
Vettori, Pietro, 122, 260, 339, 402
Vidal-Naquet, Pierre, 10n13, 14, 408
Von Arnim, Hans, 147f, 408

Weed, Ronald, 338, 408
Wheeler, Marcus, 329f, 408
Wilson, Edward O., 68, 408

Xenophon, 113n16, 194n25, 273, 366, 392, 403, 404

Zeller, 379
Zeno of Citium, 14, 95, 96

Aristotle, references to his works
Alexander, or On Colonization (lost work), 54
[Constitution of Athens], 11, 328
Organon, 56
Categories, 224
Prior Analytics, 56
70a13, 82
Posterior Analytics, 56f
1.2, 71b34, 75
2, 89b29, 21
2.16, 98b1, 57n46
Topics 6.6, 145a15, 21n2
Physics 2.8, 198b32, 170n79
Generation and Corruption, 67
1.10, 327b24, 252
De Caelo, 59, 109, 404
1.3, 270b19, 71n4
Meteorologica 1.3, 339b27, 71n4

De Anima
1.3, 407b23, 379
2.3, 414b19, 257
2.4, 415a26, 73
2.8, 420b33, 84n14
Sense and Sensibilia 1, 436a17, 26n10
Life and Death 5, 480b26, 27n12
Movement of Animals, 199n31
Progression of Animals (IA), 139
History of Animals, 69, 80f, 85, 399
1.1, 487a10, 81
1.1, 487b32, 81
1.1, 488a2, 80
1.1, 488a30, 138
4.9, 535a31ff, 84
4.9, 536b14, 88n21
8.1, 588a23ff, 87
8.1, 588b33, 90

8.28, 606b17, 132
9.1, 608a33, 168n77
9.29, 618ff, 87
9.32, 618b31–619a3, 83n13
9.39, 623a8, 87
9.46, 630b20, 88
Parts of Animals, 3, 67f, 81, 85, 401
  1.1, 642a2, 18
  1.3, 643b5, 138n49
  1.4, 644a16, 115
  2.1, 650b27–651a4, 133
  2.8, 653b35, 115
  2.9, 655a33, 116
  2.13, 657b1, 89n22
  2.16, 659b35, 120n25
  3.2, 663b–664a, 360f
  4.10, 687a8, 81
  4.12, 693b5, 56n45
Generation of Animals, 68, 85, 99, 164, 402, 404
  1.23, 731a24–b8, 73n5
  2.1, 735a17, b24, 73n 5
  2.4, 738a18, 134n43
  3.4, 755a31, 88, 359
  3.10, 760a35, 73n5
  4.8, 776b5, 98n3
  5.7, 786b21, 85
Metaphysics, 55f, 62
  E.1, 1025b25, 21n2, 22n3
  10.9, 1058a31, 92
  12.8, 1074b10, 71n4
  14.4, 1091b16, 99
Nicomachean Ethics, 107, 142, 162, 203, 231ff, 270, 374f, 377
  1.1, 1094a, 111n15
  1.1, 1094b, 38, 43ff
  1.1, 1095a, 22, 35n22
  1.5, 1095b, 375
  1.5, 1097b, 91n28
  1.13, 1102a, 38n26, 48, 374
  2.1, 1103a, 37, 137
  2.1, 1103b, 41
  2.2, 1103b26, 22, 65
  2.2, 1104b8, 31n16
  2.2, 1105a10, 31, 36, 131
  2.5, 1105b29, 22
  2.5, 1106a, 29n15, 39
  2.5, 1106b, 30, 39
  2.6, 1106b, 30
  2.6, 1107a, 39
  3.2, 1112a15, 130
  3.6, 1113a29, 23n5
  3.7, 1115b20, 136n47
  3.15, 1119a34, 34n20
  4.1, 1120b, 219n42
  5.1, 1129a26, 223
  5.1, 1129b, 227ff
  5.2, 1130a, 223f, 230
  5.3, 1131a25, 213, 225
  5.3, 1131b, 225
  5.4, 1132a, 225
  5.5, 1133a28, 108
  5.7, 1134b24, 270
  5.7, 1135a, 183, 198, 228
  5.9, 1137a, 230
  5.10, 1137b29, 269
  6.3, 1139b16, 29
  6.5, 1140b6, 88n20
  6.8, 1141b, 42, 199f, 271
  6.12, 1144a31, 199n31
  7.11, 1152b, 38ff
  7.14, 1154b23, 379
  8.1, 1155a–b, 142, 155
  8.3, 1156a6, 153n67
  8.5, 1157b19, 149
  8.7, 1158a, 154
  8.8, 1158b29, 144
  8.9, 1159b, 143n52, 149n62, 162n73
  8.9, 1160a, 79, 161n72
  8.10, 1160b, 162, 166
  8.10, 1161a, 167
  8.12, 1161b13, 152
  8.13, 1162b23ff, 158
  8.14, 1162a17, 75, 91n28

9.1, 1163b32, 151
9.4, 1166a, 23n5, 147ff
9.6, 1167b2, 151, 157
9.10, 1170b32ff, 154, 155
10.5, 1175a19, 40n28
10.6, 1177a, 140, 374
10.7, 1177b33, 219n43
10.8, 1178a, 374
10.8, 1178b7, b23, 1179a9, 77
10.9, 1179b, 32f, 41
10.9, 1180a, 41n29, 287, 390
10.9, 1180b32, 26, 390
10.9, 1181b15, 386
Eudemian Ethics, 21f, 26, 37, 46f, 75, 142, 144, 147f, 151, 153, 156ff, 222, 387, 402
  1.3, 1214b29, 34n19
  1.3, 1215a12, 47
  1.5, 1215b19, 34
  1.5, 1216b10, 22n3
  1.6, 1216b35, 21
  1.7, 1217a24, 77n7
  1.8, 1218b11, 44n33
  7.7, 1241a32, 151, 157
  7.9, 1241b17, 130n40
  7.10, 1242a, 75, 90, 157
  7.10, 1242a30ff, 140, 157ff
  7.10, 1242b, 157ff
  7.10, 1243a8, 159f
  8.3, 1249b16ff, 47
Magna Moralia, 148
Politics
  1.1, 1251a1, 60
  1, 1252a5, 76
  1, 1252a7, 113n16, 271
  1, 1252a9, 115
  2, 1252a26, 28, 72
  2, 1252a30–34, 120
  2, 1252b2, 185
  2, 1252b4, 120n25
  2, 1252b6, 139
  2, 1252b7, 114
  2, 1252b12, 74
  2, 1252b16, 74
  2, 1252b19, 185
  2, 1252b27, 74
  2, 1252b28, 76, 96, 151n65
  2, 1252b30, 75, 79
  2, 1252b31, 91
  2, 1253a1, 75, 90
  2, 1253a3, 93, 100, 134
  2, 1253a7, 80, 82, 86
  2, 1253a8, 83
  2, 1253a10, 83n12
  2, 1253a11, 82
  2, 1253a14, 93n30
  2, 1253a15, 84
  2, 1253a18, 86
  2, 1253a19, 82
  2, 1253a29, 89
  2, 1253a30, 134
  2, 1253b19, 347n4
  4, 1253b31, 123
  4, 1253b32, 123
  4, 1253a5, 123
  4, 1254a7, 123
  4, 1254a8, 123
  4, 1254a14, 124
  5, 1254a17, 119
  5, 1254a23, 128
  5, 1254a31, 73
  5, 1254b4, 130
  5, 1254b9, 121
  5, 1254b10, 138
  5, 1254b21, 124
  5, 1254b22, 128, 139
  5, 1254b23, 128n37
  5, 1254b32, 128
  5, 1254b24, 128
  5, 1254b27, 105
  6, 1255a15, 175, 218
  6, 1255a28, 124
  6, 1255a30, 135n45
  6, 1255b10, 130n40

7, 1255b11, 123
7, 1255b13, 125n32, 128, 140
7, 1255b14, 124
7, 1255b20, 114n17, 136, 253
7, 1255b33, 136
7, 1255b35, 111
7, 1255b37, 127
8, 1256a1, 112
8, 1256a32, 108
8, 1256b3, 106
8, 1256b16, 139
8, 1256b26, 106
8, 1256b36, 108
8, 1257a13, 107
8, 1257a27, 107
8, 1257a29, 107
9, 1257a41, 111
9, 1257b4, 109
9, 1257b10, 109
11, 1258b10, 112
11, 1259a3, 112
11, 1259a6, 109n14
12, 1259b4ff., 165
13, 1259b37, 195
13, 1260a10, 129
13, 1260a12, 129, 167
13, 1260a14, 165
13, 1260a15, 78
13, 1260a40, 125
13, 1260b1, 125
13, 1260b3, 130, 137
13, 1260b5, 129
13, 1260b6, 130
2.1, 1260b28, 171
2, 1261a16, 98
2, 1261a31, 63n53, 226n51
2, 1261b10, 98n2
2, 1261b11, 97
4, 1262b7, 144
5, 1264a3, 396
5, 1264b15ff, 44, 293
5, 1264b17, 140n50

6, 1265a1, 391n7
6, 1265a18, 377n26
6, 1265b12, 328
6, 1265b26, 240
6, 1265b33, 237
7, 1266b1, 280
7, 1267a13, 103
7, 1267a14, 280
7, 1267a37, 103
7, 1267b1, 103
7, 1267b30, 103
8, 1268a6, 288
8, 1268b9, 289
8, 1269a3, 289
8, 1269a6, 72
8, 1269a14, 323
8, 1269a18, 323
8, 1269a26, 288
9, 1269a31, 282
9, 1269a32, 349n5
9, 1269b3, 176n4
9, 1271b1, 221n46
9, 1271b2, 109n13
10, 1271b21, 176n5
10, 1271b23, 289
10, 1272a30, 284
10, 1272a34, 284
10, 1272a38, 285
11, 1272b25, 291
11, 1272b30, 293
11, 1273a31, 291
11, 1273b18, 291
11, 1273b21, 291
12, 1273b33, 281
12, 1273b35, 238
12, 1274a13, 294, 330
3.1, 1274b32, 171
1, 1274b36, 172
1, 1274b38, 57, 172
1, 1274b41, 172, 389
1, 1275a1, 172
1, 1275a22, 174, 256

1, 1275a26, 176
1, 1275a28, 177, 256
1, 1275a33, 257
1, 1275a34ff, 257
1, 1275a38, 245
1, 1275b13ff, 177
1, 1275b18, 177
2, 1275b25, 179n9
2, 1275b27, 180
2, 1275b36, 283
2, 1276a1, 174
2, 1276a2–5, 175
3, 1276a13, 183n15
3, 1276a30, 181
4, 1276b24, 190
4, 1276b25, 190
4, 1276b27, 190
4, 1276b33, 190, 232
4, 1276b35, 189, 191
4, 1276b36, 189n21, 191
4, 1276b37, 191
4, 1276b38, 191n23
4, 1277a1, 191
4, 1277a10, 191
4, 1277a13ff, 192
4, 1277a24, 192
4, 1277a25–29, 192
4, 1277a37, 117
4, 1277b3, 121
4, 1277b7, 114, 193
4, 1277b20, 258
4, 1277b25, 193
4, 1277b27, 158n69
5, 1278a8, 187, 197
5, 1278a11, 125
5, 1278a20, 125
5, 1278a29, 120n26, 176
5, 1278a38, 161, 178
6, 1278b8, 323
6, 1278b11, 311
6, 1278b22, 183n15
6, 1278b25, 95

6, 1278b30, 51
6, 1278b35, 137
6, 1278b35, 138
6, 1278b39, 137
6, 1279a17, 183n15, 184, 213
6, 1279a21, 215
7, 1279a25, 311n9
7, 1279a34, 248
7, 1279a37, 178, 242
7, 1279a39, 265
8, 1279b13, 380
8, 1279b16, 185n17
8, 1279b35, 210
9, 1280a1, 63n54
9, 1280a9, 216, 217
9, 1280a10, 216
9, 1280a28, 216, 226
9, 1280a32, 86, 130, 211
9, 1280b3, 309
9, 1280b35, 141, 181
9, 1281a1, 77n9
9, 1281a4, 187, 388
10, 1281a11, 179, 201
10, 1281a14, 221, 232
10, 1281a21, 221
11, 1281b2, 202, 259
11, 1281b6, 170
11, 1281b7, 202
11, 1281b9, 201
11, 1281b15ff, 200
11, 1281b19, 295
11, 1281b26, 202
11, 1281b28, 198
11, 1281b30, 202
11, 1281b32, 176n5, 202
11, 1281b35, 201
11, 1282a34, 201n34
11, 1282a38, 256
11, 1282b2, 270
11, 1282b11, 41, 227, 391
12, 1282b17, 183n15
12, 1282b20, 63n54

12, 1283a10–16, 311
12, 1283a14ff, 228n55, 309n6
12, 1283a16, 211, 336
13, 1283a30, 217, 228n39, 232n58
13, 1283a34, 217
13, 1283a40, 218, 255
13, 1283b4, 218
13, 1283b42, 194
13, 1284a3, 100
13, 1284b28, 195
13, 1284b30, 195
14, 1285a27, 299
14, 1285b13, 89n25
15, 1285b35, 205
15, 1286a5, 205
15, 1286a29, 259
15, 1286a30, 205
15, 1286b8, 89n25, 184
15, 1286b10, 185
15, 1286b12, 185
15, 1286b14ff, 186, 215n41, 238, 250
16, 1287b3, 205n37
16, 1287b32, 289
16, 1287b17, 61
17, 1288a1, 204
18, 1288a32, 286, 349
18, 1288a34, 350
18, 1288a35, 350
18, 1288a37, 195, 286
18, 1288a39, 286
18, 1288a40, 351
18, 1288b2, 351
18, 1288b5, 346
4.1, 1288b13, 275
1, 1288b21ff, 274, 275
1, 1288b24, 278
1, 1288b27, 271, 281
1, 1288b33, 278
1, 1288b39ff, 275, 279
1, 1289a1, 274, 279, 280
1, 1289a6, 281, 370

1, 1289a13, 220n45
1, 1289a15, 323
2, 1289a31, 198
2, 1289b12, 305
2, 1289b15, 351n8
2, 1289b16, 305
2, 1289b23, 306, 344n44
3, 1289b40, 309n6, 311
3, 1290a7, 323
3, 1290a11, 311
3, 1290a27, 299n9, 332n36
4, 1290b9, 210n40
4, 1290b21, 312n10
4, 1290b29, 60
4, 1290b37, 307
4, 1291a8ff, 97
4, 1291a11, 309
4, 1291a24, 60
4, 1291a39, 60
4, 1291b14, 312
4, 1291b30, 259
4, 1291b31, 312
4, 1291b32, 260, 312
4, 1291b33, 261
4, 1291b34, 313n12
4, 1291b36, 312
4, 1291b37, 260
4, 1292a1, 216
4, 1292a2, 269
4, 1292a16, 200
4, 1292a19, 200
4, 1292a32, 270, 285
5, 1292b10, 285
6, 1292b27, 213
6, 1292b32, 262
6, 1292b37, 313
6, 1293a23, 214
6, 1293a26, 315n13
6, 1293a32, 285
7, 1293b3, 270, 349n5, 350
7, 1293b10, 247, 261
7, 1293b12, 248

INDEX 419

7, 1293b24, 249
8, 1293b33, 240, 248
8, 1294a17, 240
9, 1294a41, 244
9, 1294b14, 252
10, 1295a4, 299, 315n14
10, 1295a15, 299
10, 1295a17, 205n36
11, 1295a25, 265
11, 1295a31, 266
11, 1295a36, 63n54
11, 1295b1, 308
11, 1295b4, 63n54
11, 1295b13, 143, 220
11, 1295b25, 219n44
11, 1296a8, 328
11, 1296a22, 262
11, 1296a27, 329
11, 1296a36, 263
12, 1296b13, 254
12, 1296b17, 255, 314
12, 1296b18, 287
12, 1296b22, 314
12, 1296b26, 255
12, 1296b31, 255
12, 1296b35ff, 295
12, 1296b40, 235, 295
13, 1297a15, 178
13, 1297a23, 244
13, 1297a29, 302
13, 1297b2, 256
14, 1297b35, 315
14, 1297b37, 316, 317, 320
14, 1297b39, 293
14, 1298a7, 317
14, 1298a10, 318
14, 1298a31, 318
14, 1298a33, 318
14, 1298a34, 318n16
14, 1298b10, 318
14, 1298b11, 319
14, 1298b13, 320

14, 1298b20, 258, 320
14, 1299a2, 322
15, 1299a26, 321, 367
15, 1300a8, 321
15, 1300a41–b1, 241, 321
16, 1301a10–15, 319
16, 1301a12, 319
5.1, 1301a25, 331
1, 1301a26, 212, 226n53
1, 1301a39, 232, 331
1, 1301b5, 331n32
1, 1301b6, 331
1, 1301b13, 332
1, 1301b19, 332
1, 1301b29, 212, 226
1, 1301b36, 212
1, 1301b39, 262n8
1, 1301b40, 333
1, 1302a1, 262, 333
1, 1302a2, 236, 335
1, 1302a12, 198
1, 1302a14, 259
2, 1302a18–22, 333
3, 1302b3, 338, 339
3, 1302b5, 339
3, 1302b21, 337
3, 1302b33, 296
3, 1302b36, 98
3, 1303a6, 176n4
3, 1303a7, 339
3, 1303a13, 341
3, 1303a14, 341
3. 1303a25, 180, 338
4, 1303b19–26, 341
4, 1303b28, 328
4, 1304a3, 296
4, 1304a5, 248
4, 1304a11ff, 329
4, 1304a20, 330
4, 1304a21, 332n36
4, 1304a28, 332
4, 1304a33, 332n35

4, 1304a38, 236
4, 1304b7, 330
5, 1305a12, 198
5, 1305b16, 328
6, 1306a38, 328
6, 1306b6, 341
6, 1306b16, 328
7, 1307a5, 334
7, 1307a9, 334
7, 1307a10, 207, 351
7, 1307a13, 207
7, 1307a23, 334
7, 1307b6ff, 292
8, 1307b32, 250
8, 1308a3, 250
9, 1309b5, 188
9, 1309b8, 245
9, 1309b19, 297
9, 1309b30, 214
9, 1309b32, 265
9, 1310a2ff, 302n13
10, 1310b3, 239
10, 1310b9, 301
10, 1310b40, 301
10, 1311a8, 239
10, 1311a35, 342n43
10, 1313a3, 89n25, 198n30
11, 1313a34, 299
11, 1313a36, 299n10
11, 1314a1, 300
11, 1314a31, 300
11, 1314a35, 300
11, 1315b1, 301
11, 1315b4, 302
12, 1315b11ff, 206
12, 1316a4, 246
12, 1316a39, 340
6.1, 1316b32, 322
1, 1316b39–1317a10, 322
1, 1317a2, 322
2, 1317b3, 212
3, 1318a30, 308n5
4, 1319b8, 176n4
6, 1320b32, 300
6, 1320b33, 296
7, 1321a5, 61, 189n20
7, 1321a26, 218
7.1, 1323a14, 346
1, 1323a21, 372
1, 1323a24, 29n14
1, 1323a32, 34n34
1, 1323b4, 373
1, 1323b21, 373
1, 1323b30, 40
1, 1323b41, 373
2, 1324a5, 293
2, 1324a7, 373
2, 1324a11, 40
2, 1324a17, 374
2, 1324a19, 374, 375
2, 1324a30, 375
2, 1324a34, 377
2, 1324a35, 375
2, 1324a37, 376
2, 1324a38, 381n28
2, 1324b2, 376
3, 1324b24, 376
3, 1324b28, 376
3, 1324b41, 377
3, 1325a28, 346n2
3, 1325a36, 378
3, 1325b16, 379
3, 1325b20, 379, 380
3, 1325b21, 380
3, 1325b24, 379
3, 1325b25, 379
3, 1325b29, 379
4, 1325b33, 364
4, 1325b34, 346
4, 1325b37, 277, 355
4, 1325b38, 355
4, 1325b40, 277
4, 1325b41, 365n18
4, 1326a8ff, 181n10

4, 1326a9, 40
4, 1326a16, 367
4, 1326a30, 289
4, 1326b2ff, 96
4, 1326b16, 353
5, 1326b29, 96
5, 1326b39, 276
6, 1327a14, 354
6, 1327a18, 354
6, 1327b23, 133
7, 1327b28, 139
7, 1327b29, 132
8, 1328a21, 356, 367
8, 1328a27, 309
8, 1328b5, 368, 371
9, 1328b24–1329a2, 348
9, 1328b33, 348
9, 1328b39, 349n5
9, 1329a26, 176n4
10, 1329b25, 71n4
10, 1330a25, 169
11, 1330a38, 354

13, 1331b35, 357
13, 1332a8, 63n54
13, 1332a9, 357
13, 1332a12, 357
13, 1332a17, 357n11
13, 1332a19, 358
13, 1332a22, 63n54
14, 1333a7, 122
14, 1333a11, 352
14, 1333a35, 43
14, 1333b37, 127
14, 1333b40, 124
15, 1334a18, 131
16, 1335a6, 61
8.2, 1337b11–14, 121
7, 1341b32, 61

Rhetoric
1.2, 1356a26, 38n26
1.4, 1360133, 282
1.11, 1371a14, 34n18
2.4, 1380b35, 147f
2.6, 1384b24, 34n18

www.ingramcontent.com/pod-product-compliance
Lightning Source LLC
Chambersburg PA
CBHW020119240426
43673CB00038B/529